Aristocratic Education and the Making of the American Republic

MARK BOONSHOFT

Aristocratic Education and the Making of the American Republic

The University of North Carolina Press *Chapel Hill*

© 2020 The University of North Carolina Press
All rights reserved
Set in Arno Pro by Westchester Publishing Services
Manufactured in the United States of America

The University of North Carolina Press has been a member of the
Green Press Initiative since 2003.

Library of Congress Cataloging-in-Publication Data
Names: Boonshoft, Mark, author.
Title: Aristocratic education and the making of the American republic / Mark Boonshoft.
Description: Chapel Hill : The University of North Carolina Press, 2020. |
　Includes bibliographical references and index.
Identifiers: LCCN 2019053443 | ISBN 9781469659534 (cloth) | ISBN 9781469659541 (ebook)
Subjects: LCSH: Public schools—United States—History. | Education—Political aspects—
　United States—History. | Education and State—United States—History. |
　Education—Aims and objectives—United States—History. | Social stratification—
　United States—History.
Classification: LCC LA215 .B66 2020 | DDC 371.010973—dc23
LC record available at https://lccn.loc.gov/2019053443

Cover illustration: Drawing of Erasmus Hall, 1829. Wallach Division Picture Collection, The New York Public Library.

Portions of chapter two were previously published in a different form as "The Great Awakening, Presbyterian Education, and the Mobilization of Power in the Revolutionary Mid-Atlantic," in *The American Revolution Reborn*, ed. Michael Zuckerman and Patrick Spero (Philadelphia: The University of Pennsylvania Press, 2016), 168–83. Used here with permission.

For my parents

Contents

Acknowledgments xi

INTRODUCTION
Why Academies?: Aristocratic Education in Revolutionary America 1

Part I
From Denominational Schools to Nationalist Institutions,
1730–1787

CHAPTER ONE
The Emergence of Academies: The Great Awakening and
Colonial Elite Formation 13

CHAPTER TWO
The Academy Effect: Civic Education and the American Revolution 31

CHAPTER THREE
Rebuilding Academies: Education and Politics in the
Confederation Era 49

Part II
The Culture of Academies, 1780–1800

CHAPTER FOUR
Defining Merit: Academies and Inequality 75

CHAPTER FIVE
Diplomacy and Dance: The Geopolitics of Ornamental Education 96

Part III
From Aristocratic Education to Reform, 1787–1830

CHAPTER SIX
Creating Consensus: The Politics of State Support for Academies 121

CHAPTER SEVEN
The First Era of School Reform: War, Panic, and Popular Education 148

EPILOGUE
The Legacy of Aristocratic Education 181

Appendix 185

Notes 187

Bibliography 229

Index 271

Figure and Tables

FIGURE

1.1 Manuscript map of Morristown by Mary Louisa Macculloch, November 4, 1819 6

TABLES

4.1 Pennsylvania academy locations by constitutional ratification vote 79

6.1 Date of academy opening versus incorporation, through 1800 123

6.2 Percent of academies founded by 1800 receiving charters by 1800, by region 124

6.3 Party competition in Massachusetts towns with an academy before 1800, using gubernatorial election results 127

6.4 Partisanship and academy chartering in Virginia and North Carolina, to 1800 129

6.5 Academy towns in western Massachusetts and Shays's Rebellion, 1780–1820 142

7.1 Partisanship of founders of two Massachusetts academies, 1798–1799 151

A.1 Number of academies founded from the Revolution to 1800 185

Acknowledgments

This is a book about education. It makes sense to begin by thanking those who educated me. Nobody has done more to turn me into a passable historian and make this book possible than John Brooke. Over countless meals at the Wex, John shared his wisdom, energy, and absurdly creative mind. His generosity has never wavered and his commitment to historical work remains infectious and inspiring. At Ohio State, I was also lucky to learn much about the historian's craft from Margaret Newell. I'm not sure how anyone finishes graduate school without the enthusiastic support of someone like Randy Roth. Paula Baker, Joan Cashin, Alice Conklin, Jane Hathaway, Robin Judd, and Dodie McDow were all also generous with advice.

My path to becoming a historian began at the State University of New York at Buffalo. Erik Seeman has been a steady source of support and friendship since I started showing up to his office as a sophomore. Carole Emberton treated me like a colleague from very early on and always tells it like it is. The late Richard Ellis sparked my interest in early national politics. Tamara Thornton has done a tremendous amount for me and my career. What matters most about Tamara is that she's a mensch.

I wrote and rewrote much of this book in the Arents Tobacco Collection Room at the New York Public Library (NYPL). My debt to Thomas Lannon for bringing me to NYPL is one I can never repay. Meandering conversations about Harper Torchbooks and Victor Hugo Paltsits were nice too. Thanks also to the other denizens of the third floor for welcoming me. While back in New York, the City University of New York Early American Republic Seminar was my scholarly home. Mike Crowder, Miriam Liebman, Glen Olson, Evan Turiano, and David Waldstreicher kindly let me invade their seminar and read my work.

I finally finished drafting this book as a faculty member of Norwich University, where I benefitted from the support of Sharon Smith, Katie Nelson, Michael Andrew, Emily Gray, Gary Lord, Christie McCann, Steve Sodergren, Cristy Boarman, Karen Hinkle, and Lea Williams. I was also lucky to arrive at Norwich with the likes of Jeff Casey, Sophia Mizouni, and Michael Thunberg. I thank Dean Kris Blair, John Mitcham, Drew Simpson, and all my colleagues in the history department for welcoming me to Duquesne University and Pittsburgh.

Many people have commented on pieces of this book and taught me a great deal in the process. I thank Emily Arendt, Doug Bradburn, Judith Burton, Zach Conn, John Dixon, Eliga Gould, Robb Haberman, Rob Koehler, Ned Landsman, Marie Basile McDaniel, Margaret Nash, George Oberle, Catherine O'Donnell, Peter Onuf, the late Bill Pencak, Hunter Price, Carole Shammas, Cam Shriver, Nora Slonimsky, Tracey Steffes, Margaret Sumner, and Kevin Vrevich. Mike Zuckerman and Pat Spero gave excellent feedback on an essay that is now part of chapter two. Thanks to Pat and Mike, I also got to know Kyle Roberts, who hosted me at Loyola-Chicago's Atlantic history seminar. I also shared full chapters at Yale, thanks to Zach Conn and Joanne Freeman; at Indiana University's Center for Eighteenth Century Studies; and at the Huntington Library, thanks to Carole Shammas.

It's a great feeling to be enthusiastic about revising something you've already worked on for nearly a decade. Johann Neem and Jason Opal gave me that gift when they read the manuscript for the press. Both offered feedback that made the project better and seem exciting all over again. Just as importantly, Johann and Jason taught me what it means to be a good citizen of the historical profession. At UNC Press, Chuck Grench and Dylan White demystified the publication process and helped me write the best possible book.

A few historian friends deserve special mention. Nora Slonimsky is a force—or perhaps she just uses it. Either way I'm grateful for her friendship and sage-like advice. Michael Hattem is always up for a conversation on the important things: Stax records and Fender telecasters. Emily Arendt has been there since day one at Ohio State. Maybe eventually I'll get something published without her advice. Hunter Price welcomed me to Ohio State and is a damn fine conference buddy. Patrick Potyondy is always ready to remind me why history matters.

Teachers, colleagues, and friends all taught me to be a historian. But research libraries are the lifeblood of historical scholarship. I visited many more libraries than are listed in the bibliography. Here I thank the expert staffs of all of them: Westfield Athenaeum, American Antiquarian Society, Bedford Historical Society, Bedford Free Library, New York State Archives, New York Historical Society, Westchester County Historical Society, Alexander Library at Rutgers University, Firestone and Mudd Libraries at Princeton University, North Jersey History Center, Trenton Free Public Library, Historical Society of Pennsylvania, Presbyterian Historical Society, University of Pennsylvania

Department of Special Collections, David Library of the American Revolution, University of Delaware Archives, Maryland Historical Society, Maryland State Archives, Virginia Historical Society, Society of the Cincinnati, North Carolina Division of Archives and History, Rubenstein Library at Duke University, and the Southern Historical Collection at the University of North Carolina.

Money is important too. I was fortunate to receive financial support from the graduate school and history department at Ohio State, Virginia Historical Society, David Library of the American Revolution, New Jersey Historical Commission, Society of the Cincinnati, and the Society for Historians of the Early American Republic to visit the Library Company of Philadelphia and the Historical Society of Pennsylvania. I thank Rich Morgan and the American Antiquarian Society for making me the inaugural Alstott-Morgan fellow. Norwich University awarded me the Board of Fellows Faculty Development prize to write the last chunks of the manuscript. At long last, I clicked "send" on the book while at the Fred W. Smith Library for the Study of George Washington at Mount Vernon as the Amanda and Greg Gregory fellow.

My family has taught me more than anyone and offered unending support. Thanks to Rich and Leslie Marcus, who put me up and fed me on a few occasions. In Philadelphia, Randy Freed, Tess, and Harry suffered longer intrusions, but always made me feel at home. The Dreskin clan—Billy, Ellen, Aiden, and Charlie—are the most positive and encouraging people I know. I feel lucky to call them family. For as long as I can remember, Ivy Barsky and my brother Michael have vied with one another to be my biggest cheerleader. I'm forever grateful to both of them. My parents nurtured my curiosity and made it possible to imagine history as a career. Yet when academic career woes wore me down, Michael and Emma and my parents often bore the brunt. I thank them for understanding.

Katie is one in a googolplex. I'm still not sure how to thank her for being my partner in our wonderful little life. For now, one word will suffice: Love.

*Aristocratic Education and the
Making of the American Republic*

Introduction
Why Academies?: Aristocratic Education in Revolutionary America

Education never mattered more to Americans than at the nation's founding. Neither the American Revolution nor the Constitution resolved the two central dilemmas of transitioning from monarchical to republican governance. Colonial subjects did not just wake up, Rip Van Winkle–style, in 1776 as capable citizens who could rule themselves. Nor did Americans agree about who should wield power in a society premised on equality. Americans looked to education to solve both conundrums. Deciding how and who to educate and what schools to support and fund was tantamount to designing a system of self-government.

Some Americans latched on to education to reassert elite rule, uphold hierarchy, and legitimize them both as natural in the wake of a revolution fought for equality. In the earliest years of the republic, they successfully funneled public support to schools that trained a presumptive elite. This was essential to their desire to build a powerful American state, modeled on European precedent. But others countered that education was *the key* to realizing the Revolution's most democratic ideals of equal and informed citizenship—albeit limited by racial and gender exclusions.[1] In the early nineteenth century, reformers criticized elite schools as backwardly aristocratic and pushed for education to break down elite privilege. Because of their work, which was done before Americans developed a legal definition of citizenship, claims to public influence came to rest on education. Some people even argued that public education was a right of citizens, in ways that resonate through the present.[2] In other words, the rise and fall of "aristocratic education" was critical to settling the American Revolution and making the American republic.

THE HARD-LINE FEDERALIST Noah Webster was as invested as any American in the debate over education and governance. In 1788, Webster argued for a system of education that "gives every citizen" the knowledge to exercise citizenship and hold office. This was not just desirable; it was actually "the *sine qua non* of the existence of the American republics." Webster believed it fell to government to provide this schooling. Since power "is in the hands of the people," he wrote, "knowledge should be universally diffused by means of public schools." It was clear that other Americans agreed. Five revolutionary state constitutions also called for public education and the Northwest Ordinance mandated it.[3] Yet this was a novel proposition. The closest precedent for accessible, tax-supported education was the system of New England town schools, which dated to the colonial period.

Webster's hopes were dashed. State legislatures across the early United States failed to make elementary education widespread, let alone universal. Worse, he thought, those legislatures instead supported "*academies* where people of property may educate their sons." Academies were privately run, but often state-sanctioned and -supported, secondary schools. In those schools, Webster wrote, "no provision is made for instructing the poorer rank of people." Yet the first fourteen states founded around 175 academies before 1800—one for about every 23,000 free people (see the Appendix). Through 1800, states issued more charters of incorporation to academies than to any other institution save churches, municipalities, and transportation projects. This led Webster to conclude, that in the young nation, "the constitutions are *republican*" but "the laws of education are *monarchical*."[4]

Webster called academies monarchical. But the main objection was that they seemed to re-create European-style *aristocracy*, so they might better be termed "aristocratic." In the American context, academies specialized in training elites. The schools had first emerged in the mid-Atlantic region during the Great Awakening to credential clergy. By the time Webster wrote, academies did much more. The same academy might teach basic literacy and numeracy to children and also prepare young adults for college. What distinguished academies was that they taught the classics and a full range of "ornamental subjects": dancing, fencing, French, and the visual arts. The schools appealed to the sons and daughters of wealthy and powerful families—an assumed elite—who could afford the expense.

Historians have long noted the outpouring of rhetoric in favor of public schooling. In the early republic, paeans to public schools, like those by Webster, abounded. Writers celebrated how schools could train ordinary citizens, encourage republican values, and differentiate the new nation from Europe. Americans dreamed up ambitious plans for tiered systems of public schools. Yet this all came to naught.[5] The question that remains is not why the most ambitious plans failed. After a destructive revolution, amid economic and political uncertainty, and in the face of antitax sentiment, *any* bold policy faced long odds. The question is: Why did academies thrive in the same period? Why did aristocratic education and the American republic rise together?

There were both personal and political reasons for this paradox. Anxious elites who wanted to maintain their status saw academies as a solution, not a problem. These Americans knew of no way to convey status without emulating European elites. Men and women alike embraced European trappings in their dress and in the material culture with which they adorned their homes. Their pursuit of classical and ornamental education in academies flowed from similar desires.[6] There was also clear political logic—or, at least, justification—for a European-style elite in the new nation, and thus for academies. Surely to Webster's chagrin, his Federalist allies led the charge to make academies ubiquitous. In 1787, academy boosters tended to promote the Constitution and a strong nation-state. Most remained Federalists into the 1790s. Some, though, became the vanguard of the Moderate wing of the Jeffersonian Republican coalition. Much of this book explains how these groups used academies to further their vision for the nation-state. It makes sense here to explain why they turned to academies and identify precisely what problem they hoped to solve.

The meteoric expansion of academies in the 1780s and 1790s only makes sense in the context of postrevolutionary state formation.[7] The self-styled group of wise and virtuous gentlemen who coalesced as Federalists designed the Constitution with two main problems in mind. First, they decried what they called an "excess of democracy." During the 1780s, uneducated country bumpkins had swept into state legislatures. They passed myopic debtor relief and paper money laws that catered to ordinary people, which bred internal strife and threatened the republican experiment—or so the Federalists claimed. They designed a Constitution that took power away from the state legislatures and vested it in a less accessible national government.[8] The perceived tilt toward anarchy also mattered, Federalists claimed, for securing the United States' credibility on the world stage. The framers understood that their new nation confronted a hostile geopolitical environment. The Federalists designed a fiscal-military state to project the nation's power in the Atlantic and along the western frontier. This was necessary for making the United States into a "treaty-worthy" and "civilized nation." These were polities that could control their populations and follow the law of nations: the basis for diplomatic recognition.[9] The Federalists' main project, as historian Max Edling and others have shown, was to build a nation-state that Europeans recognized as legitimate.[10]

Creating a European-style state also depended on a creating a European-style ruling elite. Many would-be Federalists were not shy about their desire to build some aristocratic elements into the new system.[11] A year before writing his essay on education, Webster admitted that "a republic is among the last kinds of government I should choose." Rather, he continued, "I should infinitely prefer a limited monarchy."[12] In the Constitutional Convention, Alexander Hamilton proposed that senators and the president serve for life, like the king and lords in Britain.[13] That same year, Hamilton helped transfer to New York's Federalist-dominated Board of Regents the full power to regulate academies. Similar impulses were at work. As one New Yorker incisively wrote, the delegates to the Constitutional Convention might "suggest legislative refinements and innovation[s]." Their work, though, would be in vain "if they do not displace from the helm, characters... who cannot enjoy that confidence and esteem which the world always give to property and education."[14] *The world* respected property and education. So too should Americans. Many Federalists did not blame the Europeans for thinking the United States was governed by rubes. They agreed, and sought to fix that.

Put differently, in 1787 the Federalists designed a system that would work best when controlled by people like them. Several constitutional provisions—the indirect election of senators, large congressional districts, and the electoral college—would act as "sieves" to keep the most "objectionable" men out of high offices and filter the most talented into them. But the turmoil of the 1770s and 1780s also led some leading Federalists to conclude that men like them were in short supply. It was not enough to keep themselves in power. The Constitution did not address this shortage; it created no institutions that made men in their image. A proposal for a national university had failed in the Convention.[15]

The Federalists, then, needed a way to reproduce themselves. They turned to institutions that they knew worked: academies. Many Federalists had attended colonial academies and parlayed a denominational education into public power. They saw themselves as living proof of the schools' capacity to produce enlightened and liberal men who saw beyond local prejudice. This reflected Enlightenment-era discourse surrounding advanced education and connected academies with the Federalist state-building project. Subsuming local prejudices to the needs of an ascendant nation as it took its place in an interconnected world was exactly what the Federalists aimed to do. Men learned to think this way through a traditional, worldly, and classical education. If prudence led most academy founders to deny the "aristocratic" label, they still valued these schools for the same reasons that they faced the epithet: the academies' colonial origins, European curriculum, and focus on training an elite.[16]

Why did Americans accept aristocratic academies, even for a time? It was a great advantage that academies were locally grounded. Founders worked with their neighbors to build academies in their communities. Usually located in prosperous rural communities, and set in the center of town, academies became central civic institutions, perhaps second only to county courthouses (see figure I.1). They hosted elections, patriotic celebrations, and visits from esteemed political leaders. Public exhibitions given by academies also became important events in their own right.[17] These academic affairs effectively took over for militia musters, which had long been the primary public displays of civic pride. Academies replaced the martial logic of the militia with the logic of improvement, inculcating ordinary Americans with a faith in social order based on education.[18] They brought into American communities what historians have long called the Moderate Enlightenment. This strand of thinking synthesized traditional values of order, hierarchy, and rule by a well-educated elite with a commitment to informed consent.[19] The academies' rootedness legitimized the central conceit behind them: that a European-style education should confer power in a republic. This local work served the academy founders' national and geopolitical goals.

It still took state governments to make this aristocratic vision viable. Significantly, most formal academies received charters of incorporation from state legislatures. Those that did not, still often acted like an incorporated institution.[20] Groups of men put up their own capital, solicited more through subscriptions, and administered schools through boards of trustees. This distinguished academies from other schools run by individuals, which offered some of the same curriculum.[21] Historically, charters of incorporation were a royal prerogative, an exclusive grant of privileges from the king. Americans turned incorporation into a tool to create and regulate institutions that served the "public good." Trustees leveraged incorporation to their advantage. It both insulated academy boards from democratic control and conferred on them patriotic credibility.[22]

Academies, then, represent a formative example of how nationalists used local voluntary associations and state governments' vast authority to bolster national strength. Much scholarship sees associations and state power as antagonistic. Other work pits state and national governments against one another.[23] Academy founders expertly navigated the early republic's murky federal system.[24] Thus, the rise of aristocratic education was not just critical to making the Federalists' desired European-style nation-state. It was also emblematic of *how* they created that state.

DESPITE THE FEDERALISTS' best efforts, many Americans continued to think of the academies as Webster had: as an anachronism. Writing a decade

after Webster, William Manning sounded a similarly dour note. The radically democratic Massachusetts Jeffersonian favored universal public schooling, in which "No student or scholar would pay anything for tuition." This should encompass "common schools for little children" and secondary education for boys and girls. Under such a system, "we should have plenty of men to fill the highest offices of state," all of whom had an education in republican principles. Instead, Manning complained, Americans invested in "academies." These schools had the effect of "running down republican principles," and they suffused American culture with "exhibitions in favor of monarchies."[25] The glut of academies had only worsened. But by the late 1790s, change was afoot.

The book ends by reframing the emergence of accessible education, aimed at producing a self-governing citizenry, as a reaction against aristocratic education. This was critical to the larger political transformations of the early nineteenth century: the decline of Federalism, the Jeffersonian ascendancy, and the rise of a more coherent American nationalism, for better or for worse. Most historians of education skip past this, to the rise of the common school movement in the 1830s. Led by men like Horace Mann, this later era of reform consolidated statewide, tax-supported public systems in many Northern states, as well as some embryonic versions in the South. Much recent work has shown, though, that schooling was already widely accessible in the North. Historians argue this was the product of local effort, unconnected to larger political developments.[26] Yet political and geopolitical changes created a sense of urgency that made widespread schooling possible. Men like Manning capitalized to renew the attack on aristocratic education. New laws challenged academies' dominance. Instead, states encouraged tax-supported public schools in ways that anticipated the later "common school revival." The "first era of school reform" not only overthrew aristocratic education, it also overthrew the Federalists' national vision that aristocratic education had helped to sustain.

The attack on aristocratic education both benefited from political changes and accelerated them. First came the Federalists' decline and the Jeffersonian

(*facing page*) FIGURE 1.1 Mary Louisa Macculloch drew this map, possibly while a student at the Morris Academy in Morristown, New Jersey. It depicts the homes and buildings in the center of Morristown, including the Morris Academy at the corner of South and Pine Streets. Manuscript map of Morristown, New Jersey, by Mary Louisa Macculloch, November 4, 1819. Courtesy of North Jersey History and Genealogy Center, Morristown and Morris Township Library, Morristown, N.J.

Republicans' rise. Nationally, the Jeffersonians rejected Federalist attempts to emulate Europe. In practice, however, the Jeffersonians did not repudiate the Hamiltonian state so much as redirect its energies. Instead of pandering to merchants in the East, they directed federal power west to colonize Native lands to spread slavery.[27] Rhetorically, though, the Anglophobic attack on Federalism jived with the antiaristocratic assault on existing academies.[28] In much of the North, the Jeffersonian takeover transformed an elite-driven political culture into a popular and responsive one. The people should rule themselves, they said. Widespread education was the means to that end.

Education was the policy arena through which Americans settled the question of "who should rule at home." Nearly every historian of early American politics acknowledges how Jeffersonians rethought the role of education and educated people in a republic.[29] But they have not explained how education policy was transformed to usher in this new political culture.[30] In part, this is because the effects of the Jeffersonian Revolution were not immediate. Moderate Jeffersonians continued to value a distinct, well-educated political elite.[31] As a result, they supported academies into the nineteenth century. Yet Moderates balked at some of the Federalists' excesses. They ultimately joined forces with more radical Jeffersonians who prioritized reform, especially tax-supported common schools. The Jeffersonian Revolution, then, was a necessary precondition for the first era of school reform. But it could not bring this about unaided.

The 1810s was the critical decade in the first era of school reform. It was bracketed by geopolitical crises. The War of 1812, along with the U.S. embargo that preceded it, brought to the fore lingering animosities between Britain and its former colonies. Then the Panic of 1819 threw into relief the growing inequalities within the United States. Americans sought to address both crises in self-consciously republican ways. Public schools looked like a panacea. The sense of crisis enabled a fusion of radical and moderate education policy. New policies took root through the same mechanisms the Federalists had used—local schools shaped by state laws. Now, however, they served a different national agenda. The need for tax-supported common schools became a popular assumption in much of the rural North. States increasingly shifted resources away from the academies and toward common education. Even more than that, widespread common schooling drove the demand for new forms of secondary and higher education. Even the academies were transformed. The former bastions of aristocratic education began to serve more than a would-be elite.[32] Rather than just topple aristocracy, education reformers hoped to elevate the bottom and democratize the top. Unlike the

Federalists' vision for education that aimed to reproduce men who thought a certain way, education reformers hoped schools would liberate people to pursue their values in private and public life alike.

Accessible, and even equitable, education for white men had become a reality in many Northern communities by the 1820s. This chronology leaves no doubt about the origins of widespread common schools. They were popular well before fears of urbanization and industrialization ran rampant. Reform was a reaction to aristocratic elements in American society, not ascendant democratic ones. If anything, the first era of school reform made democratic self-government possible. Of course, this version of self-government did coexist with other savage inequalities.[33]

ARISTOCRATIC EDUCATION FOCUSES on the politics—local, state, national, and geopolitical—that framed formal schooling in the decades surrounding the American Revolution. The primary actors here are academy founders and mainstream reformers. Almost all were white men with a formal voice in politics.[34] What academy advocates and reformers alike often left unsaid is that theirs was fundamentally a debate about opportunities afforded to white people, and mostly white men at that. They focused primarily on the influence of wealth and class on self-government. The fact that historians distinguish between "academies" and "female academies" shows how deeply their assumptions seeped into the sources.[35] The infrequency with which most white men in my sources even consider people of color is clear evidence of how they imagined nonwhites outside the body politic. In other words, the fact that reformers directed their ire at the bugaboo of aristocracy gave school reform legs, but it also circumscribed its effects. This was not an attack on slavery, patriarchy, or colonialism, and it showed.[36]

Nevertheless, the debate over education shaped the experiences of Indigenous peoples, African Americans, and white women. The era of gradual emancipation coincided with aristocratic education. Early antislavery activists made education a priority in that period, hoping to show free blacks' capacity for citizenship.[37] Americans also compelled many Indigenous people into schools with the hopes of "civilizing" them. Assimilation intended to colonize by less outwardly violent means.[38] What I make clear here is that these efforts were often set against what were termed "aristocratic" academies. Teachers imposed notions of "respectability" and "civility" modeled on the idealized version of white manhood that academies inculcated. White women's education also took shape in this context. Middling and elite women's access to education exploded in the era of aristocratic education.

But the idealized Federalist social order also circumscribed women's public influence, even as intellectual equality seemed feasible. That was the bargain.[39] When education did not undermine existing inequalities, it strengthened them. It reified the notion that academy-educated white men were a natural, not a hereditary, aristocracy.

The first era of school reform did not directly challenge racial and gender inequity in schooling. Education systems became more regionally defined, which produced different regimes of inequality. This ran the gamut. The plantation South kept enslaved people entirely ignorant and poor whites not much better off, whereas greater New England had nearly universal literacy and among the most democratic political systems in the world.[40] Especially in rural areas of the North, women and free blacks often inadvertently benefited from reform.[41]

More importantly, though, reform changed the context of educational inequity. Reformers increasingly justified public schools as tools for cultivating citizenship and self-government. This transformed education from a tool for building hierarchy into a blunt instrument of inclusion and, in turn, exclusion. This made education—especially equal access to public schools—a central battleground in larger fights over citizenship. Education became a crucial thread in the African American freedom struggle, and segregation became a tool that whites wielded against it. The dynamics were different when it came to Native peoples, who were members of separate nations. But education provides a through line in both colonialism and Indians' efforts to resist it and to maintain their autonomy.[42]

These conflicts are a product of the fall of aristocratic education. In perverse ways, they testify both to the founding generation's success in making education an arbiter of access to public power and reformers' efforts to democratize it. After the first era of school reform, education existed to produce a *representative* government. Asking who should receive a public education had become tantamount to asking who should be represented. Whites doggedly guarded their privileged access to public schooling because they knew it mattered. Education—even when publicly supported—has not always served democracy. It had to be made to do that. As Americans remake their democracy and the body politic, so too must they remake their public schools.

Part I
From Denominational Schools
to Nationalist Institutions, 1730–1787

CHAPTER ONE

The Emergence of Academies
The Great Awakening and Colonial Elite Formation

The outlook seemed bright for the First Presbyterian Church of Elizabeth Town, New Jersey. Just a few years after the church's centennial, in 1766, the board of trustees noted that the congregation had "greatly increased in Numbers and is likely to increase more & more." They also realized that their church building "in a very short time will be much too small." The congregation had only built the current meetinghouse some forty years earlier, in 1724. Nevertheless, "after full debate and serious Consideration," the trustees decided to build an addition to accommodate their new parishioners.

Even with the cost of the church expansion looming, a group of Elizabeth Town Presbyterians embarked on another construction project. They "voluntarily entered into a subscription . . . for the Building of a school House." The church board of trustees agreed to oversee the small school and kick in £100 for building "a proper house." They also set aside land for the new school, which the trustees hoped would "be of great advantage to the interests of learning."[1] The school was one of many that colonists, especially Presbyterians, built in this period, from New York to the Carolinas.

Presbyterians called most of these schools "academies," and they served a pressing need. Elizabeth Town was an epicenter of the so-called Great Awakening—a series of religious revivals and denominational disputes that began in New England in the 1730s and then spread beyond. Throughout the mid-Atlantic and upper South, revivalism gained steam amid a period of institutional failure. Populations boomed and new congregations established themselves, but many failed to find ministers to lead them. Most of British North America lacked domestic schools to train clergy. The Awakening emerged, then, out of a crisis of religious elite formation. Schools like the Elizabeth Town Academy were a response. They were institutions of elite formation, designed to train ministers to fill pulpits and restore religious order. The expansion of academies, along with colleges, succeeded at creating a new ministerial elite, answering the religious needs of Reformed Protestants, especially in the mid-Atlantic and upper South.

But academies' influence extended beyond religious matters. Religious disorder was symptomatic of a larger lack of both settled institutions and a settled elite in colonial America. British imperial officials regularly complained about the dearth of schools training men of the professional class in the colonies. Academies helped fill this need as well. Both for political reasons and in response to student demand, the schools moved their culture and curriculum in a more secular direction. Academies functioned as outposts of transatlantic Enlightenment culture, often deep in the hinterlands of colonial America, and appealed to upwardly mobile young men with secular ambitions. By the 1750s, it was clear that these religious institutions were powerful forces of elite formation more generally.

Elites, Disorder, and Education

At the turn of the eighteenth century, Britain's North American colonies differed from one to the next. Systems of labor, the organization of households, economic interests, religious traditions, and governments varied considerably from the plantation South to New England. Amid this diversity, most colonists shared an attachment to the English monarch. Patriarchy and hierarchy, in other words, remained as guiding assumptions. But compared to the situation in England, hierarchy was on a less stable footing in the colonies. Monarchical governance was built on the assumption that social status conferred political authority. This looked different overseas. To be sure, Virginia plantation owners concentrated wealth through entail, and manor lords re-created a feudal system in New York's Hudson Valley. However, these concentrated claims to power were much younger than aristocratic titles and estates in England. Outside these extreme examples, the gulf between rich and poor was not nearly as great as in England. Much as they tried to emulate British elites, most wealthy colonists could not fully re-create the trappings of English aristocrats. When political authority stemmed from social standing but the ruling class had less secure aristocratic power, if they had it at all, their authority was attenuated. This divergence between assumptions and reality left many colonies teetering on the brink of disorder in their early years.[2]

One way that the colonial-born elite differed from their English counterparts was in education. English aristocrats stood to hold political power regardless of their abilities. Most nevertheless received a formal classical or legal education. The commitment to giving English aristocrats a secondary and higher education grew in the early years of North American colonization.[3] In the colonies during the seventeenth century, though, formal education was limited. At best, ordinary colonists received an education at home and at church. Continuing a trend that dated back to Tudor England, colonists viewed the household as the fundamental unit of socialization. Household education taught youths the patriarchal social norms of early modern society and provided basic vocational training. Churches took care to inculcate young people with moral and religious standards. Beyond this, even well-to-do colonists found they had limited formal options for schools. Through the Glorious Revolution, Harvard was the only college in British North America.[4]

Many of the king's agents thought that the lack of educated colonists stifled the administration of colonial governance. When, in 1691, the lieutenant governor of Virginia proposed a plan to establish "strict enforcement of the laws in every branch of administration," he collected county-level information on militias and government offices. He also sought information about "the promoters of education." Schools were part of good government.[5] A few years later, another report on Virginia suggested that the "Administration of Justice" suffered from a lack of education. County courts had worked "irregularly" for their entire history in Virginia. But they functioned better under the English-educated gentry of a prior generation than under the current Creole generation who "have been born in Virginia, and have had generally little more education than to read, write and cast accounts, and that very indifferently."[6] In nearby Maryland, the governor complained that "Royall commands before the Generall Assembly" were rarely followed, which he blamed on the fact that there "was not any person of liberall education." The governor could not "graft good manners on so barren a stock." Time and again, the uneducated assembly failed to take any action on royal plans.[7]

Colonial officials in North Carolina likewise complained that the colony had never elected a "reasonable Assembly." According to the governor, because North Carolina has "been so long in confusion," assemblymen catered to a populace "whose ignorance and want of education makes them obstruct everything for the good of the country even so much as the building of churches, or erecting of schools, or endeavouring to maintain a direct trade to Great Britain."[8] Governor Gabriel Johnston drove at a central paradox. The lack of strong governance hindered the development of education, while the lack of education itself destabilized governance. These deficiencies were mutually reinforcing.

Imperial officials assumed that expanding education for the elite and empowering educated men would strengthen governance. In 1722, lieutenant governor Alexander Spotswood of Virginia delayed appointing a "Sollicitor of the Virginia affairs" until a candidate with "the advantages of a more liberal education" was ready to take the post. That was preferable to installing someone less qualified to the office.[9] By the 1730s, officials in New York expressed "confiden[ce] that public schools for the education of youth [would] always find countenance from" the Board of Trade.[10] Yet even at this late date, officials did not actively build or promote schools, even for the elite. A lack of formal education remained as both a symptom and a cause of political instability.

New England was the exception that proved the rule. There, religion inspired support for public schooling from the outset. Massachusetts passed its famous "old deluder Satan" laws within a generation of settlement. These required towns to create local schools to teach basic literacy, numeracy, and writing.[11] The hope was that if the people could read the Bible and understand religious teachings, they could know when Satan was tempting them. Literacy was one shield against irreligion.[12] Throughout the seventeenth century, these schools had only a modest impact.[13] Though the mid-Atlantic lagged behind New England in formal schooling, literacy rates were comparable before 1700. Large portions of the English-, Dutch-, and German-speaking migrants who came to the mid-Atlantic were already literate. By the turn of the eighteenth century, male literacy hovered just below 70 percent in both regions. Women's literacy rates were much lower.[14]

Yet during the eighteenth century, New England's relative political and social stability came to rest on formal education. By the time of the American Revolution, male literacy rates in New England shot up toward 90 percent, among the highest in the world. Female literacy rates, though, stagnated, and the gendered literacy gap grew. Town schools functioned as brutal sites of socialization that "traumatized" boys into productive laborers and citizens. These "town-born" children had a stake in the political health of their community. In exchange, young men received protection against competition from laborers not born in town.[15] Education became a central means to ground communities amid a bevy of changes: economic growth, rising land scarcity, the expansion of towns, and the creation of new ones.[16] The Bay Colony also required larger towns to keep classical grammar schools, though many ignored the edict. Harvard and, by 1706, Yale educated the rising young men of New England. In Cambridge and New Haven, the children of well-to-do families trained to fill pulpits, begin professional careers, and serve in public office. Town schools rooted poor and middling whites in their local communities, and colleges connected the clerical and political elite throughout New England.

Virginia, the oldest English colony, also stabilized during the eighteenth century, albeit in a very different way from the colonies in New England. Reflecting its aristocratic bent, Virginia's dominant slaveholding planter class was actively hostile to educating common people. In 1670, Governor William Berkeley famously "thank[ed] God, there are no free schools nor printing . . .

for learning has brought disobedience, and heresy, and sects into the world, and printing has divulged them, and libels against the best government. God keep us from both!"[17] Hierarchical Virginia depended on popular ignorance. In the wake of Bacon's Rebellion, in 1676, Virginia's elite leveraged racism and the illusion of white, male democracy to create a stable social and political regime. They also worked to bolster their own social authority. Some of the wealthiest Virginians had attended English schools or had private tutors. At the turn of the eighteenth century, domestic higher education became available at the College of William and Mary.[18]

The Puritan model was more comprehensive, and rings modern. But Virginia's race-based model of elite formation endured as well. Neither could work in the religious and ethnically pluralistic environs of the mid-Atlantic—New York, New Jersey, Delaware, and Pennsylvania—or the backcountry upper South. Without comparable levels of slavery, Virginia's race-based social order was impossible to re-create. The mid-Atlantic also lacked the longstanding tradition of local self-government that characterized New England, and which depended on local schools. Most of the middle colonies were founded as proprietary colonies, meaning an individual lorded over the territory based on a grant from the king. Later, they came under royal authority.[19]

Early on in its existence, Pennsylvania proved the difficulties of emulating New England. William Penn founded Philadelphia with a robust plan for municipal government, including public schools. During the early years of the city and the colony, Quakers administered most of the schools. Without consistent or sufficient state support, they never adequately served the whole population.[20] Moreover, education was itself a point of contention, even among Quakers. Debates over schooling were at the root of the so-called Keithian schism, the most important religious dispute in early Pennsylvania. The namesake, George Keith, was a well-connected Quaker who had surveyed the line dividing East and West Jersey and also served as headmaster of the Philadelphia Friends School. He believed that one could not understand Christ's teachings or reach salvation without knowledge and rationality. Instead of automatically accepting Quaker children as members, which was the common practice, Keith wanted them to have to testify a confession of faith. Without education, they could not do that capably. This flouted Quaker understandings of child rearing and domesticity. Most Pennsylvania Friends believed that a loving home was all that was necessary to nurture the spiritual light inside children. Keith's ideas meant that children who died young went unsaved. However, he lost. Keith and many followers became Anglicans, while Quakers continued to rule the commonwealth.[21]

By the second quarter of the eighteenth century, it was clear that the mid-Atlantic and backcountry upper South had to create their own models for education. There, the lack of education was problematic less because it inhibited the sort of governance that imperial officials prized, and more because it hurt colonists' spiritual lives. The population of these areas boomed during the first half of the eighteenth century. German- and Dutch-speaking peoples of Reformed and Lutheran denominations and pietistic sects, along with Scottish and Irish Presbyterians, flooded into New Jersey, Delaware, and backcountry Pennsylvania, then down through western Maryland, Virginia, and the Carolinas. The developing areas in which they settled lacked both strong civil institutions and churches.[22]

Religion was supposed to be a binding agent, but clergymen were few and far between. By 1740, no more than 10 percent of Pennsylvania's German Reformed and German Lutheran congregations had settled clergymen. Dutch Reformed and Swedish and Dutch Lutheran congregations fared better. Yet even there, ordained ministers still filled only about half the available pulpits. The basic problem was that these denominations' bureaucracies remained in Europe and the colonists depended on them for ministers. Most importantly, the schools that trained and ordained clergy were overseas, and college-educated ministers did not want to move to unsettled areas of North America. Clergymen who did make the journey found their power hampered by independent lay leaders, who had grown accustomed to directing their own religious affairs.[23]

Prior to 1730, Presbyterians were more successful than other mid-Atlantic denominations. They had an ecclesiastical structure—of a national general assembly, regional synods, relatively local presbyteries, and individual congregations—that proved portable. The creation of the Presbytery of Philadelphia in 1706 inaugurated a period of ecclesiastical organization in the mid-Atlantic. In the next decade, the church created the Synod of Philadelphia, which oversaw presbyteries in Philadelphia, New Castle, Delaware, and Long Island. Their ecclesiastical organization remained weak, though, in the Pennsylvania backcountry. To offset this, the synod created the Presbytery of Donegal in 1732. Colonial Presbyterians controlled no schools that produced ministers but could ordain and regulate the clergymen who came from universities in Scotland and New England. By the 1730s, even this was insufficient. More Irish people arrived in the colonies in that decade than in the preceding three combined. Regions that Presbyterians had successfully organized felt the stress of population growth and the insufficient supply of ministers. The church continued to add presbyteries and expand their ecclesiastical organization. But they could not fill pulpits with ministers fast enough to meet the demands of the immigrants who streamed in and started congregations. Like other denominations, Presbyterians were in trouble because they depended on strong clergy yet lacked domestic schools to produce ministers.[24]

Nearby exceptions make a stark counterpoint. Pietistic sects, like the Moravians, eschewed a hierarchical ecclesiastical structure altogether. They did not need college-educated ministers and were less dependent on Europe than the denominations and faced fewer growing pains.[25]

Ultimately, Reformed Protestant denominations found they needed to build domestic schools to train ministers. Of all innovations in colonial education, academies founded to train ministers were to have the largest influence on American education for almost a century.[26] The emergence of that model is the subject of this chapter; and its fate, the subject of this book.

An Awakening of Education

Evangelical revivalists became the shock troops of academy building. Beginning in the 1730s and taking off in the 1740s, a fusion of Presbyterian, Congregational, and Reformed evangelicals in New England and the mid-Atlantic set off the religious revivals that historians call the Great Awakening. Revivalism emerged to provide the laity with a path to salvation, which denominational failures had blocked.[27] In New England, the revivalists were known as the "New Light," and in the mid-Atlantic, as the "New Side." Their opponents were called the "Old Light" or "Old Side."[28] The schism was particularly stark among Presbyterians, who made the division official in 1746. The New Side created a new, revivalist Synod of New York, while the Old Side kept control of the Synod of Philadelphia. Colonial Presbyterians did not reconcile until the two synods reunited in 1758. In the mid-Atlantic, education, not revivalism per se, was the battleground of the Awakening. Competition among Presbyterians engendered a sort of cold war, an educational arms race, as the Old and New Sides each vied to train ministers who would restore denominational power. Presbyterians showed their fellow colonists the power of academies to train a domestic elite, albeit a clerical one. Given the challenges of elite formation and disorder that plagued colonial America, other denominations unsurprisingly followed suit.

The colonial craze for academies began in Bucks County, Pennsylvania, in 1727, when the Presbyterian revivalist William Tennent started the famous "Log College." Fewer than twenty men attended the school, which neither had a charter nor conferred degrees. It could hardly offset the clergy shortage that plagued the whole region, but it put momentum behind the revivalists' cause and transformed religious politics.[29] Tellingly, the Old Side focused its attacks on the New Side at the small school. They alleged that the Log College contributed to disorder because it trained unqualified men for the pulpit. This was a serious allegation from Old Siders, who believed that God "is a God of order," and thus that "all the affairs of his kingdom on earth should be done decently and in order."[30] The reality, though, was that the school deliberately addressed the underlying disorder of the time. Evangelical leaders like Gilbert Tennent—William's son—argued that the church should support more "Private Schools of the Prophets" like the Log College. These were the best hope to empower men who could restore religious authority in the region.[31]

The Log College spawned a network of small academies that stretched from the Carolinas to northern New Jersey and had a major influence on colonial education.[32] At their academies in Fagg's Manor and Pequea, Pennsylvania, Samuel Blair and Robert Smith both trained future presidents of the College of New Jersey (now Princeton University). The New Side–run college was founded in Elizabeth Town, in 1746, to "supply the very numerous vacencies [sic] in all those provinces as far as Virginia, with qualified Candidates of the Ministry."[33] It was the first college founded in the colonies since Yale, four decades earlier. Another future president of the college, Samuel Finley, cut his teeth as an academy teacher. In 1756, he boasted of "a number of hopefully pious youth ... whom have been, & now are, at my school."[34] Though he prioritized training ministers, Finley also taught many men who went on to successful careers in other professions, especially medicine.[35]

When it came to education, the Awakening eventually cut as deep in Old Side strongholds as revivalist hotbeds. In 1744, while the Old Side continued its assault on the Log College, it also moved to found a school "to educate youths for supplying our vacancies" in the clergy. They decided that a broad educational mission would draw the widest range of students and put the school on a sure footing. They envisioned an academy where "all persons who please may send their children and have them instructed gratis in the Languages, Philosophy, and Divinity." To lead the school, the synod appointed Francis Alison, an Irish-born and Scottish-educated Old Side stalwart.[36] Alison ran the school, in New London, Pennsylvania, for almost a decade. His students eventually took it over and moved it to New Castle and later Newark, Delaware, where it evolved into the University of Delaware. Students from these Old Side academies built a network of schools in Delaware and Pennsylvania to rival New Side education.[37]

As the zeal for academies spread beyond the Presbyterians, the schools took on more secular purposes. In 1749, Benjamin Franklin publicized a plan for what became the Academy of Philadelphia. Whereas the founders of denominational schools tended to harp on their importance to clerical education, Franklin's academy was ostensibly nonsectarian. He envisioned that "Youth will come out of this School fitted for learning any Business, Calling or Profession" and ready to "execute the several Offices of civil Life."[38] That did not stop teachers from trying to wrest control of the school for their respective denominations. A few years after its founding, the board of trustees also received a charter for an affiliated college (the forerunner to the University of Pennsylvania). This was one of five to open in the North American colonies within a decade and a half, more than doubling the number of colleges.[39] The others were Dartmouth College, College of Rhode Island (Brown University), Queen's College (Rutgers University), and King's College (Columbia University). Several opened under denominational control and, like Queen's College, intended to produce "an able, learned and well qualified ministry."[40] But Franklin's project portended how academies and colleges would soon turn toward the formation of a secular elite.

The Awakening even influenced the comparatively stable school system of New England. In addition to new colleges, small theological schools received a boost during the Awakening. Followers of Jonathan Edwards opened small "schools of the prophets" across New England, which trained some 500 ministers between 1750 and 1825.[41] The period even saw the first attempts at creating mid-Atlantic-style academies in New England. Former lieutenant governor William Dummer left money for an "academy" in Essex County, Massachusetts. The school opened in 1763, though it resembled a run-of-the-mill New England Latin grammar school. Luminaries in Hampshire County also attempted to acquire a charter for a school in Hatfield, though Harvard's boosters put the kibosh on this potential competition.[42]

Meanwhile, Presbyterians continued to outstrip all other denominations at building schools. The nominal reunification of the Old and New Sides in 1758 left competing factions fighting for power entirely through the schools.[43] Attempts to share control of the College of New Jersey enflamed infighting between the Old and New Sides.[44] In a telling letter to John Witherspoon—who would become the college's president in 1768—one New Side man wrote that "the old side will always be the old side till God give them grace, and then they become the new Side, and will unite, but not till then."[45] Schools remained proxies for competition well after Witherspoon took over. In 1773, the Newark Academy sent John Ewing on a fund-raising trip to Britain to raise money for the school, only to find his efforts hampered by Witherspoon.[46] Meanwhile, Presbyterians opened at least twenty academies, from New York to South Carolina, between 1758 and the outbreak of the Revolution. None developed a particularly notable reputation, but they altered the shape of local life nonetheless.[47] In the end, the New Side "won" the Awakening, and dominated the Presbyterian Church for the foreseeable future, because they had more success in building schools that trained ministers who served their interests.[48]

The Great Awakening arose out of an institutional crisis of elite formation: Ministerial shortages had created an appetite for revivalists' evangelical message. But the advent of the academy by New Side Presbyterians was just as important to their success at confronting denominational failure. Revivalists' opponents and other denominations turned to the same institutions to solve their own ministerial shortages. Academies had become the main engine of religious elite formation in a large swath of British North America, and their influence expanded from there.

The Enlightened Culture of Academies

The sheer number of new academies meant they could not all stay afloat by just training ministers of narrow religious factions. To survive, they had to broaden their appeal. Academies had always offered more than theological education, grounding their curriculum in the Enlightened ideas and curriculum of the time. Following the Awakening, they amped up their appeal to students with ambitions beyond the ministry. As academies began to teach the skills expected of men of business and politics, their potential as civic institutions of secular elite formation came into focus. The Enlightenment and religion were not just intellectually compatible in this period; they were institutionally codependent.

Many academies benefited from other currents that the Awakening unleashed in addition to revivalism. Latitudinarianism—a tolerance for variations between faiths and theologies—blossomed for a host of reasons. Revivalists preached to anyone who wanted to hear their message, regardless of denomination. German-speaking colonists had already dabbled in worship across denominational lines. On top of this, many young men who came of age during the Awakening sought an escape from revivalism. In New England, the revivals had the ironic effect of increasing membership in the Anglican Church. Some revivalists in New England thundered that Harvard had become a nest of liberal Arminianism. Many others who embraced liberal theologies during the Awakening still remained in their church. Yet they found the Awakening exhausting and balked at the commotion. Academies ultimately appealed as much to these young, exhausted children of the Awakening as to would-be ministers.[49]

Most academies and colleges created a similar and secularized culture. Schools taught young people to be lawyers, doctors, and merchants; instructed them on the finer points of philosophy; and enmeshed them in a world of literature and the arts. Academies, then, socialized upwardly striving provincials into a "Moderate Enlightenment" ethos that dominated educated circles in the British Atlantic.[50] It rested on a theory of history that taught that societies progressed by overcoming ignorance. This version of Enlightenment thinking privileged order and knowledge over equality. Educated and rational leaders would produce the public happiness that enabled individuals to pursue their personal happiness.[51]

Across denominational lines, academies offered what teachers believed was a range of modern and practical subjects. Most schools taught arithmetic and other types of math, English writing and speaking, natural philosophy (science), as well as Latin and Greek.[52] At least one student had notes on "gunnery" and "of Shooting in Mortar-Pieces" comingled with his work on math.[53] Curricular similarities included the very systems of thought that grounded all learning. Even before Isaac Watts's *Logic* was published in North America, the famous hymnist's work structured how academy students learned logic.[54] Francis Alison and Robert Smith—respectively Old Side and New Side academy teachers—both modeled their lectures on logic from Watts.[55] The library of the College of New Jersey contained a copy of Watts's *Logic* by 1760.[56] Before that, Watts's influence spread among well-connected New Side Presbyterians, including Esther Edwards Burr, whose father and husband were both presidents of the college.[57]

The capstone at most academies and colleges was moral philosophy: ethics. The colonists based their study largely on the ideas of the Scottish Enlightenment thinker Francis Hutcheson. Hutcheson argued that humans had an innate "moral sense" that led them to benevolent behavior, and moral philosophy existed to cultivate that sense. Francis Alison usually gets credit for bringing Hutchesonian ideas to the American colonies. Alison had a degree from Edinburgh and probably studied divinity at Glasgow directly under Hutcheson. Since it dovetailed with religion by examining the innate habits and senses of man, moral philosophy reflected the theological ideas of teachers more than most other subjects. Yet even Alison's theological opponents embraced it. It influenced revivalist leaders like Jonathan Edwards—who jumpstarted the New England Awakening at his church in Northampton, Massachusetts, and later served as president of the College of New Jersey. The college was relatively slow to introduce moral philosophy to its curriculum. John Witherspoon deserves most of the credit for bringing moral philosophy to Princeton and fusing it with evangelicalism. Ironically, he was an opponent of Hutcheson in Scotland. Moral philosophy ideally helped young men live up to the Enlightenment goal of serving the community, which all schools hoped to encourage in their students.[58]

Even more than curriculum, the culture of academies pushed students to help lead societal progress. The most common word used to describe how academies motivated students was "emulation." The French pioneered this pedagogy in schools and learned society essay competitions. Competition ideally would "reward individual energies in ways that would produce benefits for the rest of society." Jean-Jacques Rousseau famously catapulted himself from lowly music teacher to leading intellectual by winning an essay contest on the moral benefits of the arts and sciences.[59] Leading English educators also extolled the virtues of student communities in fostering emulation. The radical, dissenting academy teacher Joseph Priestley argued that when students had "no road of ambition open to them but that of excelling in their studies, they of course applied their time, and bent their application, that way." He valued "real emulation," which developed when teachers put students in "contests with equals."[60]

Though generally associated with the postrevolutionary United States, this ideal was commonplace in colonial academies.[61] Teachers eschewed a traditional reliance on threats, compulsion, or the specter of retribution from "Spirits and Goblins, of *Raw-head* and *Bloody-bones* that are ready to fetch them away, and devour them," as one almanac put it. Instead, they instilled a "Love of Credit."[62] Students at Robert Smith's New Side academy in Pequea, Pennsylvania, "were stimulated to exertion by being brought into frequent competition and by having conferred upon the successful candidates for distinction such honours as were calculated to awake their boyish emulation."[63] Some writers valued academies over private tutoring precisely because they fostered emulation. As one pamphleteer noted, "where there is a community" of students, "it will create an emulation, a laudable desire to excel."[64] Officials at Delaware's Old Side Newark Academy thought the pursuit of academic distinction "must be the Object of every Student's Ambition."[65] By 1771, it was already standard practice at the Elizabeth Town Academy "to excite an emulation in the youth to study & excel."[66] In the process, students learned to harness their emotional energy to benefit the community, which elevated their status.[67]

Not everyone in North America accepted the utility of emulation. It could seem impious, even at denominational schools. A 1756 pamphlet from Germantown, Pennsylvania, bemoaned that it was "too plain to need any proof" that most colonists believed "the nature of the best education of our sons" was to "stir [students] to action from principles of *covetousness* or a desire of distinction." This taught them to try and "accumulate wealth, excel others and shine in the eyes of the World." The author argued, instead, that children should "never do any thing through strife, or envy, or emulation, or vainglory." It was wrong to try and "excel other people." Students should merely strive to please God.[68] The pamphlet alerted readers that emulation might undermine piety and lead students toward an uncontrolled desire for wealth, fame, and power.[69]

The nefarious potential of emulation was not lost on academy teachers. Even staunch critics of ambition recognized that it had an equally toxic opposite: idleness. As Francis Hutcheson put it, the "most opposite temper to ambition is the love of ease."[70] And Calvinist ministers and educators contended with accusations that their teachings encouraged idleness. If everything was preordained, what could motivate someone to do good in the world?[71] Schools also combated idleness by taking students out of the home, which was important because parents' idleness often, like "Leprocy follows and spreads on their Children."[72] In justifying emulation as a pedagogical tool, teachers probably vindicated some of their own ambitions, which led them to positions of power in religion and education.[73]

Academies and Worldly Pursuits

If academies promoted Christianity and bettered society, as teachers claimed, their culture was still also competitive and appealed to the self-interest of students and parents alike. Students turned their academy education to their advantage. By the 1760s, academy alumni drew on the knowledge, skills, and networks they gained at school to make their mark in a variety of professions. They also took part in the voluntary associations and cultural practices of the British Atlantic elite. Academies emerged to produce men of the cloth; they just as often made their students men of the world.

Prescriptive literature held that education was important for social and financial advancement. Parents should realize, one almanac declared, that it was "a foolish and most absurd Piece of Thrift, for the Sake of adding 20 or

50 Pounds to a Child's Fortune, to deprive him of the Benefit of such an Education."[74] Another almanac claimed that education preserved good relationships between generations. Parents who educated their children had "far better Title to his [the son's] Obedience and Duty, than [those who gave] him a large Estate without it."[75] Another advice guide declared that education was "the surest way to preserve an estate when got" or to "amass together money enough to purchase one."[76] Many students and their families must have staked their future on the power of a good education.

Denominational schools obliged and helped students realize professional ambitions outside of the ministry. At Samuel Finley's West Nottingham Academy, students always ate meals with prominent visitors. Benjamin Rush, a student of Finley's, remembered that "the benefits derived from the news, anecdotes, and general conversations which young people are thus permitted to hear are much greater than is generally supposed." Finley also "frequently exercised his pupils in delivering and receiving letters, and in asking and receiving favors." Rush thought Finley's attention to these skills helped explain why "many of my schoolmates filled important stations, and discharged the duties of useful professions with honor to themselves and benefit to their country."[77] "Soft skills" were essential for those with ambitions of moving up in the world.

In addition, academies fostered networks that students could use as they embarked on careers. The Philadelphia Academy's constitution provided "that the Trustees will make it their Pleasure . . . to promote and establish" their students "in Business, Offices, Marriages or any other Thing."[78] Students also took much of the responsibility for themselves, and actively maintained networks after leaving school. The famous diarist, Philip Vickers Fithian, created a mutual improvement society with some of his former schoolmates. The society held meetings and debates, wrote essays for each other, and exchanged feedback. The members believed that their "personal entertainment & improvement as individuals, depends on the diligence of the Members in general." Fithian thought it was "of very considerable advantage to every diligent member of it."[79] Academies gave young men access to vast stores of social capital.

Only a small subset of colonists could take advantage of the advanced education offered in the academies. By the 1770s, around one-third of 1 percent of white men in the colonies were college graduates.[80] Costs for academies were usually lower than for colleges, yet few people could afford it and even fewer attended.[81] The supply of academies often exceeded the demand. A capacity to help students in a range of pursuits was a boon for an academy in a crowded market. Francis Alison took pride that at the Newark Academy, "farmers can educate their children, so as to fit y^m. for almost any station in life."[82] Compared with the entrenched hierarchies of England, colonial education offered social mobility to the young men who could afford it. That was still a decidedly small group, and one with aspirations to elite status.

A good proportion of students at denominational schools went into professional careers, not the ministry. Lists of academy students are hard to come by, so prosopographical analysis is difficult to conduct. But biographical data abounds for the College of New Jersey alumni. The school educated more men who did not become clergy than who did. In the quarter century prior to the Revolutionary War, only about 47 percent of graduates entered the ministry. This rate was higher than at many colleges, though it still reveals the importance of secular curriculum to the school's success.[83] During the Revolutionary War years, the proportion of clergymen dropped to 21 percent.[84]

The smaller, poorly documented academies that opened throughout the mid-Atlantic also served a clientele who used their education in pursuit of worldly gains. Take Francis Barber, the last principal of Elizabeth Town Academy prior to the Revolution. He attended the College of New Jersey because he was "designed by his parents to wear the sacred robe." To the dismay of his parents, Barber found that "this office did not suit his taste."[85] He was not unusual in that way. His two immediate predecessors were Tapping Reeve and Aaron Ogden. The former became a distinguished lawyer and founded the first law school in the United States. The latter was a businessman and namesake of the famous 1824 Supreme Court case, *Gibbons v. Ogden*.[86] While Barber and his predecessors searched for their calling, they socialized another generation into Moderate Enlightenment culture within a religious school.

The convergence in educational culture at various denominational academies was an unlikely but significant development.[87] Students usually attended an academy with the religious affiliation of their parents. As they furthered their education, though, many attended whichever school made the most sense for their chosen career. For example, John Ewing attended Francis Alison's Old Side academy, and then the New Side College of New Jersey, before working at both institutions as a teacher. He finally settled down in Philadelphia as pastor at the First Presbyterian Church and as a faculty member at the College and Academy of Philadelphia. Several of Samuel Finley's students from his New Side West Nottingham Academy attended colleges other than Princeton. Two of his students, Edward Shippen and John Morgan, helped found the medical school at the College of Philadelphia. Another of his students, Benjamin Rush, was one of the school's first professors.⁸⁸ Academy pedagogy had birthed networks that transcended the very religious divides the schools were initially created to institutionalize. By the 1760s, academies appealed to would-be elites of many traditions who were in pursuit of many ambitions.

Academies and Civil Society

Academies also aided a broader shift in the relationship between the North American colonies and the metropole. By offering an Enlightened curriculum and training students for secular professions, academies had reoriented students' relationship to Britain itself. Alumni began to fashion themselves more like men elsewhere in the Empire with a similar class and educational background. Nowhere was this clearer than in the way academies and their alumni helped open civil society and the public sphere in late-colonial America.⁸⁹

The emergence of print, consumer culture, and voluntarism took root in the elite, urbane spaces of colonial America and connected those places with British merchants and thinkers.⁹⁰ Academies were one of the very few institutions that drew this culture into the hinterlands. For practical reasons, academies tended to be rural institutions. When sending children to school, parents worried most about their health and their morals. Disease and vice were both associated with cities. Teachers and trustees strategically set up schools in rural areas that city dwellers could access easily but that were "in a very healthy Part of the Country." In these areas, "Parents of Children have the utmost Security, that can be desired, for their Morals."⁹¹ While there, students engaged with print culture and civil and philanthropic associations, more often associated with urban areas. This bolstered the academies' growing reputation as sites of secular elite formation, and furthered their students' professional goals.

Print was a key vector of new social and cultural values throughout the British Atlantic. Ideas about gentility circulated through pamphlets and literature, while newspapers made people aware of the consumer goods that became trappings of status. Academies were already enmeshed in print networks, which were central to the Awakening. Popular revivalists exploited the growing print culture to turn leading revivalists like George Whitefield into veritable celebrities.⁹² Newspapers and pamphlets spread their evangelical message faster and further than itinerant ministers could. Having been reared in the Awakening ferment, students, teachers, and school trustees understood the power of this new print culture and took part in it.

Denominational schools had the power to shape the reading habits of a generation of students. Teachers were close with publishers and booksellers. In the early 1750s, Samuel Davies—the Presbyterian minister, academy teacher, and future president of the College of New Jersey—took a fundraising trip to Britain on the college's behalf. While abroad, Davies cultivated relationships with printers in order to publish his sermons. Closer to home, he also spent time with the prominent Philadelphia printer William Bradford.[93] It seems that Bradford did good business in many academy towns.[94] While in England, Davies also built ties with the Society in London for Promoting Religious Knowledge (SPRK) and secured from them a few large shipments of books. Davies' own efforts at self-improvement created networks for sharing and spreading written works. His students reaped the benefits.[95] Through their engagement with institutions like SPRK, educated provincials also inserted themselves into the British Empire's expanding world of philanthropy, which was drawn together by print.[96]

Academies were incubators of their own culture of print production and consumption. People affiliated with schools produced new printed materials. William Smith, provost of the College and Academy of Philadelphia, helped create the *American Magazine*, which situated "the college in a network of manuscript and print circulation that was emerging around the Atlantic World." Magazine culture more generally brought the polite and refined side of Enlightenment literature to North America.[97] Even Francis Alison—Smith's Old Side Presbyterian colleague and his frequent adversary at the Philadelphia Academy—promoted the *American Magazine* to his friends and students.[98]

Literary ambition trickled down to the students. During the mid-1770s in the Cohansie region of southern New Jersey, Philip Vickers Fithian and his former school friends created their own manuscript newsletter to spread ideas and debate politics. The *Plain Dealer*, as they fashioned it, brought the dominant transatlantic print culture to a rural region. Significantly, this grew out of their "admonishing society." Before that, many of these men had participated in the College of New Jersey's Whig and Cliosophic debating societies. Those institutions probably led to other, smaller debating and improvement societies that left no traces.[99] In the Cohansie case, sociability also mattered a great deal. Fithian frequently attended singing schools around South Jersey, where he had "the opportunity of seeing" peers from throughout the region. He was particularly pleased when an "eloquent singer from Philadelphia" attended a session at a local church.[100]

Sectarian schools had ironically provided a unifying experience for students across denominational lines. Alumni seemed to bend toward imperial culture and away from purely religious divisions. If commerce, print, philanthropy, and the Enlightenment drew together elite and upwardly mobile middling people across colonial America and, indeed, the British Empire, then denominational academies were critical for socializing colonists into this broader culture.[101] Within two decades, these religious schools had developed the capacity to socialize a British-style, secular elite.

ACCORDING TO BENJAMIN FRANKLIN, before the mid-eighteenth century, "the *culture* of *minds* by the *finer arts* and *sciences*" in the colonies "was necessarily postpon'd to times of more wealth and leisure." By 1749, Franklin thought that "those times are come." He believed that "numbers of our inhabitants are both able and willing to give their sons a good education, if it might be had at home, free from the extraordinary expence and hazard in sending them abroad for that purpose."[102] To Franklin, the slow development of colonial education had stemmed from a lack of demand. According to others, supply had been the real problem. Looking back on the 1740s, when Francis Alison first began teaching students at his home in New London, Pennsylvania, the synod leaders recalled that "Learning was under great Discouragements, and Opportunities of Education scarce."[103] Outside New England, governments failed to provide inhabitants with education. Across the mid-Atlantic and upper South, religious denominations failed to pick up the slack.

All that changed with the Great Awakening. Denominational schools, like the small academy in Elizabeth Town, emerged to train ministers and remedied the institutional failures that led to early revivalism. Students, parents, teachers, and the community writ large soon realized that the academies' influence could be much greater. They learned that academies were powerful tools of elite formation, which mattered in a place that lacked more traditional bases for aristocracy. Academies helped produce a new professional class and cultural elite in the colonies. Before the Seven Years' War, the full political import of academies was still unknown. But amid that global crisis, imperial officials came to use denominational schools to strengthen the British presence in North America. Once politicized, though, academies could be turned against the British. The generation of would-be leaders educated in those schools could not only envision a world separate from the British Empire, they sparked, fought, and settled a revolution to create it. In their hands, academies became, for a time, a revolutionary institution.

CHAPTER TWO

The Academy Effect
Civic Education and the American Revolution

While conducting his duties as officer of the day on February 11, 1783, Colonel Francis Barber mounted his horse and started back toward his quarters. It was the end of a long war, and Barber was very lucky to be alive. He had suffered wounds at Monmouth and Newton, and "a slight wound in his face" from a bayonet at Yorktown.[1] More than most, Barber probably felt that the end of his service could not come soon enough. Indeed, it had not. Barber was killed that day "by the fell of a tree, which was cut down by a soldier of the American army, at the cantonment near Newburgh, a short time before the army was disbanded, and after the articles of peace had been signed."[2] Two days later, "he was buried with the honors of war."[3]

Though Barber rose rapidly through the ranks of the Continental Army, he was a soldier by neither training nor inclination. Barber taught at the Presbyterian Academy in Elizabeth Town, New Jersey through the mid-1770s, "until called from that employment to take . . . the field, for the defence of America."[4] His death might have been unusual, but the trajectory that brought Barber to Newburgh was not. Decades later, the trustees of the First Presbyterian Church of Elizabeth Town, who supervised Barber's academy, proudly recalled that "at their country's call," the "scholars ran from their masters, and with them, to the rescue."[5]

Barber and his students were part of a more common generational experience. By the 1760s, the denominational colleges and academies that emerged out of the Great Awakening had politicized. During the Seven Years' War especially, denominational academies drew praise as institutions of civil elite formation. In part, this culminated their turn toward socializing well-to-do colonists into the Enlightened culture of the British Atlantic world. Academies' politicization was also part of a broader imperial recommitment to the civic purposes of education. Academy trustees leveraged that to strengthen their schools' position within the British Empire. They claimed that academies deserved support because they trained good British subjects and potential leaders. Not long after, though, came the Imperial Crisis. Academies had encouraged students' ambitions and transformed their sense of self amid imperial political and social upheaval. Unfortunately for the British, the political importance of academies manifested most clearly when students and teachers mobilized behind the revolutionary cause. They left schools in droves to take positions of civil and military leadership during the American Revolution.[6]

Revolutions are inherently destructive. Yet successful revolutions depend as much on the consolidation of new power groups as the overthrow of prevailing power structures.[7] Denominational academies gave rise to a new cadre of power actors, a crucial group of would-be elites. To be sure, this was a uniquely mid-Atlantic story. The pattern was clearest in New Jersey and Delaware, where non-Puritan Reformed denominations—and thus academies, too—were most concentrated. The academy generation, though, found their way into the most national of institutions during the Revolution. Through these men, the colonial academy model spread to the rest of the new United States. The American Revolution showcased the power of academies as a tool of *civil* elite formation and clarified their civic purpose. Paradoxically, this was an outcome of the politicization of schools that had first served the interests of the British Empire.

Politicized Education and the Seven Years' War

Before the academy generation became vectors of Revolution, many academies themselves became institutions pregnant with political importance. This grew out of the Enlightenment commitments of academy teachers and students, who assumed that societies or nations could not develop without the exertions of educated and ambitious men. As Philip Vickers Fithian wrote, "Without Instruction & Refinement Men are advanced but a little above their fellow Creatures the Brutes."[8] It was only natural that this view of education would ignite political ambitions in students. As Francis Hutcheson put it, "where the moral sense is in its full vigour, it makes the generous determination to publick happiness the supreme one in the soul."[9] On the one hand, this was good. "A moderate degree" of ambition for power "is innocent and useful," Hutcheson wrote. It led men to "desire reputation for integrity and moral worth." However, on the other hand, when these desires "grow too violent they are restless and uneasy to the individual, and often pernicious to society."[10] Teachers had to direct political ambitions toward acceptable ends.

Colonists and Britons alike came to see academies as incubators of political talent. In this period, English education reformers made the case that schools had a duty to nurture future leaders. During the 1750s, Thomas Sheridan—an Irish actor and advocate of teaching elocution—bemoaned that English schools did little to "train up the youth destined to compose the august body of our legislature." That needed to change. "In all well-regulated states," Sheridan argued, education ought to shape students' "talents in such a way as will render them most serviceable to the support of that government."[11] Likewise, during the 1760s, the radical pedagogue and liberal political theorist Joseph Priestley wrote that it was important "to fill up with advantage those years of a young gentleman's life which immediately precede his engaging in those higher spheres of active life." Priestley criticized how most English schools focused on training ministers. In a period when "the connection of states are extended," teachers should direct their attention to "gentlemen who are designed to fill the principal stations of active life."[12] The need for schools to train a future political elite was even more pressing in the colonies, where hierarchies were not as fixed and who would hold power was harder to predict.[13]

The conflict with France in the Seven Years' War gave academies the chance to prove their political utility. As institutions that already fostered Protestantism, denominational schools were obvious bulwarks against the encroaching Catholic menace.[14] King's College in New York City best illustrated how colonial colleges claimed to serve imperial purposes. Looking back after the war, the trustees argued that their "public Seminary of Learning" inculcated "the Principles of Virtue, Religion and Loyalty." King's College deserved the "Approbation of every Friend to the Prosperity of the British Empire in America." To illustrate the point, the trustees brandished the fact that it had been "favoured with a Royal Charter" and received "the Countenance of the Government."[15] King's College had the advantage of being an Anglican school. It made sense that the state church served the state. That said, the school was legally bound to educate all Protestants equally. A vocal group of Presbyterians had secured this concession at the college's founding and also blocked a proposed requirement that all students attend Anglican services. These provisions blurred the differences between established and dissenting schools.[16]

British officials tolerated dissenting Protestant schools largely for the same reasons that they supported King's College. Legally speaking, dissenting colleges in the mid-Atlantic resembled King's. When granting charters, imperial officials mandated similar concessions that dissenters demanded of Anglicans in New York. Jonathan Dickinson, the first president of the College of New Jersey, conceded that the school's main goal was "the Education of pious and well qualified Candidates for the Ministry." But the school had to do more than train revivalist preachers. The trustees were "by our Charter obliged to admit without Distinction, those of any & of every religious Profession to the

Privileges of a liberal Education."[17] This model persisted through the Seven Years' War, and the Presbyterian Newark Academy in Delaware received a charter with similar provisions. Later, the trustees reassured potential English donors that there "is no clause in the charter, by which the least preference is given to any Protestant denomination of Christians." The trustees committed never to "remove [the school] from its present catholic foundation."[18] It served all Protestants equally.

King's College, then, was Anglican, but it might have no stronger claim to serve the Empire than any other *Protestant* school. All four chartered schools in the mid-Atlantic had received some combination of tacit or explicit support from imperial officials, including approvals for lotteries to raise money.[19] Of all the schools, the College and Academy of Philadelphia was the most overtly nondenominational. Most of the smaller, nonchartered academies had already started to appeal to children of many denominations, exploiting the Awakening's latitudinarian tendencies. They were all Protestant institutions that served Protestant children. That fact mattered during a conflict with a Catholic power.[20]

School leaders leveraged the growing connection between education and Empire. At the Philadelphia Academy's end-of-year exercises in 1754, shortly after the war broke out, Francis Hopkinson—a future signer of the Declaration of Independence—argued that "*Knowledge* is incompatible with *arbitrary Power.*" Here he clearly had in mind Catholic absolutism, not the British Empire. "THE RIGHT EDUCATION OF YOUTH," he continued, "has ever been esteemed, by wise men, one of the chief cares of the best constituted States." Thus the College and Academy of Philadelphia helped keep the British state healthy. Hopkinson would later argue that the College and Academy protected both "the true Principles of *Liberty,* and the *Protestant Religion.*"[21] Leaders of the College and Academy also positioned the school as an interdenominational, civic meeting place. When Quaker elected officials would not provide supplies for the war effort, "Free Electors" met at the school to find a workaround.[22] The next week, a newspaper published an account of George Whitefield's appearance at the "Academy-yard," where he preached "to a vast Number of People of all Denominations."[23] The two events showed how the academy helped draw the boundaries of this Protestant political community.[24]

Dissenters and dissenting schools had the most to gain from education's rising stock. Among Presbyterians, nobody saw this more clearly than the New Side minister Samuel Davies. He claimed God would inevitably side with the English and pushed his Virginia congregation to take up arms. The first Virginia militia unit to mobilize in the Seven Years' War came from

Hanover County, Davies's home. Later in the 1750s, Davies took up the presidency of the College of New Jersey and spread his patriotic message to a wider audience. Most notably, he gave his famous sermon, *Religion and the Public Spirit*, toward the end of the war. He followed that up with a eulogy for King George II. Davies believed that dissenters needed to demonstrate their patriotism to ensure political protection for their schools and denominations. Both of Virginia's wartime governors understood and honored the relationship that Davies hoped to maintain.[25]

During the war, Davies and other educators harped on how their schools nurtured virtuous civil leaders. In *Religion and Public Spirit*, Davies exhorted a Princeton graduating class that if they ever possessed the chance to "be of Service to Posterity," they must "rejoice in the Opportunity." Students should "be ambitious to survive yourselves, to be immortal upon Earth." In fact, absent public spiritedness, "all the valuable Ends of a liberal Education, will be lost upon you." Advanced education mattered only for its public value.[26] Davies's sermon used Calvinist principles to stoke political ambition, but he sounded like his Anglican counterpart in Philadelphia. William Smith told students at the Philadelphia Academy and College that they "can acquire no Authority so lasting, no Influence so beneficial" as through "*superior Talents*, joined to *inflexible Integrity*." Students developed all of this in school. But Smith would also "beseech you to avoid all Manner of Passions." To check themselves, students need to realize that often men would not "receive the full Applause of your Virtue in your own Day." They should act virtuously nonetheless.[27]

The war experience convinced many observers of the similarities between various schools and further papered over denominational differences. In a 1763 sermon, an Englishman and Anglican priest, Daniel Watson, praised how "protestant youth of all denominations are received into" the colonial colleges. Education, he surmised, "will give birth to many amiable and lasting friendships in after-life, between men of different persuasions." Schools "tend to wear off that sourness of party." Watson went on to describe America as "the school of christian knowledge, useful arts and liberal science."[28] By the end of the Seven Years' War, this is what denominational schools were known for.

Throughout the Empire, the war generated an interest in the civic purposes of education.[29] In 1765, the Englishman John Brown celebrated schools, calling them the "Foundations of civil Liberty." They directed "the Habits of the youthful Heart, to a Coincidence with the general Welfare" of society. In similar language to that used by Davies, Brown called this "public spirit, or the Love of our Country; the highest Passion that can sway the human Heart."[30] His arguments anticipated the language of republican educational reformers in the early United States. Joseph Priestley criticized Brown because he "seems to consider as the only object of education, the tranquility of the state." Priestley thought this overvalued "Uniformity," which he called "the characteristic of the brute creation." Instead, he thought that "humans are capable of infinite improvement" and schools should encourage "more variety." Doing so, Priestley concluded, was "certainly an object of the greatest importance in every state."[31]

Despite their disagreements over specifics, Brown and Priestley recognized that education could serve national interests. This logic had implications for the colonies. Brown argued that "Colonies, when peopled beyond a certain Degree, become a Burthen to the Mother Country," insofar as "they divide her compacted Strength." Yet this was just one example of "the incurable Defect of our political State, in not having a correspondent and adequate Code of Education."[32] Viewed from this perspective, cultural reform, as much as constitutional or economic integration, seemed necessary to bring together the metropole and the periphery. Denominational schools already did some of this work, so it made sense for the Empire to encourage them.

Education might also help colonists overcome the European perception of North America as a "savage" place. In his famous *Commentaries* on English law, the jurist William Blackstone noted that the "American plantations" were conquered lands, taken by force. This put them somewhat outside the control of English law until Parliament asserted otherwise.[33] The fact that the colonists readily embraced slavery and waged constant war with Indigenous peoples raised questions about their civility. Could they abide by the law of nations and honor treaties? Failing to control nonwhite populations could erode British claims to authority throughout the realm.[34] Education offered a way to "civilize" uncivil domains. In the 1750s, Thomas Sheridan claimed it should "be the first care of a nation that is ambitious to distinguish itself in the world to cultivate and refine their language ... to be a perpetual ornament and support to the state."[35] The necessity of political refinement was most pressing in North America. But the emphasis on education fit within the larger British Atlantic experience. Throughout the realm, local magistrates and officials helped establish governing authority by encouraging "civility" among the elite.[36]

The general national anxiety and geopolitical unrest that accompanied the Seven Years' War, then, imbued academies and colleges with civic importance. In recognition of education's political value, the Empire acknowledged the autonomy of Presbyterian and other Reformed churches over their schools. This comity emerged out of shared fears of Catholicism, which the war threw into relief. But it also elided how dissenters' desire for autonomy clashed with the centralizing ambitions of imperial officials.[37] The extent of these disagreements would become clear in the coming years. In 1763, though, denominational schools' perceived value to the Empire as sites of civil elite formation left dissenters confident of their place within that empire.[38]

Students and Teachers in the Imperial Crisis

During the Imperial Crisis, the politicization of education backfired on the British. Students, teachers, and trustees embroiled academies and colleges in the political controversies that ultimately led to American independence and denominational schools became a force of imperial disintegration. Much impelled students and school officials to stand against Britain. Latitudinarian impulses fractured as the Imperial Crisis brought denominational politics back to the fore. Denominational academies had also stoked the personal and political ambitions of countless students, who found an outlet in the nascent revolutionary movement. During the 1770s and 1780s, men like Francis Barber took their place on the international stage.

Perhaps Britons should have seen this coming. For all the ways they promoted a shared elite culture between colonies and the metropole, colonial schools also revealed some key divergences. "Ornamental" subjects—dancing, music, fencing, visual arts, and modern languages, particularly French and Italian—were important to English elite education. Americans would later embrace this curriculum. Prior to the Revolution, though, it seemed backward and unnecessary to all but the groups most connected with England itself: the children of urban merchants and the southern planters. Dancing masters fostered metropolitan culture by teaching young men and women the choreography—both the dances and social interactions—of balls and assemblies, the central rituals of court culture. While establishing the social status of the dancers, these practices also connected participants to the king.[39]

North American academies and colleges were firmly British, but never wholly English. American educators took their cue from the Scottish Enlightenment, which emphasized "useful" education. Moreover, colonial political traditions exaggerated the republican threads of this educational culture.[40] As a result, denominational academies were lukewarm in their embrace of ornamental subjects. Colleges and academies did teach them, but often as something extra. The College of New Jersey, which became a patriot hotbed, offered French instruction in the 1770s. Of the major schools, King's College had the most developed curriculum in modern languages.[41] Benjamin Franklin thought that French, as well as most other ancient and modern languages, served specific purposes. He argued that students at the College and Academy of Philadelphia should only learn the languages relevant to their careers. Franklin thought similarly about art. He recognized that "Drawing is a kind of Universal Language, understood by all Nations," and could benefit gentleman travelers or middling mechanics. Yet "Art is long, and their Time is short," Franklin argued. He "therefore propos'd that [students] learn those Things that are likely to be most useful and most ornamental."[42] Colonists placed unusual value on practical education.

American resistance to ornamental education was also gendered: The curriculum did not conform to colonial conceptions of masculinity. In the 1750s, one newspaper essayist proposed a sarcastic plan for an academy "better calculated for the free-born *Sons of Gentlemen*" than the "*old-fashioned*" curriculum of most colonial schools. This school would "win the Hearts of all Mothers" because "I will take care, that my Pupils shall not be over-burdened with Learning." Instead, students "shall learn DANCING to the greatest perfection." Discipline would be loose because correction "is infinitely worse than any Vice." To add to the lack of structure, students "shall go Home to their Mamma's one Week in every Month."[43] The implication was clear: old-fashioned, genteel education made men weak, dependent, and effeminate. It did not help that elite women often received an ornamental education. Some women in certain communities, like Philadelphia, had access to a more academic education.[44] Otherwise, educational opportunity for young women in colonial America was quite limited outside the ornamental education offered in urban seaports. The female seminaries that dotted the early national landscape were not yet a feature of American life. Most colonists thought of female education more as cultural finishing than an academic pursuit.[45]

The rise of republicanism deepened these gendered ideas about education. Ornamental subjects, dancing especially, seemed to embody the republican caricature that luxuries corrupted individuals and communities. Opposition to ornamental education dovetailed with boycotts of British goods that were at the heart of revolutionary resistance. In 1774, a would-be Loyalist newspaper in New York ran advertisements for "A NEW ACADEMY FOR TEACHING MUSICK, DANCING, AND THE ITALIAN and FRENCH LANGUAGES."[46] By contrast, a few months later, a student at the Old Side Newark, Delaware Academy gave a public address on "the mischiefs of luxury."[47] If virtue was masculine and its antithesis was luxury, which was feminine, then ornamental education corrupted men's virtue. A republic would cease to function if the men in power were all educated to be effete.[48] Using ornamental subjects as a foil bolstered the connection between academies and masculine political service.

Differences in educational values notwithstanding, well-educated colonists did not uniformly support independence. Location, ethnicity, and denomination conditioned the positions that men took on resistance. Regardless, schools put unusual pressure on men to engage in politics. In 1766, on the heels of the Stamp Act crisis, the College of Philadelphia held an essay competition on the "reciprocal advantages of a perpetual union" between Great Britain and the colonies. The tone of the essays was measured. Some essayists, though, did critique imperial officials for disrupting an otherwise fruitful relationship.[49] The influence of the school's Anglican provost, William Smith, tempered the arguments of both sides. Smith taught Hutchesonian moral philosophy, and through it, republican principles. Smith, though, was no radical. He never took as staunch a loyalist position as some, but rather was ambivalent about the American Revolution.[50]

Presbyterian schools, by contrast, were overtly radical. During the 1760s, dissenters detected a change in the Empire's stance toward them. It seemed that imperial officeholders were increasingly staunch Anglicans, who were determined to strengthen the Church of England in the colonies.[51] Dissenting colonists had long feared that the Anglican Church would try to assert their power by establishing a colonial bishop. Doing so would surely undermine the dissenters' control over their spiritual lives and important local institutions, including schools. Shortly after the repeal of the Stamp Act, some Anglican leaders confirmed these suspicions and raised the possibility of establishing a colonial episcopacy. The policy probably never had a chance to go into effect. But the dissenting colonists had their guard up. They reacted to mumblings about a colonial bishop within the context of imperial policies that threatened their political liberties.[52] The issue lingered. During the war, several Anglican priests faced violent retribution.[53]

At the College of New Jersey, rampant support for patriot resistance continued nearly unabated from 1765 through the outbreak of war. Students attacked imperial politics in graduation orations, signed nonimportation agreements, and even staged their own tea party.[54] Academy students took part in similar activities. Alumni from the local academy led the revolutionary movement in the Cohansie region of Cumberland County, New Jersey, where they also staged another local tea party.[55] The Old Side Newark Academy became politicized as well, albeit less dramatically. By 1772, one observer noted how Newark Academy students discussed "the most perplexing political topics," including "difficult and knotty questions, relating to the *British* constitution." Academy exhibitions made him feel as though he "was within a circle of vociferous politicians at *Will's* coffee-house, instead of being surrounded with the meek disciples of wisdom, in the calm shades of academic retirement."[56] College and academy students could not escape the political debates that would soon tear apart the Empire.

More than anything, then, education influenced how men experienced the Revolution. A large proportion of colonists—perhaps even a majority—did everything they could to avoid taking sides in the conflict.[57] Educated men found it difficult to remain neutral. The structure of educational institutions forced some men to take clear sides. Faculty members and trustees of chartered institutions often had to take oaths of allegiance to the king when they accepted their positions. During the Imperial Crisis, colonists signed their names to all manner of oaths, covenants, and boycott agreements. For patriots and loyalists alike, a signature defined one's allegiance.[58] Though many college officials took oaths well before the outbreak of imperial tensions, they were on record pledging allegiance to the king. This circumscribed their options. They could either renounce the oath, which for all intents and purposes was a revolutionary action. Or they could do nothing, which to revolutionaries looked like an affirmation of loyalism. There was little middle ground. When new state legislatures started to reissue charters for schools, they required officials to take new oaths to the state governments.[59]

There was also a growing sense that the expansion of colleges and academies had made the North American colonies more self-sufficient. By contrast, attempts to create domestic higher education in the West Indies had failed. In Barbados, the planter Christopher Codrington willed plantations and slaves to the Society for the Propagation of the Gospel (SPG) to endow a college. When it finally opened in 1743, it offered mostly elementary learning.[60] West Indian planters still needed to send their children to England for more advanced education. This was one of the bonds that connected planters with the metropolitan elite.[61]

By the 1770s, North American school leaders claimed their institutions could better serve the children of planters. Future signer of the U.S. Constitution Hugh Williamson went to Jamaica in 1772 to raise money for the Newark Academy. In an almost imperial vision for the school and the North American colonies, he argued that "this tender plant, watered by your hands, in due time shall become a great tree." The school's "branches shall cover the Continent, and extend to these distant isles, while millions that are yet unborn shall sit in peace under its shadow."[62] At the same time, John Morgan was also in Jamaica soliciting money for the College of Philadelphia's medical school.

Morgan appealed to "the large commercial connexion between these Islands and the city of Philadelphia."[63] Domestic schools buoyed a growing sense that North America had the potential to become a new metropole. They also reflected the changing relationship between schools and the Empire. When John Ewing went to England to raise money for the College and Academy of Philadelphia in 1774, he found "many discouragements" because his contacts were "angry with the Americans."[64] As many colonial schools seemed to turn against the Empire, the Empire turned against those schools.

Academies and Revolutionary Mobilization

By the onset of the Revolution, much of the academy generation was ambitious to take the reins of political and military leadership, poised to do so by their education, and embedded in larger networks of like-minded men. The public started to think of educated men as nascent elites and natural leaders. Newspaper essays argued that teachers "should be made Delegates in Congress, Assembly-men, Magistrates, &c." That would ensure that "patriots, heroes and lawgivers . . . fill the first offices of government."[65] This was not idle talk.

The academy generation transitioned directly into the revolutionary generation.[66] Francis Barber's Elizabeth Town Academy was not the only school to shutter when the teachers and students turned out for war. In Somerset County, Maryland, students and teachers at the local academy "engaged in a different scene" when the war came. They transformed from "the friends of literature" into "steady opposers of tyrannical usurpation."[67] These schools confirmed the belief that education "not only concerns the Happiness of the Individual, but the Welfare and Prosperity of Society," as one almanac put it.[68] Students and teachers harnessed the networks they formed at school to help their colonies mobilize for revolution.[69] In joining the Revolution, students could claim to serve their community while also raising their own status. They did exactly what the curriculum and culture of academies taught them to do, but against the British rather than for them.[70]

How widespread was this? The best data are for the College of New Jersey, where over 70 percent of the living alumni in 1775 served in the military or held public office during the Revolution.[71] Precious few student lists survive from the colonial academies. Evidentiary problems notwithstanding, academies clearly were integral to revolutionary mobilization in New Jersey and Delaware. In these states, many academy-educated men filled the ranks of the Continental Army officer corps and political offices. Of the twenty-four men who served as majors, lieutenant colonels, and colonels in the New Jersey

Continental line, at least one-third had a direct connection with an academy as either a student or a teacher.[72] Some came from Enoch Green's Deerfield Academy, where Philip Vickers Fithian and his friends were educated. The central node of the New Jersey officer corps was Francis Barber's school, the Elizabeth Town Academy. For most of the war, the commanding officers of both the first and third regiments had important Elizabeth Town connections. Academy-educated officers also frequently took on logistical and administrative jobs, as paymasters, adjutants, and aides-de-camp. They pushed the paper that allowed the Continental Army to function.[73]

The Delaware line was much smaller, but it also felt the influence of the academy generation. Colonel David Hall was educated at an academy in Lewes, Delaware, and then commanded the Delaware line for most of the war. Both his immediate subordinate and successor also studied at academies. So, too, had the regimental surgeon before he attended medical school.[74] Francis Alison's influence on the Delaware line was particularly clear. He felt comfortable writing the Committee of Safety to recommend his own nephew as someone "who may be set to act" as "a Lieutenant or Ensign if appointed."[75] The officer corps looked the way it did, in part, because the Awakening expanded the pool of educated young men in the colonies.

While they served in the army, educated officers continued their pursuit of cultural refinement. Though the Continental officers tended to come from wealthier families than enlisted men, they were still not a hereditary elite. An officer's rank did not convey his status; rather, status depended on rank. As a result, cultural distinctions mattered more in the Continental Army than in European armies. Officers established strict rules to enforce the social separation from enlisted men.[76] As one historian put it, officers held themselves to "standards of ostentatious conduct."[77] Academies had taught some officers these standards in the first place.

Like at school, officers honed their status as a group. Sociability was crucial to the officer experience.[78] While stationed at Ticonderoga, "Major [Francis] Barber and sundry of the officers went to Crown Point in sleighs for a pleasure spell."[79] At another time, Ebenezer Elmer recalled that he "went up and played a few games of whist with some of the officers."[80] All this could look unbecoming. Elmer snidely noted that "much of the folly of gallantry is to be learned in the army."[81] Enlisted men also sensed what was happening. One soldier in the New Jersey line commented that many officers "would not pass unnoticed in the politest courts of Europe." To an extent, that was the point.[82]

Education helped solve a central challenge of the Revolution, which emerged first in the army: how to justify hierarchy in a society founded on equality. The same rigidly enforced cultural differentiation that supported military rank would become important to the republic generally. Senior officers and continental congressmen saw the officer corps as both a model for, and incubator of, gentlemen leaders for the new republic.[83] If the officer corps did become a source of leaders and ideas about status, then education would maintain its critical civic role once the war ended.

To a degree, that is what happened. Most academy men were new to positions of leadership. Though in many ways they looked and acted the part convincingly, their aspirations to higher elective office had been stifled during the colonial era.[84] None of the academy-educated officers from New Jersey had served in the colonial legislature before the war. Very few of their fathers held colony-wide office either, though several held lower-level local offices such as justice of the peace and sheriff. The families of Delaware's officers had slightly more success before the war. Yet many of the educated officers from both states who survived the war rose to high-level political office in the 1780s. A few peaked as state assemblymen or council members, and others as governors.[85]

Critically, many of the earliest national officeholders were educated at denominational academies. This included many delegates to the Constitutional Convention and members of the first United States Congress. For example, Delaware and New Jersey both sent five men to the Constitutional Convention in Philadelphia in 1787. Three from each state had academy backgrounds.[86] A fourth from New Jersey, David Brearley, grew up near Princeton and probably attended the local grammar school, but it is not entirely clear.[87]

The academies' influence was greatest in New Jersey and Delaware, where Reformed education did the most to solve the colonial challenge of elite formation. New England mobilized almost ancient patterns of communal leadership for the revolutionary cause, and in the South, the planter elite retained its power. The mid-Atlantic academy experience, though, represented the future. It remains significant that the influence of academy students was pronounced in the period's few national institutions: the Continental Army, Continental Congress, Constitutional Convention, and later, Freemasonry and the Society of the Cincinnati. By the 1780s, these national institutions greased the wheels for the expansion of academies beyond the Reformed mid-Atlantic. That work may have begun during the war, as one anecdote suggests. The Leicester Academy, in Worcester County, Massachusetts, was one of the first New England academies when it opened in 1784. Among its early supporters were General Rufus Putnam, the second man to serve as the army's chief engineer, and Jeduthan Baldwin, the assistant chief engineer. On at least one occasion, Baldwin "Drank Wine & Supt." with Francis Barber. Might the men have shared notes on their backgrounds and discussed academies? We can never know.[88]

Either way, the American Revolution allowed the academy generation to realize some ambitions that the social mobility of the colonial period had fostered, but that the political immobility of the period had frustrated. Their experience was not part of some wholesale democratization of officeholding.[89] Education mattered to these men, not because it made them more like their constituents, but because it was exclusive and taught students to differentiate and distinguish themselves.[90] Education may not explain why these men played such prominent roles in the Revolution. Yet their collective ascent showed Americans that education—and especially the academies—had a civic purpose. They were a powerful tool of elite formation in a world premised on equality.

War, Destruction, and the Future of American Education

Even with this educational model in hand, Americans had their work cut out for them. The transition back into civil routines was not so simple, least of all when it came to education. Never before had New Jersey mobilized teachers and students for war. In fact, since 1704, New Jersey had exempted those responsible for governance "from being listed in any Troop or Company." This included legislators, judicial officers, coroners, sheriffs, and key professionals such as ministers, doctors, and also teachers.[91] The war, then, interrupted schooling in unprecedented ways. It also upended much of the educational infrastructure colonists had built in the mid-Atlantic since the Awakening, which shaped the development of schools going forward.

The fighting was particularly virulent in the New Jersey. After George Washington's surprise attacks on Trenton and Princeton in December 1776, a protracted "forage war" for supplies wracked the Jersey countryside.[92] Though education was "essential to the Prosperity of every Community," the legislature noted it "hath been greatly interrupted, and in many parts totally prevented by the Necessity of subjecting Instructors, as well as Scholars, to military Duty." In response, New Jersey passed the 1778 "Act for the Encouragement of Education." Because education was so integral to "well-regulated Governments," the state granted military exemptions to "each and every Master or Teacher," with some minor technical restrictions.[93]

This law notwithstanding, teachers still found themselves wrapped up in the violence of war. During June 1780, a young teacher named John Stockholm kept track of his reading habits and the days he "kept school." Rather suddenly, amid the quotidian detail, Stockholm noted that "the militia were alarmed by the landing of the British and Hessian troops at Elizabeth." He mustered at the news. A few days later, though, Stockholm marched back home. Some weeks after that, Stockholm again found himself in a "pretty sever [sic] skirmish with the enemy." This was the last combat that Stockholm saw, but not his last encounter with the military. In 1781, he "had an interview with Col Lamb," from New York. During that encounter, he also saw "his Excellency General Washington—who is but a man—tho' a very superior one." With the war won, Stockholm returned to his earlier routine. He organized a public exhibition for his students, which "exceeded my expectations." Stockholm then prepared to resume his education at college in Princeton.[94]

The war's greatest long-term impact on education was physical. The British regularly targeted Elizabeth Town because they hoped to capture or kill New Jersey's governor, William Livingston, who lived there. In an attempt in January 1780, "the Rebel Posts at Elizabeth Town & Newark were completely surprized and carried off, by different detachments of the King's Troops."[95] The British failed to capture Livingston, but they damaged the patriots' infrastructure, including repurposed Presbyterian institutions. In Elizabeth Town, "the Presbyterian parsonage then used as barracks," and other buildings, "were found deserted, and in the rage of their disappointment the enemy set them on fire and they were burned down." The British also burned down the "academy, adjoining the Presbyterian burying ground, [which] had been used for storing provisions for the troops."[96]

Later that same night, the British entered Newark. They again "seized possession of the academy, which the rebels had converted into a barrack." The loyalist newspaper reported that the local militia attempted "a momentary defence," which failed. "7 or 8" were killed and another "thirty-four noncommissioned officers and private men were taken prisoner."[97] Patriot newspapers conceded that the British "plan was well concerted, and as well executed." The night finally ended when the regulars "burnt the academy, and went off with precipitation."[98] After the war, the Newark Academy trustees estimated that with their "New Elegant building burnt," and other property destroyed, losses amounted to £1,400.[99] At other points the American and British armies had used Nassau Hall—the main building at the College of New Jersey—as a barracks or hospital. The college suffered from the handiwork of British regulars. A mark from a cannon ball is still visible on an exterior wall.[100]

Academies elsewhere fared similarly. The British fired cannon at the Newark Delaware Academy, in response to gunfire from inside.[101] The trustees of the Wilmington Academy noted that, during the war, "this Building designed for the most quiet use of Society was thought necessary for the Accommodation of Troops & Military Stores." The war left the academy in "so shattered a Condition" that they estimated the repair costs at £500.[102] In Maryland, the trustees of an academy in Somerset County described how the "rapid advances of the school were soon checked by the war with Britain." As was true elsewhere, "exposed to the ravages of the enemy ... the great business of education paused for a while."[103] The war, in short, proved destructive to education.

Most Americans thought the British attacked academies because of what they became during the war—barracks, hospitals, and so on—not because of what they meant before it began. In some cases, the violence visited upon academies might have had more significance. As the Revolution devolved into civil war, it enflamed denominational tensions and ensnared religious institutions in a web of violence. Throughout the Raritan Valley, the British Army left a trail of destroyed churches in their wake. In New Brunswick, the Presbyterian meetinghouse suffered £400 worth of damage at the expense of the British, while the Dutch Reformed Church claimed twice that amount. The Anglican Church in town, however, required only a little over £40 in repairs. The Presbyterian meetinghouse in Princeton required upward of £160 in repairs, while the most damaged Anglican church in Middlesex County, in Piscataway, was left about £110 worse for wear.[104] Nearby in Somerset County, the regulars caused £80 of damage to one Presbyterian meetinghouse and £250 to another. At the latter church, in Millstone, the British seem to have completely taken the building apart, making off with 11,000 feet of white pine boards.[105] American forces seem only to have destroyed one (unsurprisingly, Anglican) church in Trenton.[106] In the context of civil war, religion likely became a proxy for revolutionary affiliation.[107] Academies also had denominational associations. Even more than churches, academies had enabled religious groups to mobilize their collective strength for political ends. This exposed them to the ravages of war and created challenges for the new republic.

Individual Americans did not escape the war unscathed either. In Essex County—home to Elizabeth Town—one-tenth of householders applied for restitution for damages sustained at the hands of the British. Economic depression then followed the conflict and lasted into the early republic. Nationally, wages fell relative to prewar levels while labor force participation stagnated; trade did not recover and internal markets failed to pick up the slack; and currency inflation followed by the rise of banking and a modern financial system hurt ordinary farmers.[108] Americans, then, had much to rebuild but limited resources at their disposal. Postwar recovery would be a major political project, and the fate of academies hung in the balance.

MUCH OF THIS DESTRUCTION must have been on the minds of Francis Barber's friends, colleagues, and fellow soldiers as they mourned his death in 1783. Barber's eulogist, Ebenezer Elmer, celebrated his valor and leadership. Elmer remembered how "the popularity of Colonel Barber" allowed him to put down "the unfortunate mutiny of the soldiers of the Pennsylvania and New Jersey lines" in the winter of 1780–1781. He invited mourners to recall Barber's conduct in battle, especially in engagements when he suffered wounds. Yet as they tried to come to terms with just "how great the loss" would ultimately be, they also looked to the future. Barber's death was certainly tragic. It was also untimely. As Elmer put it, Barber had been "Cut off in the full meridian of life, health and *usefulness!*"[109]

While Elmer paid tribute to Barber's role in making American independence possible, the eulogy also betrayed apprehension over the nation building that lay ahead. For Elmer at least, Barber's death made these anxieties ever more acute. After the Revolution, Americans faced the task of building and rebuilding all manner of infrastructure: from governments and political norms, to more mundane things like churches and schools. In his eulogy, Elmer foresaw the prominent role that the academy generation, Continental officers, and their allies would play in rebuilding. They needed to take the lead in developing civil society and promoting an American state, and in the related work of building schools.[110] Nervous though they were, they were not inexperienced. As they sought to create national independence in a global world of nations, these Americans embraced the lessons of their colonial past to shape the future.[111]

In no realm was this clearer than schooling. Fourteen volumes of Elmer's orders, notes, and journals survive from the late 1770s, documenting his experience as an officer and surgeon in the Continental Army. Once the fighting stopped, Elmer grew less persnickety about keeping records. During the early 1780s, he used one volume as both a notebook and account book. It depicts Elmer's personal transition from the military back into civilian life, as well as a sliver of New Jersey's transition into a new postrevolutionary routine. In the back of the book, Elmer listed £42 that he received from subscribers in support of a proposed academy in Bridgeton, New Jersey. Located in Cumberland County, Elmer's native Bridgeton sits a little over five miles southwest from Deerfield, where he received his early education at a small academy. The list of subscribers includes men that Elmer knew from his school days and others from the broader network of young, educated Presbyterian men that had congregated around Bridgeton, Deerfield, and Fairfield in the 1770s. Several had served with Elmer as officers, chaplains, and doctors in both the militia and the Continental Army. The paper trail on the Bridgeton Academy begins and ends with this list; it probably never went into operation.[112]

But others would succeed where Elmer failed. Even though many colonial academies did not survive the war, by 1800, more academies dotted the mid-Atlantic countryside than ever before. They spread well beyond the narrow confines of that mostly Presbyterian world, reaching deep into the South, and northward into New England. This was because academy boosters survived the war and spread the gospel. Men like Elmer were living proof that academies were a tool of civil elite formation. They showed the important civic role that education could play in the new republic. In the decades following the Treaty of Paris, men like Elmer turned academies—an unusual institution forged in the Reformed world of the mid-Atlantic and upper South—into a hallmark of American civil life.

CHAPTER THREE

Rebuilding Academies
Education and Politics in the Confederation Era

Almost fifty years after Ebenezer Elmer failed to build an academy, Alexis de Tocqueville arrived on American shores. "Americans," Tocqueville observed, "make associations to give entertainments, to found *seminaries*, to build inns, to construct churches, to diffuse books, to send missionaries to antipodes; in this manner they found hospitals, prisons, and *schools*." Education—including in academies, which were sometimes called seminaries—was one main outcome of Americans' predilection to "constantly form associations."[1] Tocqueville no doubt saw his fair share of academies during his 1831 tour of the country. By the time he arrived, there were thousands scattered throughout the United States. Tocqueville was right to treat academies alongside the Benevolent Empire, which came into its own at the time. Like the thousands of Bible and tract societies, temperance unions, and missionary organizations that sprang up, academies harnessed Protestant denominational power and melded it with civil associational energy in service of national ambitions. Yet unlike the Benevolent Empire, the academy was not a newfangled institution.[2]

Following the American Revolution, the idea that education was an essential component of republican governance became a cliché. Academy founders drew on this rhetoric, no doubt. But the education academies offered was not what many Americans had in mind when they discussed republican education. They envisioned state-run public schools offering a "practical" curriculum aimed at creating an informed citizenry. These proved difficult to create amid the disorder and financial challenges of the Confederation period. Academies, though, could come about from informal group initiative, as Tocqueville pointed out. Overlapping networks of Continental Army officers, Confederation-era politicians, and nationalist civil associations took action. They provided the social and financial capital to found academies designed to train the next generation of political leaders in their image.

Their goals were secular. But they still needed help from the denominational networks that had brought academies to North America in the first place. Religious officials obliged. Clergy recruited teachers to staff academies and helped maintain the schools once they opened. Denominations supported education to compete in the religious marketplace and influence public life in an era of disestablishment.³ Between the Revolution and the advent of the U.S. Constitution in 1787, these nationalist and denominational interests vied with each other to direct academies.

By 1787, the nationalists had won. Academies had grown more secular prior to the Revolution, to be sure. Yet they retained denominational ties. During the 1780s, civil elite formation became the primary and avowed purpose of academies. Elite demand, fast-changing domestic and international politics, and the power of nationalist academy leaders all eroded the denomination-building function of academies. The schools increasingly drew together citizens from different denominations as opposed to reinforcing distinctions between them. Trustees reoriented academies to serve their own political hopes and their children's secular ambitions.⁴ In that process, academies spread beyond the Presbyterian mid-Atlantic and upper South and infiltrated the rest of the nation, including New England. Academy builders successfully forged a national education policy without a national mandate.

Jacob Green's Hopes for Denominational Education

By the time the Revolutionary War ended, Jacob Green had spent nearly four decades educating young men. Born in Massachusetts in 1722, Green studied at Harvard in the early 1740s, at the height of the Great Awakening. The revivals captivated Green, as they did with many other students, and he came under the influence of Gilbert Tennent and George Whitefield. Green's initial post-college plan to work at Whitefield's ill-fated Georgia orphanage quickly fell apart, so he became a minister. Two leading New Side Presbyterians—Jonathan Dickinson and Aaron Burr, who would become the first two presidents of the College of New Jersey—brought Green to their home colony. In 1746, he took over the pulpit at the Presbyterian Church in Hanover, Morris County, where he spent the rest of his career. Green's evangelicalism was a constant. He oversaw revivals in his congregation in 1764 and again ten years later, on the eve of the Revolution. His interest in education also held steady. The same year he arrived in Hanover, the College of New Jersey took shape in nearby Elizabeth Town. Green became a founding member of its board of trustees. He also taught local children in what he called—owing to his New England upbringing—a Latin grammar school. Among his students was his son, Ashbel Green, a future president of the College of New Jersey.⁵

During 1780 and 1781, the elder Green published a series of essays in the *New Jersey Journal* under the pseudonym "Eumenes." The essays tackled the issues of the day—paper money, taxation, liberty, slavery, and education. Green's arguments about the last topic were hardly original. "The education of youth is a matter of importance to Church and State," he opined. Written in what Green called "an ironical mould," the piece read like a satirical advice column for parents and children. "Eumenes" advised mothers and fathers to dote over their children and not to discipline them. Sons and daughters should lie, cheat, steal, and take up all the vices they could. Green warned children that "civil government" might attempt to "regulate" their behavior. "This opposition should not discourage you," he counseled; "the laws you must elude." Religion, too, would try to tame children and stifle "those pleasurable exercises which have been the delight of your lives." They should fight this as well.[6]

Green addressed education only obliquely in his "ironical" essay. The implications were obvious nonetheless. Following the essay's advice would threaten both religion and civil government. By contrast, good education would strengthen both piety and the state. For Green, good education was explicitly Christian. He also invoked the state because he cared deeply about the future of the republic. During the 1770s, Green ardently supported independence, writing pamphlets, working on revolutionary committees, and serving in the New Jersey Provincial Congress.[7] But Green's writings about education only make sense in the context of the religious path he tried to blaze during his lifetime. The Awakening was the formative event in Green's life and framed his worldview into the 1780s.

A fixation on training clergymen for an ever expanding number of congregations—the central problem of the mid-Atlantic Awakening—united Green's educational work.[8] In 1779, Green withdrew his church from conventional Presbyterian governance. Green objected to the synod's power over the "ecclesiastical business" of congregations.[9] Elsewhere he wrote that overarching church institutions were an "absurdity."[10] He objected, in particular, to the prevailing Presbyterian system of ordination, which required candidates both to obtain a college degree and to train with a minister for a year. Green could not abide this "double imposition." Taking a position common to Awakening revivalists, Green argued "that a gospel minister ought to be allowed to preach where he is invited & thinks he has a prospect of doing good." Synods or presbyteries should not get in the way. Green's solution was "to form into" what he called "Voluntary associate Presbyteries." He oversaw the first one, in Morris County.[11]

This ecclesiastical innovation blended Presbyterian and Congregationalist structures. "I am for Presbyterian ordination" but "Independent church government," Green wrote in his autobiography.[12] The new type of presbytery "will meet in synod as a voluntary society," and "shall have unrestrained liberty to license and ordain, for the gospel ministry, any person whom they shall think proper."[13] Congregations would still lack the power of ordination. The plan nevertheless chiseled away at synodal authority. It resembled Presbyterian revivalists' attempts during the Awakening to ordain Log College students. Recognizing that the plan might appear extreme, Green and his colleagues clarified that they were "very sensible of the importance of a learned ministry, and are determined not to introduce unsuitable men." Nevertheless, "of the degree of learning necessary, and of other qualifications," he thought "they must judge for themselves."[14] Under Green's plan, academies would be more critical to Presbyterianism than ever before. If a voluntary presbytery controlled an academy, it could ordain students trained in their chosen theology.[15]

Green argued that the Revolution ushered in a civic culture in which the plan could work. Now was "a proper time" to undertake these changes because "civil and religious liberty is attended to," he wrote. A vibrant culture of voluntary association would normalize the type of church governance that Green favored.[16] Making the case that denominational academies served republican governance was thus more than a shrewd argument for religious education in postrevolutionary America. Education that inculcated republican values was critical to Green's proposed form of church governance. It would train men who valued voluntarism. In turn, that meant that Green's voluntary religious organizations, with pulpits staffed by academy alumni, could also thrive. Green had much at stake in arguing that the fates of both religion and the state rose and fell together at the mercy of education. He wanted denominational academies to function in the new nation the way they had in the late-colonial period. This model had worked for Presbyterians when they were legally a dissenting religion. There was little reason to doubt that it would work in a period of disestablishment—or so Green thought.

Denominational Challenges

The Revolution created obstacles to Green's vision for reinvigorating sectarian education. First, his plan ran up against a shortage of money and resources that followed the destructive military conflict. Many colonial academies and colleges ended up as barracks, storehouses, or hospitals during the war. Some had fallen into disrepair. Others, along with many churches and public buildings, were simply destroyed during the carnage. Revamping education might have been a high priority for Americans, but it was on a very long list. Outside New England, Americans also had a checkered history of funding schools.

Colonists had relied on transatlantic denominational networks to sustain American academies and colleges, and fund-raising trips to Europe were commonplace into the 1770s.[17] The American Revolution wrecked transatlantic religious cooperation, as divisions between coreligionists overpowered Christian fellowship.[18] In some arenas, Britons and Americans reconstructed philanthropic networks on humanitarian, as opposed to imperial, terms. Medical knowledge, humane society efforts to prevent drowning, and eventually antislavery all relied on transatlantic cooperation. This did not translate into education because of its centrality to nations. Americans were left scrambling to find new ways to support schools. Jacob Green's goals hung in the balance.[19]

The United States' new relationship with Great Britain most directly influenced colleges. The ink was scarcely dry on the Treaty of Paris before John Witherspoon—the revolutionary politician, Presbyterian minister, and president of the College of New Jersey—planned a trip to Britain to raise money for the school. Witherspoon arrived in spring 1784, and quickly found that his was no straightforward task. John Erskine, of the Scottish Presbyterian Church's Popular Party, first informed Witherspoon of the obstacles he faced. Erskine relayed the opinion of their mutual friend Charles Nisbet, a Scottish educator and minister, and later the first principal of Dickinson College. Nisbet doubted that Scots felt "a spirit of reconciliation" enough to support American schools. Erskine had already told Benjamin Rush the same. If he came to Britain to raise money for the newly founded Dickinson College, he should not expect even to offset the cost of his trip. Others warned Witherspoon that "prejudices once taken, are not easily removed." The problem was that "the far greater part of the people in Scotland, are as yet no means friends to America." Animosity between Americans and their erstwhile imperial brethren survived the Peace of Paris.[20]

Equally important, Witherspoon's correspondents argued that merely asking for money abroad hurt American claims to nationhood. Ever candid, Erskine counseled that it was "a great abusement of the Majesty of the United States to send a late member of Congress a begging in England." Doing so might even be "contrary to law."[21] Benjamin Franklin, who was still in Europe after successfully negotiating the Treaty of Paris, agreed. He believed that "the very Request would be disgraceful to us, and hurt the Credit of Responsability we wish to maintain in Europe." Taking any foreign money signaled that the United States was "too poor to provide for the Education of their own Children." Even worse, according to Franklin, the opposite was true. Americans could easily support "every Means of public Instruction." Franklin only wondered why "our Legislatures have generally paid so little Attention to a Business of so great Importance." European support would absolve the state legislatures of their responsibility to fund education and make the whole nation look weak in the process.[22]

At stake in these conversations was the United States' very independence. In a stern letter, written the day after Franklin's, John Jay made this point. When "our country remained part of the British Empire," it made sense "that the younger branches of the political family should request and expect the assistance of the elder." After independence, though, the "United States neither have, nor can have, such relations with any nations in the world," least of all Great Britain. In claiming the status of a sovereign nation, the United States implied it could "provide for all the ordinary objects of their government." To Jay, this included education. It was thus not "consistent with the Dignity of a free and independent People to solicit Donations for that or any other purpose, from the *Subjects* of any Prince or State whatever."[23] Building domestic schools was part of building an American nation. Witherspoon had worked hard for American independence, later supported the United States Constitution, and made Princeton a hotbed of Federalism. He understood the stakes very well, and he followed Franklin, Erskine, and Jay's advice. Witherspoon even anticipated their arguments. He laid the blame on the "Trustees of the College of New Jersey [who] contrary to my Judgement and Inclination" assumed that "this would not be an improper Time to solicit" foreign money.[24]

Having failed in "their foreign sollicitations," the College trustees hesitantly turned inward. They first unsuccessfully requested support from the Continental Congress, which had met for a time at Princeton. Increasingly desperate, they next appealed to the Presbytery of New Brunswick. At the same time, they hatched a plan to "make a general application to the friends of religion & learning in this country." Supporting the college would serve "our civil & religious interests," they claimed. Up to this point, the trustees had avoided asking local Presbyterians for aid because the war was destructive in their communities. Church coffers were spread thin already. Members of the Synod of New York and Philadelphia ultimately failed to drum up much money and the college remained in a precarious state.[25] By foregoing foreign support, Witherspoon's commitment to the nation hurt the denomination his college ostensibly served.

This was not a uniquely Presbyterian problem. In nearby New Brunswick, the trustees of Queen's College confronted similar troubles when they requested denominational support. The Reformed Synod hoped the school would rise out of "obscurity." But it was "impracticable at present to attempt a general collection of money in their respective congregations for the use of this institution." All the synod could promise was to solicit scattered donations for the school.[26] As was true among Presbyterians, the Dutch Reformed Church suffered during the war. Even members of New Brunswick's own Reformed congregation had to prioritize other projects above the college. In particular, they needed to scrounge up £800 to repair their church.[27]

At their most desperate, the trustees of Queen's College and the College of New Jersey broached the idea of merging. The proposed 1793 plan would have converted Queen's College into a theological seminary with an affiliated academy, while the College of New Jersey would have continued to grant college degrees. Dutch Reformed officials scuttled the plan.[28] By the 1810s, each denomination ran both a college and a separate theological seminary. None other than Jacob Green's son, Ashbel, oversaw the creation of the Princeton Theological Seminary during his first year as president of the College of New Jersey. Presbyterian theological education lost a key connection with republican education.[29] Instead of enabling denominations and the state to work together, the Revolution undercut the connection between denominational and civic education.[30] Jacob Green's hopes for academies crashed against similar challenges.

Many of the same broad transformations that influenced colleges trickled down to academies. The severing of transatlantic denominational support hurt the academies indirectly. Nor was the war less destructive in academy towns than in college towns. In 1782, New York governor George Clinton lamented that the "calamities of the war" had created "a chasm in education, extremely injurious to the rising generation."[31] Yet academies were also a different sort of institution than colleges. While colleges operated at the state or even national level, academies were county institutions. This created a separate set of problems revolving around the challenge of pluralism. As a result, as compared to colleges, academies more starkly and more rapidly transformed from denominational into nationalist institutions.

This turnabout was particularly clear in Pennsylvania. During the Revolution, militant republican ideologues took control of the Pennsylvania state government and ratified a radically democratic constitution. Presbyterians rode this wave of change in the 1770s, taking power for the first time. Troubled by widespread Tory sympathies among the Anglicans they had replaced, the Presbyterian-dominated legislature banned them from many professions, including teaching at colleges and academies. Their main target was William Smith, the Anglican priest who had long run the College and Academy of

Philadelphia. The new legislature went even further, and revoked the charter of the College and Academy. They replaced it with the Presbyterian-controlled, though ostensibly nondenominational, University of the State of Pennsylvania.[32]

Across Pennsylvania, citizens opened academies amid the upheaval at the state's most important school. In 1785, the board of trustees of the Protestant Episcopal Academy of Philadelphia met to revive the old Academy of Philadelphia. That same year, the Episcopal Church opened another academy in York.[33] The trustees claimed that "children of every denomination will be received" at the school. How convincing this was to parents is unclear. A few months later, a bookseller advertised a Church of England catechism, "used in the Academy."[34] In any event, critics pounced. They charged that the Philadelphia Episcopal Academy was an inherently divisive institution, which had been created to challenge the new state university and undermine the public good. The Episcopal Academy's most vocal public enemy wrote under the pseudonym, "Uniformity." To him, even the "very terms episcopal academy, amount to a declaration of hostilities against all other religious societies." It was as ridiculous of a notion as an "Episcopal ship—A Presbyterian rope walk—Or a Quaker brewery." The academy revived "toryism." Its trustees were "*half whigs*" who threatened the revolutionary possibility that "religious distinctions would have ceased to divide the citizens of these states."[35] In other words, the threat was pluralism itself. It revealed divisions in the body politic.

Despite his pseudonym, "Uniformity" could not help but betray his own sectarian logic. Toward the end of the essay, he adopted a menacing tone and reminded Episcopalians that they no longer had "the hierarchy of the church of England to fly to." Given their new, "insignificant situation," the Episcopal Academy trustees "should remember that their hand is now in the lion's mouth, and not to provoke him." To head off any unpleasantness, "Uniformity" proposed that all schools should have to receive a license from the superior court or the board of trustees of the state university. Of course, Presbyterians dominated both institutions.[36]

If pluralism was a problem in Pennsylvania, it was because of the people "Uniformity" defended, namely, the board of the University of the State of Pennsylvania. The Presbyterian takeover of that school had already mobilized education in denominational conflicts. "Uniformity" attempted to preempt this critique by downplaying how the university had emerged to undercut the influence of Anglicans-turned-Episcopalians. He celebrated the university's "catholic spirit," and the fact that it offered "equal privileges" to all citizens. But the foundation of the school belied any ecumenical and consensual rhetoric.[37]

In a strange reversal, Episcopalians—the former establishment—took up the pluralist argument and advocated stridently for denominations to remain involved in education. "An Episcopalian" argued that as "religion without learning is apt to run into enthusiasm, so learning without religion is apt to produce infidelity." Education needed a religious foundation, and denominational academies would provide it. "An Episcopalian" also reminded his readers that "separate education for the youth of distinct societies, is no new thing in" Pennsylvania. Presbyterians controlled several schools, including the recently founded Dickinson College in Carlisle. These schools strengthened denominations by giving them a way to inculcate their religious principals in youth. At the same time, they provided an important religious inflection in education to the benefit of society writ large. "An Episcopalian" merely argued that the Episcopal Academy would do the same. It would "promote learning and religion in the state, without which liberty cannot long be preserved." Like Presbyterian schools, the Episcopal Academy was "entitled not only to the toleration, but to the patronage of government."[38] Echoes of Jacob Green came from the lips of his theological antagonists.

Other writers defended "An Episcopalian's" belief that denominational education could unite Americans. "A Friend to Equality of Freedom and Learning in Pennsylvania" claimed that "EVERY good man beholds with satisfaction the exertions of various religious societies within this state, to revive literature and science, since the revolution." Looking at Pennsylvania, he pointed to recent Presbyterian efforts, the newly founded Episcopal academies, as well as Quaker and Catholic schools in Philadelphia. With each "religious society" caring for education, he argued, "the whole republic must undoubtedly feel the beneficent consequences." In fact, educating students in denominational schools cultivated "harmony and christian friendship." Dividing students religiously could unite the people politically. At the very least, it might limit religious conflict. "A Friend's" argument was counterintuitive to many Pennsylvanians, and possibly antithetical to the commonwealth.[39]

Benjamin Rush understood better than anyone the panoply of challenges facing American education. Rush believed deeply that religion should have a role in schools. He maintained that teachers should use the Bible as a schoolbook. Rush, though, opposed his fellow Pennsylvania Presbyterians' education policy. During the conflict over the Episcopal Academy, Rush published a letter critical of the new University of the State of Pennsylvania. He questioned the manner in which the legislature overthrew the old leadership. By revoking the charter and depriving the original trustees of their corporate property, the legislature set a precedent that threatened the sanctity of charters altogether. Rush feared especially for the "security of the charter of Dickinson college," which he recently had helped found. He also acknowledged the danger to "all the other literary and religious institutions in the state." Rush had no issue with an educational landscape dominated by denominationally affiliated schools. He celebrated the Presbyterian-run Washington Academy in Somerset, Maryland, a Catholic academy in Maryland, the Episcopal Academy in Philadelphia, and his Presbyterian Dickinson College in Carlisle. But this educational development was merely proof that "to God it belongs to bring good out of evil." Whereas Pennsylvanians' recent actions had shown the propensity of "man to bring evil out of good." In other words, denominational competition might as easily have stifled education as expanded it. When one group took power, they might undercut other denominations' schools, as Presbyterians had done. Nothing less than divine intervention could explain why schools continued to open in such an environment.[40]

The major problem with competitive pluralism in a republic was that it represented a source of division. Republics were supposed to be, if not homogenous, at least unified. Religious pluralism might work because a town could sustain many churches. Moreover, whether religion was a public or private issue was a matter of debate. No such ambiguity surrounded education. Because Americans believed that education played a major role in teaching republican values, all schools effectively had a public function. To educate students by denomination was tantamount to dividing the body politic.[41] Americans accepted denominational higher education because college was still necessary for ordination in many faiths. Colleges expected to serve a homogenous, self-selecting population. But almost every academy needed to serve a relatively heterogeneous population. The majority of counties had, at best, one academy.[42] Most people did not have a choice of academies unless they were willing to send their children far from home. Whether denominational schools could serve a diverse population was a contested question. Academies' rootedness thus created pressures that lessened their sectarian role.

The Pittsburgh Academy took a very different approach than the Episcopal academies, one that paved the way for the future of education in Pennsylvania. In 1786, Hugh Henry Brackenridge began the effort to found this academy, which eventually became the University of Pittsburgh.[43] Brackenridge grew up in Presbyterian schools. After receiving his early education at the academy in Fagg's Manor, he graduated from the College of New Jersey and then taught at a Presbyterian academy in Maryland. Though licensed as a Presbyterian minister, Brackenridge grew disillusioned with the church and opted for a life in politics and literature.[44] But he did not entirely escape his past. Samuel Barr—a Glasgow-educated Presbyterian minister—was the first name on the Pittsburgh Academy's original list of trustees. Presbyterians also made up a large chunk of Pittsburgh's earliest residents. At the same time, Barr attempted to establish a Presbyterian congregation in Pittsburgh. Brackenridge, though, lent his support to an ecumenical "Christian society." He similarly ensured that the Pittsburgh Academy claimed no denominational affiliation. The school's rules stipulated that "persons of every denomination of christians be capable of being elected trustees."[45] The Pittsburgh Academy would exist, not to benefit Presbyterians, but rather to "provide for the cultivation of genius in every part of the government."[46] Reorienting academies to a nationalistic mission and building them through interdenominational cooperation would become the norm elsewhere.

Over time, educators devised new ways to cultivate cross-denominational appeal for their schools. Academy advertisements conveyed trustees' desire to see "amity reign between societies of various denominations."[47] Into the early nineteenth century, academies advertised that they instructed students with prayers that were "approved of by all Christian denominations."[48] Often academies educated students of different denominations together, while separating them for religious services. In Dutchess County, New York, for instance, an academy run by a single minister advertised that nearby there were "Clergymen of reputation, of the Dutch, Episcopalian, and Presbyterian churches" to attend to students' spiritual needs.[49] Many of the earliest chartered academies in New York stemmed from interdenominational effort. The quintessential example was the Union Hall Academy, which the Episcopal, Presbyterian, and Dutch Reformed Churches in Queens County cofounded.[50] In Newark, New Jersey, the local Presbyterian minister tried but failed to run an academy on his own.[51] Ten years later, the school got off the ground when he teamed up with Episcopalians. Symbolically, the new trustees acquired a site "about an equal distance from the Presbyterian and Episcopal churches." The local ministers of both churches would always have seats on the board.[52] When they laid the cornerstone for the school, the local Anglican and Presbyterian ministers cooperated on the ceremony.[53] All these communities used religious pluralism to create educational unity, and in the process sacrificed denominational education on a national altar. Religious educators conceded that academies should be civic institutions.

The Nationalist Elite and Academies

A range of forces curtailed denominations' ability to provide sectarian education. At the same time, many academies with denominational origins also consciously changed in response to demand from Americans who could afford an education for their children.[54] Like many colonial academy students, young men in the early republic looked to academies to achieve secular ambitions. Newspaper advertisements made clear that academies prepared students for the professions, like law and business. As one critic noted, "Seminaries" were "calculated to answer the views of youths destined to fill some learned profession."[55] This environment not only crowded out denominational academies, but also stymied the creation of public common education. Schools that answered the "wants" of those who aimed for "no higher than common stations and employments ... have not been heretofore attentively regarded," complained another writer.[56] In short, academy boards followed the money.

The ideal of a self-governing informed citizenry dated back to seventeenth-century Britain. In creating a republic, the American Revolution thrust that ideal to the center of political life. The 1780s saw a marked increase in newspapers and other forms of print media. State governments and, later, the national government protected and encouraged this diffusion of information. They guaranteed press freedom, protected copyright for authors, and subsidized the spread of news through the post office.[57] Yet it was one thing for people to have access to information, and another for them to process it capably. That is where education came in. Pennsylvania was one of several states to include a provision for public education in its state constitution. Benjamin Rush also drew up a system of free public schools in the state.[58] Most famously, in 1779, Thomas Jefferson proposed a comprehensive plan for public education in Virginia. He envisioned a pyramidal system, with universal primary education for white boys and girls at the base. Qualified boys would filter up through district schools into county grammar schools, and then finally into the College of William & Mary.[59]

Early calls for public schools often flowed from a conservative mistrust of popular sovereignty. Without education, the people could not govern responsibly, or so the elite thought. The very thing that led some elite Americans to believe in widespread education made it difficult to enact. In fact, many state legislators questioned the motives behind public education and opted not to tax themselves for education at all.[60]

In many cases, the elite also prioritized their own education over that of other people. While Pennsylvania failed to make available widespread common schooling, it successfully transformed the academy sector. North Carolina and Georgia's constitutional provisions for public schools were equally ineffective. Conservative opposition to paying for the education of poorer Virginians scuttled Jefferson's plan.[61] Yet Southern states met the elite demand for academies during the 1780s. In that decade, more academies opened in Virginia (twelve) than in any other state. In a story endemic to postcolonial nations, the members of the American elite were anxious about maintaining their status. They demanded the kind of education that supported their status claims and used their influence to get access to it.[62] As Tocqueville understood, new civil associations, which tended to be elite run, made the expansion of these schools possible.

The failure of public schools and the expansion of academies occurred amid sustained political upheaval. The American union was thin, held together first by necessity in the Revolutionary War and then by compact, with the Articles of Confederation. Before the framers offered up the Constitution as a solution, elite voluntary associations attempted to create national cohesion. Though nationalists were a minority, they were a coherent one. Continental Army officers and Continental congressmen provided a base of support. These groups were unusual in that they experienced the Revolution as a national event. Most of them eventually supported the U.S. Constitution. Beginning well before that, they built voluntary associations that crossed state borders and drew together the elite from across the nation. Most conspicuous was the Society of the Cincinnati, which was founded in 1783 as an organization of former Continental Army officers. The society originally intended to have hereditary membership through primogeniture, but public outcry led most state branches to rescind this plan. Yet the society still had big ambitions. In addition to the thousands of former officers who joined, many influential politicians entered its ranks as honorary members.[63]

Though less exclusive than the Society of the Cincinnati, the Free Masons shared similar goals and grew quickly during the 1780s. In fact, the Masonic experience was a driving force behind the society's founding. By the end of the Revolutionary War, Continental officers had created ten Masonic lodges within the lines. Membership was open to company-grade—captains and lieutenants—and higher-ranking officers alike. The lodges also welcomed professionals and bureaucrats, from doctors and chaplains to adjutants and quartermasters and paymasters. Only one lodge admitted noncommissioned officers. While Masonry tempered the otherwise sharp distinctions between different levels of the officer corps, it divided officers from enlisted men. Members imbibed Masonry's Moderate Enlightenment ethos, which celebrated societal improvement through diffusing knowledge coupled with a belief in the power of benevolent leadership by rational elites. Through Masonry and the Society of the Cincinnati, the Continental officer corps became a relatively unified coalition and lobbying force. These networks spread their political vision for the republic across state lines. The Masons, more successfully than the Cincinnati, even made themselves appear disinterested and apolitical.[64]

These groups supported other organizations and institutions that they believed served similar goals, including academies.[65] Take New Jersey. In the mid-1780s, former officers and other would-be nationalists groused that the state did not meet congressional tax requisitions, which were necessary to pay officer pensions.[66] At the same time, informal networks of Continental officers and nationalistic civil officeholders led efforts to build academies. The first academy to open in New Jersey after the Revolution was in Trenton. Local leaders offered the deepest financial support. Isaac Collins—publisher of the *New Jersey Gazette*, the state's first newspaper, which was then based in Trenton—subscribed for four shares. Only Stacy Potts, who would become mayor of Trenton, donated as much. The initial burst of subscribers to the academy also included men with unassailable nationalist bona fides. Two future signers of the U.S. Constitution, David Brearley and William Churchill Houston, both subscribed for shares. Brearley also became a founding member and vice president of the New Jersey Society of the Cincinnati. His colleague in that group, Joseph Bloomfield, likewise owned one share in the Trenton Academy. By the middle of the decade, the Trenton Academy also counted Aaron Dickinson Woodruff as a subscriber. He was master of the Trenton Lodge, the fifth local lodge created by the Grand Lodge of New Jersey, whose grand master was David Brearley. The web of nationalist associations in Trenton was dense and there was much overlap with academy boosters.[67]

In some cases, Mason Lodges and academies physically rose together. In 1785, Virginia Masons led "all Lovers of Literature" in supporting a new academy. Like many public parades, the one in honor of this school began with a procession and ended with a dedication. Lodge no. 39 left its mark on the foundation stone of the academy, which "was laid the 7th of September, 1785, in the ninth year of the Independence of the United States of NORTH AMERICA." The marker itself connected the academy with the republic's history and future.[68] Another academy in Powhatan County, Virginia, even bore the name of the Masonic Lodge that sponsored it.[69]

Academies and nationalist associations often shared physical space. On the opposite end of New Jersey from Trenton, the Newark Academy provided Masons with a lodge room for indefinite periods of time.[70] In its early years, the Fayetteville Academy in North Carolina paid a nominal fee of five shillings per year to operate out of the local Mason lodge.[71] Masons in Cooperstown, New York, in the 1790s, held a number of meetings and ceremonies at the local academy.[72] We can easily imagine academy trustees adjourning a board meeting only to convene a lodge meeting down the hall. Academy buildings, in other words, were often not just schools, but also the physical manifestation of a larger, elite vision for social improvement.

Educational Politics

Academies were clearly part of a growing nationalist movement, though trustees tried to show that they could also adapt to local needs. Serving children of all denominations, for example, was one way. Nonetheless, not everyone agreed with their vision. When academies emerged in New England—and especially western Massachusetts, the most unquiet place in all of Confederation America—the nascent political fault lines around them came into sharp focus. To secure academies' place in the new republic, their boosters needed to win contentious political battles.

Unlike in the mid-Atlantic and upper South, the emergence of academies in New England marked a break from the colonial past. The only prerevolutionary school to resemble an academy was in Byfield, north of Boston. Lieutenant governor William Dummer willed property to create an "academy" in his name. This school was similar to the Latin grammar schools that the colony required that large towns maintain: an edict that many ignored; such was the power of the town. Dartmouth College also began as an academy to train Indians as Christian missionaries, but it received a charter allowing it to grant college degrees by 1769. Finally, Israel Williams, one of Hampshire County's "River God" oligarchs, led a failed attempt in 1762 to found Queen's College, in Hatfield. Though its boosters wanted a college, the bill that passed the assembly shortly before the plan died a convoluted death referred to the proposed institution as an academy. At other points during the deliberations, legislators and petitioners called it a "collegiate school." Either way, it would have been something less than a degree-granting college. To most of Hampshire's residents, the proposed school was nothing more than an overwrought, ambitious plan hatched by hated, county oligarchs.[73]

The failed plan in Hatfield helps explain both why academies came late to the region with the most robust educational system in the world and the deep roots of the Bay State's contentious education politics. Political and religious life in New England—especially Massachusetts—revolved around the town. Church governance happened at the congregational level, which did not cross town lines. Towns, not certain numbers of people, had representation in the General Court. And town schools traumatically socialized children into the rhythms and mores of town life. In exchange, "town-born" kids gained political membership.[74]

Academies fit uncomfortably in a town-centered world. They took shape in the pluralistic environs of the mid-Atlantic. At the very moment that New Englanders adopted academies, they grew increasingly interdenominational everywhere else. Just as important, liberal education, as well as institutions like the Masons, were wrapped up with the rise of "liberality." This outlook challenged local prejudice and celebrated cosmopolitanism. New England elites embraced it even though it flew in the face of the region's localism.[75]

The organization of academies embodied these liberal ideas. Unlike the compulsory institutions of town life, academies were voluntary institutions that operated across town lines. Phillips Andover Academy's charter was the first granted to an academy in New England. It stipulated that a majority of the trustees had to reside outside the town of Andover.[76] That provision reappeared in subsequent academy charters. Massachusetts academies had a legal obligation to buck the power of the town. In 1797, the General Court finally issued a report proposing regulations for academies. It recommended that an academy should not receive support "unless it have a neighbourhood to support it, of at least thirty or forty thousand inhabitants." Under this plan, academies would serve an area around the same size as congressional districts, which Anti-Federalists, in 1787–1788, widely ridiculed as too large to represent the people.[77] Elsewhere in New England, academies worked similarly. The Plainfield Academy was the first to open in Connecticut through voluntary association. The trustees' petition for a charter celebrated the school's ability to draw students both from other towns and from outside the "Land of Steady Habits."[78]

Academies' threat to town life was clearest in western Massachusetts. The General Court incorporated the first academy in the region at Leicester, Worcester County, in 1784. Like earlier academies in the eastern counties, the charter provided that half the trustees had to reside outside Leicester. It was the first institution created by Congregationalists in the region that crossed town lines.[79] In practice, as in law, the Leicester Academy was a county, if not regional, institution. Before the ratification of the Constitution, only one other academy opened in western Massachusetts, in Williamstown; it later became Williams College. Together, these academies served enormous numbers: More than 140,000 people resided in central and western Massachusetts. By contrast, the three academies to open in Essex County before 1790 served a mere 60,000.[80]

The rise of academies dovetailed with other postrevolutionary threats that portended a transfer of authority from the towns to the counties. Fears of this shift sat behind the most infamous event of the 1780s: Shays's Rebellion. The Regulation, as its proponents called it, began in the three western Massachusetts counties of Worcester, Hampshire, and Berkshire to the far west. In the years before tensions boiled over in 1786, Hampshire County, and to a lesser extent Berkshire County, experienced civil unrest and extralegal conventions that anticipated the court closings of the Regulation. Debt was the root cause. Struggling revolutionary soldiers sold, for cents on the dollar, the securities they had received as payment for their service. They then found themselves taxed heavily to repay men who speculated in this government debt. Many people could not afford the taxes. The dynamics of unrest in these places tended to revolve around the accessibility of justice: Would debt questions be adjudicated at the town level, which had long been the locus of public life? Or would justice be meted out at the county level, which less-accountable gentry leaders had dominated since before the Revolution? This fight played out differently in each locale. Suffice it to say, though, that the Shaysites challenged a rising county-level political and judicial elite. They believed that the shift of power out of the towns smacked of royal government, which before the Revolution had entrenched itself through county courts, judges, and magistrates.[81]

The issues raised by both academies and the Regulation were not just similar, they were actually connected. From their very first meeting, the board of trustees of Leicester Academy accepted tuition and subscriptions in either "money or public securities." The board acted like a speculator. It gave the treasurer the power to sell government securities "on the most advantageous terms" to fill the coffers. The treasurer also defined acceptable public securities and calculated how much interest the academy stood to collect from different types. By 1797, the academy held some £1,500 in securities and just over £2,500 in specie.[82] On top of this, during the 1780s, all but one of the nonclergy members of the academy board held judicial office. These men presided over the debt cases that so infuriated the Shaysites. Perhaps unsurprisingly, the trustees stood firmly with the government and against the regulators in 1786. Two of the founding members even raised regiments to put down the Regulation.[83] Two decades after Shays's Rebellion, the president of the Leicester Academy board celebrated the Constitution for having "restored public credit, and of course revived this institution."[84] The academy itself was literally invested in putting down the rebellion and securing public credit, as were its trustees.

The connection between liberal education and the Regulation extended beyond academies. Brookfield was another Worcester County town torn apart by Shays's Rebellion. The gentry there did not build an academy; wealthy children from Brookfield probably went to Leicester. But in 1789, Brookfield residents created a mutual improvement organization. The Minervaean Society met to debate topics of intellectual and political interest, including issues surrounding public debt. In one meeting, the majority agreed with speculators that discriminating between original holders of government securities and those who purchased securities "would not be good policy."[85] The improvement-driven and incipiently nationalistic worldview of academy founders and their ilk sat at odds with the regulators' localist attachment to the traditional order of the town. Academies, improvement societies, and other voluntary local associations—including fire clubs, agricultural societies, and, as was true throughout the United States, Masonry—all represented challenges to traditional New England life.[86]

Academies in New Hampshire took shape amid similar sorts of social strife. In summer 1786, Reverend Stephen Peabody made the rounds to gather support for the Atkinson Academy, the second academy in the state. But he found his attention consumed by a "mobb" that presaged Shays's Rebellion. As he shuffled between meetings with fellow trustees, he also took the time to "look over & correct ye piece" that some of his neighbors wrote "respecting paper money." By September, the "mobb" had attempted to close the courts in Exeter. It took the militia to disperse the crowd. When Peabody heard that "a number of ye heads of ye mobb are in jail," he wrote that "I am glad of this—tho' I fear ye consequences." Tensions in civil life continued to shape the academy when the trustees organized themselves more formally at the decade's end. In June 1789, opponents of the academy—"ill-natured obstinate ignorant fellow[s]," according to Peabody—refused even to attend a town meeting to discuss it. Peabody dismissed one critic for "talk[ing] as he always does like a fool!" Other "unreasonable" people opposed the academy, characteristically, "without reason."[87]

These battle lines persisted well after the end of the Regulation. Academies came late to Hampshire County, the heart of Shays's Rebellion and the site of the failed colonial-era academy in Hatfield. When the county's first academy finally opened in Westfield, in 1793, General William Shepard was at the helm. Shepard famously led a force of some 1,200 men, largely drawn from towns along the Connecticut River, to put down the Regulation. In perhaps the most dramatic moment of the whole episode, Shepard ordered his men to fire cannon at regulators in Springfield. Four men died and another twenty were injured. In the immediate aftermath, Shepard received death threats. He never lived down his part.[88] Like prior charters in the state, Westfield Academy's stipulated that a majority of trustees must reside outside of town.[89] Those trustees included men like Justin Ely, who frustrated people to the point of rebellion in 1786. During the regulation, the Shaysites ransacked Ely's business.[90] Later in the 1790s, another academy opened in Hampshire County, in Deerfield. Men who played a conspicuous role in suppressing the Regulation sat on that board too.[91]

Academies in Hampshire County undoubtedly irritated the defeated Shaysites. This new Connecticut River Valley elite had all but re-created the patterns of rule characteristic of the leading colonial River God families.[92] In some towns—like Northampton—the elite so dominated local politics that they could use town funds for elite education in grammar schools, rather than common schools. Usually, they needed to circumvent the towns and create academies.[93] There was still no chartered school in Hatfield. But the Westfield and Deerfield Academies looked like what the River Gods had attempted thirty years earlier with Queen's College. Unlike grammar schools—which the towns controlled and often chose not to fund—academies were subject only to the whims of county elites. Shepard and his allies accomplished something that their River God predecessors had not. Might that mean the postrevolutionary county elite was even more powerful? To downtrodden rural residents of Hampshire County, academies must have represented the triumph of the very forces against which they fought the Revolution in the first place.[94]

These incipient partisan lines held true outside the counties afflicted by the Regulation. In the rest of New England, groups that feared the Shaysites and became Federalists partially because of the Regulation proved most comfortable flouting the traditional town-based order. They tended also to provide the staunchest support for academies. Three of the four Massachusetts academies that were chartered before 1785 were in towns in the Boston hinterlands that lined up behind the Constitution during the ratification controversy. The first academy in New Hampshire opened in Exeter. While no town-level election returns on ratification survive, by 1800, Exeter was still almost uniformly Federalist.[95] Generally, academies opened in commercially oriented towns, where residents felt most threatened by the Regulation.[96]

Academy critics did not oppose education generally. The loudest voices against New Hampshire's Atkinson Academy were local officeholders—militia officers, deacons, and selectmen. Despite their vitriol toward the academy, they tended to support district schools unthinkingly.[97] Vermont chartered only two academies before 1800, but it enacted laws that empowered towns and districts to set up common schools.[98] The problem was that academies undercut these more accessible schools. This argument appeared as early as March 1784. In the same month the General Court granted the Leicester Academy charter, the *Boston Magazine* published an essay on "the destructive consequences and tendency of establishing PRIVATE ACADEMIES." These institutions were "pregnant with evils," and would "lay a foundation for a total destruction of the constitution." The problem was that men of means built academies without any "particular consideration for [their] neighbours." The schools only served those who could afford to go. If academies did not exist, those same men of means would instead support public schools in which "the youth would all have it in their power to receive an advantage which they would not be likely to obtain any other way." And schools that educated rich and poor children together best served the common good.[99]

Another essay picked up this theme in the next issue of the *Boston Magazine*. The writer agreed that "the establishment of so many Academies will interfere with this very wise and useful law" that mandated town schools. Ultimately, he concluded, "if Academies take place of schools, though there may be a greater number of superior scholars—yet there may be much less useful knowledge."[100] Some academy advocates did not even try to disguise how academies bolstered the power of the many over the few. One Boston essayist conceded that the schools served only "the wealthy and the great." Yet the writer believed that "men possessed of property are entitled to a greater share in political authority." It was good if those men were educated. For that reason, "public academies are . . . greatly promotive of the public weal."[101] The transfer of educational authority from town schools to academies raised fears about the future of democracy in Massachusetts. Before long, these fears defined the debate over academies across the rest of the North.

None of this is to say that Shays's Rebellion or other less famous upheavals caused people to build academies. Rather, debates over academies and the proper balance of local and county authority mapped onto broader conflicts over the future of the republic. The men who built the earliest New England academies thought of themselves as friends to government and order, and vested their hopes in a new more powerful nation. They trusted academies to train students to act like the cosmopolitan academy trustees who had stared down the barrels of agrarian rebels' guns. To be sure, in New England, their supporters were mostly Congregationalists. In fact, Congregational ministers often made up large chunks of out-of-town trustees on academy boards. But academies were on the leading edge of a fundamental reorganization of public life in New England. They epitomized a new way to create stability in the postrevolutionary world, outside of the traditional structures of town and church.[102]

Though opposition to academies was less widespread in the South, academy boosters fought similar battles. The most obvious scuffle over education came in Maryland in 1785. The state legislature hatched a plan to fund two existing academies as a proto–state university. In the House of Delegates, there was a clear split on the issue between those who represented creditors and debtors. The former supported the college plan, while the latter opposed it. A series of newspaper essays laid out the debtors' objections. Most importantly, they objected that the plan provided "for gentlemen's children to be educated at the public expense."[103] Another essayist claimed that the plan would "plunder the treasury" and become a "burden to the people." Worse, it was unnecessary. Based on "pompous accounts" of the academies in the newspapers, the writer concluded the two schools were in fine condition without state funding. The writer conjured up an image of state-funded academies "striding across the bay like a huge coloss." This "idle foolish whim" was clearly the brainchild of the elite "and never would have occurred to men of common sense."[104] As in the North, undemocratic financial policy fused with state support for elite-run schools.

The fight over academies was bound up with the most contentious political issues of the 1780s and framed by the ideals of the American Revolution. Opponents attacked academies for reintroducing aristocratic forms that stifled the Revolution's democratic potential. The perceived need for public schooling, then, flowed from dissatisfaction with how elite white men dominated politics. Education reform might address these issues without helping women or people of color. Strikingly, debates about education rarely considered female academies in the same pieces as male academies and public schools. The very way that academy boosters and opponents alike discussed education crowded out more potentially expansive visions of reform.

The Lingering Importance of Religious Networks

Across the United States, an elite vision for academies geared toward nationalist ends eclipsed both local and denominational traditions of schooling. Yet the rise of these academies did not undercut religion's general importance in American life. If anything, religion grew more important following the Revolution.

As a result, the idea that schools should inculcate piety never waned. Religious leaders still had clout and academy trustees needed to court their help to secure the triumph of the nationalist educational vision.[105]

Even the most politically driven schools in New England could not escape their dependence on the Congregational Church. Ministers had access to religious networks, which remained among the most far-flung of the period. As part of their earliest fund-raising efforts, the trustees of the Leicester Academy relied on ministers in neighboring towns. They sent a circular letter to Congregational ministers throughout the county, asking "them to use their influence to procure subscriptions."[106] Ministers themselves also drew on extensive personal networks. In his efforts to build the Atkinson (New Hampshire) Academy, Stephen Peabody met with neighbors "respecting [the] money" needed to finish the school. On other days, he drew "up some rules for ye Academy" with one colleague, then met with another to talk "about some regulations we are about proposing for ye Academy." A few days later, he checked in with the "joiners ... at work upon ye school-house." Constructing the school building occupied him for quite a while. A colleague named Atwood received several letters about it, "for which he [was] very angry." Peabody had to put out that fire too, a task made all the more difficult because Atwood had "been drinking again." Even the mundane tasks of ensuring that pupils paid their tuition on time fell to Peabody. The Woodstock Academy in Connecticut relied on the similar efforts of a local minister.[107] Put simply, building schools was not easy, experience counted, and religious leaders had it.

More than any other region, the South relied on religious networks to create academies. The first academy to open in Maryland during the 1780s was in Somerset County and began as a Presbyterian school in the colonial period.[108] The trustees rechristened it the Washington Academy to explain its new nationalistic purpose. They also guaranteed that "No preference shall be shewn to any particular religious denomination."[109] Nevertheless, Presbyterians continued to run the school.[110] After the board twice failed to recruit a teacher, it sent one trustee to a synod meeting to identify someone who wanted the job.[111] After recruiting a candidate, the board still needed the synod to transfer this minister into their presbytery. The success of this nationalistic institution depended on the Presbyterian Church's cooperation.[112]

Denominations also oversaw colleges, which remained the main source of capable academy teachers. Many early southern academies were beholden to the College of New Jersey. In 1783, prominent men in Hillsborough, North Carolina, banded together to create an academy. They were led by William

Hooper, who made his name putting down the North Carolina regulators in the 1760s, served in state-level office during the Revolution, and then built a legal career defending Loyalist property in the 1780s. For his efforts, he saw his public career come to an end in 1788 when he failed to gain election to the constitutional ratification convention.[113] Hooper and other trustees' political connections proved useful. They acquired 140 acres of land, confiscated from a Loyalist, to endow the school.[114] Even still, they needed religious networks to find staff. College of New Jersey President John Witherspoon recommended that the board hire a 1784 graduate named Zadoc Squire. He took over the Hillsborough Academy in 1787.[115]

A steady stream of Presbyterian educators moved South and enabled the expansion of academies in Virginia during the 1780s and 1790s. College of New Jersey alumni served as the founding principals at the first three academies to open in postrevolutionary Virginia. Two of those schools were directly under the control of the Hanover Presbytery. Yet as the names of two early Virginia academies—Liberty Hall and Washington-Henry—suggest, politics figured into their creation.[116]

Why did the denominations lend their support to schools with overtly secular missions? Denominational leaders still valued an informed laity and an educated clergy, which academies created. Perhaps, too, they hoped that through education they might retain an influence on American culture. Education remained one way Protestantism stayed relevant in American life from Monday through Saturday. Yet every time ecclesiastical organizations or informal denominational networks mobilized in support of academies, they subordinated themselves to the nation. It was a process that would repeat itself time and again.

JACOB GREEN'S VISION OF a symbiotic relationship between denominational academies and the new republic was dead by 1787. That same year, Green and colleagues in Morris County received a charter of incorporation from the New Jersey State Legislature. It was not for an academy, but rather for a "Society instituted in Morris County for the Promotion of Learning and Religion."[117] This was the second chartered educational institution in the state, after the Trenton Academy. The society aimed to "assist poor and pious youth in obtaining an education, and support itinerant evangelicals... to promote learning and religion in the destitute parts of our land." A cross between a school and a missionary organization, the Morris Society sent men from New Jersey to start churches in Westchester and Dutchess County, New York, as well as in Connecticut. They also founded new associated presbyteries in these places and another outside of Albany, to serve the northwesternmost white populations of New York State.[118]

Green finally created the educational institution he envisioned, but it was deliberately *not* an academy. Academies had ceased to suit his vision. Green continued to see academies in terms set during the Awakening, as denominational schools. Most other Americans thought little about the sectarian squabbles that so defined Green's worldview. They repurposed the Awakening's critical innovation—voluntarily organized academies—for their own needs. Academies' capacity for elite formation was an unintended outcome of the spread of colonial academies. In the first decades after the war, elite Americans made this the primary purpose of academies. This served trustees' own interests. But they also reoriented academies toward the political challenges confronting the new republic. Shorn of their original denominational purpose, academies provided a durable model for improving associations and institutions that defined American civil society. Indeed, buoyed by a nascent nationalist politics that coalesced around the Constitution, academies continued to spread rapidly after 1787.

Across the United States in the 1780s and 1790s, academies offered elite young men a European-style curriculum that served their personal and professional ambitions. Students and community members alike learned to think of the nationalist-turned-Federalist cultural values that academies taught as American values. Even more, those values would outlive the original Federalist coalition. As Federalists evolved from the faction that supported the Constitution into an organized party, their popularity waned. By the mid-1790s, many supporters of both the Constitution and academies jumped ship to the Moderate wing of the Jeffersonian Republican Party. Even amid these political changes, academy curriculum and culture stayed remarkably constant. It is to this academy culture that we turn next.

Part II
The Culture of Academies, 1780–1800

CHAPTER FOUR

Defining Merit
Academies and Inequality

The residents of York, Pennsylvania, had much to celebrate on July 4, 1788. It was the twelfth anniversary of American independence, "that great event which gave us rank among the nations of the earth," as one newspaper report put it.[1] Just over a week earlier, Virginia had also become the tenth state to ratify the United States Constitution. Naturally, the town held a party. The festivities began at ten in the morning with a procession to a church, where the audience heard a sermon. From there, the revelers headed to a barbeque. Before the crowd could eat, they heard some more speeches.

For most of the day, the local militia led the procession along with students from the York Academy. Twelve students had the honor of carrying white flags, each of which had the name of one of the "*twelve* states which had been represented in the grand convention." The rest of the academy students followed behind in a double-file line, while the community watched and cheered. Rhode Island had refused to send delegates to the Constitutional Convention. That state's flag "was black, and carried by a negro boy in crape, in the rear of the procession." The Rhode Island flag also carried four lines of verse: "I will divide her among the nations. I will take away her name. For her iniquity hath abounded. Her unrighteousness hath vex'd the land."[2]

The York Federalists organized this procession to celebrate the Constitution's adoption. It also conveyed to the community their ideal vision of political hierarchy in the new nation. Educated young men took center stage, symbolizing their role as future stewards of the nation. Other white men took part as full citizens, supporting their leaders. African Americans were present as a foil, relegated to a place outside the body politic. However, unlike in Rhode Island, they had no choice in the matter. Women expressed their patriotism and made their civic contribution indirectly, by participating in the "entertainment" that followed the procession.

It was a particularly special day for one student, who was singled out from his peers. John Spangler gave a patriotic oration as part of the festivities. He celebrated the events that gave the United States "a name among the nations" and reminded his academy peers that "our wisdom and virtue alone can give that name renown." They were the future of the republic and their education taught them how to lead responsibly.[3] The procession, then, suggested a new justification for power: academic merit. In aristocratic societies, schools educated children who were preordained to hold power. Academy officials were at pains to show, instead, that they identified *meritorious* Americans and set them on a path to power. Resting authority on education and talent and rejecting hereditary authority theoretically amounted to a fundamental break with the old world.[4]

In practice, the change was not quite so stark. Academies charged tuition, so wealthy children could more easily attend an academy. Culturally, too, academies did not break starkly from the past. The academies had emerged in the first place to meet elite demand, and elites founded and administered the schools. They were an insecure bunch, amounting to a quintessentially postcolonial elite who measured themselves against the ruling class of Great Britain. Unable to shake a European view of status, American elites aspired to it. Academies catered to their insecurity. These schools offered neither a theological education, as colonial academies had, nor a new practical and American form of education, as reformers advocated. Rather, they offered a European-style education, focused on the classics and oratory, as was popular in Europe. Appealing to existing elites shaped the student body at academies and tended to reinforce existing inequalities, even if they were no longer, strictly speaking, hereditary.[5]

Even still, academies did not perfectly replicate existing hierarchies. Access to academies was not limited solely to the wealthy, nor did all wealthy children attend. Rather, through academies, elite nationalists-turned-Federalists accomplished something both less direct and more fundamental. They defined the routes to influence, the very foundations of civil authority, to mirror their values and to favor the traditional markers of status to which they aspired. All Americans who sought power needed to conform to these ideals, and the academies taught them how. This meant that academies socially reproduced the existing elite, even when it provided pathways for non-elites to gain power. Through patriotic public events like the York procession, elite Federalists made a public case that this benefited the nation. Academies, then, both served the political goals of their founders and laundered the privilege they and their children hoped to maintain. By 1800, the United States was home to an unequal educational system that did little to make possible what we now call meritocracy. Yet American schools claimed to produce a leadership class defined by merit.[6]

Education and the Ratification Debate

At its most radical, the American Revolution threatened the long-standing assumption that social and political power were of a piece. In particular, revolutionary governments went after traditional sources of hereditary power and undercut families' ability to pass down wealth. Every state that had allowed entail during the colonial period abolished it after the Revolution. Primogeniture fell as well.[7] Deference to social betters was on the wane more generally, and Americans grew more comfortable electing ordinary people to office.[8]

Other Americans thought the declining influence of traditional elites created "an excess of democracy," which bred new problems. Taking stock of the 1780s, many nationalists-turned-Federalists concluded that while the Revolution had successfully toppled hereditary hierarchy, it had not actually replaced it with anything. Unworthy demagogues had filled the void. Nationalist Americans—Continental officers, national politicians, Masons, members of the Society of the Cincinnati, and, indeed, academy founders—raged that the allegiances of too many citizens remained with the states at the nation's expense. Most notably, at various times, single states scuttled a proposed 5 percent impost, which many congressmen believed was necessary to put the country on a stable financial footing. The inability of Congress to raise revenue meant it could not pay the money it owed to soldiers. In 1783, this almost led to a coup among the Continental officers. All told, nationalists blamed new and uneducated officeholders for undermining public credit, creating tensions between states, and hurting the young nation.[9]

To the Federalists, things were no better within the states. States issued paper money and passed laws that catered to debtors and threatened the sanctity of contracts. Even when the states managed to pass corrective laws, local officials sometimes refused to enforce them. This was the case in parts of Pennsylvania where law enforcement officers would not foreclose on property. Others stood by idly while farmers closed roads and prevented officials from enforcing laws and collecting overdue taxes.[10] The ineffectual government under the Articles of Confederation could do little to assist state governments.[11]

In 1787, the Constitutional Convention met in Philadelphia to address nagging problems ostensibly created by democratic state governments and the ineffectual national government. The framers hoped to create a government that returned power to the educated. Supporters of the Constitution claimed "to wish for a Government administered by the *better sort* of people;

who have had something of a liberal education."[12] Educated men supported the Constitution, in turn. As an observer wrote to John Quincy Adams, "there is not a man of Education that dare speak in opposition to" ratifying the Constitution.[13] One essayist concluded that the Constitution served "the interest of all men, whose education has been liberal and extensive." Under it, "there will be a theatre for the display of talents, which have no influence in State Assemblies."[14] At some level, educated people's support for ratification was self-interested.

Anti-Federalists, who opposed the Constitution, even complained that the Federalists touted the educational imbalance between parties to stifle debate. It was "one of the leading arts of the aristocratick faction," claimed a Massachusetts Anti-Federalist, "to depreciate the abilities" of those with "less fortune, education" who opposed the Constitution, as though that proved the Federalists had the better argument.[15] Some Federalists turned this complaint against their opponents. Writing to James Madison, Rufus King noted that "the Opposition complain that . . . men of Education are all in Favor of the constitution, & that for this reason they appear to be able to make the worst, appear the better cause."[16] In other words, everyone agreed that educated people supported the Constitution. The question was whether this was evidence of its wisdom.

The Constitution created a political environment that was more conducive to the success of well-educated men. Yet the Constitution itself did nothing to educate would-be elites or inculcate respect for education among the public. Academies, though, could do both. It is no coincidence that the York Academy was involved in the ratification celebration. In Pennsylvania, support for academies and the Constitution overlapped. Five counties were home to academies before the Pennsylvania ratification convention. The majority of delegates from three voted for the Constitution, one voted against, and one county split its vote. But the only academy in an Anti-Federalist county was in Pittsburgh, and was founded by outspoken western Federalist, Hugh Henry Brackenridge. The pattern persisted beyond 1787 (table 4.1). Counties that voted for ratification were more likely to have an academy before 1800 than counties that opposed it.

In Pennsylvania and elsewhere, Federalists supported local academies as part of their broader state-building efforts. Nobody made this logic clearer than James Wilson. A future law professor and Supreme Court justice, Wilson signed both the Declaration of Independence and the Constitution, and in 1787 led the Pennsylvania Federalists' ratification campaign. Wilson believed in the paramount importance of commerce. Commercial nations

TABLE 4.1 Pennsylvania academy locations by constitutional ratification vote

Ratification Vote, 1787	Total No. of Counties	No. of Counties with Academy by 1800
Majority Yes	11	9
Even Split	2	2
Majority No	6	3

Note: For the ratification vote, see "Pennsylvania 1787 Constitutional Convention," *A New Nation Votes.*

needed both strong laws that upheld contracts and "men of intelligence" to enforce them.[17] "The advantages of an aristocracy," he said in a defense of the Constitution, "are experience and the wisdom resulting from education."[18] This was a hierarchical, even reactionary, view of political power. Wilson's Old World sensibilities no doubt stemmed from his upbringing in Scotland as much as his recent experience in Pennsylvania. As he elaborated later in his law lectures, "education and experience ... are excellent for forming and finishing the habits and characters of statesmen." His frame of reference here was the English aristocracy and the education he imagined was also European. Wilson thought he could adapt aristocratic education for American sensibilities. What he hoped to change was who received advanced schooling. In England, children of the elite would gain the "preeminences of aristocratick power" with or without school. Wilson thought that was backward. Aristocracy would work better if people believed power came from education, and that their "prospects of success in publick life must depend on the qualities, acquired as well as natural." Then men would value liberal education for "justifying that good opinion" of their peers.[19] Academies emerged to help create this more natural—and potentially more intractable—aristocracy.

Merit and American Conceptions of Aristocracy

Federalists like Wilson had a clear goal—rebuilding a traditional elite—and the academies provided a way to achieve it. Academy boosters still had to convince the general populace that this was not just a retreat to hereditary aristocracy. Wilson's notion that power would flow from talent—merit—became the justification, as it would in many democratic societies. Merit was a useful concept because it embraced hierarchy yet justified it as natural.[20] In the United States, proponents described this theoretical new elite as a "natural aristocracy of merit."[21] The turn toward merit flowed from the experience of the Revolutionary War. The erstwhile Continental Army officer corps and the hereditary fraternal organization they created, the Cincinnati, obsessed over status, hierarchy, and order and ironically trumpeted the power of merit.[22] The Federalists embraced merit because it upheld the link between social and political power without appearing to reintroduce hereditary privilege. It reconciled republicanism with inequality. In this new world, whoever defined merit and how to measure it also determined how democratic or egalitarian that society would be. Trustees and teachers worked to make academies the arbiters of merit.

Understandings of merit were in flux across the eighteenth-century Atlantic World. In France, merit captured the nobility's imagination during the latter years of the *ancien régime*. As in the United States, military officers championed this change.[23] That merit could exist in a monarchy highlights its ambiguities. In monarchical societies, traditional emblems of status and outward refinement tended to connote merit. Enlightenment figures wondered whether outward appearance could predict internal worth. Ideologically, the answer had to be no. Yet in a meritocratic society, men of merit would most likely become wealthy and might embrace traditional trappings of status. That made it hard to overturn assumptions that conflated outward status with internal merit.

Americans confronted this conundrum first through the work of English writers. Vicesimus Knox, an English education reformer, wrote that "Internal dignity, corresponding with external, cannot but carry with it great influence." Outward appearances and personal virtues went together.[24] Similarly, Lord Chesterfield's *Advice to His Son*, which Americans read widely, tried to make sense of the relationship between appearance and merit.[25] Chesterfield wrote that young men should mingle in "Good company," which consists "chiefly (though not wholly) of people of considerable birth, rank, and character"—all traditional markers of status. At the same time, they would not be "admitted into it, if not distinguished by any peculiar merit." Chesterfield encouraged his son "to keep company with people above you," though not "with regard to their birth; but with regard to their merit, and the light in which the world considers them."[26] The easiest way to find people of merit remained socializing with those whose status was outwardly evident. But social standing, birth, rank, or appearance did not necessarily guarantee that a person possessed merit.

Americans embraced merit in ways that mirrored changes in Europe. But their need to square their social order with republican principles offered a unique twist. In a wide-ranging 1787 essay written under the pseudonym, "A Foreign Spectator," the Philadelphia Swedish Lutheran minister Nicholas Collin argued that American inequality was different. It "proceeds then from this: that the improvement of the human mind has not kept pace with the progress of wealth." As a result, in America "we often behold an amazing disparity of merit in persons of the same fortune and occupation."[27] It was easier to gain the wealth to cultivate appearances than it was to improve oneself. Consequently, there was less overlap between appearance and merit in the new republic. While Collin believed that "superior merit alone will procure the sublime glory and happiness" for the young nation, even he could not figure out how to judge it.[28] The difficulty of measuring merit threatened to undermine people's faith that natural aristocracy could bring about stable rule without just remaking arbitrary aristocracy.

This confusion was endemic to the thinking about merit in the period. Academy founders grew up with a conception of what scholars have called "essential merit." Unlike more modern "institutional merit"—which is based on specialized knowledge, aptitude, and evidence of potential—"essential merit" was understood as more or less innate. An understanding of merit as essential seeped into the language of noted early American educators and led them to conflate merit with social standing.[29] David Ramsay wrote to Benjamin Rush to introduce a young man with whom "I have no personal acquaintance." Ramsay nevertheless told Rush that "I have reason to believe he is a young gentleman of merit." He came to this conclusion from the young man's "own appearance" and the "character of the gentleman who introduced him to me." Ramsay asked Rush to give "Mr. Wright" advice on medical education. From some mixture of birth, wealth, or social standing, this young man seemed meritorious. Nevertheless, education offered something to Mr. Wright, who, Ramsay explained, "proposes to elevate himself."[30]

Essential merit in the early republic depended on institutions for legitimacy. All these conditions played into the Federalists' hands. They both understood the reactionary potential of merit and were experienced institution builders. The Continental officers created the Society of the Cincinnati to institutionalize their claims to distinction. The academies would do the same for later generations. This shared emphasis on merit provides a link between academy education and the Cincinnati. At a July Fourth celebration at the Wilmington Academy, presided over by the Society of the Cincinnati, Delawareans toasted "virtue and merit," which they hoped would "ever be the best claims to distinction and regard."[31] These projects both put institutional weight behind claims of merit that otherwise might seem to rest on a very traditional foundation: an officer's commission or exclusive education.

Re-creating aristocracy through education was a clever strategy in a republic because other Americans looked to schools to create new opportunities for exceptional men of humble birth to hold positions of communal leadership. The New York City Society of Associated Teachers was bullish about education's power to democratize social and political order. Before the American republic, society did not understand the importance of teachers and education to governance. Now, though, it was clear that teachers "inculcate the first principals of Knowledge and Virtue, which is our Political Base." It fell to their "profession to perpetuate our republican form of Government." Thanks to the Revolution, "unmeaning names of Titular Distinctions, and hereditary privilege are discarded." And thanks to teachers, "in their stead" Americans embraced "the standard of merit."[32] The Associated Teachers were not Federalists, but rather affiliated with New York City's radically democratic Jeffersonian Republicans. That they of all groups extolled merit in the mid-1790s shows that the Federalists' sleight of hand had worked. A wide range of Americans conceded that schools should measure merit, and merit in turn should confer power.

Students on Display

Members of the Society of the Cincinnati had military exploits as evidence of their merit. The younger generation who attended academies also needed to prove their merit publicly. This is why academies and students featured prominently in the growing culture of parades and public ceremonies through which Americans cultivated a national identity.[33] James Wilson understood the power of these events better than most. "Publick exhibitions" and "publick processions," Wilson wrote, "instruct and improve, while they entertain and please." At best, they show "great political truths."[34] Events like the York procession certainly aimed to convey a political truth: that the archetypal natural aristocrat was academy educated. Through their influence on academies and these events, then, the Federalists reified understandings of merit that upheld their vision for social order, all under the guise of patriotism.[35]

Academy founders foregrounded their nationalist motives. Some of the earliest academies in several states—New York, Maryland, Virginia, and the Maine District of Massachusetts—bore George Washington's name. Patriotic names aimed to underscore an academy's benefit to the nation. The trustees of the Washington-Henry Academy, in Hanover County, Virginia, for instance, claimed "to support and promote the public weal, from an unaffected attachment to the interest of the American states in general."[36] This sort of rhetoric was widespread among academy founders. The trustees of the Trenton Academy believed their project served "the good order of government" at a moment when that seemed fragile.[37] In 1782, Alexander McWhorter set about opening an academy in Newark, New Jersey, where he had taught before the war. He did so confident that "every attempt to promote literature in this infant government, will be so readily acknowledge by all" as of "high importance."[38] Education was one way that local communities could help make the nation from the ground up.

Other academy boosters drew on imperial rhetoric. A Pennsylvania writer pointed to Maryland as "an example that deserves the imitation of everyone who has an eye to the future grandeur of this young and rising empire."[39] The Baltimore Academy trustees hoped their school would "augment the glory of a new-born Empire."[40] This logic extended to women's education. A poem read during a female academy exhibition in Philadelphia declared that "form'd by nature over hearts to reign, / From science learnt that empire to maintain."[41] An account of another of this academy's exhibitions noted that "the cultivation of letters, is one mark of the progress of society towards its most improved period, and I doubt not, will be productive of much good to this rising empire."[42]

Regardless of whether they hoped to strengthen an American nation or an empire, trustees argued that academies trained civic-minded men to guide the United States. At the opening of an academy in Lewes, Delaware, its principal claimed that the school would shape students into "blessings and ornaments to the rising generation."[43] It might seem as though academies only "instruct youth in dead languages." Really, though, they inculcated in students a "duty to their God, to themselves, to their neighbor, and their country."[44] Academies existed to "exercise the vital Springs of Action, and animate the Students, with an inviolable Love and Attachment to the Services of Almighty God, [and] their native Country."[45] In some places, training a new generation of leaders amounted to an official duty. During the Revolution, New Jersey exempted academy teachers from militia service, jury duty, and town offices that might "interfere in any Degree with [their] Duty as an Instructor."[46] The implication was that academy teachers already held a public trust.

To show that students were following the path that had been set out for them, academies hosted public exhibitions and examinations. The watchword at these events remained "emulation," as historian Jason Opal has authoritatively shown.[47] And as in the colonial era, the competitive rhetoric of emulation tried to spur students to excel among their peers and work for the greater good. Much as this rhetoric sounds tailor-made for American democratic ideals, Europe's influence was strong. The English saw a competitive socializing experience as essential for students who, by birth, would inevitably hold positions of power. William Barrow, an English academy master and writer, argued that "If the youth be designed for any active station in publick life... he ought to have a public education."[48] By a "public" education, Barrow meant schooling in a group, not private tutoring. Americans knew that there were European precedents for academy pedagogy. While touring through Europe, "R. Sullivan" wrote and published in a Philadelphia newspaper an essay titled, "The Advantages and Disadvantages of a Public and of a Private Education." The essay described how public education ensured that a student "feels an exultation in rising to be foremost of his class." When this happens, "his incitements to morality become equally strong." This was emulation in action.[49]

As a practical matter, academic events helped students launch public careers. They made students known to the immediate audience that watched them and the larger audience that read about them in newspapers. Exhibitions also gave students access to important connections. Trustees often planned exhibitions at times when luminaries could be judges. At early examinations, Trenton Academy students performed in front of the lieutenant governor, state assemblymen, Richard Henry Lee (then president of the Continental Congress), and the Baron Von Steuben.[50] In 1787, "General Washington" attended a portion of the Alexandria Academy's exhibition.[51] The judges were largely there for show. Yet newspapers gladly noted when they "gave many signal testimonies of their approbation."[52] Even when national figures could not attend, "a large concourse of respectable citizens" turned out for academy events.[53] Visitors furthered the academy founders' mission of socially reproducing certain kinds of men. Students could assume their success depended on appealing to the sensibilities of an existing elite, which saw academies as important. Even more, students had the chance to prove their mettle to local, regional, and national power brokers. It is hard to know if and how often relationships formed. But this experience was part of the social and cultural capital that academies offered.[54]

Students understood the stakes of public examinations and hoped their performances could pave the way for political influence. One Philadelphia academy student congratulated his peers for achieving "a stamp of character, and an attestation of merit, which cannot fail to make the most favourable impression upon the publick mind."[55] Roger Taney, the future chief justice of the United States, remembered his Dickinson College valedictory address as his entrance into public life.[56] Given their importance, exhibitions could arouse deep anxiety. When tapped to give a prominent oration at a July Fourth event, one student hoped "the honor bestowed on me will not expose my ignorance to shame."⁵⁷ Students internalized the connection between academic merit and power.

Important as they were for students, public ceremonies also served a didactic function for audiences. Newspapers frequently published accounts of these ceremonies. In one conspicuous example, a group in Baltimore planned to publish "a REPOSITORY OF SCIENCE and INTELLIGENCE" called *The American Spectator*. The editors hoped to spread information about education initiatives in different states. They also asked for the "Gentlemen who superintend the great Business of EDUCATION" to inform them of "meritorious Performances of the Youth under their Care." The editors hoped "that such a general Display of their Abilities will tend to excite a Spirit of Emulation" beyond academy walls. In sum, the Baltimoreans wanted "to catch, living as they rise, the Manners' of this young but great and rising Empire."⁵⁸ The *Spectator* does not seem ever to have been published. The plan nevertheless suggests that academy promoters hoped they could influence less-educated Americans through published accounts of exhibitions. Others claimed that as academies spread, "the spirit of ambition has operated, with success in different parts of the union." As a result, "no country has ever displayed so extensive a field to rising merit."⁵⁹ But how extensive and broad was access to merit? Who could claim it?

Class and Merit

Even among white men, the new emphasis on education and merit did not overhaul the social order. Academies offered a range of curriculum, from the "three Rs" to classical language training and other college preparation. In between, they usually taught some combination of advanced English grammar, bookkeeping, geography, navigation, and other subjects that appealed to middling young men who wanted to work as clerks or merchants. This middle-level curriculum—which private "venture schools" run by entrepreneurial teachers had long offered in colonial cities—was most important for creating social and economic mobility.⁶⁰ These were not the subjects celebrated during academy exhibitions. Rather, the emphasis remained on the classical languages.⁶¹ If academy exhibitions forged the connection between education and political power, they also then betrayed the disjuncture between the values of a rising middle class and the elite who ran academies. As one newspaper essayist put it: academies taught students to "speak in a different dialect from other people, and assume a style of behavior peculiar to themselves."⁶²

"Premiums"—effectively, recognitions of excellence—were the main reward offered at exhibitions. Trustees and visitors conferred them on "those who distinguish themselves by superior merit."[63] One set of academy trustees claimed to use "sundry premiums" for both "the encouragement of merit, and as a stimulus to future exertions."[64] Students, though, showed merit through success in an advanced curriculum. One academy board, for instance, offered premiums "to inspire the youth with a laudable ambition to excel in every branch of *polite* learning."[65] The Georgetown Academy only publicly examined students in Latin, Greek, and French.[66] Similarly, in 1786, the Alexandria Academy only gave prizes in the classics and oratory.[67] For over three years, the trustees of the Protestant Episcopal Academy of Philadelphia kept a register of notes on exhibitions. In 1786, the Episcopal Academy only ranked the best students in Latin, not in English or math. Those upper-level Latin classes included many well-connected Philadelphians. Benjamin Franklin's grandson William Bache, Tench Coxe's son Charles, and James Wilson's sons Bird and William all went through this class. Even once trustees began to grant premiums in math and English, they reserved the most effusive praise for the Latin students.[68]

The biggest fanfare at public exhibitions was for oratory. Orations translated the social authority of elite children into nascent public power.[69] As one academy advertisement declared, "A taste for, and emulation to excel in public speaking, has always been a characteristic of every wise and great nation." Therefore, it "ought not to be neglected by those who wish to be distinguished in life."[70] Newspaper accounts of another academy's July Fourth exhibition noted that three students "delivered orations ... fully expressive of patriotism and virtue," characteristics of good leaders.[71] John Spangler's 1788 speech was not the only one that the York Academy highlighted in newspapers. Others celebrated "the Advantages of public Examinations" or the work of classical authors.[72] As academies turned oratorical skill and classical learning into proxies for merit, they set up class barriers around the natural aristocracy of merit. The irony here is that most Americans did not have a classical education, yet they identified merit based on academic excellence.

This may not have troubled academy educators, who saw their niche as preparing students for their destined role in society. Education would not sort people; they were already sorted. Academy teachers devised separate curricula for different students depending on their likely profession. That "lads who are not intended as pupils for an university should receive a different management from those, who are" was acceptable pedagogy.[73] Burgiss Allison of the Bordentown (New Jersey) Academy advertised "that gentlemen may have their children either fitted for any particular class in a public seminary, or such as prefer a private school, have their education finish'd."[74] Another set of trustees celebrated how their students made progress toward their "high *destiny*" of serving as "fair candidates for office."[75] The structure of academy curriculum, in other words, belied rhetoric that celebrated mobility.

Even academies that aimed at the middling sorts taught students differently depending on their class background. The Baltimore Academy trustees believed that most academies catered to would-be professionals. They, instead, served "others, who only aim at being prepared to discharge the ordinary occupations and employments of life." Yet the board did not propose to equalize education across classes. Rather, the Baltimore Academy taught a curriculum without classics that might prove "beneficial and ornamental to the Trader, the Farmer, or Private Gentleman."[76] They reasoned that this will "qualify Youth for the ordinary Business of Manhood," and "tend to prepare them for their destined Employment in active life."[77] Many academies and private teachers also ran night schools, which were marketed to "pupils intended for the Counting House."[78] Students could learn a "practical curriculum" at convenient hours that would "not interfere with their business."[79] If academy advertisements reflect reality, then the schools taught young men the skills they needed to fulfill a station they already assumed they would occupy, precisely what James Wilson thought that European education did.

Nonetheless, the American emphasis on the classics and the rhetoric about destiny did not eliminate mobility per se. While it did add years to schooling, Latin was not significantly more expensive than other subjects. Rather, this language of destiny suggested that certain types of education corresponded with certain stations. One observer complained that this "undiscriminating mode of education" assumed "that classical studies are of such a nature as will be equally important to all men, who wish to make a distinguished figure in society." As a result, "no person can be eminently qualified for a conspicuous station" without classical learning. To this writer, that made little sense. "That all must be confined to an exact similarity of classical education" ignored that there are "different geniuses" in the world.[80] Academies, then, forced politically ambitious young men to embrace trustees' traditional ideas about education. That was the rub for critics, who hoped that the Revolution had overthrown such a constricted view of education. Nor were their complaints anti-intellectual. Noah Webster and Benjamin Rush—among the most important intellectuals of the period—both decried the hegemonic importance of the classics. But they fought an uphill battle against an American elite who sought European markers of status.[81]

The socioeconomics of attendance confirm that academies offered only limited mobility. Academy students were often wealthy. Within academy towns, the families who sent children to the school owned anywhere from 50 percent to 300 percent more property on average as other households.[82] Yet this only captures a small sliver of the social demography of academy attendance. Most towns did not have an academy during the first two or three decades of independence. New Jersey had the highest rate of academies per capita of any state by 1800, and there were still only twenty. The majority of students came from elsewhere to attend an academy. As late as 1817, for example, only around one-third of the ninety students at the Leicester (Massachusetts) Academy hailed from the town. Those thirty-odd students comprised only 10 percent of Leicester's free white boys and girls between the ages of ten and sixteen. Another 50 percent or so of Leicester Academy students came from elsewhere in Worcester County. The remaining 15 percent were drawn from even further afield.[83]

Given the high cost of room and board, out-of-town students unsurprisingly came from even wealthier families. An extant county-wide return from the 1815 federal direct tax allows for a partial reconstruction of Leicester Academy classical students' family wealth. Of the three from Leicester, two came from families in the town's top decile, while the third fell lower but remained in the top half. Of the nine identified classical students from other Worcester County towns, eight came from families in at least the top quarter of their town's tax list; most were in the top decile. The last student was a bit further down the tax list but still from a family in the top half of wealth.[84] Undoubtedly, academies were more exclusive even twenty years before this data, when they were fewer in number. They would be similarly less exclusive twenty years later. But in the early republic, academies were not yet middle-class institutions.[85] Access to the aristocracy of merit was limited, though not impenetrable.

Gendered and Racial Limits of Merit

The rhetorical emphasis on merit may not have opened up as much opportunity for ordinary white men as promised. It did even less for women and free African Americans. No doubt, they tried to illustrate their merit to claim a role in public life. But they faced steep obstacles. Elite white men had defined themselves as the epitome of merit, which made it an inherently gendered and racialized ideal from the outset.

Women's public role expanded during the American Revolution. Their participation in nonimportation agreements, labor in making homespun clothing and war supplies, and work on the home front made victory possible. After the war, their role changed to recognize their contributions. As "republican mothers," women were responsible for preparing their sons to be good citizens. Since good citizenship was informed citizenship, women needed a meaningful education to rear sons for public life. But women's education, such as it was in the colonial period, focused on ornamental subjects and was criticized as merely finishing school. Something needed to change. Nearly 200 female academies opened in the half-century following the Revolutionary War. Many other academies that mostly served men also had "female departments." One writer in the 1790s noted that "female academies are everywhere establishing." A veritable "revolution" was afoot.[86]

As at male academies, educators made the case that female academies benefited the new nation. Benjamin Rush set the tone in his "Thoughts upon Female Education," written to commemorate the opening of the Young Ladies' Academy of Philadelphia in 1787. Rush proclaimed that schooling should "be accommodated to our state of society and to the forms of our government." Thus, even if academies encouraged European-style ornamental education (as the next chapter shows), they still made changes so that schools prepared women to serve the republic. It was especially important "to make ornamental accomplishments yield to principles and knowledge in the education of our women," Rush wrote.[87] To help their family members become men of merit, women needed an academic education. The way Rush and other men framed female education denied the equality of the sexes. Women would accrue influence while they upheld a hierarchical society that circumscribed their public voice.

But some women writers argued for women's innate equality. Most notably, Judith Sargent Murray published, "On the Equality of the Sexes" in the *Massachusetts Magazine* in 1790, and followed that up with *The Gleaner*. Both works argued that unequal education created an illusion of inequality between men and women. Justice demanded that women must receive equal education so that they can realize their true equality with men. Yet Murray reassured readers that women still "will not be assuming." They would not use their education to challenge the social order. Tellingly, many American advocates for women's education distanced themselves from Mary Wollstonecraft, the English radical and noted proponent of women's rights. Wollstonecraft's personal life—including publicized affairs and an illegitimate child—suggested that educating women brought instability.[88]

In practice, most early national academies offered women something new. Second only to white men on a classical academy track, academy women had the greatest opportunity to gain public recognition for their academic prowess.

Benjamin Rush argued that in a female seminary, "emulation may be excited without jealousy, ambition without envy, and competition without strife."[89] By 1788, Philadelphia's female academies held frequent public exhibitions to "facilitate the proficiency of the pupils, and to excite a noble emulation."[90] Young women received public accolades for their performances. In 1795, the *Aurora* published an account of one exhibition that trumpeted the "surprizing" success of the Young Ladies' Academy. The writer commended "the spirit of emulation which Mr. Poor has artfully infused into the minds of his pupils."[91] Some newspaper accounts of exhibitions published the names of girls who received awards for their academic work.[92] The Litchfield (Connecticut) Female Academy even had women judges award a "prize of merit" at one exhibition.[93]

There were, of course, differences in how academies educated men and women. Female academies, as much as any institution, ingrained the idea that women should only influence public life indirectly.[94] Whether female academy students should give public orations, for instance, was a contested question. So far as people could imagine, women would never hold positions of political leadership. Why, then, should they learn oratory?[95] Some female academy students ultimately gave public orations. Just as often, they wrote speeches that their teachers read to the audience. Harriet Beecher Stowe claimed that her proudest moment came when a teacher read one of her compositions at a Litchfield Female Academy exhibition. Her father gave it a hearty round of applause before he knew his daughter was the author.[96] Under any circumstances, women had less latitude in the subjects they could cover in their orations. Moreover, most women did not learn classical languages, though in later periods some did.[97]

At many academies, young women learned to navigate male-dominated social spaces. Critics alleged that coeducation elicited passions in young men that had no place in schools. When the Newark (New Jersey) Academy started admitting women, one writer railed that this would lead to the "total putrefaction of the moral air."[98] Despite these criticisms, the school kept its female department.[99] Even in social settings at schools, women performed for a public audience. One poem by a female academy student, entitled "The Woman of Merit Described," outlines this dilemma. "Without pride or meanness familiar and witty," the meritorious woman "acts what she thinks and thinks what she says / Regardless alike of both censure and praise / Her thoughts and her words and her actions are such / That none can admire or praise her too much."[100] Coeducation rewarded unassuming women who exerted influence without upsetting gender norms. It was a delicate balance.

But powerful men saw heterosociability as necessary for a stable polity.[101] The conservative vision for women's education won in the short term.

Like women, free African Americans hoped that access to education would help them gain a public voice. White organizations provided some education for African American children during the early republic. Several academy boosters were members of the New York Manumission Society, which in 1787 created the New York African Free School. Just as often, young black men appeared in academy records as property, not as students. The boards of both the Washington-Henry Academy in Virginia and the Newark Academy in New Jersey received slaves as "donations," which they "were empowered to sell . . . for as much money" as they could.[102]

White educators set lower expectations for black students than for white academy students. The African Free School's rules revolved around controlling behavior. Trustees admonished students to "attend to their business in silence, avoiding unnecessary whispering and moving from seat to seat." Teachers reminded students "not to quarrel." Scholars took a "vow to live in love and friendship," as though it could not occur naturally. Black students also had to clean the school "according to the direction of the master."[103] By contrast, poems read at white academy exhibitions hoped that "Within these walls may friendship reign; / Trustees, and tutors join; / And pupils, hand in hand attain / Those arts which all refine."[104] Educators assumed that white children could motivate each other but that black children would corrupt one another.[105]

Support for the African Free School stemmed from many motives. Some advocates believed education might help African Americans prove their capacity for citizenship to skeptical whites. One account of a 1796 exhibition argued that "the most prejudiced advocate of African slavery, if present, could have his favorite argument weakened" by the students' performances. Exhibitions showed that African Americans could be "rendered capable of discharging the duties of citizenship."[106] At some point during the nineteenth century, the African Free School established a "Class of Merit." It provided "an example not only as regards advancement in learning, but also in a very high degree, and in a more important view, by its weight of character." Students in the class took on some responsibilities for the management of the school, held meetings, and kept a minute book. In his history of the Free School, Charles Andrews—the longtime, white principal—wrote that "this little society operates in a small sphere, similarly to those institutions, establishd [sic] among men."[107] It was a voluntary association in miniature.

In other cases, support for the African Free School stemmed from a belief in black incapacity for citizenship, and served less enlightened goals. After witnessing an exhibition, one self-described "friend to emancipation" hoped that New Yorkers who used bound labor would see the advantages of the school. He argued "that by cultivating the minds of their servants, they will probably encrease their sense of moral obligation, and thus render them more worthy of their confidence." "Having servants of his own," the writer concluded, "he has experienced the importance of instruction to them."[108] This was a peculiarly northern view. In the South, slave literacy loomed as a threat. It had been a key ingredient in insurrections. In the North, the notion that education could control blacks persisted, even among the most ardent supporters of black education. Charles Andrews recounted that "the behavior of the children was orderly" at every exhibition he oversaw. As late as 1824, newspaper accounts drew attention to the students' "order, neatness of dress, and cleanliness of person." For Andrews, perhaps the most telling evidence of his success was that none of his students ended up in prison.[109]

Whatever educators' motives, black schools created a distinct cadre of educated free African Americans, which bred class tensions. The Free School's culture of respectability irritated the black working class just as academy education perturbed some poorer whites.[110] Nevertheless, white men rarely acknowledged in black students the same kind of merit they saw in white men. Academies, then, inculcated in Americans a belief in the connection between academic merit and civic leadership, which idealized a certain type of well-to-do white man.

Institutional Realities and the Shaping of Merit

Academies often reaffirmed prevailing views of power and authority in part because they catered to the children of existing elites. Many parents were academy educated. They then founded and helped build schools, and they molded them to their liking.[111] Subscribers—the people who donated money to academies and thus had the right to vote for trustees—also commanded a good deal of power. The trustees were more beholden to them than to the parents of aspiring children who merely attended the school. This was clearly the case at the Baltimore Academy. The board stipulated that if they had too many students, "the Children of Subscribers and Contributors shall always have a preference."[112] In other instances, subscribers garnered even greater special treatment. One Philadelphia female academy stipulated that "no lady unacquainted with English grammar, can be admitted, except the children of members."[113] Even if the elite admitted the need to justify power in new ways, financial, cultural, and social capital allowed them to shape to their benefit the institutions that conferred authority. Therefore, academies were organized around class, as much as curriculum.

As the only large schools to consistently offer high-level subjects, the academies influenced lower-level schools. Small, private "venture schools" spread widely in the 1780s. They were consistent only in being ephemeral, which blunted their potential to challenge academies. Academy teachers and trustees also wielded significant indirect power over them. The trustees of the Protestant Episcopal Academy believed the cause "for the inferiority" of one of their classes was that the students "have been but a short time in the academy." Instead of taking their elementary instruction at the academy, most students "were admitted from some private schools in this city, which have of late been dissolved."[114] If venture schools could not teach students well enough for them to assimilate into academies, they would have a hard time succeeding. Some academy principals also believed that good early education should be exclusive. John Lowe, an academy master in Stafford County, Virginia, required prospective students to provide "sufficient testimony of their natural talents, and unwearied application to study." Without that, he would not admit them. Too often, he had to dismiss "gentlemen from his tuition" because "their continuance with him was only robbing their parents of a sum of money."[115] Students' success in academies depended on an earlier education that prepared them well, and thus their parents' financial standing.

Academies' exclusivity clashed with trustees' claims that they were communal institutions. But local boosterism was powerful, and community members often came to value academies that they or their children would likely never attend. At the most basic level, academies were a financial boon. Rich kids brought money to academy towns. Sometimes this bred animosity between the haves and have-nots. Academy boosters retorted that this was the price of the progress that they brought to small towns.[116] One visitor to Westmoreland County, Pennsylvania, for instance, claimed that for many years, people there "in appearance, dress, and manners could with difficulty be distinguished from the Indians." After an academy opened, the region started to produce gifted orators. This was seen as evidence of progress from "savagery" toward "civilization." Understandings of civilization came largely from magazines. Usually published in seaports with connections to the Atlantic World, magazines apprised Americans of European standards of taste and refinement. After this academy opened, booksellers in the Westmoreland County area started to stock magazines. One ordered fifty sets of both the

American Asylum and the *Columbian Magazine*. Taken together, the academy in Westmoreland brought "to us the blessings of good government," even if it did not directly serve most people.[117]

Academy trustees also attended to some of the educational needs of middling and poor people. Some academies effectively doubled as lyceums and hosted lectures for the general public.[118] Others opened their doors to a small number of scholarship students. During one Trenton Academy examination, "friends and proprietors of this Academy" announced their intention "to establish a fund for the tuition of poor children." They claimed "this laudable undertaking ... met with considerable encouragement."[119] Other academies found "great success in procuring subscriptions for the endowment of [an] English school, so as to make education in it entirely free."[120] Students at the Baltimore Academy performed *Cato* at a Baltimore theater to raise money for "charitable purpose[s]."[121] This public generosity made it harder to attack academies, even as they worsened social inequality. To criticize academy founders was to attack the very men who also provided some education for the less fortunate.

More generally, trustees claimed that the schools helped produce an informed citizenry. The board of an academy in Burlington, New Jersey, believed that "liberal education is among the most effectual means of forming useful and virtuous citizens." The "establishment of seminaries" was their contribution to this "desirable object."[122] The founders of the Hagerstown Academy made a similar argument. The academy would induce "wealthy men to settle among us," who would broaden the tax base such that "education would be more generally diffused, and would easier be obtained by the youth of every class."[123] Trustees at least attempted to make the case that academies were not antithetical to the interests of nonelite whites. This all buoyed their broader goal of using education to organize the hierarchies of American civic life.

WHEN JOHN SPANGLER STEPPED to the stage to give his oration at the York constitutional ratification parade in 1788, he seemed to have launched a public career. Nearly twenty years later, in 1805, Spangler stood as the Federalist candidate for York County coroner and won. That was the only elected office he ever held.[124] It might seem that Spangler failed to live up to the fanfare of the 1788 procession. Viewed another way, though, Spangler was an academy success story. Federalists built academies and included students in nationalistic processions to ensure that future leaders had received a good, liberal education and would act in ways that befit that education. Coroners like Spangler had less power over law enforcement than the sheriffs, constables, and justices of the peace whose conduct in the 1780s had so alarmed Pennsylvania's Federalists. The coroner was nonetheless a related office. James Wilson, the intellectual force behind Pennsylvania Federalism, believed that Americans who "neglected, perhaps despised," coroners did so at their peril. It was "an office, both ancient and dignified." A good coroner made up "no inconsiderable part of a complete juridical system."[125]

It is impossible to know how common Spangler's trajectory from academy to public office was. Yet it is clear that by the nineteenth century, the Federalists had successfully made both merit the ostensible basis for power and education—particularly academies—the arbiter of merit. Building social order around academic merit may have reified existing hierarchies. Yet filtering social order through education served a larger purpose. If academies played a role in the development of political leaders, those leaders would feel compelled to support education in the future. As one school advertisement declared, "the ambition which operates in the bosoms of many of our countrymen to represent their fellow subjects in the legislature of their country, should stimulate them to furnish their children with the rudiments of wisdom."[126] The aristocracy of merit was tough to oppose because it lent support to the idea that education mattered to citizenship and power. It conceded that hereditary status had no place in a republic. These *were* democratic ideals—or at least they could be. Even as education created hierarchy, it also held out the possibility of breaking it down. That served to naturalize inequality, which made it all the more powerful.

In the short term, by allowing nationalists to rebuild a more hierarchical political order without completely flouting republican principles, academies helped them confront the so-called excess of democracy and entrench their own power. In the long term, however, their decision to solve this problem through education cemented the civic ideal that schooling served the public good. It ensured that the values that led Federalists to build academies would outlive them. It also meant that attempts to make American society and politics more equitable would necessarily require school reform.

CHAPTER FIVE

Diplomacy and Dance
The Geopolitics of Ornamental Education

One of the most important educators in 1780s America was French. Alexandre-Marie Quesnay de Beaurepaire was the grandson of François Quesnay, King Louis XV's physician and founder of the physiocrat school of economics. The younger Quesnay came to North America as a captain in the French Army and served briefly during the Revolutionary War, though illness cut his tenure short. While he healed in Virginia, Quesnay began to think about opening a "French Academy" where he would teach the "polite arts"—dancing, singing, fencing, drawing, and painting—in addition to French.[1]

In 1779, Quesnay set off to Philadelphia to open such a school. The curriculum Quesnay offered was demonstrably European and flouted Americans' growing rhetorical commitment to practical and republican education.[2] Unsurprisingly, he met with opposition. Yet as attempts at democratic and republican education reform floundered in the 1780s and 1790s, this extreme manifestation of aristocratic education grew entrenched across the United States. Quesnay even came closer to creating a national university than anyone else at the time. Though his grand plan for a national institution stalled, Quesnay's curriculum became an expected part of the academy experience by the 1790s.[3]

As with the rest of academy education, the American elite provided the demand for the polite arts. Many students had unassailable patriotic credentials. Former Continental Army officers proved particularly interested in what Quesnay was selling. But this education was considered ornamental, which marked it as something different from academics and outside the rhetoric about merit. How did trustees and teachers justify a curriculum that so clearly butted up against republican ideals and gender norms?

Both groups justified the curriculum by claiming that it was geopolitically necessary. Those same Americans who supported ornamental education also wanted to see the United States take its place as a treaty-worthy nation within the dominant global community of civilized states.[4] To do this, to gain diplomatic recognition, the republic needed to meet European expectations of what a nation was. These diplomatic considerations propelled the movement to create the Constitution and a more powerful federal government. There was also a performative side to state formation. Civilized nations needed to meet certain cultural expectations. If Britain offered the model of a fiscal-military state, France provided the cultural model. Of course, in the 1790s, French radical republicanism would radicalize American politics. Before that, France's reputation for cultural refinement shaped American society with very different effects.[5] French culture influenced the republican court that took shape in the nation's capital in its early years.[6] Likewise, Quesnay and others pointed to French schools as evidence that the United States was, in fact, civilized.

In other words, it was geopolitically necessary for American elites to know how to dance.[7] Refined statesmen bolstered the credibility of the United States in the eyes of other nations' diplomats. That American schools reared these statesmen helped prove that the United States could sustain itself.[8] The nation's claims to independence, then, rested in some measure on domestic ornamental education. Academies, and ornamental education especially, reveal how two postrevolutionary impulses—fostering national character and building national strength—were at odds. Academy boosters stoked fears about the United States' precarious geopolitical position to justify education that served their own interests. By applying geopolitical logic to education, the very institution charged with creating a more egalitarian society, they stymied the advent of that society.

French Schools in the Critical Period

When Quesnay arrived in 1779, Philadelphia was in turmoil. The city was only a year removed from nine months of British military occupation. Patriots chafed at men and women who had socialized with the occupiers, including during an elaborate farewell ball for British officers, called the Meschianza. Aristocratic culture seemed to have run amok. At the same time, runaway inflation and merchant price gouging led artisans and workers to demand price controls. This culminated in the so-called Fort Wilson Riot. Militiamen marched on the home of James Wilson, where merchants had congregated, and shooting ensued. As many as seven men were killed, and more were wounded. The fight between republican values and European culture was live in revolutionary Philadelphia.[9]

Quesnay was undeterred. He took note of "the pleasure and satisfaction which the Public appear to take in learning the FRENCH LANGUAGE." Feeling encouraged, Quesnay opened an academy where "LADIES" and young men would attend at separate hours.[10] He continued the French academy in

Philadelphia throughout the early 1780s.[11] In 1782, Quesnay moved to a larger location and opened "his ACADEMY of POLITE SCIENCE, in Southwark," a neighborhood that would claim a large French community by the mid-1790s. Quesnay added that the school's opening occurred in the "presence of a very brilliant and numerous concourse of ladies and gentlemen of the first rank." He always associated himself with Philadelphia's elite.[12]

As time wore on, Quesnay set his sights beyond Philadelphia. He expanded first into Trenton, New Jersey. Then, in summer 1784, he plied his trade in Elizabeth Town and Newark, centers of revolutionary resistance in New Jersey. The towns were "agreeable and wholesome places," and conveniently located for New Yorkers to send their children there. All were also home to existing academies. Impressed with "the gentility and politeness with which their inhabitants ha[d] treated" him, Quesnay hoped to reopen his schools in New Jersey every spring. This would not come to pass because demand was not what he anticipated.[13] Quesnay moved next to New York City for a stint.[14]

Over the years, Quesnay offered an increasingly comprehensive range of polite arts. In addition to teaching French, Quesnay taught the "Art of Fortifications," as well as "Painting likenesses, landscapes, flowers, &c."[15] He also invited musicians to teach in his schools.[16] By the time he acquired the newer, bigger building in 1782, Quesnay and his assistants offered all this under one roof. That new building used to be a theater. He informed the public that "the pit will be raised level with the stage; the scenery dismantled, and the whole will form a most capacious and elegant ball-room." These renovations telegraphed curricular changes.[17]

Dancing schools became an important part of Quesnay's operation. By fall 1782, Quesnay hired a new dancing teacher, a Frenchman named Louis D'Orsiere, who had run a dancing school independently for a time.[18] In Philadelphia, Quesnay's employees held a dancing academy for young women "at the Freemason's Lodge, in Lodge Alley," as well as "An evening school for the gentlemen." He made it so the dedicated student had "free access to the different schools (drawing excepted) till he is perfected."[19] Dancing instruction helped Quesnay corner the market on polite education in Philadelphia and provide a finishing school for the city's elite.

Yet Quesnay was not the only person teaching the polite arts in the urban North. Numerous entrepreneurial teachers opened small schools that taught one or two of the subjects that Quesnay offered. Andrew Brown's school in Philadelphia was typical. In 1784, when Quesnay was in New York, Brown added a drawing and dancing school to his French language academy.[20] He faced competition from Benjamin Blyth, who opened one of the first schools dedicated solely to the visual arts, in 1784.[21] The sort of art instruction offered in the 1780s was unmistakably ornamental. Students learned to paint and draw portraits, miniatures, and landscapes. They worked with a variety of materials in addition to paper, including silk, glass, satin, and calico, as well as "shading in India ink."[22] James Cox opened a painting and drawing school "at the request of several respectable characters" for whom art was a leisure pursuit, not a career.[23] Of those teaching the visual arts, only Quesnay consistently offered architecture. That, along with fortifications, was probably directed at the military clientele to whom Quesnay frequently pandered.[24]

Women also made a living through teaching the ornaments. In Maryland, "Mrs. Alcock" taught young women needlework and embroidery, along with music and dance.[25] "Mrs. Pine" taught a similar range of subjects and also displayed her students' artwork for the public.[26] On occasion, couples opened schools together in which the wife taught ornamental subjects and the husband more traditional academics.[27] Women came to dominate ornamental teaching in the early 1800s, well before teaching in general came to be seen as a woman's profession.[28]

Dancing became the most important part of ornamental curriculum. It was the most overtly public skill, and most indebted to European fads. Dancing masters tended to teach dances "both in the English and French modes."[29] When Quesnay hired D'Orsiere, he claimed to "teach all sorts of dances most in fashion in Europe."[30] Teachers argued that dancing taught bodily comportment that was recognizable everywhere. It gave "to the human form, the power of displaying its natural beauty, and symmetry." Quoting the Englishman Vicesimus Knox, the advertiser continued that "a skill in this art ... enables young people to join in a diversion, which, in decent company is as innocent as it is pleasing."[31] Beyond that, it taught "graces and manners" that were applicable outside the ballroom.[32] Knowing how to dance, then, allowed a young person to take part in elite society.[33] The emphasis on bodily control and grace was also important in oratory, which men who hoped to enter politics needed to master.[34]

Dancing offered students frequent opportunities to display their refinement in public. As with academics, this helped "create emulation among the scholars."[35] Schools generally scheduled lessons so that the male and female students learned separately. But as often as once a week, dancing teachers would open their ballrooms to the public "for the advantage and amusement of his Scholars, and the Ladies and Gentlemen of the city." The entire process separated the "respectable" attendees and students from the masses. One dancing teacher went so far as to install a separate staircase so students could get to his ballroom without having to enter through a tavern.[36] Reports of these events focused on the attendees' social status. After Quesnay held one ball, a newspaper reported that it "was filled with ladies of the first rank and beauty." It went on to highlight "the great variety of elegant dresses, with which the fair visitors were adorned." This all showed Quesnay's "superior abilities" in refining young men and women.[37]

The other way that men learned comportment was through fencing. A Frenchman named Le Maire was the most widely advertised fencing teacher in the urban North. He claimed that fencing, like dancing, "gives also grace, ease and vigor to the body."[38] By teaching the "most noble motions," fencing "produces a generous confidence in those who know its excellencies."[39] Of course, fencing also had a military connotation. Le Maire sold his fencing academy as a place to learn "military science."[40] Ever eager to please his military clientele, Quesnay offered fencing too. One teacher he hired came recommended by the Marquis de Lafayette.[41] The military function of fencing connected polite education with the revolutionary cause, but the practice was never divorced from its role in refining Americans on European terms.

Quesnay marketed his services directly to Continental Army officers and their families in other ways. He made special provision that his "Academy will be open to the American officers at all times." Usually Quesnay was more stringent in admitting students. He once advertised that besides "gentlemen of public character, no person will be admitted without being presented by some Academician."[42] The same rules applied for admission to his dancing schools. All prospective students needed a recommendation, but "with respect to gentlemen of the army, their commissions, on being produced, will serve as a recommendation."[43] Appealing to the officer corps was shrewd business.

Throughout the Revolutionary War, the officer corps had shown a deep interest in cultivating gentility. George Washington was famous for his dancing prowess, which inspired his subordinate officers. The Continental officer corps also came to admire the masculine self-control and polite manners of their opposition, especially John André: the British officer with whom Benedict Arnold conspired in his treason against the United States. André's calm, grace, and even artistic skill as he awaited execution endeared him to the Continental officers. The enlisted men, however, could not wait to see him hanged.[44] The officers' pretensions were neither lost on the Americans nor above reproach. In response, in 1787, Royall Tyler wrote *The Contrast*, a play that critiqued the aristocratic ambitions of some American officers and raised questions about the basis of authority in the new republic.[45]

Quesnay and other teachers nevertheless hoped that marketing to the officer corps would help their public image and make them seem patriotic. On opening his first dancing school, Quesnay claimed that "as a foreigner and friend to America," his goal was "to promote and furnish useful amusement for those gentlemen of the army, who have sustained innumerable hardships, and bravely ventured their lives in service of their country."[46] Quesnay offered free instruction to *thirteen* children every year. These "children are to belong to respectable inhabitants of this State, whose private fortunes may have been injured by the war, and those of officers and soldiers of the army of the United States."[47] Quesnay also honored well-known war heroes. At other assemblies, his students performed "La Fayette's Departure, an English Country Dance," and "Washington's Resignation" to celebrate the general's decision to relinquish power and return to his plough like the great Roman Cincinnatus.[48] When he could, Quesnay gleefully reported the support of men whose patriotism was beyond reproach. Quesnay recounted that at one of his assemblies, "the amiable marquis de la Fayette was present at the last entertainment, and expressed his determination to support the interests of the academy."[49] If people like Lafayette wanted to promote these students and schools, it followed that so too should the people.

Gender, Class, and Critiques of Polite Education

All this pandering betrayed an underlying weakness: The kind of education offered at French schools seemed out of place in a republic. Ornamental education was flagrantly European, perhaps the best evidence of American education's aristocratic bent. In fact, it had not had much of a presence when the Americans were still colonists. Unsurprisingly, it came under withering attacks from essayists and satirists. Some sought to connect critiques of polite education and academy education's more general deference to Europe. Often, too, these attacks were noticeably gendered.

In 1787, a Philadelphia essayist returned from Europe and derided how in England and France, frivolous manners and behaviors conveyed much about one's social standing. The author began the essay by claiming that despite "all I had read of London, I was perfectly sick of it in three weeks." To claim a certain stature, Britons needed "to study a long time in the academy of compliments." "No man here dares," he continued sardonically, "to venture into the presence of his superiors, or attempts going in or out of a room without a previous education on that purpose." A woman could not "even venture to move her fan, without being previously taught." The essay appeared in the

Anti-Federalist-friendly *Freeman's Journal*, and it was intended to illustrate differences between Europe and America.[50] But many readers must have wondered how different things were in the United States. In almost any other Philadelphia newspaper, they found incessant ads for French, dancing, and drawing teachers who taught Americans to cultivate airs in much the same way as the Europeans.

To many Americans, similarities in education across the Atlantic showed the degradation of republican values. Noah Webster believed that education helped societies advance from a primitive to a flourishing state. At some point, though, education became a source of corruption. This happened when, in the "opulent part of civilized nations, [education] is directed principally to show and amusement." Put differently, there was a clear distinction "between a good education and a showy one, for an education, merely superficial, is a proof of corruption of taste and has a mischievous influence on manners." To Webster, the latter kind of education was gaining ground in the United States. Ornamental education and a "too general attention to the dead languages" in American schools revealed "the absurdity of our copying the manners and adopting the institutions of monarchies." Americans needed to realize that "it is dishonorable to waste life in mimicking the follies of other nations and basking in the sunshine of foreign glory."[51]

Webster was a cultural elite, but he found support from the radical Anti-Federalist Robert Coram, who even quoted Webster in his writing. Coram contended that "in the civilized state education is the most imperfect part of the whole scheme of government." European education distracted from the practical pursuit of useful knowledge. Schooling was just about the last thing on which Americans should defer to Europe.[52] The advocate for women's education Judith Sargent Murray recognized the power of this critique. She attacked parents who taught young women that "ornamenting our exterior ought to be the principal object" of school. Murray tried to leverage this to create new opportunities for women. Since ornamental education was unrepublican, she argued that women should receive substantive and equal academic education.[53]

The critique of ornamental education as a corrupting luxury was gendered. During the Revolution, elite men conveyed patriotism by touting their civic and martial virtue, attributes understood as strictly masculine. Women showed their patriotism in an equally gendered way: by producing homespun cloth. Men then wore that cloth to signal their rejection of European luxury.[54] A gendered division of labor underlay the whole project. Even more, republicanism cast luxury as antithetical to virtue. If virtue was masculine, then luxury was, by implication, feminine. Ornamental education played havoc with all of this. It celebrated luxury and appealed to both genders, and yet men embraced it as a route to political power. In other words, dancing and the like feminized elite formation.[55] Thomas Jefferson, among others, believed France was emblematic of how polite culture led to effeminate men holding power.[56] Worse, this erosion of gender norms could lead to other vices. Quesnay, for instance, had to warn his "enemies" that he would prosecute anyone who disgraced him by bringing a "Woman of *ill-fame*" into his academy.[57] Quesnay was susceptible to these sorts of smear campaigns because of the gendered connotations concerning ornamental education.

Satirists picked up the argument against ornamental education. One advertised a fake academy that taught dice and cards to "fashionable youth" and "young Men of Fortune and Family." In case the meaning was not clear, the ad went on to call "gaming" a "polite art." This writer also blended critiques of polite and academic curricula. The fake academy would offer "Oriental Languages and a Hebrew Professor for those who, having finished their studies, have occasion to do business with the Jews."[58] Another fake "academy for instructing young gentlemen in the science of hair-dressing" advertised in a Philadelphia newspaper. Mocking pompous academy teachers, the author added that his methods conformed "to the most approved authors and latest discoveries made in that valuable branch."[59] In popular portrayals, academy students came off as effete and consumed by superfluous concerns.

Other satirists tried to convey how elite education hurt students' virtue. One concocted a character named "*Superficialis*," as "a mirror in which the great of the literary world may see themselves." The writer hoped that in this character they might "discern every feature of their insignificance." "Superficialis" possessed a "lively sense of his own external excellence," which through "flattery and indiscretion at length swelled into *vanity*." This happened "under the watchful eye of his preceptor, while at *Academy*." By the time he finished school, "*Superficialis*, though in reality contemptible, in appearance commanded some attention." As polite culture grew more ubiquitous, "Supeficialis" found it ever easier to hide "his real littleness."[60] This caricature underscored the criticism that American academies often created small-minded and haughty men, and not the virtuous republican leaders they claimed to train.

None of these criticisms of ornamental education were baseless. Quesnay, for one, tried to head them off, and claimed he did "not mean to introduce the LUXURIES, manners or fashions of Europe." Quesnay tried desperately "to convince the inhabitants of the United States . . . that my only desire is to be useful to them."[61] He believed it was useful to teach those "branches of education common in Europe, [which] are wholly unknown, or light attended to, in this country."[62] But to defuse criticisms, Quesnay and others had to invent new and more compelling arguments for ornamental curriculum.

Manners and Diplomacy

Quesnay voiced stronger justifications for his schools in 1786, when he undertook his most ambitious project yet. That year, Quesnay returned to Virginia and chose "Shockoe-Hill" in Richmond as the site for an "Academy of Polite Arts." The Richmond Academy received great fanfare from the outset. Quesnay obtained the financial support of a host of important Virginians to build his own building; he had always rented previously. The local lodge of Free Masons supported "this laudable undertaking, founded on the plan of enlarging the education of our youth in the polite personal accomplishments." The Masons led a ceremony to lay the "foundation stone" of the academy "under a salute of cannon."[63] Quesnay based the curriculum on his observations of European academies. It would include math, drawing, civil and military architecture, painting, sculpture, engraving, music, "horsemanship," and dancing, alongside science, history, and other common academic subjects, especially foreign languages.[64] The plan was similar to Quesnay's schools in New York, Philadelphia, and New Jersey, but on a much grander scale. He envisioned the Richmond academy as comprehensive and centralized, with branch schools throughout the mid-Atlantic.[65] It would function almost like a national university.

Quesnay returned to France to recruit faculty and raise money for the new academy. To that end, in 1788 he published a memoir that discussed his previous schools, explained his vision for the new one, and laid out the broader purpose he thought polite education served. Though written in support of an exceptionally ambitious project and directed at a French audience, Quesnay's *Memoir* offers insight into justifications for polite education in the United States more broadly.[66]

Simply put, Quesnay believed that there were compelling geopolitical reasons for the United States to support polite education. Before his schools opened, parents who wanted "to accomplish a youth" were "under the necessity of sending them to Europe."[67] By providing a domestic option, Quesnay could claim that he made the United States more independent. Earlier in his career, Quesnay explained that Europeans "already view with astonishment, your abilities in the fields of war and politics." Americans only needed to "convince them also of your taste for the polite arts and sciences."[68] A major academy would do that. Promoting the "fine arts," Quesnay contended, was "sound policy" for the United States.[69] According to Quesnay, "Academies are capitals of the sciences, of which it is not believed that the capitals of empires should or even can be deprived." Polite education bolstered the appearance the nation projected to the world. Beyond polishing the American elite, Quesnay's academy would teach architecture at a time when the nation needed stately government buildings.[70]

Quesnay appealed beyond just a status-anxious elite, to all Americans who were worried about the republic's place in a world of nations. Like individual Americans, the nation writ large needed to prove its civility to Europe. Education was caught in the middle of these individual and collective anxieties because civilized nations were comprised of civilized people. It was not that far-fetched to say that the United States' geopolitical existence depended, in part, on conformity in education.[71]

Quesnay's plan for the Richmond Academy made sense in the geopolitical context of the late eighteenth century. Part of what connected the dominant European nations was a shared commitment to arts and education. Quesnay positioned the Richmond Academy as an early foray into the global world of cultural institutions. Article IV of the academy guidelines required school officials to "correspond with the Paris Royal Academy of Sciences, Painting and Sculpture, the Royal Society of London, the Royal and Imperial Society of Brussels, and other learned societies of Europe."[72] In this way, the Richmond Academy would "form that much needed bridge over the divide which separates Europe from America."[73] Quesnay thus made a strong case that Americans who hoped to "see the bonds of the various nations of Europe with America perpetuated" should think of polite education as essential.[74]

Quesnay also argued that polite culture would foster commercial interactions with Europe, a necessity for the fledgling nation. Until the 1795 Jay Treaty stabilized relations with England, the United States had a vexed relationship with the former metropole. During the 1780s and early 1790s, many Americans turned to the French for capital.[75] Quesnay freely acknowledged his desire to increase "the relations of France with America, and of binding America to my country by new bonds of gratitude, similarity of tastes, and very intimate intercourse." His French supporters saw commerce as among the most desirable potential outcomes of his plan. They hoped the Richmond Academy would "promote light and knowledge in all parts of the world, and [perhaps] even become very useful to commerce." The "friendly interchange of the sciences and arts" served the economy, promoted "the happiness of humanity," and could "unite all nations."[76] Polite education fostered all manner of exchange.

Ornamental curriculum was seen as a way to ease the United States' entrance into a global economy. Dating back to Benjamin Franklin's 1749 *Proposals Relating to the Education of Youth*, Americans recognized that French was a practical necessity for merchants.[77] Teachers at ornamental academies marketed their schools to aspiring men of commerce. Andrew Brown, one of the most widely advertised French teachers in Philadelphia, offered instruction at night "for the convenience of Gentlemen engaged in business."[78] Joseph Carrier, an émigré from Marseilles, also opened an evening school, in which his students took Italian, Latin, and Greek; fencing; dancing; and navigation. Carrier thought that all these branches were "calculated for the inhabitants of a City of Commerce."[79] Like Quesnay, these teachers claimed that their schools were necessary given the United States' precarious global position.

Some of the most perceptive American nationalists bandied about arguments like Quesnay's in the nation's most prestigious schools. When he enrolled at Harvard, John Quincy Adams brought with him a unique perspective for a student. Adams had already accompanied his father on diplomatic missions to France and the Netherlands and served as a private secretary to another American diplomat in Russia. Adams put his experience to good use in Harvard debating society meetings, where education was a frequent topic of discussion. In an essay that he presented in 1786, Adams argued "that the progress of every virtue, and of every amiable Quality in a Nation . . . is always in Proportion to the progress of civilization." Since "Civilization is to a State what Education is to an Individual," Adams continued, then the "advantages which are derived from Education" were "a subject on which the welfare of States and Empires . . . depends."[80] In short, education was a foundation of civilized nations.

But what kind of education was best? Like Quesnay, Adams departed from the conventional wisdom that there was a unique relationship between education and republics. At a later meeting of the same society, Adams noted that "the most civilized Nations extant are governed by despotic Monarchs." He knew of what he spoke; Adams had received some education during his time in Europe. From this "it must follow," Adams concluded, "that republics are not so much civilized," and that "the prospect which every citizen in a free Government, has, of obtaining Offices of State" is "rather prejudicial than advantageous to Literature" and civilization.[81] The republican ideal of widespread and practical public education aimed at producing an equal citizenry could be detrimental. Instead, since monarchies were more adept at civilizing their people, it might follow that their education systems had something to recommend them. Adams probably said what he did for the sake of debate. Yet his argument that aristocratic education might cultivate civilization better than republican schooling was not beyond the pale. In building academies, Americans had come close to institutionalizing the educational vision that Adams advocated. Quesnay's work brought Americans closer still.

For their part, academy boards touted their ability to meet the standards of European schooling. One academy ad boasted that "the Regulations are similar to those of the principal Academies in Europe." European lessons helped schools "animate the Students, with an inviolable Love and Attachment to the Services of Almighty God, their native Country, and Fellow-men."[82] Teachers with European credentials were also in high demand. Academy ads bragged about hiring teachers who had "presided with great Reputation and success over an Academy in Europe."[83] Another teacher was lauded as "a gentleman whose character is well attested both from Europe and America, and whose ability and fidelity, as a teacher, are known and approved."[84] When a teacher was "highly esteemed among the learned in different parts of Europe," that helped to "ensure success" of a "seminary."[85] Those who had never taught in European schools emphasized their European education. One teacher "received a liberal and classical education in one of the most celebrated Academies in England." Others highlighted degrees from Edinburgh, the "University of Paris," or the "University of Dublin."[86] This gave them credibility in an insecure republic. They might also give an insecure republic credibility in the world.[87]

American nationalists took an expansive view of what legitimacy on the global stage looked like. Their vision drew together culture, commerce, politics, and state formation. Quesnay's main contribution was to help Americans develop the culture that underpinned the United States' connection with Europe. French and polite education, he claimed, served American independence. That idea gave cover to an education that status-anxious American elites wanted anyway.

Polite Education and Union

A year before Quesnay published his memoir in France, but after the foundation stone for his academy was laid, Nicholas Collin penned "An Essay on the Means of Promoting Federal Sentiments in the United States, by a Foreign Spectator." Collin was a Swedish Lutheran minister, member of the American

Philosophical society, and an ex officio member of the board of the new University of the State of Pennsylvania. Though Collin called himself foreign, he had lived in the mid-Atlantic since 1770. Printed serially in Philadelphia newspapers from August to October of 1787, Collin's essay is something of a curiosity. The first numbers appeared during the waning days of the Constitutional Convention, and the last during the early weeks of the ratification debate. The extended essay was more than just another Federalist volley in the war of words over the proposed Constitution. Collin tackled a range of topics, from the problem of fashion and luxury to the need for a stronger fiscal-military state. The unifying theme was his desire to cultivate "Federal Sentiments" within a "SENTIMENTAL POLITICAL UNION."[88] By this, Collin meant that Americans—the elite, at least—needed to feel connected across the vast expanse of the new nation. The union could not exist without these emotional bonds, and polite education could help forge them.[89]

Writing for an American audience, Collin stressed domestic issues more than Quesnay had. Collin complained especially about what he called the "defective police." The term encompassed a range of infrastructural deficiencies that plagued the young nation.[90] Collin lamented that "frequented roads are often impassable in the winter—public bridges are often for years out of repair, and sometimes till passengers have been in great danger."[91] Even more broadly, the "internal police" connoted government's basic power of regulating society for the public good. Though rooted in early modern Europe, Americans grew obsessed with the idea in the aftermath of the Revolution. It sat behind the vast expansion of the power of the states to regulate individual behavior.[92] But Quesnay believed that empowering the states was insufficient to address the challenges that the United States faced.

Confused jurisdictions and inconsistencies in legal cultures across space exacerbated the problems of defective police. As James Madison did in his "Vices of the Political System of the United States," Collin called this the "multiplicity of laws." States simply passed too many laws, which was bad enough. Then the law also changed as one crossed state lines. The ensuing confusion effectively undermined faith in the rule of law generally.[93] Both the defective internal police and the multiplicity of laws laid bare the difficulty of creating a workable national union in the United States. "What idea must this give a reflecting person of the government," Collin wondered, if the United States lacked "the sense or power to redress the grievance?"[94] Was it a government at all?

Colonization into the western territories would only amplify the problems of the defective police and multiplicity of laws. Without careful planning,

Collin argued, "this part of the union can neither be civilized, governed, nor secured."[95] No doubt, Collin's insecurity stemmed from the common depiction of the West as "savage" and dangerous. From Collin's perspective, then, the United States' biggest potential strength was also its greatest vulnerability. The breadth of the nation embodied its future potential, but it also depended on cooperation between states and regions, which proved difficult. Sentimental union, though, could put the different parts of the union in sync with one another.

For Collin, the lack of legal stability was a cultural problem. "Laws," he wrote, "have a near connexion with manners."[96] He was not alone in arguing that law and order rested on a cultural foundation. Cesare Beccaria, the famous Italian philosopher, also believed that "the sciences, education, good order, security and public tranquility" should be "all comprehended under the name of police" and as an "object of public economy."[97] James Wilson, too, wondered, "What are laws without manners?" Like Collin, he believed good law could not "be formed, but by a proper education."[98] In particular, ornamental education taught manners. Thus, Collin argued that polite education was a solution to problems that hindered American nationhood. Collin acknowledged that his arguments "will appear nonsense to some grave sensible people." He nonetheless maintained that "rational, innocent, ingenious, social amusements are of great consequence to manners and national felicity." For example, a dancing "Assembly room in every township . . . would excellently promote civilization" in very tangible ways.[99] Collin did not explicitly mention or defend Quesnay and his academies. But he made a similar argument about the importance of polite education to the United States.

Though Collin focused on domestic problems, they troubled him because of the United States' precarious geopolitical position. Here Collin agreed with many leading Federalists. In one piece, he quoted a speech Alexander Hamilton gave in the New York state assembly, which warned that "if there are any foreign enemies, or domestic foes to this country; all their arts will be employed to effect a dissolution of the union."[100] Respectable nations did not have to live in fear of sudden attack. Internal vulnerabilities, like the defective police or multiplicity of laws, invited it. If the United States could not create a unified legal system, how could it put up a united front or follow the law of nations?[101]

Like Quesnay, Collin hoped that the United States would create substantial institutions to teach politeness and manners on a grand scale. To that end, the "Foreign Spectator" supported plans for a federal university. More generally, Collin argued that "public education throughout the states, is a great federal concern, as without it no state can be well governed, nor act its part in the confederation with dignity, honor and a federal spirit."[102] But he did not prioritize the sort of elementary education that most proponents of public schooling did. Collin thought the belles lettres deserved "particular attention . . . because they humanize and refine the human heart." Polite literature was "not merely ornamental," he added, "but extremely useful [for] innobling those affections which are the bands of civil society." Collin went so far as to propose "an academy of Belles Letters . . . under the patronage of Federal Power."[103]

Collin thought his proposed academy could help solve most of the problems he identified. "In proportion as elegant learning is cultivated," Collin argued, "it will structure manners, religion, laws, and government," all of what he saw as lacking.[104] The academy's main purpose would be "qualifying men in several respects for all the important offices of government." The belles lettres would teach these men "political eloquence," which they would use to spread federal sentiments.[105] "When after a finished education" alumni "depart to their different stations, and places of residence," he wrote, these men "will be so many capital links of the federal union[,] . . . so many powerful centripetal forces to give it stability."[106] James Wilson likewise believed "a union of hearts and affections . . . is the very life and soul of a confederated republic." Education created an "esprit du corps" that would connect elites across the union.[107] Americans could win the West one minuet at a time. Collin flagrantly ignored the underlying violence that Americans unleashed on Native peoples in the Northwest, which made his theory plausible.

Collin's goal was decidedly not equalitarian. As he put it, "When the public education shall distinguish many by political abilities and a polite taste; and enable great numbers to esteem these qualities; the most eminent character will be chose [sic] for the legislature, civil administration, and military command—consequently the government will not only in reality be so much better, but acquire that love and respect from the people, so necessary for its efficacy."[108] Polite, educated men, to whom ordinary people deferred, were the solution to the defective police and the multiplicity of laws. If that was not enough, Collin reminded his readers that "in foreign negotiations a great deal depends on the address, wit and genius of a minister."[109] American leaders who were trained in the belles lettres could handle European diplomacy. Like Quesnay, Collin argued that polite education was a geopolitical necessity. It would create elites who could both function on the diplomatic stage and counteract democratic disorder at the local level.

"An Assembly Room in Every Township" Realized

Every president before Andrew Jackson advocated in vain for a national university. Quesnay's Richmond Academy was arguably the closest Americans came to founding one during the early republic. Richmond had "warmly patronized his academy," and enough funding materialized to build a stately school building.[110] The French Royal Academy of Painting and Sculpture, the Paris Royal Academy of Sciences, the French Academy, and Louis XVI all pledged to work with Quesnay. Then the French Revolution threw these institutions into disarray and the funding dried up. Quesnay himself took an active role in the conflict, first as a pamphleteer and then as a soldier, finally realizing his unfulfilled martial ambitions. He never returned to the United States. Without Quesnay at the helm, the school failed.[111] Grand plans for national institutions teaching the polite arts proved untenable. All the while, smaller French academies paved the way for the future of polite education in the United States. These schools began opening their doors around the time when Quesnay started teaching in Philadelphia. Thanks to these French academies, ornamental education became ingrained in the mainstream academy curriculum for both men and women during the 1790s.[112] Collin's vision of "An Assembly room in every township" designed to "excellently promote civilization" took root in a decentralized fashion.[113]

The emergence of female academies vastly expanded women's education and, in the process, helped spread ornamental education. To be sure, female academies were rigorous; their curriculum rivaled that of colleges during the early republic. Republican ideology suggested women needed an academic education to raise the men in their life into capable citizens. At the same time, female academies offered polite and ornamental subjects, and these subjects reached more young women than ever before. A 1788 advertisement for a French and painting academy for young women in New York City was fairly typical. Students spent the morning working on academics and the afternoon on needlework and drawing. Some took additional music lessons later on, before ending the day with prayer.[114] In Philadelphia, a women's boarding school opened in 1788 to teach "useful Learning and ornamental Accomplishments." The curriculum included reading, writing, geography, needlework, French, music, and dancing. The proprietor also advertised a drawing school, "Distinct from the above Plan."[115] Female academies combined traditional polite education with their new emphasis on academics.

In urban areas during the 1790s, men and women chose from an ever growing number of entrepreneurial French, dancing, painting, and drawing teachers.

Immigrants, largely from France, ran many of the schools. In 1791, a dancing teacher who claimed to come from the Royal Academy of Paris held three dancing balls in Philadelphia. Weeks later, a "French Painter" advertised that he planned "to teach a few students in any branch of drawing."[116] He was not alone. In 1794, two French architects came to Philadelphia from Paris and offered drawing classes.[117] Another teacher, "from Cape François," fled the Haitian Revolution and opened a French school in Philadelphia in 1793, around the time of a devastating Yellow Fever epidemic. Despite his bad timing, by year's end he competed for students with at least one other new French arrival in the city.[118] Philadelphia drew the most French educators largely because it had a growing French neighborhood, made up of people who had fled the Revolution.[119]

Yet other urban centers fostered markets for polite education. New York welcomed a private academy in which a team of teachers—one from Edinburgh, the other from France—offered ancient and modern languages, including "HEBREW AND ORIENTAL LANGUAGES."[120] For a time, the city was also home to a fencing teacher from the Academy of Paris and a "professor of Eloquence" from Trinity College, Dublin.[121] A pair of brothers, Archibald and Alexander Robertson, educated New Yorkers in the visual arts for over a decade. Archibald arrived first. The limner—a portraitist—promptly opened a school, which he christened the Columbian Academy.[122]

These private teachers often glommed onto the clientele of existing academies, which brought polite education to smaller northern towns. For example, both Lansingburgh and Albany, New York had academies that hosted French schools. Mr. Griffiths, who ran the Albany school, had worked for Quesnay in New York City during the 1780s before heading upriver. In Lansingburgh, Charles Cruzeau sustained himself by offering his services to nearby academies, in addition to running balls out of an assembly room.[123] This was part of a larger refinement of the upper Hudson Valley, which included a boom in French-style buildings. Architects arrived from France, did business in New York City, and then came north to build country homes for elite families.[124]

In the upper South, a similar influx of immigrants opened schools near existing chartered academies. As was often the case, these men claimed impressive credentials. "Rev. Dubourg" came to Baltimore from Paris, where he had run an academy. Baltimore's female academy advertised that their French teacher had been president of a "college" in France.[125] Barring impressive credentials, schools seemed eager to advertise when their French teachers were native Frenchmen.[126] By 1798, Baltimore, Norfolk, and Alexandria—all towns with formal academies—had teachers offering some combination of drawing, dancing, and French. Two separate dancing schools, one of which also offered fencing, competed for business on Maryland's eastern shore.[127]

Boards of chartered academies capitalized on the rage for ornamental education. In their petition for a charter, the trustees of Virginia's Winchester Academy highlighted the "study of polite learning."[128] Many academies made formal arrangements with French teachers and dancing masters.[129] Of the fifteen academies founded in New Jersey by 1795, information is available on the curriculum of twelve. Seven of those offered either French, ornamental instruction, or both. Another two offered foreign languages, though not explicitly French. Most academies in New Jersey offered at least the French language, which kept French teachers employed and left open the possibility of broadening the polite curriculum.[130] Throughout New England, too, French and dancing masters found a ready market as early as 1784.[131]

In most cases, academies offered ornamental subjects as additions to the main curriculum. Though a few schools made French part of the general language course of Latin and Greek, it too usually cost extra. One academy advertised that "the French language will be taught at such hours as will not interfere with those generally appropriate to ordinary studies."[132] Another advertised that their students could study dancing, singing, fencing, or visual arts "at the usual prices, by the most eminent masters," which had been hired by the school.[133] Separating out ornamental subjects added to the cost of academy education. The George-Town Academy in Washington, D.C., charged twenty-six dollars for the academic curriculum, and twenty-eight if the student did not board at the school. Drawing instruction cost an additional nine dollars every three months, and dancing classes, an additional eight.[134] The most expensive part of an academy education remained boarding, which could be four or five times more than tuition.[135] But the added cost for French or ornamental education was hardly insignificant and thus further distinguished certain students from others.

The adoption of ornamental subjects by formal, chartered academies secured the long-term viability of polite education. As a group, ornamental educators did not have the best reputation. Quesnay once compared himself with most other teachers who had been chased out of their home countries for "recklessness or misconduct." These hucksters traveled "from town to town" and left behind "pupils whom they are able to teach nothing more, and to whom often they have taught nothing."[136] Surely too, some foreign teachers claimed contrived titles and inflated their credentials. The market separated some of the wheat from chaff. Certain teachers had long and distinguished careers. James Cox honed his craft while bouncing around Philadelphia, its outskirts, and as far afield as Albany. In 1798, Cox thanked Philadelphians for supporting his ventures for fourteen years.[137] Knowledge of teachers spread through word of mouth. Southerners corresponded about which Philadelphia teachers ran the *"fashionable* Academy" that served "the most wealthy and respectable of the Community."[138] Academy boards provided yet another layer of vetting and brought the polite arts into the mainstream.

French Academies and Party Politics in the 1790s

As the French Revolution reshaped American party politics during the 1790s, it also affected polite education. In New Jersey, the ornamental curriculum first caught on in strongly Federalist towns. The Trenton, Elizabeth Town, and Princeton Academies offered the most robust polite education in New Jersey. All these towns and schools were connected to a strand of Presbyterian Federalism that emanated from the College of New Jersey.[139] This Federalist bent makes sense, considering the nationalist vision that undergirded defenses of the polite arts.

Jeffersonian Francophilia changed the political dynamics of polite education. Though it was another staunch Presbyterian town and the former home of the College of New Jersey, Newark was a major Republican enclave in Essex County. From an early date, its school had a French teacher.[140] The trustees proudly hosted several native Frenchmen at their 1797 student exhibition. Their guests claimed that the Newark Academy taught French "on easier, more familiar and more useful principles, than in any seminary they had ever seen in this country."[141] The Union Hall Academy—located in Jamaica, New York, in Queens County—was another school in a staunchly Republican town that vested French education with a political purpose. There, French proved more popular than Latin, despite costing more. Students learned French alongside French immigrants, as they did in Bordentown, New Jersey.[142] Another academy in Philadelphia served as the meeting site for a society that assisted recent immigrants to the United States.[143]

Generally speaking, Federalists were more comfortable with the polite culture of ornamental education. Nonetheless, they feared that French immigrants would bring Jacobinism to the United States. This created an odd dynamic. Federalists tended to support polite education but to crack down on the French immigrants who most frequently taught it. The Republicans supported French immigration to the United States, and Republican educators found French language instruction to be politically useful.[144] Prior to this point, though, they shied away from other ornamental subjects that Frenchmen often taught. They thus supported the immigrants themselves even though they were uncomfortable with one of the chief ways in which they made a living. Ultimately, these peculiar partisan dynamics ensured that French and ornamental education remained widely available. Moreover, Jeffersonians began to moderate their views in the 1790s as Federalists grew increasingly reactionary, and academies became a more bipartisan institution (see chapter 6).

Through it all, polite educators continued to argue that they strengthened the image the United States projected to Europe. The notion that French and "the European languages" were "useful to those in the mercantile line, and ornamental to the private gentleman" remained.[145] Teachers bragged that they instructed their "pupils in the graces and manners necessary to be observed in all genteel societies."[146] They also continued to tout their European connections. A duo in Baltimore advertised that they would teach dances that they "had the honor of introducing in London and many fashionable circles of Europe."[147] Artists, too, continued to paint and teach miniatures "in the present London style."[148] Most starkly, elite Americans' veneration of Major John André reemerged through ornamental education. "A MONODY on the unfortunate MAJOR ANDRE," was made available to "Country merchants, Academy's, and Public Library's . . . on the most reasonable terms" by an art teacher in 1792.[149] European touchstones drove the rage for politeness through the 1790s.

Writing in 1797, a French drawing teacher at an academy in Bordentown, New Jersey, came closest to reviving Collin and Quesnay's line of argument. Amable-Louis-Rose De Lafitte Du Courteil disparaged parents who "refuse to their children the exercise of horse, dance, fencing, drawing, music, &c. all of which are agreeable and often useful arts." Americans should learn from old regime France, where "academies or societies of men of letters patented by the king" benefited the nation. Courteil thus challenged Americans to "naturalize the arts and sciences in your own country," and bring "glory to a polished nation." Courteil favored a national institution, but he did his part by teaching polite arts at a local academy.[150]

The fact that American academies offered the polite arts kept American education from devolving into a full-blown dependence on Europe. While the American elite admired European education, they balked at sending their children overseas for it. First, it was expensive to send a child even as far as England. Secondly, they feared that aristocratic culture might overawe the students' republican values. When traveling abroad, colonists and later Americans often socialized with each other as they tried to make sense of what they confronted. Far from their parents at an impressionable age, there was no telling what habits young Americans might learn. Americans saw a big difference between receiving a European-style education and studying abroad. At least it was a useful distinction for elites who sought out polite education.[151]

In similar ways, fears of economic dependence deepened Americans' commitment to domestic polite education. Every American who went to Europe for an education took capital out of the United States at a time when the economy was struggling.[152] In the "Foreign Spectator," Collin made an analogous point about European fashion. He estimated that Americans spent nearly £900,000 a year on imported goods. This money left the borders of the United States, likely never to return. Collin claimed that he was "not an enemy to elegancies." Yet he still opposed Americans' predilection for buying European luxuries because, he explained, "I would sometimes rather live on potatoes, than owe money for meat." It was more than the drain of specie or the creation of simple fiscal indebtedness to Europe that frustrated him. Rather, this tendency to send money to Europe for fashion "mark[ed] a want of an independent spirit, which is the characteristic of a free people." It was especially problematic in a republic. Collin's advocacy of strong, domestic schools, based on European educational culture, followed a similar logic.[153]

BY THE MID-1790S, some Americans concluded that by emulating European education, they had strengthened the republic. The trustees of a female academy in Philadelphia claimed that "Ambitious to profit from all European patterns, America still is rising to an elevation above them." In particular, the "very rapid improvement" of students was "synonimous [sic] with equal advances which our country is experiencing in her public prospects." Educational progress and national strength went together, and not just in the abstract. The "synonimous" relationship between the two helped explain why "our roads improved, our communications, inland opened, our code of laws softened and ameliorated, our charitable and useful establishments augmented, and the general welfare of America promoted."[154] Polite educators argued that they could help the United States become a powerful nation-state. Perhaps they had succeeded.

By the early nineteenth century, the United States had survived twenty-plus years of independence, a change in constitution, the geopolitical knot of the French Revolution, and a peaceful transition of power between political parties. Yet Americans continued to measure themselves against Europe.[155] Many academy trustees' deference to Europe does not mean they were insincere in linking their schools to the nation-building project. The reality was that traditional curriculum and culture might do more to legitimize American education than newfangled forms of schooling. That postcolonial anxieties manifested so starkly in education is perhaps the best evidence of academies' centrality to American state formation.

At some point, the logic became inescapable: Though adopted to legitimize the United States in the world, ornamental education had come to shape American political culture. The polite arts provided another way for elites to separate themselves from the body of the people. Political and social hierarchies in the new republic rested on cultural authority that was cultivated in academies and looked deliberately European. In the name of independence, polite education thrived. But it left standing some retrograde behaviors, distinctions, and values that the Revolution had supposedly destroyed, just as academy supporters had intended.

Part III

From Aristocratic Education to Reform, 1787–1830

CHAPTER SIX

Creating Consensus
The Politics of State Support for Academies

The Federalist Party in Morristown, New Jersey and the board of the Morristown Academy were one and the same. When the academy was founded in winter 1791–1792, New Jersey's entire congressional delegation supported the Federalist administration. Yet by the next congressional elections in 1794, the Republicans began to make headway and the Federalists' fortunes took a turn for the worse.[1] By 1800, Morristown was a Republican stronghold, voting ten-to-one against Federalist candidates for U.S. representative.[2] Undeterred, academy boosters still wore their Federalism proudly. That year, the lone Federalist candidate for state assembly from Morris County was William Campfield, an academy trustee whose father was its founding president. The Republican candidates trounced him, garnering about three times as many votes county-wide and four times as many in Morristown. Campfield did not take the hint. He ran again for assembly in 1803 and scrounged up only eleven votes from his townsmen, who sided almost forty-to-one against him. At least two votes likely came from other academy leaders who were also on the Federalist ticket. John Doughty, who would become the academy's president in 1805, received four votes. Daniel Phoenix Jr.—a founding member of the board and its treasurer—garnered a comparatively respectable eighty-one votes.[3]

Despite the waning Federalist presence in Morristown, the academy continued to thrive. It educated many New Jersey children, some of them Jeffersonians like Daniel Mulford. Mulford was born in 1781, came of age during the 1790s, and could not decide what to do with his life, so he enrolled at the Morristown Academy. There, the twenty-one-year old did not hide his Republican politics. During the academy's winter session in 1802, he went to see John Leland preach. The Massachusetts Baptist minister stopped in Morristown "on his return from Washington, where he had been to deliver Mr. Jefferson the mammouth cheese." A month later, Mulford "spoke the first part of Mr. Brackenridge's [sic] speech for the abolishing of the additional Judges of the Federal Courts."[4] John Leland and his congregation in the uniformly Republican town of Cheshire, Massachusetts, made the half-ton cheese to celebrate Jefferson's election as president.[5] It was a quintessential example of the new forms of democratic participation that the Republicans encouraged.[6]

Kentucky Senator John Breckenridge's speech critiqued the Judiciary Act of 1801. The so-called Midnight Judges Act had created new federal court positions that lame-duck president John Adams packed with Federalists.[7]

While Daniel Mulford bucked the trustees' politics, he subscribed to the cultural ideals that they inculcated. During his time in Morristown, Mulford took part in nationalistic parades with his fellow students; he diligently noted in his diary when he "took the first premium of Fifty for Latin Grammar," and when he "lost the Head of the Grammar Class"; and he "composed a constitution for the Morris Academical Society," a mutual improvement group.[8] His ambitions and self-worth conformed to ideals concocted by Federalist academy trustees and depended on credentials from Federalist institutions.

The Morristown Academy's story is emblematic of how many Jeffersonians came to embrace academies despite their Federalist origins. Trustees spent the 1780s lobbying state governments to support the academies, in the hopes this would prove that they served the public good. They were successful until the increasingly vitriolic partisan politics of the early 1790s engulfed academies and put them on the defensive. Yet later in the 1790s, academies seemed more secure than ever before. As the most reactionary elements in the Federalist Party responded to the French Revolution with utter paranoia, they shifted the entire political system and drove away more moderate men. The Jeffersonians absorbed some of these less hard-line Federalist defectors into their ever-more capacious coalition. In the process, they took over the moderate center of American political life. A large swath of Jeffersonians accepted the Federalist sociology of the relationship between ruler and ruled, which the academies epitomized. Most academies, then, had not changed. Nor had support for them expanded to new constituencies. Those individuals were now simply spread across party lines. This moderate fusion diluted the critique of the academies as aristocratic, which had seemed ascendant in the mid-1790s. As support for academies became a bipartisan point of consensus and state backing continued to bolster their reputation, they looked more like the nation-building institutions their founders had always claimed they were.

State Support of Academies

Early American state governments possessed extensive powers to make laws and regulate society, all under the banner of police powers. By the advent of the U.S. Constitution, charters of incorporation had become a popular way for state governments to enact their will. Most charters went, not to business

TABLE 6.1 Date of academy opening versus incorporation, through 1800

State	No. of Academies Incorporated in Year of Opening or Earlier	No. of Academies Incorporated after Opening	Percentage of Academies Incorporated in Year of Opening or Earlier
New Hampshire	4	4	50
Connecticut	1	3	25
Massachusetts	15	5	75
New York	11	15	42

Note: This table skews to the North because newspapers were more widespread there, which made it easier to know when academies opened. For further explanation of my methods for tracking academies, see the Appendix.

corporations, but rather to groups that would fulfill some communal need. Corporations, it was thought, existed to serve the public good. That phrase—"the public good"—was frequently bandied about, though its meaning was subjective. Through their power to grant or deny charters, state governments decided what did or did not aid the public good. Legislatures then used their chartering power to regulate voluntary organizations and ensure they promoted public purposes, not the private interests of their founders. Charters of incorporation did this by defining institutions' legal rights and setting limits on how much property they could amass.[9]

It was through incorporation that states most directly influenced education in the early republic. States that had colonial religious establishments led the way in chartering academies. The Congregational establishment survived in New Hampshire, Connecticut, and Massachusetts well into the nineteenth century. Traditionally, the only corporate bodies in New England were the town and the Congregational Church. There, academies epitomized a new public culture that threatened to shatter ancient traditions and the town-based establishment. The New England states wanted to ensure that other institutions could not accumulate enough power to threaten the establishment. Incorporation became their tool. Academy leaders in Massachusetts sought charters of incorporation from the very beginning, and most schools did not open until they received one. Academies in the other New England states with established religions also received charters, though in Connecticut the charters often came well after the schools were founded. Charters endorsed nonestablished institutions as stewards of the public good and stymied criticisms of them as threats to a unified body politic (table 6.1).[10]

TABLE 6.2 Percent of academies founded by 1800 receiving charters by 1800, by region

Region	Academies Founded before 1800	Percentage of Pre-1800 Academies with Pre-1800 charter
New England	35	94%
Mid-Atlantic (ex. N.J.)	60	45%
South	60	87%
Total	155	72%

Note: New England: New Hampshire, Massachusetts (including Maine), Vermont, Rhode Island, and Connecticut. Mid-Atlantic: New York, Pennsylvania, Delaware, and Maryland. I left out New Jersey because I could not determine how many academies the state chartered. South: Virginia, North Carolina, South Carolina, and Georgia.

Places that overthrew an established church saw a similar pattern. The former Anglican strongholds of Virginia, North Carolina, South Carolina, and Georgia all rushed to disestablish the state church. So too did Maryland, which, during the colonial period, coupled an Anglican establishment with a legal commitment to the toleration of Trinitarians and Catholics. Southern states also began incorporating academies immediately (table 6.2).[11]

This actually flew in the face of the South's general apprehensions about incorporation. The Southern states effectively repudiated the Elizabethan law of charitable uses, which had long allowed religious and charitable organizations to exercise corporate-like powers without a charter. Though most of the Southern states joined the rest of the Union and allowed local churches to incorporate, Virginia balked at even this. Like in New England, the South's experience with religious establishment framed their incorporation practices. Yet the purpose of charters was different than in New England, where incorporation protected the establishment. Southern states used charters to restrict churches' rights in order to aid in disestablishment. More generally, they used charters as an egalitarian cudgel to regulate institutions through which elites might concentrate power. Ironically, restricting incorporation meant that in the South, charter rights went only to associations like the Masons and educational institutions like academies that mostly served the elite.[12]

Only the mid-Atlantic states moved slowly to charter academies. At the behest of academy founders, those states eventually devised the most innovative policies. While charters placed some restrictions on academies, they also lent credence to claims that the schools served the public good. This was something that academy founders desperately wanted to prove, so they eagerly sought out charters. The trustees probably hoped that when public funding for education materialized, incorporated schools would have the best claim to it. Pressure from academy boosters led to a novel academy system in New York. The Empire State overthrew a weak legal establishment and then institutionalized the pluralism that had always characterized the mid-Atlantic. In 1784, the state legislature created the board of regents to oversee the transformation of King's College into Columbia College. The law explicitly divested education of denominational control.[13] Three years later, in 1787, Alexander Hamilton and other Federalists proposed revisions to the way the state governed Columbia. But at the urging of Federalist state senator Ezra L'Hommedieu, who would serve a long term on the board, the state also expanded the regents' power to include chartering and overseeing academies.[14]

Academy supporters had successfully forced the issue. By 1787, New Yorkers had formed, or put in motion plans to form, seven academies spread across six of the state's thirteen counties. Notably, in 1786, an academy in L'Hommedieu's home county of Suffolk applied to the legislature for a charter. That same year, another Federalist-run academy in Kings County received permission—in a copyright law—to accept a land grant from the Dutch Reformed Church.[15] These gambits had the desired effect. The 1787 regents statute explained that "academies have been erected and instituted in different parts of this State, by the free and liberal benefactions of corporations."[16] Private initiative created the need for state intervention.

Despite its Federalist origins, the 1787 Regents bill generated bipartisan support. L'Hommedieu introduced the bill, which passed the state senate by voice vote and the assembly after a bit of rancor.[17] Republican Governor George Clinton signed it into law. Bipartisan action gave regents academies the state's imprimatur that they served the public good. Yet the board of regents was a Federalist institution. Of the thirty-one men appointed to the board before 1800, thirteen were either ministers or ex officio members. Fourteen of the eighteen remaining members had either supported the ratification of the Constitution, held office as Federalists, or both.[18]

In New Jersey, too, Federalist-driven developments in civil society led to bipartisan laws that benefited academies. During the first two decades of independence, New Jersey founded more academies per capita than any other state. Yet through 1794, it incorporated only one, in Trenton. Then, later that year, the state passed an "Act to Incorporate Societies for the Promotion of Learning." This made it easy for all schools, "which now are or hereafter may be," to incorporate. The law mostly regulated the composition of boards of trustees and granted them the power to sue and be sued. The bill passed the assembly unanimously.[19]

This pattern—of Federalist support for individual academies coupled with bipartisan support for incorporation—was starkest in New England. The rage for academies in Massachusetts cooled noticeably after the first few opened in the early 1780s. Between 1785 and 1790, the legislature chartered none. Then the floodgates reopened. In 1791 and 1792, the General Court chartered four academies in Maine.[20] During spring and summer 1792, two academies in Massachusetts proper received charters, as did three more in 1793. Of these, only one—in Marblehead—bucked the trend and drew the bulk of support from non-Federalists. It also deemphasized the classical curriculum.[21]

Elsewhere in Massachusetts, the familiar pattern repeated and avowed Federalists built academies.[22] Men who stood against Shays's Rebellion in 1786 and became Federalists led the group who built the Westfield Academy in Hampshire County.[23] The two academies founded in Middlesex County in 1792–1793 have a similar history. At least two trustees of the Westford Academy went on to serve as Federalists in the state senate.[24] In Groton, the board was dominated by Federalists, one of whom would later attend the Hartford Convention.[25] The founders of the Taunton Academy included three of the minority of Bristol County delegates to vote for the Constitution at the 1788 state ratification convention.[26] No members of the board ran for office against the Federalists until the 1810s.[27]

Academy founders, then, were disproportionately Federalists, even in Massachusetts where the party was strong. Despite the perception that they dominated the Bay State, Massachusetts Federalists always felt under siege. A strong opposition movement flowed from the Regulation, through the state's strong Anti-Federalist showing in 1787–1788, and into the early 1790s.[28] The French Revolution amplified the Federalists' fears of this opposition. They worried that radical republican ideas would cross the Atlantic and bring violent disorder to America. The fate of the fragile nation, which the Federalists saw as their creation, hung in the balance.[29] They suddenly pushed to charter more academies in 1792 and 1793, just as the French Revolution began to infect American politics.[30]

The most embattled Federalists pushed hardest to found academies. Often, academies opened in towns that the Federalists did not control. Of the four Federalist-backed academies chartered in 1792 and 1793, three opened in towns—Taunton, Westford, and Groton—whose delegates to the ratification convention in 1788 voted against the new Constitution. Massachusetts did not grant another charter for an academy until 1795, when Federalists in northeastern Worcester County opened one in New Salem, another town to vote against ratification in 1788.[31]

TABLE 6.3 Party competition in Massachusetts towns with an academy before 1800, using gubernatorial election results

Year of Gubernatorial Election	Academy Towns with Federalist ≥80% of the Vote	Academy Towns with Jeffersonian ≥80% of the Vote	Academy Towns Where Jeffersonians Overperformed
1788	6/15	0/15	9/15
1796	2/15	6/15	9/15
1797	1/14	3/14	9/14
1800	2/15	2/15	11/15

Note: Based on Massachusetts gubernatorial election returns, *A New Nation Votes*.

These political alignments extended to state politics. Federalists opened academies in towns with a strong Republican presence. In 1788, John Hancock routed the Anti-Federalist candidate for governor, Elbridge Gerry. But Gerry performed better in towns that had an academy before 1800 than he did statewide. In the few other relatively competitive contests for governor before 1800, Republicans overperformed in academy towns. When Federalists took the governorship in the late 1790s, it was while losing academy towns. In 1800—the closest contest of the period—Federalists won 58 percent of the towns in Massachusetts. However, they won only four of fifteen (around 27 percent) of academy towns. Deerfield and Hingham were the only academy towns where Federalists consistently won by large margins through 1800. It made sense to open academies in conflicted towns, given that the founders hoped to shape cultural values. The unconverted might ignore academies a few towns over; they had to engage with those in their own communities (table 6.3).

In New Hampshire, too, Federalists invested in academies to shore up their influence. But here they built them in Federalist strongholds. The first gubernatorial election with extant town-level returns was in 1800. Seven of the eight New Hampshire towns with academies by that point voted for the Federalist candidate, John T. Gilman. Yet statewide, he won only 60 percent of towns. And while Gilman received 63 percent of all votes, in academy towns he garnered an impressive 78 percent.[32]

Despite the clear Federalist edge of most New England academies, they retained a veneer of nonpartisanship through the mid-1790s. Academies successfully petitioned for charters regardless of which faction controlled the state governments. In Massachusetts, John Hancock—a popular and ideologically slippery governor, who did not identify as a Federalist—signed fifteen of the state's twenty academy charters before 1800. Jeffersonian governor Josiah Bartlett signed more than half of the academy charters issued by the Granite State before 1800.[33] This bipartisan legal support affirmed the pledges of academy founders that the schools were public institutions, not partisan outposts.

By contrast, academies in the South never experienced a bipartisan moment before 1800. A general fear of active government intertwined with the logic of slave societies to drive opposition to academies. Southern reformers periodically called for common schools to teach poor whites how to exercise citizenship. Yet opposition was fierce. Others feared that schools threatened the South's racial hierarchy. To say that education could make someone a capable citizen conceded that some Northern antislavery activists were right: When nurtured properly, people of African descent might become citizens too. If they were honest, all white Americans admitted that enslaved people could learn. Dating back to the Stono Rebellion of 1739, whites curtailed black access to literacy because they connected it with resistance. Ultimately, the argument that schools were necessary to elevate whites undermined the racist and aristocratic fictions that sustained slave societies. It seemed better just to uphold the assumption that people were born into their proper station and white people were capable citizens because of a natural and immutable racial hierarchy. In such an environment, the purpose of education was unclear. But large slaveholders still wanted academies for their children's education. Subsidizing it on the public's dime, though, was obviously a regressive redistribution of resources to the wealthy. Slavery, then, threw into relief the academies' elitism.[34]

For a time, the Southern fight over academies broke along party lines. North Carolinians and Virginians annually chose their state representatives, who then appointed a governor. The governor's party identification makes a good proxy for the state's partisan composition. In both states, Federalists chartered a disproportionate number of academies relative to their time in power (table 6.4).[35] Evidence for the rest of the South is more impressionistic. Georgia voted overwhelmingly Republican. Augusta, Richmond County, and Savannah, Chatham County, were the only places with a Federalist Party organization or newspaper. Yet six of the seven academies founded in Georgia before 1800 opened in these or neighboring coastal counties.[36] South Carolina founded the fewest academies per capita of any state before 1800. Federalist governors signed the laws creating all of those schools, as well as the College of Charleston.[37]

TABLE 6.4 Partisanship and academy chartering in Virginia and North Carolina, to 1800

State	Years Governorship Held by Party (Percentage of Total Years)		Academies Chartered by Party (Percentage of Total Academy Incorporations)	
	Federalist	Anti-Federalist/ Jeffersonian	Federalist	Anti-Federalist/ Jeffersonian
NC	9 (50%)	9 (50%)	16 (76%)	5 (24%)
VA	6 (75%)	2 (25%)	10 (91%)	1 (9%)
Total	15 (58%)	11 (42%)	26 (81%)	6 (19%)

Note: I could clearly discern the governor's partisanship in North Carolina between 1782 and 1800, and in Virginia between 1792 and 1800. To identify incorporated academies in Virginia, I used Hening, *The Statutes at Large*. My number of academies matches the number given in Heatwole, *History of Education in Virginia*, 127. Most historians say North Carolina chartered upward of thirty academies before 1800. See Tolley, "A Chartered School in a Free Market," 62. Tolley follows the numbers in Curtis, "Bingham School and Classical Education," 328; and Connor, *North Carolina*, 439. I could not corroborate that higher number in the session laws. I use only those academies with an incorporation date that I confirmed.

Many states also subsidized academy budgets. As with incorporation, states reserved funding for institutions with a public purpose. At first, states funded the schools indirectly, largely by authorizing lotteries. American experiments with lotteries date back to the colonial period and have generally been used to fund churches and transportation projects. Into the early republic, lotteries remained a somewhat subversive technology. Timeless criticisms of gambling often reared their head in opposition to them. Some lotteries also operated without public sanction. People wondered whether so-called managers would ever draw the lottery or just abscond with the proceeds of ticket sales. State-authorized drawings, though, suggested that the object of a lottery would serve the public good.[38] The Chesapeake states authorized the first academy lotteries. Virginia granted permission to the Hampden-Sydney Academy to run one during the American Revolution.[39] Maryland authorized a few lotteries during the 1780s, including one for the substantial sum of £1400.[40] North Carolina acted more slowly, but it began authorizing lotteries during the 1790s.[41] In the North, Massachusetts experimented with academy lotteries as early as 1785.[42] Though indirect, lotteries had the advantage of making support for academies volitional. One did not have to play a lottery at all, let alone one that supported an academy. Doing so lent support to the academies.

New Jersey made extensive use of lotteries during the early 1790s. The first few in the state indemnified towns or associations for damages from the Revolutionary War. In 1791, the assembly authorized a lottery in Elizabeth Town to raise money to rebuild both the local courthouse and the academy: Francis Barber's academy. These buildings had been "occupied for the use of the United States, and burnt by the enemy" during the war.[43] The assembly passed the bill and the council concurred unanimously.[44] After they failed to convince the U.S. Congress to help them, the trustees of the Newark Academy used a similar argument to win the state's permission to hold a lottery. The funds would "enable them to complete the Academy, which was destroyed during the late War by Fire, while it was appropriated by the late American Army as a Guard-House." The bill passed the assembly by twenty-nine to six.[45] Other academies rode this wave of patriotic goodwill. In 1794, the legislature passed a single bill granting seven academies the right to hold lotteries.[46] It convincingly passed the assembly by twenty-two to fourteen and the council by eight to four.[47] This decision predated, and perhaps precipitated, the state's 1794 general incorporation statute for institutions of learning. In both cases, across party lines, New Jerseyans agreed that academies served the common good and supported them.

Of any state, New York offered the most direct support to academies. In 1790, the legislature gave the regents control over state lands at Fort George, Ticonderoga, Crown Point, and Governor's Island, in New York harbor. Massachusetts also used land grants to support academies, but it gave the lands to individual academy boards.[48] In New York, the regents created a committee to manage their real estate profile. The committee held auctions to lease their land and invested money in foreign credit markets to fill the regents' coffers.[49] Two years later, in 1792, the legislature gave the regents £1,500 per year, for five years, to distribute among the state's academies.[50] Senators from the Federalist-dominated southern district, around New York City, voted unanimously for the bill. The Clintonian Republican–controlled middle and eastern districts—encompassing the middle and upper Hudson Valley—were more divided. Nevertheless, Republican governor George Clinton signed the bill into law.[51]

Nearly every state in the union, then, frequently granted charters of incorporation and other support to academies. The Southern Federalists needed to control state legislatures to get academies chartered. But in New England and the mid-Atlantic, non-Federalists accommodated the academies. Bipartisan legal and financial support confirmed founders' claims that academies served the public good, not partisan ends. This was no small feat. Like the Constitution, academies had transformed from a pet project of the Federalists into a widely accepted part of public life.[52] Unlike the Constitution, by the mid-1790s, academies became yet another contentious issue in an increasingly divisive partisan environment.

Challenges to Bipartisan Support for Academies

The states became increasingly involved in education during the first five years under the new Constitution. Everywhere, Federalists dictated education policy, which meant that state support went mostly to academies. It also meant that state intervention in schooling did little to expand educational opportunity. Most academies remained expensive and exclusive, and they were geared toward an existing elite. As privately run schools, they were impervious to democratic reform. This all became increasingly obvious by the mid-1790s and a reaction against academies emerged, albeit with sectional variations. If, in the South, Jeffersonians opposed state-funded education outright, in the North, the fight turned on the equitable distribution of state support for schools.

As the most developed school bureaucracy, the New York State Board of Regents best shows the depths of Federalist influence on the academy system. Of the eight academies founded in the state before 1787, six eventually received charters. Yet only two did so immediately after the regents began chartering schools: Erasmus Hall Academy in Flatbush, Brooklyn, and Clinton Academy in Suffolk County. Both schools had important connections with leading Federalists who had been involved in creating the board of regents. Erasmus Hall's uniformly Federalist founding board of trustees included John Livingston and Matthew Clarkson. The former served in the state senate when it gave the regents power over New York's academies, while the latter was a regent from 1784 through 1825.[53] Though not uniform in its politics, Clinton Academy's board of trustees included two of Suffolk County's five losing Federalist candidates for the state ratification convention in 1788. The board relied on Ezra L'Hommedieu—another of Suffolk's failed Federalist candidates—to shepherd through the academy's application for a charter.[54] Men like L'Hommedieu and Clarkson had an interest in making the regents work for academies that they already supported. By contrast, there was the Kingston Academy, whose president was the Anti-Federalist John Addison. Though it predated both Erasmus Hall and Clinton, Kingston Academy did not receive a charter until 1795. By that point, Addison had become a Federalist.[55]

The board of regents was not in the business of creating new schools. It existed to control the pace of educational expansion. The 1787 law required academy boards to meet stringent property requirements to receive a charter, which the regents doggedly upheld.[56] They only grew stricter after 1792, when the board gained funds to dole out. At that point, the regents decided they would not so much as help with the greatest capital expense in founding an academy: the building itself. They worried that underfunded groups would apply for incorporation or support and then fail to complete a school, leading to "much embarrassment."[57]

In practice, no academy in New York could receive state support without men first volunteering to build one. Yet men did not associate with equal effectiveness. Melancton Smith, a leading Anti-Federalist, probably put it best during the ratification controversy. While the "great easily form associations," he noted, "the poor and middling class form them with difficulty." Another Massachusetts writer complained that the "only means by which the Few carry their plans into execution is by their associations." Smith worried that "the great" leaned toward the Federalists. He generally opposed charters of incorporation, including for banks and turnpikes, because he thought they bred aristocracy. With the regents law, New York had endorsed freedom of association but accepted an obvious inequality of association.[58]

The regents, then, birthed a tiered educational system in New York, and a regressive one at that. State support flowed exclusively to regents academies that already had strong backing. Academies that did not meet the standards for a charter and needed help could not receive any. Meanwhile, the state ignored the common district schools. Moreover, the regents did little to check the power of groups that successfully acquired a charter. The state placed less restrictive limits on regents academies' property ownership than it put on churches.[59] This situation was not unique to New York. In New Jersey, some academies carved out a curriculum that appealed to middling tastes. Most state support, though, still went to academies with a classical curriculum.[60] Republicanism cast education as a means to break down existing hierarchies. The regents—and state support of academies generally—ensured that the diffusion of education depended on the elite's beneficence and stewardship of schools, just as it had before 1787.[61]

The fact that state legal and financial support went primarily to elite schools generated a backlash by the mid-1790s. Critics of academies in the North tended to question both the public worth of academies and the public spiritedness of their leaders. Lotteries became an early target. In 1793, after the New Jersey state legislature granted Newark Academy the power to hold a lottery, the "managers" issued the "scheme" for its implementation.[62] This was how most lotteries worked. The institution that stood to benefit appointed men to decide on how many tickets to sell, at what cost, and with what odds of winning. These managers also sold the tickets and drew the lottery. The scheme told an "adventurer"—one who played the lottery—how much of the gross income went to prizes and how much went to offset costs. Upon seeing the Newark Academy lottery scheme, "A Friend to the People" denounced it because he calculated that the trustees would take in around £400 more than the law authorized. His math was wrong, though, and the Newark trustees quickly dispensed with "A Friend's" accusation.[63]

Nevertheless, "A Friend" cast doubt on the trustees' claim that they served the common good. In a second essay, "A Friend" used the lottery, in and of itself, as evidence that the trustees did not have pure motives. Lotteries appealed to the most vulnerable members of the community, while academies benefited the most affluent. In buying a ticket, one vied to win "the property of the poor, the widow and orphan, which infatuated, have thrown in their little stock." Beyond bilking the poor, lotteries nurtured "in the adventurer a covetous disposition." Even if the proceeds aided the public good, lotteries themselves did the opposite. They eroded social bonds and absolved citizens from having to act for the public weal. Buying a ticket might "assist in promoting some useful purpose." The question remained: "is public utility our object in purchasing and holding tickets"? Or was it the potential winnings? "A Friend" thought it was the latter. "Experience proves," he wrote, "that public utility is not our principle of action, and that we are prompted by a selfish motive."[64] If academies were a common good, surely the state could support them without subverting communal spirit or preying on the downtrodden.

Others cut to the heart of the matter and questioned whether academies could ever benefit the public good since they served an exclusive clientele. This line of argument proved effective in New England, where it had first surfaced in a series of essays published in the *Boston Magazine* in 1784. According to one essay, "a general diffusion of knowledge is better adapted to our situation than general ignorance, with only a few individuals who shine with very sublime splendour [*sic*], and have really all the learning in the state." Educational inequality made no sense in a republic since "every one hath to act a part."[65] Academies flouted these republican assumptions and ensured that the wealthy "monopolized all the knowledge." This allowed them also to "acquire the reins of government." Instead of providing equal knowledge for an equal citizenry, an academy-dominated system meant that "the offices of government . . . will be filled up from those whose parents have taken care to qualify them." Academies thus all but guaranteed that "the government will be subverted from a republic to an aristocracy." The essay was reprinted in

1786. Its criticism, that the rise of "PRIVATE ACADEMIES" ensured that "the importance of publick schools will be diminished," appeared again in 1787.[66]

The fear that academies undermined both town schools that served all children and republicanism persisted into the 1790s. The Salem Unitarian minister William Bentley noted in his diary a widespread belief that "academies are too numerous, that their model is not purely republican." A friend wrote to Bentley that academies' rise meant "Town Schools would be neglected." As a strong believer in diffusing information broadly, Bentley was sensitive to these critiques.[67] Vermont saw perhaps the clearest conflict between academies and town schools. One set of trustees argued that their service on an academy board should exempt them from public school taxes. Representatives of the district school countered that removing these "men of interest and ability" from the tax base "destroys the benefit of district-schools." The legislature ordered the academy trustees to pay their school taxes.[68]

By the mid-1790s, the critique that academies siphoned resources away from accessible town schools took on a partisan flavor in Massachusetts. Samuel Adams took over as governor in fall 1793, when John Hancock died. Neither man identified as a Federalist, yet they still disagreed on much, including academies. Hancock signed nine academy charters during his last fifteen months in office. By contrast, only three academies received charters in the four years during which Adams sat in the governor's chair. Perhaps the market was saturated. But Adams also had his reasons. In his 1795 address to the Massachusetts General Court, Adams acknowledged that only "the more wealthy, generally speaking, can avail themselves of the benefits of the Academies." Worse, Adams feared "that multiplying [academies] may have a tendency to injure the antient and beneficial mode of Education in Town Grammar Schools," in which "the poor and rich may derive equal benefit." The ultimate problem was that academies "detach the attention and influence of the wealthy, from the generous support of town schools."[69] That is what almost happened in Vermont, and what the 1784 *Boston Magazine* essays had predicted. The state senate acknowledged Adams's point and vowed to regulate the academies in order to "protect the whole."[70]

Academies looked particularly reactionary in New England because there they endangered the most robust public school system in the world. Some New England states resisted the pull of academies. Connecticut chartered only two academies before 1800, both before 1785. Instead, at the urging of Republicans, they used the proceeds from sales of its Western Reserve lands in Ohio to endow a common school fund.[71] Vermont also chartered only two academies before 1800. The state instead mandated a system of district common schools and public, county grammar schools. These schools were funded initially through local taxes, but the state also began providing direct aid by the late 1790s. Connecticut and Vermont had opposite political cultures. The former, a "Land of Steady Habits," operated under its colonial charter until 1818, much to the delight of its Federalist majority. The latter used the revolutionary crisis to declare its own independence and adopt one of the most democratic state constitutions. New England's longstanding commitment to public education (save for Rhode Island, which lent no support to schools at all) united them. Both New Hampshire and Massachusetts also reaffirmed laws requiring town schools.[72] Yet at the moment when the utility of public education was most evident, these states also opened academies that many believed could undermine the town schools.[73]

As the critique that academies hurt public schools gained steam, the expansion of the academies slowed. New Hampshire chartered no academies between 1794 and 1805—even with Federalist John T. Gilman serving as governor. Distrust of academies still ran hot in 1801. That year, William Bentley described how in Exeter, New Hampshire, the "Town School House stands on the side of" Phillips Exeter Academy. The layout "seems to preach, while the Academy towers over it, the doctrine so much believed that Academies destroy Town Schools."[74] Massachusetts took a different tack. Two years after Adams's 1795 address, the state limited the spread of academies and gave the state more power over them. The legislature restricted land grants to schools that could serve at least 30,000 people and already had "permanent funds."[75]

Though the dynamics were different from those in New England, the backlash against academies trended across the North around 1795. That year, the Pennsylvania legislature considered a bill to make a "permanent provision for the education of youth." The bill would have both created county boards to oversee schools and provided limited funds to cover parts of teachers' salaries. Writing under a populist pseudonym, "A Citizen" argued that this bill could not realize its stated goal of creating permanent schools. The bill merely declared that "the people themselves may, if they please, erect and support academies!" This made certain that education would continue "fluctuating with the warm zeal of a few abettors," and that it would remain "out of the power of any, except the opulent, to give a liberal education to their children."[76] Ultimately, a bill that merely supported voluntary action did nothing to challenge the status quo or equalize access to schools.

New Yorkers learned that same lesson through their experience with the regents. A sense that academies served only a small subset of New Yorkers began bubbling up by the early 1790s.[77] In 1793, even some members of the board of regents argued that "numerous advantages" would accrue from funding the "lower branches of education."[78] In his 1795 gubernatorial address, the Republican George Clinton pledged his support for common education over academies. While Clinton "commended" efforts to build academies, he maintained that "they are principally confined to the children of the opulent, and that a great proportion of the community is excluded." State support of the academies redistributed funds from the people to an elite hobbyhorse. This demanded reform. "The establishment of common schools throughout the state" was Clinton's preferred solution. Concrete proposals soon followed. The legislature considered Clinton's recommendation in 1795 alongside a petition from the African Free School to fund schools for black children in New York City. Agreeing that it was "not expedient" to provide extra funds "for the African children in the City of New-York," the legislature instead included them in the common school bill already under consideration.[79] In 1795, New York appropriated £20,000 a year for five years to fund "English"—elementary—education. This first foray into supporting common education was meaningful but insufficient.[80] Compared to earlier appropriations for academies, the per-pupil funding was miniscule.[81]

Rather suddenly, education became a fault line in New York's factional politics. Clinton had pitted common schools against academies. The 1795 funding law explicitly barred academies from accessing the new money, even if they offered an English education track. Shifting some power over schools away from the regents hurt the Federalists, who continued to dominate the board. Unsurprisingly, then, the strongest backing for the bill came from Clintonian Republican stalwarts.[82] When the Federalists retook the governorship in 1796, they amended the 1795 bill to allow academies to access this 1795 pot of money.[83] Most Federalists' allegiances lay with the board of regents, while the Clintonian Republicans sided with reform.

Academies became entangled in New York's larger partisan debate over internal improvements and public finance. In 1797, the legislature created the office of state comptroller at the urging of Federalist state senator Samuel Jones. He also became the first man to fill the post.[84] The senate passed the bill to create the office by voice vote, albeit with some grumbling from Clintonians about the comptroller's salary.[85] The Federalist-majority assembly voted overwhelmingly in favor, while the Clintonians provided more than half of the votes against.[86] Why was there a partisan opposition? The comptroller's office changed public finance in two key ways that served Federalist interests. First, chartered banks instantly gained a more direct role in government. The comptroller could borrow money to pay for appropriations when the treasury lacked sufficient funds.[87] Until Aaron Burr managed to create a bank out of a water company in 1799, Federalists dominated banking in New York.[88] Second, the comptroller would oversee lotteries. These were fast becoming a major funding stream for both academies and turnpikes, critical cogs in the Federalists' developmental agenda.[89] John Jay's Federalist administration issued a flurry of charters for public works, which the expansive fiscal powers of the Comptroller's Office aided.[90] Proponents had hoped that state support of academies would cement the notion that they benefited the public good. Ironically, public funding made academies a contentious, political issue. Distrust of incorporated institutions and concentrated power in New York would only grow in coming years, which hurt academies.

The Northern critique of academies as regressive received its fullest expression in a 1795 essay contest sponsored by the American Philosophical Society (APS). The prompt asked entrants to design a "system of liberal education, and literary instruction, adapted to the genius of the government." After struggling to inspire submissions, the APS finally chose the winners in 1797. Two Jeffersonians shared the prize. Samuel Harrison Smith went on to a successful career as a Republican newspaper printer. He is probably best known as the husband of Margaret Bayard Smith, the great chronicler of life in the early national capital.[91] The other winner was Samuel Knox, an Irish-born Presbyterian minister and educator whom the University of Virginia Board of Visitors later considered appointing as a professor of language.[92] The APS's prompt foreclosed any answers that rejected education's *national* importance. Nevertheless, the entrants disagreed about many things: the relative emphasis that should go to classics, the proper place of religion in schools, and the value of coeducation.[93] And yet, as Smith declared in his winning entry, there was "universal agreement of all men in this country as to the necessity of a reform in education." The problem remained that Americans' "professions disagree with their actions."[94] They talked a lot about the need for widespread, republican education, only then to support schools for the few.

Academies were the most glaring example. The APS essayists echoed criticisms that existing schools failed to educate the whole population. One of the losing essays, by "Academicus," claimed that "the wealth of a republic, may be said to consist in the quantity of wisdom" in the citizenry. When education "becomes a Monopoly in the hands of the rich, the liberties of the state become a boon to the highest bider [sic]." The United States was verging close to such a situation.[95] Another essayist argued that universal education should be the goal. Unfortunately, "hitherto only a small number of those, who were capable of receiving useful learning, have had it in their powers to pursue it."⁹⁶ The most strident critique of academies came from Knox, who was himself an academy principal in Frederick, Maryland. Knox bemoaned that "Immense revenues and donations have, indeed, been applied to the founding of... seminaries." At the same time, "the poor... have been left almost totally neglected." In this, the United States had "fallen in with the error of many even of the most enlightened countries of the world." Education in a republic was supposed to be different because the people governed themselves. But Americans emulated "the policy of those governments that existed by the slavish ignorance of the people."⁹⁷ There were uncomfortable similarities between American and European—aristocratic—education policy.

The very nature of these critiques, though, placed limits on reformers' attacks and solutions. Reformers criticized how education reintroduced aristocratic forms in a republican nation by undermining the equality of opportunity that many Americans thought delineated republics from societies with hereditary power. This was not a racially expansive reform vision; advocates of change quietly left people of color out of their discussions. Elsewhere in the Atlantic World, similar ideas about education and citizenship were turned to reactionary ends. Hoping to regain control of Haiti in the midst of its revolution, French planters argued that formerly enslaved revolutionaries were too ignorant to govern themselves. Down the line, white northerners made the same arguments about free black Americans. Of course, the Haitian revolutionaries lacked education because they had been enslaved. The revolutionary leader, Toussaint Louverture, countered that even though slavery had denied them an education, formerly enslaved revolutionaries still had the right to self-government. The Haitian Revolution's commitment to universal human equality and equal participation regardless of circumstance far exceeded that of American education reformers.⁹⁸ Even on its own antiaristocratic terms, American reformers' critique had its limits. They were not attacking an actual aristocracy, and unlike French revolutionaries, most did not couple support of public schools with radical plans to redistribute wealth. The 1790s critique of aristocratic education left ample opportunity for compromise.

The Northern Jeffersonian Embrace of Academies

Jeffersonian critiques of academies treated school funding as a zero-sum game. When academies received too much support, widespread elementary education suffered. Yet the latter was more important for teaching citizenship and establishing self-government. This critique proved to be resilient in the long term. More immediately, countervailing political forces strengthened the academies. Those who believed in the necessity of a distinct and well-educated elite continued to support academies. By the late 1790s, they no longer divided neatly along partisan lines.

Congressional politics had the curious effect of leading some Jeffersonians to defend academies. The cause was the proposal to create a national university, which Congress considered in 1796, during the waning months of George Washington's presidency. This was a pet project for Washington, who donated stock to fund the proposed school. Yet the idea for a national university originated in 1787 with Benjamin Rush. Both he and Washington envisioned the national university as a kind of graduate school for future statesmen. After taking their elementary and liberal education elsewhere, exceptional students from across the nation would come together to study subjects relevant to public life.[99] This would foster national sentiments, and create a national network of good republicans. The idea sounded reasonable to many, including several of the APS contest entrants. By 1796, Alexander White, a member of the board planning the new federal city in Washington, D.C., opined to James Madison that "the utility of a National University seems generally admitted."[100] He was too sanguine.

Washington's plan for a national university was imperiled before Congress even considered it. As an annoyed Washington told Thomas Jefferson in 1795, opponents of the plan, "without any just cause that I have been able to discover, are continually sounding the alarm bell of aristocracy."[101] The proposed national university enflamed a debate about the proper limits and ends of federal power. To many Americans, the Federalists' aggressive national agenda seemed tone-deaf so soon after overthrowing the British Empire. Beyond that, Federalist policies tended not to serve all Americans equally. Wealthy merchants clearly benefited more from the Bank of the United States than most Americans, for example.[102] The proposed university was invasive, designed to inculcate values in young men. Moreover, its avowed purpose was to create a national elite, something opponents only feared the national bank *might* do. Opponents of the university thus adapted arguments about undemocratic big government that Anti-Federalists had used in 1788 and their heirs would use for decades to come.[103]

Federalists in Congress anticipated these attacks. To head them off, they demurred from asking Congress to create a "national university." Instead they proposed incorporating a board of commissioners to collect donations "towards the establishment of a university" in Washington.[104] Proponents feared that the university "would not pass if brought into the House without disguise." According to another supporter, they "anticipated the objections which have been made to a National University, and have purposely avoided inserting it in their memorial."[105] This approach backfired. John Nicholas, a Jeffersonian from Virginia, raged that like many other Federalist schemes, this one "was so covered as not to show half the mischiefs which would attend it."[106] The Jeffersonians, then, successfully used the Federalists' cageyness against them.

Congressional Jeffersonians also harped on how the national university might hurt local education. Surprisingly, they focused on how it could damage existing academies. The fiery western Massachusetts Jeffersonian William Lyman said that the university would tax poor and middling people from "remote parts" to pay for an education they would never receive. Worse, it might undermine "small Academies." These, he claimed, "are as useful as" the university, but actually within the reach of the "middling classes."[107] Lyman's was a populist argument for academies. Likewise, John Nicholas railed that "every district of [the] country was competent to provide for the education of its own citizens."[108] Faced with the specter of the federal school, Jeffersonians found academies acceptable.[109] Both Lyman and Edward Livingston, a New York Republican, reasoned that if citizens near Washington wanted a school, they should ask Maryland for a charter.[110]

Lyman and Livingston thought this would be an easy request. They were mistaken. These congressional debates coincided, almost to the day, with the stunning implosion of a plan to support an academy in Baltimore. The Maryland legislature approved a £3,000 loan, over five years, for the Baltimore Academy trustees to rebuild the school after a fire. Religious tensions undermined cooperation.[111] At play beneath sectarian strife were fears of government intervention that had made the academies a partisan issue in the rest of the South. Since at least the time of the failed 1785 plan to turn two academies into a state college, Marylanders had worried about state involvement in education. As in Massachusetts, where positions on Shays's Rebellion were predictive of academy support, public finance and education policy intertwined. Maryland debtors opposed that "huge coloss" and creditors favored it.[112] Jeffersonian fears that incorporated institutions consolidated power remained live in the mid-1790s. Only when the Federalists retook the Maryland governorship, in 1798, did the state pass a bill to fund existing academies.[113] In much of the rest of the South, too, the politics of academies did not change. Federalist legislatures continued to grant most of the academy charters. The Southern Jeffersonians did not come to terms with academies until after 1800, when the Federalists had all but disappeared.

In the North, though, the politics of academies changed considerably. This allowed academies to recover from the deluge of criticism they faced between 1793 and 1795. It also explains why some Northern Jeffersonians defended academies in Congress. Take Lyman himself. Though he quickly came into the Republican fold, Lyman shared a background with many Massachusetts academy founders. During Shays's Rebellion, he served under William Shepard, the most notorious friend of government and the future founder of the Westfield Academy. By 1794, though, Lyman had to fend off a challenge from Shepard to win reelection to Congress. He is indicative of a broader transformation in support for academies.[114]

The sort of gentry alliances that in the 1780s underlay many academies gave way to an increasingly competitive and vitriolic partisan politics.[115] Partisanship divided academy boards, like that of the first academy to open in Lyman's western Massachusetts district, in Williamstown, which later became Williams College. One of the founders, Thompson Skinner, served as a delegate to the state ratification convention and voted in favor of the Constitution. By the 1790s, Skinner was a leading Republican in a strong Republican county. Other trustees—like Theodore Sedgwick and Woodbridge Little—remained Federalists into the 1790s.[116] This shared background provided a latent moderate streak among some Northern Jeffersonians. It led them to stomach the chartering of academies through the mid-1790s, and to oversee the continued expansion of academies in the 1800s. Despite the Jeffersonian revolution, then, there were important continuities in academy support. In western Massachusetts, for example, the connection between Shays's Rebellion and academy founding persisted through at least 1820 (table 6.5). Most academies opened in towns that divided over the Regulation and were home both to leading regulators and government militia captains. In other words, academies tended to still draw support from similar sources. The politics of the 1790s simply diffused it across party lines.

Yet not all Jeffersonians took to academies equally. The party was born divided. On the one side were erstwhile Anti-Federalists, often called Old Republicans. In the South, Old Republicans tended to oppose any sort of developmental agenda. In the North, Old Republicanism had a radical valence. They were particularly vigilant to ensure that institutions remained under democratic control and benefited "the people." These radicals distrusted chartered corporations, which seemed, by their very nature, to undermine the public will. On the other side were Moderates, many of whom supported the United States Constitution, only to grow disillusioned with the Federalists. They remained sure that active government was necessary to foster economic

TABLE 6.5 Academy towns in western Massachusetts and Shays's Rebellion, 1780–1820

Year Academy Founded	No. of Academies Founded in Shaysite Towns (Total No. of Shaysite Towns)	No. of Academies Founded in Pro-Government Towns (Total No. of Pro-Government Towns)	No. of Academies Founded in Contested Towns (Total No. of Contested Towns)
1780–1799	0	1	4
1800–1820	1	1	4
Total	1 (32)	2 (31)	8 (45)

Note: I identified the position on Shays's Rebellion of Worcester, Hampshire, and Berkshire County towns using the appendices of Brooke, "Deacon's Orthodoxy," 230–35. I included New Salem (Worcester County) in the contested list. Though it was not home to any government militia leaders, the town was deeply divided over the regulation because of religious infighting. For the town totals by category, see Brooke, "'To the Quiet,'" table 6, 455.

development and promote the public good and that chartered corporations were a legitimate way to do this.[117]

Support for academies became a defining feature of *Moderate* Jeffersonianism. Looking back from the 1800s, this is clear in places like Massachusetts and Pennsylvania, where intraparty divisions were pronounced. Turnout was high in the 1803 and 1804 Massachusetts gubernatorial elections, which pitted Federalist Caleb Strong against two very different Jeffersonian candidates. Elbridge Gerry had opposed the Constitution, spent some time as a Federalist, and then served as the Republican standard bearer in yearly gubernatorial elections from 1800 to 1803. In 1803, Gerry underperformed in towns that had an academy before 1800. He won 20 percent of those, but 24 percent of towns statewide. By contrast, James Sullivan was the quintessential Massachusetts Moderate Jeffersonian. In his 1804 gubernatorial run, Sullivan overperformed in towns with an academy. He won 47 percent of academy towns, but only 40 percent of all others. The increase in support for Jeffersonians between 1803 and 1804 marked the leading edge of a wave that gave Moderate Jeffersonians the governorship in 1807.[118] In Pennsylvania, the Moderate candidate in the critical 1805 gubernatorial election was Thomas McKean, who had served as an inaugural trustee for the reestablished Newark (Delaware) Academy. McKean garnered 60 percent of the vote in academy towns, as opposed to 53 percent statewide. He also overperformed in three-quarters (nine of twelve) of academy towns.[119] Towns with academies before 1800 were the vanguard of the Moderate Jeffersonian movement in key states.

Often, academy trustees led this transition. The rise of Moderate Republicanism was particularly stark in Middlesex County, Massachusetts. In 1804, Lawrence Academy trustee Samuel Dana first challenged his Federalist co-trustee, Timothy Bigelow, for the town's seat in the General Court. By 1807, Dana was the president of the state senate, having defeated both Bigelow and the Westford Academy trustee Ebenezer Bridge.[120] In Worcester County, Leicester and its academy remained Federalist through the 1800s. But key Republican leadership came from the academy board, including Timothy Newell who resigned from his position as a trustee in 1797. Other leading Republicans, like Thomas Denny, stayed on the board.[121] Nationally, Moderate Republicans successfully installed Joseph Varnum of Massachusetts as Speaker of the U.S. House in 1806. Varnum had worked to put down Shays, voted in favor of the Constitution in 1788, and then helped to found the Westford Academy.[122]

Academies and Moderate Jeffersonians

Political competition among academy trustees reveals the turn toward bipartisan support of Northern academies. More broadly, academies were one instance of how the Jeffersonian coalition absorbed some Federalists and their policies around 1800. In this same period, these Moderate Jeffersonians took over Freemasonry and continued efforts to professionalize the bench and the bar and formalize legal training. All three put a premium on advanced education. This convergence suggests that the Moderates supported academies because they believed that a distinct elite should rule and used the same institutions as Federalists to inculcate that ideal.

The Jeffersonian infiltration of Freemasonry is a peculiar story. During the late 1790s, a swirl of innuendo crossed the Atlantic and convinced a swath of Federalists that a secretive branch of Masons called the Bavarian Illuminati was behind the French Revolution. The most unapologetic Federalists concluded that this same group had infiltrated the American order. In response, they renounced Masonry. None of it was true, but the conspiracy theory itself led to a shift in support for Masonry. As the most reactionary Federalists lurched right, they took the entire political system with them. Middle-of-the-road Jeffersonians ended up in control of Freemasonry, a traditional home for self-styled Moderates. They did so without displacing some disgruntled Federalists who balked at their party's paranoia and kept their Masonic ties.[123]

Even with Jeffersonians in power, Freemasonry continued its traditional efforts to build a republican elite. This was no small thing. Jeffersonians had made "principles not men" a slogan for much of the 1790s, which signaled their faith in democratic ideals rather than virtuous leadership. Once they were on the cusp of power, though, Jeffersonians associated themselves both with men whose virtue seemed beyond the pale and the institutions that claimed to create them. Masonry and the academies were conspicuous examples.[124] The death of George Washington—a prominent Mason—in 1799 marked a turning point. For example, the staunchly Republican town of Newark, New Jersey, held a memorial service for him at the local academy. Alexander McWhorter—the local Presbyterian minister, academy founder, and a Jeffersonian—gave the oration. A published account of the ceremony drew attention to the presence of "the fraternity of Free Masons." Their "share in the Procession attracted every eye, and gave solemn dignity to the whole."[125] Like the Federalists before them, the Jeffersonians used Masonry to associate themselves with Washington and prove their virtue. They, too, implicated local academies in the effort.

The Jeffersonian embrace of academies and takeover of Masonry happened more slowly in the South.[126] Jeffersonians wrested control of North Carolina and Virginia in 1800 and 1802, respectively. Prior to this point, the Jeffersonians chartered few academies. Yet in the nineteenth century, Southerners continued building academies and Jeffersonian-controlled legislatures continued chartering them. Virginia passed laws to charter or support an academy in all but two years between 1800—when Jeffersonians won the governorship and eighteen of the state's nineteen U.S. house seats—and 1812. North Carolina passed at least one bill to create or support an academy in each year between 1802 and 1812. Jeffersonians held the reins of power in that state for ten of those eleven years. Maryland also began to support academies more regularly. The state passed laws to benefit academies in every year between 1800 and 1812 save three. In the South as in the North, academies survived the decline of Federalism.[127]

Southern Moderates used the academies to transmit their conception of gentry rule across generations. The Society of the Cincinnati maintained its close association with academies through the Jeffersonian ascendancy. Popular blowback had forced the organization to abandon hereditary membership. In some states, the society reverted to the original plan once the clamor died down. The Virginia society, though, did not. By 1800 it was not long for the world, though its coffers were full. Pension payouts to members' families demanded only a small part of the endowment. The membership realized they needed to do something with their funds before the original members all died.[128]

Without entertaining other possibilities, the Virginia Cincinnati agreed to donate the remaining money to academies in the state. Here they followed Washington, who gave generously to a few schools.[129] A few members contested the decision, questioning whether this was a legal use of the society's money. Nonetheless, they approved in principle.[130] Trustees of one academy claimed that "every member of the Cincinnati Society, are convinced of the propriety of giving funds to some Seminary of learning."[131] The challenge lay in deciding which school or schools to endow. Some wanted to see all the money go to their preferred academy. Other members believed that they should diffuse their largesse across the commonwealth. The funds eventually went to the Washington Academy, one of the schools to which Washington had donated.[132] The Washington Academy trustees appealed to society members' vain aspirations to be associated with Washington. If endowed by the society, the academy would forever sit as a "literary monument, in which your names will be enrolled with that of your immortal and beloved GENERAL."[133]

The debate over which academy to fund betrays how the Cincinnati aimed to serve their own interests. In endowing an academy, the Cincinnati would secure their place in history. Many members also hoped to send their children to whatever academy the society endowed.[134] Even as late as 1812, society funds directly paid for the education of members' children.[135] Ultimately, the Cincinnati found another means to maintain their collective power across generations. Postrevolutionary Virginia proved inhospitable to legal aristocracy.[136] But through academies, the Cincinnati kept alive a republican aristocracy of merit that benefited them and their children.

The society was still careful to preserve the notion that their academy existed to benefit the greater good. In the bequest to Washington Academy, the Cincinnati charged the state treasurer with disbursing the funds once the group folded. Their donation would go through the state's coffers. This final touch made the Cincinnati appear as much like benefactors of Virginia as of a school that would serve their interests. It did both, while defining Virginians' understanding of the public good to reflect the Cincinnati's faith in an educated elite.[137]

Equally striking is the absence of a connection between academies and more radical civil associations. Only on rare occasions did academies open their doors to Democratic-Republican Societies, the institutional center of Radical Jeffersonianism. When they did, academies met with allegations of partisanship that they never faced for affiliating with Freemasonry. John Poor, who ran the Philadelphia Young Ladies' Academy, came under attack because his "*academy* has long been a rendez-vous for the *Democratic society* and the

United Irishmen," another radical group.[138] In New York, it was not academies, but rather the Jeffersonian Society of Associated Teachers that had a close affinity with the Democratic Society.[139] On a few occasions, Federalists created similar partisan groups, like the Constitutional Association in Elizabeth, New Jersey. At least two of its officers served on the local academy board.[140]

Finally, the connection between academy culture and legal professionalization persisted into the nineteenth century. The earliest organized efforts at legal education in the United States sprouted in the same fertile educational soil as the early denominational academies: the Presbyterian mid-Atlantic region, especially Newark and Elizabeth Town, New Jersey. In 1783, several men in the two towns started a moot court society called the Institutio Legalis. Many of the founders were the sons of men who built academies throughout New Jersey.[141] More famously, Tapping Reeve founded the Litchfield Law School in 1784. The first dedicated law school in the United States, Litchfield trained over 1,000 young men. Reeve was a product both of the New Side schools that emerged after the Great Awakening, and of the College of New Jersey. He taught at the Elizabeth Town Academy before moving to Connecticut with his wife, Sarah, who was the daughter of former College of New Jersey president Aaron Burr, Sr.

At first, these were firmly Federalist efforts. The same combination of debt relief, paper money legislation, and court closings that raised the Federalists' hackles also sparked lawyers into action. They believed that only an orderly legal system, designed and implemented by trained professionals, could uphold contracts and maintain economic order. Moderate Jeffersonians did not repudiate any of these beliefs after 1800. Though the Institutio Legalis went into hiatus shortly after its founding, it reemerged in the mid-1790s and often met at the Newark or Elizabeth Town academies.[142] The Federalists continued to fare well in Elizabeth Town, but Jeffersonians dominated Newark, including the academy. Tapping Reeve's sympathies clearly lay with the Federalists. Yet he drew a fair number of Moderate Jeffersonians to his school. Many became influential political and judicial figures during the early republic.[143] These institutions, and the legal system they supported, threatened informal traditions of exchange and dispute resolution. Erstwhile Anti-Federalists turned Old Republicans feared and opposed legal formalization.[144] This was another policy designed by Federalists and closely associated with academies, which became a dividing line within the Jeffersonian coalition.[145]

BY THE END OF the eighteenth century, academy boosters probably felt their institutions and ideals were as secure as ever. Aristocratic education, which was intended to create an ostensibly meritorious elite, enjoyed state support across the nation. In the South, Federalists still offered the firmest support for academies. But academies grew less partisan over time. The Southern states chartered twelve academies in the first half of the 1790s and twenty-one in the second half. In 1798, Kentucky pledged a chunk of its state lands to fund academies.[146] And when the Federalists disappeared from the South over the next decade, academies remained. Meanwhile, Northern academies weathered a political assault in the mid-1790s and emerged with bipartisan support. This was symptomatic of how Moderate Jeffersonians kept alive the Federalist faith in a separate ruling elite, which was distinguished by education.[147] More than any other institution, the academies inculcated this ideal among the general populace. This unlikely bipartisan acceptance of aristocratic education was made possible by geopolitical crises and strange turns in partisan politics. In the next three decades, those same forces conspired against academies and created a new opening for popular, public, and common education.

CHAPTER SEVEN

The First Era of School Reform
War, Panic, and Popular Education

By the mid-1800s, Federalists were again worried about the republic's future and thought education was to blame. Writing in spring 1807, deep into Thomas Jefferson's second term as president, Rufus King captured the mood. He complained to Noah Webster that "in nothing has this Country suffered a greater and more injurious change of opinion than on the subject of Education." In a bygone era, education commanded the "most anxious solicitude, of our forefathers." But now, King wrote, "wealth & power have become the ruling passion of our people." That "these may be acquired without the possession of learning," he argued, explains the "neglect of, and prejudice against, learning." The people had come to view schools as "nurseries of inequality and enemies of Liberty."[1]

King was right that change was afoot, but he was wrong to say that Americans had lost faith in education generally. Rather, they had lost faith in aristocratic education and the kind of elite formation it encouraged. Academies' late-1790s bipartisan moment did not last long. Instead, a new vision for education was ascendant that, if anything, made education more important to public life. During the first era of school reform—roughly the first quarter of the nineteenth century—egalitarian forms of education began to challenge then supplant the prevailing academy-centered model. Reformers privileged widespread access to knowledge through public schools coupled with democratized secondary and higher education. And they managed to shift the priorities of many state legislatures toward enacting their vision. The goal was to make possible self-government through widespread informed participation in political life.

A series of interconnected political crises propelled the first era of school reform. The increasing relevance of the French Revolution followed by the Jeffersonian ascendancy left Federalists and their education policy increasingly embattled. Jeffersonians' democratic rhetoric, too, reinvigorated support for popular education. The geopolitical crises of the War of 1812 and the Panic of 1819 further challenged the country's remaining Federalists and spurred the demand for more accessible forms of education. Moderate Jeffersonians who still valued academies now had to compromise more often with their radical compatriots, who favored equal education for all, than with the Federalists. Slowly, many Federalists and emergent Whigs realized that if they wanted to keep alive some semblance of an aristocracy of merit and secure rule by an educated elite, they had to shape ascendant popular forms of education rather than resist them.[2] Widespread education remained a democratic idea with democratic potential. But as it took root across the North, it no longer seemed so radical. This shift contrasted sharply with the slave South, where aristocratic education survived alongside an aristocratic social and political system.

Visions of Reform

The emergence of Moderate Jeffersonians in the mid-1790s was critical to the academies' survival. Moderates supported academies because they believed in the logic that led Federalists to create them in the first place. Yet they were not Federalists. The way in which each group envisioned academies within a wider educational landscape helped differentiate them. If Federalists first proposed replacing hereditary power with merit-based hierarchy, Moderate Jeffersonians believed there was yet more to do before schools could capably identify the meritorious. They thought that academies could only identify and train a stable elite if there was a strong base of public common education. This led prominent Moderates to call for some democratization in education. Here, they also responded to their more radical Jeffersonian counterparts, whom the Federalists had blissfully ignored. These radicals questioned whether political leaders needed an advanced education at all. Instead, they argued the state need only provide for equal common education. The radicals took aim, not just at the academy curriculum, but also at the corporate form that sustained it, which they dismissed as a tool that the elite used to entrench their power.[3]

To critics, Federalist education policy was altogether sinister. In a 1799 pamphlet, the New Hampshire Episcopal priest John Cosens Ogden borrowed the Federalists' own conspiratorial rhetoric to criticize them. Ogden claimed that Northern Federalists had constructed a homegrown, American Illuminati. At the center of this were Congregational and, to a lesser extent, Presbyterian clergymen and schools. As Ogden explained, the Illuminati's influence spread through Yale, Dartmouth, the College of New Jersey, and the Litchfield Law School. These *"Illuminated Societies,"* as Ogden fashioned them, handed out degrees to *"political characters."* Degrees did not signal academic achievement, but rather indoctrination into a way of thinking. Members of this Illuminati "denounced good men at elections" simply because they lacked certain credentials. Taken together, the Federalist educational agenda had "called off the public attention from the schools and children of the yeomanry in general, to the promoting of the children of the Illuminati, and the colleges subservient to them." Under such a system, Ogden concluded, "Merit is neglected."[4] It was a sharp critique: The Federalists undermined the very merit-based natural aristocracy that they claimed to value.

Ogden's essay was over the top but hardly unprecedented. He picked up on old arguments that came from both within and outside the Federalist coalition.[5] Noah Webster had noted that privileging seemingly arcane subjects like Latin was an "absurdity." Among the people, it was "the subject of common complaint." Webster did not want to eliminate classical learning; he thought it should be "a distinct profession." Yet he acknowledged that the critics had a point. In a 1791 essay, so did Benjamin Rush. The "common people," he argued, "do not despise scholars, because they know more, but because they know less than themselves." Existing education had "a tendency to destroy the prejudices of the common people against schools" altogether.[6] Academy educators had not made a strong enough case for the utility of the curriculum they offered. Neither Webster nor Rush were anti-intellectual. Yet both still feared that aristocratic education sowed a general resentment of education, which undermined informed citizenship.

Ogden correctly identified the networks that drew together the Federalist educational world. Surely, too, he knew that academies were intertwined with his Illuminati. Presbyterian and Congregational clergymen sat on numerous academy boards. Men who had been educated at Yale and the College of New Jersey or were affiliated with Litchfield Law School founded and staffed many academies. And while Ogden wrote, Congregationalist Federalists in neighboring Massachusetts continued to found academies. Three of the most flagrantly Federalist academies—in Deerfield, Milton, and Bridgewater—received charters between 1797 and 1799 (table 7.1). Around that same time, students at Leicester Academy showed that they imbibed the values of Federalist consensual civil society. A group of students, "desirous of improving in the art of speaking, voluntarily assembled" to found a social fraternity. They were "sensible of the advantages, which might arise from a society of this kind, to preserve order."[7] No doubt the perceived democratic excess of the French Revolution was an implicit foil.

Yet academies escaped Ogden's ire, if not his notice. Ogden thought the Illuminati had designs on academies. Their reach extended into New York, where he alleged that they conspired to turn several regents academies to

TABLE 7.1 Partisanship of founders of two Massachusetts academies, 1798–1799

Academy	Federalists (Percentage of Total Trustees)	Anti-Federalists and/or Jeffersonians (Percentage of Total Trustees)	Ministers (Percentage of Total Trustees)	Non-Ministers, but No Party ID (Percentage of Total Trustees)	Total Trustees
Milton	6 (43%)	1 (7%)	7 (50%)	0 (0%)	14 (100%)
Bridgewater	13 (50%)	2 (8%)*	5 (19%)	6 (23%)	26 (100%)
Total	19 (48%)	3 (7%)	12 (30%)	6 (15%)	40 (100%)

Note: I established partisanship by finding trustees as candidates for office in *A New Nation Votes*. The table leaves out the Deerfield Academy, founded in 1797, because the town gave not a single vote to the Republican gubernatorial candidate that year. I also exclude the academy opened in Framingham, in 1797, because most of its trustees never ran for public office.
 * Both voted against ratification in 1788.

their ends. Nevertheless, Ogden thought they had not succeeded. Federalists may have dominated the board of regents, but they prohibited sectarian academies.[8] The academies also probably avoided Ogden's acid pen because many had bipartisan support. Even Ogden himself had given an oration at the opening of a female academy in New Hampshire in 1791.[9]

Moderate Jeffersonians shared Ogden's belief that Federalist education focused too narrowly on elites. Yet they never denied the importance of higher education. Here again the American Philosophical Society (APS) contest essays are suggestive. According to Samuel Knox, the academies could not "be considered as the most effectual provision for diffusing the blessings of general knowledge or scientific improvement throughout the STATE." The problem was that they depended on "proper subordinate nurseries of students, prepared for entering and attending such dignified seminaries." And most of the country lacked elementary-level schools that prepared students well for academies. Why, then, did the academies "absorb or swallow up the greater proportion of public patronage"? This left little money over to create the needed "subordinate nurseries."[10] Ultimately, Moderates hoped to sustain academies by strengthening the schools below them. This impulse provides a through line from Moderate Jeffersonians to the eventual emergence of the Whig Party.[11]

Besides Noah Webster, Federalists seldom advocated for expanding access to common education. Rather, they extolled education's importance for stabilizing social order.[12] Joseph Lathrop, a Federalist minister caught up in the

Bavarian Illuminati fervor, went so far as to claim that expanding access to education could lead to a "corruption of sentiments and manners."[13] Lathrop also served on the founding board of the Westfield Academy. He thought it "necessary there should be some in society, who have an education superior" to that offered in town schools.[14] To Moderate Jeffersonians, men like Lathrop exposed the fatal flaw of Federalist education policy: They opposed the most obvious ways to create a natural aristocracy of merit.

Moderates advocated for widespread access to common, public education. Only this could create a pathway for poorer Americans to ready themselves for a liberal education, which was indispensable to organizing society around merit. This idea undergirded the systems proposed by each Knox, Smith, and several losing APS essayists. The most common solution on offer was a pyramidal system of public education, with universal common education on the bottom, academies and/or state colleges in the middle, and in some cases a national university at the top. States would foot the bill for some number of exceptional students to receive advanced schooling that they otherwise could not afford.[15] The idea went back at least as far as Thomas Jefferson's 1779 plan for Virginia. He wanted to expand elementary education to make it possible for the meritorious to rise through higher levels of education and to teach the people to select worthy leaders.[16] Critically, some APS essayists wanted public schools that served all white men to be the established route to political power. Samuel Knox would have prohibited students who did not attend public common schools from enrolling in public academies. Likewise, only students who attended a state college could move on to the national university.[17] Benjamin Rush's plan for a national university proposed that only alumni should be eligible for national political office.[18]

Support for universal public education was strongest in the North, but some Southern Jeffersonians parroted it. In South Carolina, Richard Beresford suggested that "every citizen of the republic, from the wealthiest planter to the needy peasant, and all in equal and most ample measure, be furnished at the publick expense with opportunities of instruction." This was in a 1797 pamphlet, *Aristocracy, the Bane of Liberty; Learning the Antidote*, which called for free schools and accessible republican colleges.[19]

Yet some Northern Jeffersonians thought the Moderates did not go far enough in repudiating the Federalists. The Moderates wanted to ensure that all white men had better access to higher education and, in turn, the public trust. More radical Jeffersonians questioned whether well-educated people should have a greater claim to rule than anyone else. They saw no clear connection between educational attainment—as it currently looked—and one's ability to represent their constituents. This insight flowed from a particular understanding of representation. As Anti-Federalist Melancton Smith argued at the New York ratification convention, politicians should "resemble those they represent; they should be a true picture of the people." An academy education made one unrepresentative. Smith conceded that leaders should understand "extensive political and commercial information, such as is acquired by men of refined education." That just was not enough. Representatives needed also to understand the "common concerns and occupations of the people." It seemed clear to Smith that "men of the middling class of life are in general much better competent" at this "than those of a superior class." When it came to taxes, for example, they understood "how the burdens imposed will bear upon the different classes."[20] Against Federalist and Moderate Republican paeans to wise leaders, Smith claimed that fairness depended on mutual understanding between ruler and ruled. Too much education could impede that.

Smith never proposed an alternative education policy, but a group of Radical Republicans did. They made the case for equal, state-run education that prepared all men for political life and public service. Like the Moderates, they advocated public common schooling. They differed in saying that this alone was sufficient for both citizens and leaders. To them, self-government depended on citizens being able to think for themselves and not merely defer to, or emulate, an existing elite. Schools, therefore, should not socially reproduce people, as Federalist academies did. They should supply to all citizens the tools that allowed them to pursue their own values.

Nobody articulated this position more clearly than the Delaware Anti-Federalist Robert Coram.[21] "Education," he wrote in 1791, "ought to be secured by government to every class of citizens, to every child in the state." Coupled with large-scale redistribution of property, this was the only way to foster *equal* participation. Coram did not frame his essay as an attack on academies. Yet he clearly had no need for them. Coram asserted that "the first step of such reformation" of education "will be by turning private schools into public ones." Moreover, his belief in direct participation by the citizenry led him to see schools that created a separate elite as illegitimate. It was "a scandal to civilized society" that education often taught some men "to cheat the rest of their liberties." American education did not make a natural aristocracy. It allowed men to "create an artificial inequality among themselves and then cry out it is all natural."[22] Schools too often did little more than launder privilege.

Coram later became a leader in the Democratic-Republican Society of Delaware, which endorsed his position.[23] The Delaware Society hoped to guarantee "to every member of the community, the means of acquiring a knowledge of those duties" they had as citizens. The society also attacked their opponents for doing "nothing in the business," which led to "a torpor on this subject." The Pennsylvania society likewise declared that "the establishment of public schools ... will be the best means of impressing every class of citizens in the community with a true sense of their rights, duties, and obligations." Members of the New York society toasted "the progress of education" and hoped it would "cause a speedy abolition of every species of dangerous distinction."[24] Across the nation, Democratic-Republican societies trumpeted a vision of public education sufficient to prepare all white men for public trusts.

The radically democratic-minded Massachusetts farmer, William Manning, shared these sentiments. Manning grumbled that elites "are continually crying up the great advantages of costly colleges, national academies, and grammar schools," which "greatly promote the views and interests of the Few." Instead of republican values, these schools "teach [students] to reverence [sic] and worship great men in office." For many Federalists, this was the point. They founded academies, in part, because they believed the influence of the elite had attenuated far beyond what was safe. Citizens should respect wise and educated men, and students should aspire to be like them. Manning disagreed. Even worse, he thought that "learning necessary for the Many to have might be better promoted with half the costs." Manning envisioned a free school system with tuition-free academies that taught advanced English and trained men and women as teachers.[25]

1790s-era education reformers, whether from the North or the South, rarely extended their analysis to include people of color. They often ignored how, at the same moment, antislavery societies founded schools for free black children in many Northern states. The New York Manumission Society opened its African Free School in 1787, with the intention of showing white men that black children could be nurtured into becoming capable citizens. In 1798, the black leader Primus Hall opened a school for free black children in Boston, and the Pennsylvania Abolition Society did the same in Philadelphia in 1799. Yet reformers paid this little heed. The Moderates did not explicitly incorporate people of color into their plans for national school systems. Jefferson's own racist ideas, for example, left him unable to imagine that any black man could excel among whites and become a natural aristocrat. Some of the more radically democratic voices, like Coram, were antislavery activists. But many others, including Manning, did not incorporate free black people into their democratic visions for schooling or otherwise. Moreover, as partisanship hardened during the 1790s, the Jeffersonian Republicans increasingly drew strength from their cross-sectional appeal. Even the Radical

Northern Jeffersonians tempered their antislavery and racially equalitarian language in deference to their Southern compatriots.[26]

By 1800, the political battle lines in education were clear. Did stability depend on rule by an educated and propertied elite, as the Federalists claimed? Was a meritocracy based on more equal opportunity the key to making a republic work, as the Moderates thought? Or was equal and public education for an equal white-male citizenry the surest route to republican self-government, as the Radical Northern Republicans insisted? The three-way fight over education was a proxy for a larger debate over how to govern a republic.

The Educational Revolution of 1800: New York as a Test Case

The view that state-run common education would give all white men the tools to govern themselves found its greatest evangelist in Jedediah Peck. The "father" of New York's common schools was hell bent on, as he wrote in 1799, "bring[ing] improvement within the reach and power of the humblest citizen." This was because, "in all countries where education is confined to a few people, we always find arbitrary governments and abject slavery."[27] Peck's support for common education also came from his distaste for Federalists' pretentiousness, which academies epitomized. At the same time as he promoted common schools, he opposed providing further state funds for academies. As New York's Republicans grew stronger, Peck's arguments eventually yielded policy changes.[28]

But in the early nineteenth century, the Moderate focus on meritocracy and academies was still winning. New York's 1801 "Act for the Encouragement of Literature" authorized a series of lotteries to raise $100,000 for schooling in the state. The law earmarked half the proceeds for regents academies and the rest for a common school fund. It did not provide for free, universal, or compulsory education. It did not even prescribe if or how the state should create common schools.[29] Yet the bill had more bipartisan appeal than gambits to fund academies in the mid-1790s. A Republican-controlled assembly proposed the bill and the Federalist-majority senate passed it.[30] Federalist governor John Jay signed it into law. The 1801 law showed at least a superficial commitment to common education. At the same time, it bolstered the power of academies. It was premised on an idea of democracy as an imperfectly merit-based society—one with slightly less flagrant inequality of opportunity—for white men. Bills like this allowed Moderate Jeffersonians to peel off enough support from the Federalists and co-opt just enough of the radicals' egalitarianism to cast both to the margins.[31]

The year 1801 turned out to be a last gasp for the older order in New York. Later that summer, Republican George Clinton defeated John Jay in the gubernatorial election and put the Federalists on their heels. This emboldened New York's Radical Republicans and forced the Moderates to compromise with them. Equal participation by an equally educated citizenry became the rhetorical goal of New York Jeffersonians. By that fall, Republican essayists began publishing newspaper essays calling for school reform. Evidently, the 1801 law was insufficient. Since the "government is chiefly *democratic*," free public schools were necessary for the "triumph of republicanism," declared one writer.[32] Another essayist, who went by "Viator," thought New York ought to adopt a New England–style system of education to produce *"republican equality."* He also supported trading regressive lotteries for progressive taxes. Since children are "the stock" of the state, he wrote, "it is fitting that the rich, who are not *always liberal*, should be obliged by law to contribute to the instruction of the children of poor families." Meanwhile, the Federalists still beat the drum for academies. Viator responded to them with an old New England argument: Encouraging academies might "discourage common schools, by withdrawing from them and engrossing the patronage of wealthy and fashionable people." The common schools, though, "are the most generally useful." A flurry of articles appeared in support of Viator's call for New England–style public education.[33]

Viator would have found much to like in Clinton's first annual message of his new term. The governor lamented that the 1795 "system for the encouragement of common Schools" was "discontinued." Clinton evidently did not see literature lotteries as a sufficient replacement for direct common school funding. Since the benefit to "good government, arising from the general diffusion of knowledge" was "universally admitted," Clinton encouraged the state to rebuild something like the 1795 system. "The failure of one experiment for the attainment of an important object, ought not to discourage other attempts," he concluded.[34] In response, the legislature called committees, made up mostly of sympathetic Republicans, to look into schooling.[35] They made suggestions that went nowhere. Clinton issued similar calls in subsequent years, which produced more committee reports for legislators to ignore.

Nonetheless, Clinton's governorship was a turning point. During his term (1801–4), universal common schooling became a feasible political goal, and it would remain an important issue in subsequent gubernatorial contests, including the notorious 1804 election. That year, George Clinton left New York politics to take Aaron Burr's place as vice president. The disgraced Burr tried to make things symmetrical and take Clinton's place back in New York. But

Alexander Hamilton's opposition, among other things, cost Burr the governorship. This, in turn, cost Hamilton his life at Burr's hand. The main beneficiary of the sordid contest was Morgan Lewis, who became New York's new Republican governor. Lewis mentioned education in his 1804 address to the legislature, celebrating free public schools and "higher seminaries" alike.[36] Some Republican observers took heart and saw Lewis as a friend to education.[37] Others thought his message showed milquetoast support for universal education.[38] The Federalists liked what they heard from Lewis and saw him as a friend to academies.[39] Ultimately, Lewis's term helped public education. In 1805, the state allotted 500,000 acres of land and thousands of shares of bank stock to build an endowment for common schools.[40] That same year, a trio of Quakers founded a Free School Society in New York City. DeWitt Clinton, the Moderate Republican mayor of New York, lent his support.[41] Momentum was building in support of public common schools.

But a rift between Governor Lewis and many Republicans had opened over education. Lewis took the old Moderate position and tried to balance support for both academies and common schools. By the mid-1800s, the center on this issued had moved and Lewis got the balance wrong. The Jeffersonians smeared Lewis for "leaguing with the federalists" and dropped him from the ticket in 1807.[42] Instead, the Republicans backed Daniel Tompkins for governor. Lewis, in turn, accepted Federalist support, though he tried to claim he was still the education candidate.[43]

In the 1807 election, Peck's position had become the Jeffersonian position: universal state-funded common schools were a priority. Tompkins won and eventually oversaw the construction of New York's common school system.[44] First, the common school fund had to generate a usable endowment. That happened by 1810, when Tompkins stood for reelection against the Federalist, Jonas Platt. The Federalists again made education an issue. They alleged that Republicans had misappropriated the school funds.[45] The Republicans responded that claims of corruption were a smokescreen to distract voters from the fact that the Federalists had never supported public schools.[46] One Republican essayist put it in stark terms: "*ignorance* and *slavery* afford the richest soil for rearing federal plants, while republicanism is the spontaneous production of education and independence." Those who "wish for a destruction of the *School Fund*, and the advancement of *Tories* to office," should "vote for the federal ticket." But should "you wish your *children educated* . . . rally round the Republican Standard."[47] The centrality of education to the election played into Republicans' hands. Tompkins kept the governorship, and the Republicans held the senate and retook the assembly. Though the Federalists made a slight comeback during the War of 1812, Republicans controlled New York for the next decade.

Public education became a fixture in New York during the 1810s. In 1812, Tompkins asked the legislature for a report on common schools. Fittingly, Jedediah Peck took the lead. The report was the culmination of a decade of Radical Jeffersonian activism against academies and for common schools. Peck and the committee proposed a comprehensive system of public schooling—the first outside of New England—and justified it in opposition to chartered academies. The report proposed the "establishment of common-schools... spread throughout the state, and aided by its bounty." Quoting himself from over a decade earlier, Peck argued that only this "will bring improvement within the reach and power of the humblest citizen." The report also dismissed "all other methods, heretofore adopted" as "partial in their operation and circumscribed in their effects." In particular, "academies and universities, understood in contra-distinction to common-schools, cannot be considered as operating impartially and indiscriminately, as regards the country at large." Schools that were privately created—even those chartered by the state—would never be universal, even for white men. Yet in the United States, "where political equality is established and where the road to preferment is open to all," universality had to be the goal. As far as the report's authors were concerned, those who wished to "become acquainted with the higher branches of science" could still attend an academy. The state just needed to focus its resources elsewhere.[48]

The 1812 law laid out a statewide system of common district schools. The plan was to fund them with a combination of local property taxes, the school fund endowment, and tuition to make up the difference. An 1814 revision to the law forced communities to create school districts that the 1812 law encouraged. Critically, the board of regents would not control the new system. In fact, though they were the state's main educational administrators, no member of the regents sat on the committee that wrote the report. One regent, DeWitt Clinton, submitted a letter about the New York City Free School Society's activities as a supportive addendum to the report. The law instead created a superintendent of common schools, a bureaucratic innovation that Massachusetts and Connecticut would adopt to further reform in the 1830s.[49]

In the span of a decade, New York caught up with New England states that had publicly supported schools since the seventeenth century. In part, education in New York started to look more like education in New England as the two regions came to resemble one another more generally. Migrants from New England poured into New York's new northern and western counties during this period. Yet it was the Jeffersonians who built a permanent common school system in New York. Politics mattered.

The impact of the Jeffersonian ascendancy was clearest in New York because public schooling was new there. But even New England, where public schools long thrived, saw change in this period. New Hampshire's support of town schools dated back to the colonial era, though the Revolution threw education into disarray. In 1789, the state repealed all existing education laws, created new requirements for towns to keep schools, and introduced a new system of taxation. It again redid that system in 1804 after the Republicans took the legislature. Reform built up a head of steam. Successive laws in 1805, 1807, and 1808 empowered towns to divide into school districts, raised the proportion of taxes for education, and expanded the ambit of the common schools.[50] In Vermont, Republicanism was stronger than in the rest of New England. But even there, the one-party rule that Republicans secured in 1810 was unusual. That year, the new governor, Jonas Galusha, urged the legislature to look beyond "the higher institutions of literature." Vermont should instead ensure that education was "liberally imparted to all." The legislature raised town school taxes and made them obligatory. Access to common education grew for white boys in much of the North after the Jeffersonian Revolution.[51]

There is some indication, too, that increased state control of schools in the period benefitted ordinary white women. Most Radical Republicans envisioned little public influence for women. But the Northern Federalists turned Moderate Republicans with whom they allied held the most egalitarian gender ideals of the time. Publishers of this partisan bent catered to women readers, for example.[52] Education also had a role to play. Women's literacy advanced considerably in the thirty years following the American Revolution, especially in New England and New York.[53] In New York, state intervention made a difference. By the 1820s, the legislature essentially required districts to fund the "summer" schools that served women.[54]

Similar changes to school laws made a difference in Massachusetts (including Maine), which had the oldest tradition of public schooling. In 1789, the state legally allowed towns to divide into school districts, affirming an existing, informal practice. In setting the rules for schools, the law mentioned the role of both the school "master" and "mistress." This mattered because women teachers tended to teach summer "woman's schools" for girls and very young boys. Now they could receive state funds. Massachusetts went further still. A new law, in 1800, gave school districts the power to raise taxes that were distinct from town taxes. The state then granted those districts corporate status in 1817. This offered the districts flexibility. Historian Kathryn

Kish Sklar has shown that these new laws broadened young women's access to schools. Middling and poorer communities appropriated minimal funds for elite education, and instead turned to cheaper summer "woman's schools." These districts were also already under economic stress, and they valued educated women who left the farms to contribute to their families and communities. Under the new laws, elite-dominated towns could no longer funnel disproportionate amounts of tax dollars to grammar schools. This, no doubt, deepened the elite embrace of academies, which bucked the power of towns, and reinforced the opposition between them and the town schools.[55]

The Second War for Independence and Informed Citizenship

New York, Vermont, and New Hampshire Republicans all expanded public schooling at the very beginning of a long international crisis. Not long after Jedediah Peck finally won the battle to create a common school system, the sexagenarian readied himself for another war. This was one was real.[56] A legislative battle for public education and the War of 1812 might seem unrelated. Yet Jeffersonians like Peck saw similar values at stake. As the Napoleonic Wars raged in Europe, the British impressed American sailors into service in Her Majesty's Navy. The British claimed they could do this since subjecthood was permanent. Of course, the Americans had renounced it en masse with the Revolution. The British argument nullified American notions of volitional citizenship: that one consented to their nationality. To many Americans, this was the essence of the republican experiment, and it implicated education. A consenting citizen was informed and engaged—in a word, educated. The War of 1812, then, clarified education's importance to the break that Americans had made with the Old World.[57]

American success—such as it was—in the war unleashed a wave of patriotism and encouraged a more confident nationalism. This was clear first in the economy. Leading political economists like the Philadelphian Matthew Carey sought both to curb American dependence on Europe and to create a unified, interregional economy. Between 1815 and the decade's end, support grew for a protective tariff to encourage domestic manufacturing. The war also accelerated the dispossession of Indians in the Northwest, which hastened the admission of new Western states. This opened, not just land for white families, but also potential markets for eastern goods. Northern political economists had no illusions that westward colonization meant the growth of slavery; men like Carey counted on it. Slavery made the grist for the northern textile mills. This interregional economy also depended on communications and transportation. Internal improvements—roads, turnpikes, and canals—became a central political football of the day.[58] As the United States carved out an economic identity, white Americans sought to reassert a national identity based on active citizenship.[59] Most notably, over the next decade, ten states removed property requirements for the vote or joined the union without them, largely to enfranchise veterans. This only added to the sense of urgency on the subject of public education.[60]

Banking drew together postwar economic and cultural projects and made public education more viable in many states. To pay for its common schools, New York combined direct taxation with an endowed school fund. During the 1810s, the latter was more plausible in most states, where antitax sentiment was insurmountable. Famously, Congress chartered the Second Bank of the United States (2BUS) in 1816. The rise of state banks had a more direct impact on most Americans. State banks were relatively rare before 1810, but their number in the North increased almost fourfold in the 1810s, from 66 to 200. States chartered these private corporations and either invested in them or taxed their profits to raise revenue.[61]

In much of the country, bank finance was a revelation that made school funds possible. At points during the 1810s, New Jersey, Delaware, Pennsylvania, Maryland, and North Carolina drew more than 20 percent of their revenue from banks, and sometimes as much as 45 percent. Maryland used the money immediately to create a school fund. Delaware shored up an existing school fund that previously had relied on taxes on tavern licenses. New Jersey and North Carolina took longer to create school funds but banks provided a main revenue source. Over time, even most New England states used bank revenue at least to supplement local school taxes.[62] Taken together, postwar banking strengthened public education where it was already strong and created new possibilities for it to develop in parts of the mid-Atlantic and the upper South.

Yet changes following the War of 1812 did not bring public schools to most of the slave South. Georgia built both a literary fund for academies and a "poor school fund." The former, though, was more successful.[63] Following peace with Britain, the governor of North Carolina urged the legislature to consider "the subject of public instruction." They appointed a committee, which proposed a plan for primary schools because it was from these that most students "will pass into active life and take rank with their fellow-citizens." The problem was that, to date, the "early education of youth [was] left in a great measure to chance."[64] Archibald Murphey—the ambitious reformer who chaired the committee—pushed even harder the following year,

1817. He drew up a plan for a unified, publicly funded education system, including free tuition for talented students to move through higher schools. Murphey thought now was the time to act because the United States was at "peace with foreign nations and free from domestic inquietude." Party rancor had even died down in North Carolina.[65] But the plan did not garner a serious hearing. Southern conservatism fended off the attack on academies and stymied reform.

Virginia at least debated public schooling, though the result was similar. Thomas Jefferson's 1779 plan for a universal system of public elementary through higher education had failed to overcome conservative resistance to redistributive taxes. The state, though, did build a literary fund, which accumulated a sizable endowment. Following the War of 1812, Jefferson positioned himself to pursue his educational goals. He realized it was not feasible to get the whole system funded. Would Jefferson choose to focus his attention on the base or the tip of his pyramid? Jefferson ultimately cast his lot with aristocratic slave owners from eastern Virginia, who had little need for common schools, and created the University of Virginia. He clearly focused on the university instead of universal white common schooling, even though he conceded the latter was more important. At the time, there was some agitation among Western farmers for common schools. They found their champion in the Federalist Charles Fenton Mercer. It was not that Mercer's motivations were particularly democratic, however. Agitation to eliminate property qualifications for the vote led him to embrace public schools. And his vision for primary schooling was much more top-down than Jefferson's 1779 plan, which called for local control. Nevertheless, Mercer's plan would have changed education more than Jefferson's university, which was yet another school for the elite.[66]

Schools and the Politics of Panic

The University of Virginia received its charter in January 1819, just in the nick of time. Americans had never experienced a national economic depression before the Panic of 1819. But this bust was general. It hurt commercial farmers, merchants, and manufacturing laborers alike. Especially outside New England, a political-economic crisis, coupled with democratization, transformed what was politically possible. Notably, obstinate conservative opposition to public education—of the sort that Jefferson had exploited to found his university a few years earlier—became increasingly untenable outside the Deep South. As in the 1780s, when the Federalists accused the American people of creating the nation's economic and political woes, conservatives blamed the Panic on ordinary people's moral failings. Moral causes required moral solutions, and conservative antirelief men pushed to fund public education. In part, they hoped to divert blame away from the financial elite and head off calls for redistributive economic "relief." They also may have seen an opening to strengthen their vision for a republic governed by an aristocracy of merit. If they truly believed that popular moral failings led to the Panic, then supporting a system that recognized the authority of an exceptional elite was a logical response. Like earlier Moderate reformers, they sought to strengthen academies through increased funding, but also by expanding common schools to filter talent upwards. Meanwhile, relief advocates would not accept the point that ordinary Americans had brought about their own desperate situation. They believed the educated political and financial elite had failed them and, in turn, revived calls for schools aimed at creating and empowering an informed and self-governing citizenry.

The Panic interrupted a thriving American economy. At the end of the Napoleonic Wars, Atlantic trade reopened amid crop failures in Europe and the price of American agricultural exports skyrocketed. On top of this, British manufacturers demanded as much cotton as American plantations could produce. Speculation in Western land, which depended on credit, grew frenzied. The ever-growing number of state banks were eager to offer it. So too was the 2BUS, dashing hopes it would check inflationary expansion. At the same time, though, British manufacturers dumped finished goods on the United States. American tariffs were no match, and this caused a drain of specie out of the republic and across the Atlantic. Nothing sat behind all of the credit that banks offered. When agricultural prices fell, British creditors called in loans, the 2BUS followed suit, and the money supply contracted. Some eighty-five state banks folded, which amounted to 20 percent of all the nation's banks. The economic lives of many more individuals crumbled.[67]

Demands for relief from the "hard times" were immediate and widespread, and they came in a few different forms. Stay laws postponed the execution of debts, while replevin laws allowed debtors to reclaim property seized by creditors. Both proved popular out West. Minimum appraisal laws empowered local boards to set minimum prices at which creditors could sell debtors' property when executing a debt.[68] Some radical "relief" advocates thought that interposing between creditors and debtors was insufficient. In Kentucky, many blamed unscrupulous state bankers for the depression and advocated "bank-smashing." This plan to revoke all bank charters in the state gained wide support, but ultimately failed.[69]

The 1819-era relief measures recalled the state laws that had so alarmed would-be Federalists during the 1780s, and which Article 1, Section 10, of the Constitution was meant to prohibit. Conservatives responded accordingly and tried to slow down relief. They argued that the Panic was the result of moral failings. Too many people had forsaken industry and virtue for speculative fervor and brought this crisis on themselves and their nation. By this logic, one could dismiss relief as something that absolved those who were at fault. Direct economic relief would not fix the Panic; it might worsen the moral rot that had created it in the first place. Yet even antirelief advocates admitted that there were some deserving debtors, legitimate victims who had been swept up in a crisis. Given how bad things were, the antirelief men had to offer some solution, lest they seem callous. Instead of addressing people's immediate economic needs, the antirelief forces encouraged moral reformation. They proposed new forms of poor relief to inculcate temperance, middle-class family values, and piety. And they tethered that to support for manufacturing and, often, education.[70] This played out most clearly in Pennsylvania and Kentucky, where the Panic realigned politics around relief.

Governor Gabriel Slaughter of Kentucky was known for his education advocacy. In his 1816 gubernatorial address, he called on the state to provide "country seminaries and schools for the education of all classes of the community."[71] The next year he proposed that Kentucky tax banks and corporations to fund his plan.[72] When the Panic hit, Slaughter proved sympathetic to some relief. Yet he stood firm against "bank-smashing" radicals during their heyday in late 1819. Instead of direct relief, he proposed prison reform and internal improvements and revived his call for education. Slaughter's successor, John Adair, toed a similar line. When it came to education, he called for "establishing schools or seminaries of learning . . . in every section of the state."[73] Neither Slaughter's nor Adair's plans were particularly novel. Kentucky had supported academies since its admission to the union in 1792 but did little for common schools. Recommendations to fund academies appealed mostly to antirelief advocates. Relief men dismissed Adair as a Federalist who proposed piddling solutions to an unprecedented crisis. They wanted monetary relief and checks on creditors.[74]

The "general calamity" of 1819 also led Pennsylvanians to demand that the legislature do something "to mitigate their sufferings." They called a committee to diagnose the Panic's causes and recommend solutions. William Duane Jr., son of the Republican radical who edited Philadelphia's *Aurora*, chaired the committee. Though he was a stalwart of Philadelphia's city democracy and an old-school Republican, Duane took an antirelief line. Those who saw the

Panic as an economic crisis were "substituting cause for effect," he said. Pennsylvania was suffering "the effects of human imprudence" born of a "*want of knowledge.*" Duane dismissed stay and replevin laws as "unsound in policy and unjust in principle." Likewise, he joined with the Federalists to reject a proposed loan office that would offer currency, backed by landed security, to cash-strapped debtors. Duane argued that to stave off future calamity, the best solution "next to the care of heaven, will be the universal instruction of the rising generation." Other legislators rejected Duane's analysis. Much as they might value a "liberal system of education," they denied that the Panic "is immediately connected with that subject." Substituting new schools for statutory relief "would be but a sorry consolation to a family about to be sold out of house and home." Worse, it implied "their misfortunes were the consequences of their ignorance." Education proposals turned attention away from the real economic issues at play.[75]

Antirelief support for education spending was limited in practice. Pennsylvania's antirelief governor, Joseph Hiester, whom Duane supported, did not even push for new state appropriations for schools. Rather, he endorsed a convoluted plan from Maryland to have the federal government fund education in the eastern states. Maryland started a common school fund after the War of 1812, but progress faltered during the Panic. State senator Virgil Maxcy envisioned a solution in the West. The Northwest Ordinance had set aside 1/36th of public land to fund schooling in the states carved out of the Northwest Territories. Maxcy argued that since the Western lands were national lands, the Eastern states should receive the same benefit. He calculated 1/36th of the acreage of each Eastern state and argued they should receive that amount in Western land to fund public schools. He also wanted another 1/5th of 1/36th for academies.[76] The plan drew support from states hit hard by the Panic. But the Western states blocked the plan in Congress with help from Massachusetts and New York congressmen. These Northerners feared that the plan stoked sectional tensions, and they were unsympathetic anyway since their states had already built public schools.[77] Maxcy's plan was symptomatic of antirelief education policy: It demanded little of the existing elite and required only minimal changes to local education funding. To relief advocates, it was all a way to dodge needed economic reforms.

Yet as calls for monetary relief faltered, relief advocates became the most radical voices for public spending on education. Like the Radical Jeffersonians before them, they sensed that the Panic gave them a political opening and unabashedly made universal common education their goal. Academies were not important to relief advocates' vision. In fact, they dismissed antirelief supporters of milquetoast school reform as "Federalists," just as the Radicals had dismissed the Moderates in New York. In Pennsylvania, Joseph Hiester's more relief-friendly successor, John Schulze, responded to this shift. In his inaugural address, he said the state should "diffuse the means of rudimental education so extensively, that they should be completely within the reach of all—the poor who could not pay for them, as well as the rich who could."[78] Tennessee saw more of the same. The hard-line antirelief candidate lost the 1821 gubernatorial contest, successfully painted by his opponent as a "Federalist." The victor, William Carroll, claimed that stay laws were unconstitutional and did not champion relief. But he promoted banking policies to benefit farmers and mechanics, and pushed for internal improvements, manufacturing, and public education. His Northern-style program terrified ardent antirelief men like Andrew Jackson, who also despised Carroll for personal reasons.[79]

Relief education advocacy came earliest and was strongest in Kentucky, where the ringleader was Amos Kendall. He later became famous as a member of Andrew Jackson's kitchen cabinet, and the author of his famous 1832 bank veto. In 1819, though, Kendall was on the opposite side of things, a testament to the Panic's convoluted politics. Kendall was from Massachusetts, where he went through the town schools. While he appreciated his town school, he disdained the elitism he found when he attended an academy and then Dartmouth College. During the Panic's early days, Kendall went along with the education bills passed in Slaughter's last year. Yet Kendall "did not like these measures in the aggregate." Like other public school advocates, he fumed that the laws "devote the public means, readily available, to the higher seminaries, leaving common schools to depend on a meagre and precarious resource."[80] The latter, though, were more important.

In late 1819, Kendall took to the newspapers and proposed more aggressive school reform. In the first of six essays, he rehashed the conventional wisdom that "a republic cannot be well governed, unless all, or a great majority of the people, are capable of governing." When education was a rare commodity, it "creates an aristocracy." That kind of ruling class was even more intractable than a traditional aristocracy because "the superiority which knowledge gives is real" and people recognize it. In actual aristocratic systems, rank was usually "fictitious, and the people acknowledge it by compulsion." Here, Kendall went after Kentucky's existing education policy, which mostly benefitted academies and Transylvania University. Those funds may as well be "expended in London," he added. Kendall concluded that while "a system has been established for the rich," it was time to "have one for the poor—for all classes and descriptions of society."[81] Other relief men picked up Kendall's call. The former bank smasher, Robert M'Afee, argued that Americans should "set up the splendid example of a government providing for the education of the whole body of the people."[82] By contrast, Transylvania's president, Horace Holley, came out against relief.[83] The battle lines over the Panic had engulfed education.

To Kendall, the obvious remedy was a system of universal public schools. Kendall's next five essays explained how to build one. First, Kentuckians needed a school fund.[84] He also hoped Kentucky would mimic New England, where people gladly paid taxes "for a most useful public object." This system allowed many "children of poor parents" to receive a liberal education.[85] If Kentucky taxed the wealthy, Kendall thought they could achieve the same result. According to his calculations, the amount that the elite already paid to educate their children was enough to educate the whole state.[86] Kendall's plan entailed wholesale change. It could not "be accomplished by our institutions of learning, as at present organized."[87] To continue sending most funds to academies was to "choose an aristocratic Government—because it is better than none."[88] To relief men, anything less than systemic change perpetuated unrepublican schooling.

Reformers won some victories, but Kentucky schools did not reach the scale that Kendall wanted. In early 1820, relief forces successfully passed a law to use court fees to fund schools. Later in Adair's term, they used bank taxes to build a literary fund. Some support for currency expansion also came from a desire to create public schools.[89] This was still not enough. The notion that relief men favored common schools and antirelief men opposed them cropped up again in the 1823 gubernatorial campaign.[90] Likewise, Pennsylvania did not pass an effective education law until 1834. Panic-era politics did not transform any state's education system the way New York's had during the 1810s. Nevertheless, states that had made little progress before 1819 saw a change in the conversation about public schooling. The Panic had primed ordinary people to think about how the balance of political and economic power affected their lives. Men like Kendall leveraged this political-economic critique of elite power to build support for common schools.

The Second Party System and Moderates' Support for School Reform

The experience of the 1810s chastened conservative opponents of education reform. After overthrowing Federalists and fighting off the British, Americans began to envision public schools as necessary to fulfilling the nation's revolutionary promise. The Panic, too, made public schools appear both more pressing and less radical, when compared with redistributive economic reforms. In the coming decade, common school evangelists drummed up more support for universal primary education to create widespread informed citizenship. But unlike in the 1790s, education funding no longer seemed zero-sum. Even the most unrepentant democratic reformers recognized that universal common schools could not work without well-educated teachers. The most logical schools to train them were academies. This gave academy boosters an opening. They offered new forms of secondary and higher education that strengthened common school reform, rather than sitting in tension with it. But this also served their ends. Supplying teachers for the common schools legitimized the academies, maintained their currency in American life, and kept alive the possibility of rule by an educated aristocracy of merit. The ultimate outcome was that Northerners built a more unified education system, which was premised on equality at the bottom and opportunity at the top. Conservatives in the South felt less pressure to adapt, and there, aristocratic education held sway much longer and the sectional gulf in education grew.

Female academy teachers created the model that elite reformers later followed to transform secondary schools and colleges. In 1819, Emma Willard—an academy teacher in Vermont—sent a pamphlet to the New York legislature urging it to fund a women's college. Willard knew her audience. This school would not only help women, it would also benefit their sons, husbands, and brothers and "inevitably raise [the character] of the other sex." Currently, though, "female education has been left to the mercy of private adventurers"—in other words, "to chance." Willard drew on the growing spirit of reform, celebrating how "male education flourishes" thanks to "the guardian care of legislatures." Her plan deserved similar support. Like other reforms, Willard's would help the republic slough off "shackles of authority and precedent." Willard thus asked "patriotic countrymen" to support her and bring "national glory." Though the New York legislature denied her request, a group of Federalist men in Troy, New York, invited Willard to their city. The Troy Female Seminary opened in 1821 and served children of Republican and lingering Federalists alike.[91]

By the 1830s, teacher education became a primary argument for women's advanced education. Willard's school trained a generation of teachers who staffed common schools and academies throughout the North. Likewise, Catharine Beecher published pamphlets that used teacher training to justify state-funded female academies. Later, so too would powerful male education reformers like Horace Mann. In North Carolina, Susan Nye Hutchison petitioned the state to charter and support an academy to train women teachers.[92] During this period, the curriculum at female academies grew more advanced, to the level of many colleges. Hutchison was at the vanguard of bringing math and science into women's education. She even offered Latin. Other female academies in the North did too, though students seldom took advantage.[93]

Willard and her ilk deliberately oriented their students' minds, and American education, to the nation. Female academies were the proving ground for American history curriculum. Many academy teachers—including Willard and the pioneering women's educator, Sarah Pierce of Litchfield, Connecticut—wrote history textbooks. Compared with earlier editions, Willard's sought to produce *national* history.[94] Geographic knowledge was another key part of nation making. Jedidiah Morse published the first American geographies in the republic's earliest years. He believed Americans should learn about their country from domestic, not British, sources. But Americans long remained dependent on European books and apparatus for this work.[95] Graphic literacy was part of early female academies, though students tended to make local or world maps. Willard pioneered a curriculum of map drawing that focused on the full United States and spread this curriculum through her network of educators. Maps produced by women students made the nationalistic potential of education tangible in new ways.[96]

In time, male and coeducational academies throughout the North reinvented themselves in similar ways. They broadened access to the schools, tailored a republican curriculum, and trained teachers for common schools. This was all new. Prior to around 1820, education politics tended to pit common schools against academies. For example, New York's 1812 common school law did not address academies, even though it implicitly depended on them to train teachers. The regents fought this. Teacher training threatened to change academy culture and curriculum, since teachers did not need a classical education. In 1817, the regents doubled down and tied funding to enrollment in classics.[97] Other academy supporters realized that compromise would better serve academies. Academy curriculum had remained static during the regents' first four decades. By one count, New York academies offered a total of twenty-three subjects before 1825. Then academies collectively introduced one hundred more in the subsequent fifteen years. The year 1825 alone saw eleven new subjects, most of which were of interest to middle-class students: from Spanish and German, to branches of math and science such as algebra, chemistry, trigonometry, and logarithms. If bottom-up demand drove much of this change, legislative action made it possible. In 1827, the legislature bucked the regents, increased the literature fund, and connected disbursements to enrollment in a teacher preparation track. Finally, in 1834, the board bowed to pressure and offered a system explicitly for teacher training.[98]

In New York, erstwhile Federalists and longtime regents worked to democratize the state's academies. Simeon De Witt was an important transitional figure. He joined the regents in 1798, during the height of Federalism, and was chancellor in 1834, when the board adopted a plan for teacher training. Following De Witt's death, the manor lord, Stephen Van Rensselaer, succeeded him and implemented the new plan. This suited Rensselaer, who in 1825 had served on a committee that urged the regents to promote schooling that better fit "the situation and condition of our country."[99] The rise of common schools had impelled them to act. They also found that reform could give new life to academies by increasing demand, which served their project of building a republic governed ostensibly by men of merit.

Beyond New York, the need for teachers led common school advocates to try and democratize academies, rather than eliminate them. The Kentucky relief and public school advocate, Robert M'Afee, called academies "nurseries of the Teachers of the *primary schools*." Virgil Maxcy's plan to use western lands for schools would have funded academies because any "policy which destroys [them] . . . is fatal to the primary schools."[100] The Virginian Charles Fenton Mercer advocated granting scholarships to poor students to attend academies. They would then "supply the want of competent teachers in the schools of primary or elementary instruction." John Maclean similarly argued to make "provision for the education of teachers" in his proposal for a common school system in New Jersey.[101]

As common schooling grew more prevalent and academies democratized to train teachers, demand for secondary education rose.[102] To keep up, the New York legislature began to charter academies independent of the regents.[103] Between 1820 and 1839, ninety-six academies received charters from the state legislature. The board of regents chartered only fourteen in that span.[104] New York went from having one academy for just over every 30,000 people in 1800 to one for just under every 20,000 free people in 1850. In New England, Academies became even more accessible. By 1830, the free population served by each academy was a third of what it had been in 1800.[105] The best aggregate national data on attendance come from the 1850 census. In chunks of the North and Midwest, around 15 percent of white children received some secondary schooling. That rate may have reached as high as 50 percent in academy towns.[106]

On the one hand, these rates pale in comparison to common school attendance in free states, which may have hit 80 percent. In Massachusetts, there were fourteen students enrolled in public school for each one attending an academy. On the other hand, secondary school attendance rates would not climb demonstrably higher until the early twentieth century.[107] Academies increasingly served the growing middle class, infused communities with capital, and gave children a path "beyond the farm." They were no longer criticized as "bastions of prestige" with near the frequency of the late eighteenth century.[108] This transformation flowed from the challenge to aristocratic education.[109]

Finally, the rise of public school reform led to new proposals for higher education. Agricultural colleges first became a popular idea in the period. The schools promised to fulfill the needs of the nation in the wake of the War of 1812 and Panic of 1819. They offered new forms of higher education that also promised to improve the domestic economy. The idea for agricultural schools grew out of the fertile ground of county fairs, begun in Pittsfield, Massachusetts by the entrepreneurial Federalist-turned-Republican Elkanah Watson. Fairs awarded premiums to men for raising exceptional livestock, and smaller rewards to women for domestic manufactures. The county fair movement spread through a growing scientific agricultural press and inspired emergent agricultural societies across the North. These were a key vector of middle-class formation, which also diffused faith in education.[110]

In New York, the same regents who reformed academies became the biggest boosters of agricultural colleges. Simeon De Witt published the most important early pamphlet on the subject in 1819. De Witt bemoaned that "thousands of wealthy citizens in this state who do not know what to do with their sons" ultimately decided, "without any determinate object in view," to "give them a liberal education." This was a "ridiculous notion of merit!" De Witt clearly drew on the existing critique of aristocratic education. It was obvious that "men filling the professions, exclusively called *the literary*, have too great a preponderance in our political machinery." An "*esprit du corps*" among these literary elites "unavoidably" formed. Worse, their values "cannot be expected always to harmonize with the general interests of the community." Shades of the Anti-Federalist Melancton Smith came from the lips of a patrician reformer. In sum, when it came to education, Americans often "have been the mere copyists of foreign establishments." De Witt thought that "the happy peculiarities of our country require something different." Agricultural education could replace aristocratic education with a more American means of elite formation, yet still uphold a merit-based hierarchy. De Witt's proposal is indicative of how academy boosters hoped to use reform to maintain faith in, and make possible rule by, an aristocracy of merit.[111]

The first major attempt at an agricultural college also happened in New York. After De Witt failed to convince New York State to fund a college, the legislature created a state board of agriculture, which lasted only a few years. Amid these failures, Stephen Van Rensselaer founded what became Rensselaer Polytechnic Institute, just over the Berkshire Hills from Elkanah Watson's home. The school promoted agricultural and scientific knowledge. Bucktail Republicans criticized this as yet another elitist pursuit, an accusation that rang true to many New Yorkers. Not only was Rensselaer a former Federalist, he was also one of the last true manor lords in the United States. New York's archaic patroon system did not die until he did, in 1839. Yet patrician backgrounds did not stop these men from laying the groundwork for reform. Decades later, in the Republican Party's hands, agricultural colleges became a democratic tool.[112]

The Morrill Land Grant Act of 1862, which created public agricultural colleges, also owed something to the earliest private military schools.[113] As much as anyone, Alden Partridge reclaimed the "academy" moniker for a republican people. Vermont born and Dartmouth educated, Partridge was an early graduate of West Point. He served in the Army Corps of Engineers and then as a professor and superintendent of his alma mater. A dispute there led not only to his ouster, but to his resignation from the army. In 1819, Partridge returned to his hometown of Norwich, Vermont, and founded the American Literary, Scientific, and Military Academy, which evolved into Norwich University. Partridge added to the critique of secondary education already on offer. In the brief justifying his new "system" of education, Partridge decried the "anti-republican and monastic" schools that dominated the country. He took special aim at West Point, declaring "there is not on the whole globe an establishment more monarchical, corrupt, and corrupting."[114] Though Partridge was a Democrat, his emphasis on training citizen-soldiers with a mix of practical and liberal education reappeared in the language of the Republican Party's Morrill Act. Partridge also spawned a network of private military academies across the United States. They were for the South what agricultural colleges were for the North: a bedrock of the middle class.[115]

More radical circles of the commercial-rural North turned to manual-labor education, in which students worked to pay for their tuition, room, and board. The hope was that the schools would broaden access to liberal education while also modifying it to better suit American life. Nevertheless, manual-labor schools faced opposition. The Genesee Wesleyan Seminary in Lima, New York, which eventually became Syracuse University, was founded on the model. Local workers saw it as an economic threat, and quickly scuttled the plan. The idea also had a revolutionary edge. Abolitionists experimented with integrated education at manual-labor schools, including both New York's Oneida Institute and Ohio's Oberlin College.[116]

Eventually, post-1819 reforms made it to places where earlier reforms had not. This included two of the most obstinately pro-academy states: New Jersey and North Carolina. If academy-style voluntarism laid the groundwork for common schooling, we would expect New Jersey—which built the most academies per capita—to have led the way.[117] Instead, it took a new commitment to state intervention to build public schools. New Jersey sent banking revenues to its school fund starting in 1817, and then passed laws to protect this money between 1819 and 1828. This happened against the wishes of many academy boosters.[118]

But as was the case elsewhere, reform flourished when academy advocates realized it was necessary. The College of New Jersey was a Federalist bastion and an incubator of academies, yet, it led reform efforts. During the late 1820s, the college hosted lectures on public schools by Charles Fenton Mercer and math professor John Maclean. Mercer proposed "a system of popular education adapted to a political community wherein no privileged orders exist." As monarchies provided education to the sovereign king and the hereditary aristocracy, Americans needed to provide it to the sovereign people. Mercer particularly admired how New England common schools abolished "the odious distinction between the children of the opulent and of the poor." He tried to reason with the well-to-do: New Jersey could educate "all the youth" for less than what rich parents collectively paid for schooling.[119] Maclean made virtually the same argument, that rich parents could educate their children for a shilling on the dollar. In a universal system, he hoped the state could disperse aid based on need, which made sense when the goal "is to put all on more of an equality." Maclean wanted to hand off control to a superintendent and board of education.[120] Both men thought academies were still necessary to train teachers.

The Panic of 1819 ruined Archibald Murphey, but it gave new life to his vision for public schools in North Carolina.[121] Joseph Gales picked up the mantle. The English-born Paineite radical arrived in Raleigh in 1799 by way of Philadelphia. In his early life, Gales melded a rejection of hereditary aristocracy with support for public pensions, wealth redistribution, and the pursuit of universal reason through universal education. In Raleigh, though, he joined up with a set of middle-class reformers. They positioned themselves between Federalists, who seemed backwardly aristocratic, and radical "jacobinite" Republicans. The Moderates focused on expanding opportunity: creating meritocracy. Gales worked with the Federalists to protect the University of North Carolina and helped found the Raleigh Academy in 1801. At first, this was a standard academy. By the 1810s, though, Gales had tried make it more accessible and attached to it a preparatory school. But parents of tuition-paying academy students revolted against sending their children to school with poorer children. The Raleigh Academy closed by 1828. As a printer, Gales continued to advocate for common schooling. He looked now to public solutions, and through his writings helped make that idea seem moderate. North Carolina created a school fund in 1825 and laid out a school system in 1839, with bipartisan support. But the Whig Party—which united former Moderate Republicans and Federalists—won centralized oversight of public schools.[122]

The pattern of Whigs pushing for centralization held true in places with stronger traditions of public schooling. In Massachusetts and Connecticut, respectively, Whigs appointed Horace Mann and Henry Barnard as the superintendent of schools to create top-down oversight. The 1830s common school reformers differed from the Federalists, who saw schools as a tool to socially reproduce themselves. They also went beyond earlier Jeffersonian reformers in arguing that it was not enough to spread the capacity for citizenship. Rather, schools should help children build a sense of self and unleash their imaginations. In sum, elite reformers like Mann and William Ellery Channing envisioned a system with widespread access to both primary and secondary education. This would help children build their selves, and it would improve meritocracy by ensuring equal opportunity.[123]

Over time, centralizing reformers came to believe that academies—no matter how democratized—were incompatible with their vision. Much as academies changed, it took voluntary associations to build them in the first place. That limited their reach and made it impossible for states to guarantee universal access. In 1853, the New Yorkers threw up their hands and passed the Union Free School Act, which created a legal basis for public secondary schools. Common school districts could form a union—hence the name—to create "academic" or secondary departments. Alternately, localities could take over private academies, fund them through taxes, and govern them democratically. New York strengthened the system in 1864 by eliminating rate bills. These new democratically controlled public high schools still operated under the regents' control.[124]

If the rise of high schools in New York was instructive, their emergence in Massachusetts was more formative. In 1827, the Bay State became the first to require larger towns to build high schools. By 1860, Massachusetts had 167 high schools; New York had the second most, with 76. Elsewhere, their presence was more haphazard, though every Northern state had at least one high school before the Civil War.[125] In some communities, secondary school attendance shot up as soon as a high school opened. More often, liberal education remained a tough sell. Some viewed high schools as a clever tool for the elite to shift the cost of secondary education from their own pockets to the broader tax base.[126] Yet high schools differed from academies, which drew together the elite from across a region.[127] What defined academy attendance was not curriculum or pedagogy—they taught students of all levels—but class. High schools, though, organized students by age and educational progress, which undermined socioeconomic segregation.[128]

Education politics had shifted dramatically by the 1820s. No longer did partisan politics pit universal common education and academies against one another. To be sure, the radical position—support for equal education, and opposition to schooling for a meritocratic aristocracy—stayed alive with laborers in the Workingmen's Party and the Locofoco Democrats. Most democratic reformers, though, realized that universal access to common schooling (in the North) to train a widely informed citizenry depended on secondary schools that taught teachers. The Whigs picked up the Moderate vision for a merit-based social order, which still celebrated advanced education. But they realized that the legitimacy of merit-based hierarchy rested on universal elementary education. The two reform visions had become codependent, which took reform beyond the democratic Jeffersonian educational vision of universal common schools. Advanced, liberal education for all now seemed like a feasible goal.[129] Nothing captured this turnabout from "aristocratic education" better than the reactions of European visitors, who marveled at how Northern schools fostered equality among white men.[130]

Taken together, "the first era of school reform" in the North prefigured a system of American education that sounds strikingly modern. The shift to state-funded elementary education made universal access a goal. Attempts to democratize secondary education helped drive the rise of public high schools. Finally, agricultural colleges anticipated the fusion of liberal and "practical" education in land-grant colleges. These diverse proposals all stemmed from a shared distaste with the prevailing aristocratic model, which privileged elite education above all else. On the one hand, these reforms made possible equal citizenship among white men. On the other, the revolution in access to schools entrenched the ideal of meritocracy even further. It now seemed plausible to more Americans that academic achievement might actually reveal who was best suited to lead. This preserved the notion that there was a legitimate basis for inequality in a republic.[131] That government had created this possibility unleashed among some Jacksonians a new form of antistatist sentiment, shrouded in the language of democracy.[132] Still more Northern Democrats came to accept public schooling even as they continued to oppose other internal improvements from the Whigs.[133]

By contrast, the South fought reform and maintained an essentially aristocratic social and educational system. Maryland, Virginia, South Carolina, and Georgia all failed to provide free schools to its citizens before the Civil War. This was true across most of the cotton South, too. These states were hardly incapable of mobilizing state power: They developed transportation and other infrastructure that served the plantation economy. State governments used enslaved labor to realize these goals. When it came to moral and cultural improvements, like public education, slavery was an obstacle. Sometimes, limited school funds went to pauper schools. But many families opted to forego that opportunity, and the surplus funded elite academies. Deep Southern states programmatically denied poor whites access to education as part of the logic of maintaining slavery. An educated citizenry was dangerous. At a more practical level, to expand public schools, northern states had empowered local publics to build this common good. This drew on vast stores of communal social capital that was comparatively lacking in the South, where enslaved people vastly outnumbered citizens in many communities.[134]

Race, Gender, and the First Era of School Reform

If Northern education reform looked remarkable when compared with Europe or the American South, it still had its limits. To some extent, those limits were set by the very fight reformers waged. By imagining universal education in opposition to aristocratic education, they framed reform around the problem of class and privilege in a republic. Their critique did not fundamentally extend to inequalities of race and gender. Only the most radical abolitionists and utopian communitarians thought of universality in racially and gender-inclusive ways.[135] Mainstream reformers, then, may have had blinders similar to those of most Americans. But by casting education as universal, and then still denying it to some people, reformers transformed education from a tool of hierarchy to an arbiter of inclusion and exclusion. There were now those who received public education and those who did not. For most white men, this strengthened their claims to civic belonging. But for other Americans—Indians, free and enslaved black men, women, and even non-Protestant white men—education often looked like a tool wielded by the powerful to disenfranchise the weak.

Reform had countervailing effects on white women. Driven out of formal politics during the Jacksonian era, academy-educated women undertook literary and moral campaigns to improve the nation. They sparked public controversies over religious issues like Sabbatarianism, and also more obviously political matters. Their petitions against Indian removal and the spread of slavery thrust these issues into public debate, often against the wishes of leading politicians. There is a striking correlation between female academy curriculum and the ways educated women exercised public influence during the nineteenth century. Women reformers framed all of their advocacy as for the good of the nation, which their teachers had taught them was their duty to guard. Moreover, they often spoke through men. Congressmen read women's petitions just as male teachers had read student compositions at female academy exhibitions. This political ventriloquism kept alive antislavery sentiment in Congress over Southern objections. Women also used morally persuasive writing, which they learned at academies, to effect political change. Harriet Beecher Stowe's *Uncle Tom's Cabin* arguably did more to ready the antebellum North for a long war to end slavery than any other event. Yet women's power rested on adopting a distinct and subordinate role in public life.[136]

Schools were central to the United States' "Indian Civilization" program. The idea was fairly simple: Americans wanted Indian lands, but military conquest was expensive. Instead, Americans incentivized Indians to adopt European agriculture. They hoped that this would erode Indian cultural autonomy and lead to assimilation. During the 1790s, the federal war department directly encouraged agricultural education for Indians. In the coming decades, they used missionaries, especially Quakers, as a proxy to do the same. At the same time, the federal government erected a series of "factories"—trading posts—to monopolize the Indian trade in the Ohio Valley and trans-Mississippi West. They hoped that making Indians into trade partners would incorporate them into the American economy, and thus American notions of law and property. After the Panic of 1819, though, commerce no longer seemed like the best school of civility. That year, Congress opted instead to pursue civilization though education. They created a "civilization fund," which put $10,000 a year toward Indian schools. The federal government did not give Western lands to Eastern whites to fund education—as Virgil Maxcy of Maryland had proposed. But they supported Indian education to hasten the conquest of more western land.[137]

As citizens of sovereign nations, most Indians preferred to educate themselves. Historian Christina Snyder shows that Choctaws ultimately built one of the most comprehensive school systems of the 1840s. Choctaw public education far outstripped what their colonizers managed to build back in Kentucky. Well before even most northern states eliminated rate bills, the Choctaw offered free common schooling to their youth. Choctaw educators often helped other Native nations establish schools, while some contracted out the work to missionary groups. Before their removal, Choctaw leaders had attended Choctaw Academy—a federally funded school run by Richard Mentor Johnson, who became Martin Van Buren's vice president.[138]

In a very different setting—the urban Northeast—Catholics balked at the assimilationist goals of the public schools. Reformers' Protestant values ostracized the Catholics who arrived in droves in the decades prior to the Civil War. Catholics found ways to educate their children, and they only grew better at forging compromises with Protestants in the postbellum years.[139] It mattered, though, that Catholic children often went to school outside the public system that reformers worked hard to connect to the body politic. Did that mean that Catholics had a different relationship to the nation from Protestants? Did this diminish their citizenship claims?[140]

When it came to Indians and Catholics, education was a tool of subjugation through assimilation. The challenge for policy makers was that these marginalized groups did not want to attend the schools that policy makers endorsed. When it came to free black men, the opposite was true. Dating back to the era of gradual abolition (1780–1804), antislavery activists looked to schooling to help integrate free blacks into Northern society. Under Federalist-dominated aristocratic education, schools reinforced African Americans' subordination. But that was true also of ordinary white Americans; the education of both groups differed from that of elite whites by degree. In some sense this made inclusion through education seem feasible.[141]

As education became more equal in the nineteenth century, it transformed into a foundation of *equal* citizenship for ordinary white men. Jefferson, among others, predicted that white prejudice would overwhelm commitments to black uplift through education when it portended equal citizenship.[142] That is precisely what happened. In the 1820s and 1830s, a growing portion of white Americans objected to the very presence of free blacks in northern society. Facing rising northern white support for colonization—the removal of free black Americans to Africa—black activists made the case for citizenship and, relatedly, equal and sometimes integrated education. The first black newspaper, the *Colored American*, began publication in New York City in the 1820s. It emphasized education above all else. Other northern cities with large free black communities began sounding similar notes, nowhere more clearly than in the Colored Conventions of the 1830s. These meetings put a premium on civil or moral uplift, especially through schooling.[143]

Many white education reformers paid this black activism little mind. Worse, a grassroots movement to curtail black schooling grew in tandem among whites, and it was often violent. Most famously, in 1834, Prudence Crandall's High School for Young Colored Ladies and Misses shuttered in the face of threats, harassment, and violence. Popular pressures led to laws that made the school illegal. In litigation over the case, Connecticut courts questioned the possibility of black citizenship. Between the 1830s and 1850s, Delaware, New Jersey, Connecticut, Ohio, Pennsylvania, Indiana, Illinois, and New York all condoned or required school segregation. This was part of a concerted effort to deny black men the rights and privileges of citizenship.[144] The 1840 census was the first to include school attendance and literacy statistics. It collected that data for whites, but ignored free and enslaved blacks, as if to wish away their educational achievements.[145]

White backlash, no doubt, also responded to the rise of radical abolition, which had connections with black education. Many children who attended the New York African Free School grew up to become leading abolitionists. The networks they formed at school provided a foundation for collective action.[146] African American students—including some young women from Crandall's school—wrote essays that challenged escalating white racism in the North.[147] Schools, in short, were sites of black political mobilization. Black men and women tested their political mettle during the 1830s and 1840s through fights over access to schools.[148]

Black citizenship and schooling became the central problem of the American future. The Reconstruction amendments guaranteed citizenship and civil rights to black Americans, and congressional Republicans imposed public schooling on the South.[149] Congress understood that law can only do so much. It ostensibly guarantees the privileges and immunities of citizenship. Yet the reality of equal citizenship requires more than parchment. It depends on the uniform enforcement of laws, which is shaped by politics. Participation matters. Beyond voting and serving on juries, people need a voice in the public sphere to protect their rights. Education was and is the arbiter of access to that critical arena of persuasion.

The potency of educational exclusions, then, make clear how the first era of school reform had reframed Americans' understandings of education. Academy advocates had long felt free to ignore questions about the education of marginalized groups because they had never made universal access or equity a priority. But the first era of school reform made equal citizenship a rhetorical goal. Access to schools that teach the skills of citizenship and give people a public voice had become essential for those trying to protect their equality before the law.

Epilogue
The Legacy of Aristocratic Education

"Academy" is the 510th most common road name in the United States. Over 1,000 roads bear the name, only around 30 fewer than are named "university." Both fall well short of the 2,500-plus "school" streets.[1] Why a street is named "school" or "university" is usually obvious to even the most oblivious jogger or dog walker, but not so for academy streets. Most are no longer home to academies, though some academy buildings have survived. Erasmus Hall Academy in Brooklyn, for example, became Erasmus Hall High School, and the original building from 1786 still stands on the grounds. In addition to academies-turned-high schools, it is not unusual to find town offices, public libraries, and historical societies occupying former academy buildings.[2] Walking along an academy street or setting foot in a repurposed academy testifies to their once prominent place on the landscape. These traces also show how academies became a relic of the past, to which most Americans need pay no mind. The obfuscation of the academies' legacy has more devastating consequences when it comes to education policy than to local history.

Academies emerged in the United States, not to instill republican self-government, but rather to train an elite to govern nominally unruly populations. At first, this was a religious imperative. Feeling their hold over a growing population weaken, denominations turned to schools to train ministers who would again command the respect of ordinary people and thereby strengthen church authority. Facing a similar challenge to its authority, the British Empire encouraged these developments, hoping academies might produce a class of colonists that would help sustain British rule. This backfired on the British Empire but shaped the future of their former colonies. Ambitious and educated colonists helped bring about the American Revolution, but they never relinquished an understanding of education as a means to bolster elite authority over ordinary people—as essentially a tool of aristocracy. The displacement of aristocratic education took decades of work and was bound up in the dramatic political changes of the early nineteenth century. The reformers' victory reified the notion that education is an agent of republican self-government and made aristocratic education seem aberrant.

The academies that survive from the aristocratic era are those that best embodied their original ethos—Philips Andover and Exeter, for instance—and still fit uncomfortably in American life. As they have for over two hundred years, these tony prep schools feed children of means into Ivy League colleges and the halls of power. Access to this meritocracy does not come cheap: Tuition at Andover and Exeter runs over $55,000, similar to the median family income in the United States.[3] These schools lay bare the persistence of informal hereditary privilege in the age of liberal democracy. Yet that contradiction is less contentious now than at the turn of the nineteenth century because, unlike in 1800, only a small proportion of secondary education happens in these schools. On top of this, these two schools are now rich enough to have need-blind admissions.

Moreover, we think of places like Andover and Exeter as private schools, not public schools. This owes to the work of early reformers. At their founding, these academies received public charters and public support and claimed to serve the public interest. Reformers who challenged aristocratic education had to make the case that, because they did not serve all the people—however narrowly defined—academies were private institutions that worked for private ends. In forgetting how we came to view these schools as private in the first place, we have lost sight of how aristocratic education drew strength by blurring public-private distinctions. Our Manichean understanding of aristocratic schools as always private has created an opening for reactionary groups to further inequality by claiming the schools they support are public in some way.

In fact, the chartered academy itself has lived on in pernicious ways. They reappeared as segregation academies soon after *Brown v. Board of Education* made intentional school segregation illegal. Like nineteenth-century academies, these private schools depended on public sanction and support. Southern states provided tax exemptions and tuition grants to white students so they could afford to attend. Subsidies to segregation academies siphoned resources from the public school systems that still served black residents. Segregation academies reconstituted the separate and unequal systems that *Brown* ostensibly overturned. Cleverly, though, proponents couched their support for these schools in rhetoric about choice, freedom, and religious liberty.[4]

That language reappeared when this book was written, during what might be called "the second age of academies." Since the early 1990s, "charter schools" have emerged as the most prominent wing of a growing movement to privatize education and bring corporate-style "accountability" to schools. Self-consciously or not, many modern charter schools call themselves academies. In a variety of ways, they have worsened socioeconomic and racial segregation. In parts of the South, middle-class whites have turned to charters to avoid integrated schools and preserve their privilege. In the Charlotte-Mecklenburg Schools in North Carolina, charters helped undo three decades of progress that followed a 1971 desegregation busing order, which had made the district an integration success story.[5] More often, modern chartered academies serve a different population. Throughout much of the North, children of color attend charter schools and advocates promote them as an alternative to struggling urban school systems. Meanwhile, most of the white upper-middle class receives its education in socioeconomically segregated suburban public schools, where chartered alternatives seem unnecessary.[6]

No doubt, most modern charter schools differ from early national academies in not educating the elite. Yet defenders of public education make similar arguments against modern charter schools as earlier reformers did against academies. Charters, they say, give unelected and unaccountable elites profound power over education policy. Wealthy Americans are often the driving force behind modern charter schools. The schools reflect a perennial elite impulse to organize education by class, which protects existing privilege.[7]

Integration depends on making a more unified school system; charters undercut that. By focusing attention on charter schools that claim to offer opportunity to children of color, well-to-do northern whites shifted the focus away from how existing school inequality benefits them. As debates rage in states and cities over whether to expand caps on the number of charter schools, to increase funding, or to increase oversight, systemic policy proposals like integration fade from view. This allows lilywhite, upper-middle-class suburbs with high property taxes to continue to hoard resources and curtail access to so-called good public schools. While charter schools might appear opposite to places like Andover—or segregation academies—they work in similar ways to prop up an unequal and divided system, even if they did not create it.

The very sort of institution that public schooling was designed to overthrow, then, is now heralded as a solution to reform public education. Every recent president has called education the civil rights issue of our time. Each has also supported expanding educational choice, especially through charter schools. Might knowing the history of academies temper the modern reformers' hubris? Might it lead them to ask why, if chartered academies have *never* served equality and democracy, they think they now will? And might it force reformers to confront the fact that any semblance of equal and common education is fast disappearing from the United States?

The return of chartered K–12 schools is part and parcel of a broader retreat from education as a shared and equalizing civic experience. Steadily, schools have racially resegregated.[8] Even in white communities, the division between the haves and have-nots has grown.[9] Nor has the expansion of higher education corrected for all that has gone wrong at the K–12 level. The degree to which college offers upward mobility is limited and declining at a moment when a bachelor's degree is at its most valuable. A precious few public institutions—namely, the University of California and the City University of New York systems—still regularly open up opportunity for underprivileged students. But austere state governments have slowly decimated them with budget cuts.[10] The word meritocracy came into use in 1958 and seemed to signal the hard-won emergence of an egalitarian social order. Under the meritocrats' watch, American education has once again become a tool of the privileged.[11]

The story of early American academies offers no easy lessons for the present. But the rise and fall of aristocratic education reminds us of the necessity of educational equity to life in a democratic republic. The founding generation saw how faith in education deteriorated when Americans thought it was a tool of the elite to secure their power. Given the importance of education to democratic citizenship, this threatened also to erode self-government itself. Blinkered as the first era of school reform was, at least its avowed goal was undermining a system of education that reproduced status. Nineteenth-century reformers offered a powerful, if imperfect, solution. They attempted to make democratic forms of liberal education accessible to all citizens. To do this, they advocated for children of different economic backgrounds to attend school together because they believed that education would be best if the whole community invested in the same institutions. Their vision is enduring yet unfulfilled. So too is the revolutionary promise of government by an informed and equal citizenry.

Appendix

TABLE A.1 Number of academies founded from the Revolution to 1800

State	No. of Academies Founded by 1800	1800 Free Population	Free Population/ Academy
New Hampshire	8	183,850	22,981
Massachusetts (+ Maine)	20	574,564	28,728
Vermont	2	154,465	77,232
Connecticut	4	250,051	62,513
Rhode Island	1	68,742	68,742
New York	26	565,437	21,748
New Jersey	20	198,727	9,936
Pennsylvania	20	600,839	30,042
Delaware	4	58,120	14,530
Maryland	10	215,383	21,538
Virginia	26	534,404	20,554
North Carolina	24	344,807	14,367
South Carolina	3	199,440	66,480
Georgia	7	102,987	14,712
Total	175	4,051,816	23,153

The data in this table derive from a few sources. To identify New England academies, I relied on a remarkable dissertation: Richard Gerry Durnin, "New England's Eighteenth-Century Incorporated Academies: Their Origin and Development to 1850" (Ph.D. Diss., University of Pennsylvania, 1968). Durnin's appendix G contains the founding and incorporation dates for pre-1800 New England academies. I follow Durnin in differentiating Vermont's "academies" from its county grammar schools; I include the former, but not the latter. The only addition I made to his list was of one academy, chartered in Rhode Island in 1800, identified in *Charter of the North-Kingstown Academy. State of Rhode-Island, &c. In General Assembly, June session, A.D. 1800*, Evans no. 38383. The "data sheets" on each academy in Durnin's appendix H contain valuable information on the organization, curriculum, and teachers at each school. It also transcribes the lists of founding trustees from each academy's original articles of incorporation. My interpretation of the partisan backdrop of academies rests on these lists.

I identified academies in the mid-Atlantic and the South using both newspapers and governmental records. State session laws—and in New York, the *Journal of Meetings, Minutes of the Board of Regents of the University of New York*, volume 1, which I obtained on microfilm from the New York State Archives in Albany—allowed me to identify charters issued to academies. Especially in the mid-Atlantic, many academies did not incorporate.

In 1794, New Jersey passed a law that allowed academies to incorporate without a special act by the legislature, so they cannot be traced through session laws. Newspaper advertisements helped me to fill in the blanks. To differentiate academies that resembled chartered academies from the various proprietary schools that adopted the moniker, I include in this list only schools that I could determine had officers or a governing board. Usually, that became clear when various officers or board members signed advertisements or, better yet, when a newspaper printed a notice of an upcoming trustees meeting.

Notes

Abbreviations in Notes

INSTITUTIONS

AAS	American Antiquarian Society, Worcester, Mass.
DLAR	David Library of the American Revolution, Washington Crossing, Pa.
HSP	Historical Society of Pennsylvania, Philadelphia, Pa.
LCP	Library Company of Philadelphia, Philadelphia, Pa.
LVA	Library of Virginia, Richmond, Va.
MdHS	Maryland Historical Society, Baltimore, Md.
MHS	Massachusetts Historical Society, Boston, Mass.
MSA	Maryland State Archives, Annapolis, Md.
NCDAH	North Carolina Department of Archives and History, Raleigh, N.C.
NJHC	North Jersey History & Genealogy Center, Morristown Public Library, Morristown, N.J.
N-JHS	New-Jersey Historical Society, Newark, N.J.
N-YHS	New-York Historical Society, New York, N.Y.
NYPL	New York Public Library, New York, N.Y.
NYSA	New York State Archives, Albany, N.Y.
PHS	Presbyterian Historical Society, Philadelphia, Pa.
PUL	Manuscripts Division, Department of Rare Books and Special Collections, Princeton University Library, Princeton, N.J.
RUL	Alexander Library, Rutgers University, New Brunswick, N.J.
SOC	Society of the Cincinnati Library, Anderson House, Washington, D.C.
TFL	Trentoniana Department, Trenton Free Public Library, Trenton, N.J.
UD Archives	University Archives, University of Delaware, Newark, Del.
UPenn	Rare Book and Manuscript Library, University of Pennsylvania, Philadelphia, Pa.
VHS	Virginia Historical Society, Richmond, Va.

COLLECTIONS AND PUBLICATIONS

CSP	*Calendar of State Papers, Colonial Series*. 45 vols. London, 1860–1994.
DHRC	Merrill Jensen, John P. Kaminski, et al., eds., *The Documentary History of the Ratification of the Constitution*. Madison, Wis., 1976–.
KYSJ	*Journal of the Senate of the Commonwealth of Kentucky*. Published with various titles.
MA	*Resolves of the General Court of the Commonwealth of Massachusetts*. Published with various titles.

NJ Assembly Journal	*Votes and Proceedings of the General Assembly of the State of New-Jersey*. Published with various titles.
NJ Council Proceedings	*Journal of Proceedings of the Legislative Council of the State of New-Jersey*. Published with various titles.
NJ Laws	*Acts of the General Assembly of the State of New Jersey*. Published with various titles.
NNV	A New Nation Votes: American Election Returns, https://elections.lib.tufts.edu.
NYAJ	*New York Assembly Journal*. Published with various titles.
NYSBR	Journal of Meetings Minutes, Board of Regents of University of New York, reel 1, New York State Archives.
NYSJ	*New York Senate Journal*. Published with various titles.
NYS	*Laws of the State of New York*. Published with various titles.
VT Assembly Journal	*A Journal of the Proceedings of the General Assembly of the State of Vermont*. Published with various titles.

Introduction

1. The best history of this ideal is Brown, *Strength of a People*.

2. My approach follows women's and gender historians of female academies. Female academy founders designed the schools to shape conceptions of society and governance as well as individuals' relationship to the state, which made them an important site of contestation over civic belonging. No book informed my approach more than Kelley, *Learning to Stand & Speak*. Also see Nash, *Women's Education*; and McMahon, *Mere Equals*. On the way in which voluntary associations and public institutions, rather than just the law, shaped membership in the body politic, see Brooke, *Columbia Rising*; and Novak, "Legal Transformation." On cultural and literary foundations of citizenship, see Hyde, *Civic Longing*, esp. 6–9; and Kaplan, *Men of Letters*. For a contemporary claim that education conferred citizenship, see Yates, *Rights of Colored Men*, 1–15. For state governments and citizenship, see Bradburn, *Citizenship Revolution*.

3. They were Vermont, North Carolina, Pennsylvania, Georgia, and Massachusetts.

4. Webster, "On the Education of Youth in America," in Rudolph, *Essays on Education*, 66, 46 (italics mine). Between 1780 and 1800, over 5 percent of all charters issued by the Massachusetts legislature went to academies. A similar pattern holds true in the South, which was much more reticent to issue charters. In South Carolina, between the Revolution and 1835, academies or seminaries and colleges accounted for nearly 15 percent of charters of incorporation, second only to churches. Incorporation statistics for Massachusetts come from Kaufman, "Corporate Law." For other states, see Bloch and Lamoreaux, "Voluntary Associations."

5. As the historian Lawrence Cremin wrote: "no theme was so universally articulated during the early decades of the Republic as the need for self-governing people for *universal* education." See Cremin, *National Experience*, 203. Likewise, historian Richard D. Brown has written that American educators tried to "create an institutional environment in America that would nurture republican citizens"; Brown, *Strength of a People*, 72–73. Gordon Wood calls the outpouring of writing about education, "unprecedented"; see *Empire of Liberty*, 471. The question historians have grappled with was whether the push for public education

aimed at liberation or social control. See Tyack, "Forming the National"; Kaestle, *Pillars*; Rush, *Essays, Literary*, i–xxxi; Pangle and Pangle, *Learning of Liberty*; Cleves, *Reign of Terror*, 194–229; many of the essays in Justice, *Founding Fathers*; and Cutterham, *Gentlemen Revolutionaries*, 37–65. For a critique of the focus on early national education pamphlets, see Moroney, "Birth of a Canon."

6. Yokota, *Unbecoming British*.

7. Here I push against the notion that academies were born of a narrow outlook. George Thomas argues that academies and colleges in the early republic "were parochial state institutions with clear sectarian affiliations unlikely to promote the nationalizing and liberalizing sentiments deemed instrumental in helping to secure and perpetuate the new constitutional order." See Thomas, *Founders and the Idea*, 6. Similarly, Nancy Beadie argues that outside of men who "had revolutionary military experience or belonged to a Masonic lodge," support for academies did not derive from political commitments. See, "Education, Social Capital," 30.

8. Main, "Government by the People"; Wood, *Creation of the American Republic*, 471–518; Holton, *Unruly Americans*; and Bouton, *Taming Democracy*.

9. Golove and Hulsebosch, "Civilized Nation." For "treaty-worthiness," see Gould, *Among the Powers*. My gloss on this literature is indebted to Cutterham, "International Dimension."

10. On the fiscal-military state, see Edling, *Revolution in Favor*.

11. Robertson, "'Look on This Picture'"; McConville, *King's Three Faces*, 313–16; Wood, *Empire of Liberty*, 53–94; and Breen, *George Washington's Journey*. My sense of monarchical survivals in American culture falls short of what Eric Nelson suggests in *Royalist Revolution*.

12. *Connecticut Courant*, November 20, 1786. For identification of this as Webster, see "Monarchical Tendencies in America," in *DHRC*, 13:169.

13. Quoted in Taylor, *American Revolutions*, 377–78.

14. "Americanus," *New-York Daily Advertiser*, August 1, 1787, in *DHRC*, 19:183. On the centrality of education to Federalist defenses of natural aristocracy, see Wood, *Creation*, 480, 492; Cornell, "Aristocracy Assailed," 1162; Cutterham, *Gentlemen Revolutionaries*, 3; Klarman, *Framers' Coup*, 8; Edling, *Revolution in Favor*, 26; and Wilzentz, *Rise of American Democracy*, 76, 100, 102.

15. On sieves, see Wood, *Creation of the American Republic*, 512–13, 614–15.

16. Opal, "Labors of Liberality," 1083–85, 1088, 1093–94.

17. Waldstreicher, *In the Midst*; and Travers, *Celebrating the Fourth*.

18. A new literature shows that the future Jacksonians would not accept this lying down and instead reinvented a martial and violent logic of national sovereignty opposed to social improvement. See Leonard, "Party as a Political Safeguard"; Brooke, "Patriarchal Magistrates"; and Opal, *Avenging the People*.

19. May, *Enlightenment in America*, pt. I. Similarly, Robert Wiebe describes a widespread commitment in this period to "gentry governance," a belief that the character of leaders was integral to the success of the nation-state. See *Opening of American Society*, esp. 1–125. Another conduit of these values was the culture of sensibility and sentimental literature, in which many academy students partook. See Knott, *Sensibility and the American Revolution*; and Kaplan, *Men of Letters*, esp. 42–86. On the colonial period, see Sloan, *Scottish Enlightenment*.

20. On the rise of legal formality within associations, see Butterfield, *Making of Tocqueville's America*, 12–38.

21. On the range of schools called academies in this period, see Beadie and Tolley, "School for Every Purpose"; and Tolley, "Mapping the Landscape."

22. My understanding of the politics of incorporation owes primarily to Maier, "Revolutionary Origins"; and Bloch and Lamoreaux, "Voluntary Associations."

23. William Novak is the historian most responsible for recovering the immense state power that shaped nineteenth-century life; see Novak, "Myth of the 'Weak.'" Yet Gautham Rao argues that "the nature of the relationship between Novak's strong state built upon the state police powers and the emerging strong federal state that worked through a more diverse set of actors and institutions remains unclear." See "William J. Novak's," 231. Likewise, Gary Gerstle notes in his recent synthesis of American governance that "few recent accounts of the 'American state' know what to do with the states." *Liberty and Coercion*, 55. Nevertheless, Kyle G. Volk suggests that "Gerstle's position that the federal and state governments were ideologically antagonistic for most of U.S. history necessarily places these entities in tension. Little space remains to consider the conduct of federalism: the ways that the federal and state governments worked as complementary parts of the whole." "Apply Liberalism Liberally," 56.

I hope this history of academies offers an example of what such an analysis might look like. My approach is inspired by scholars of European states, especially the English state. Michael Braddick, for instance, explains how English government in the seventeenth century "depended on the co-operation of unpaid local officials, and these local brokers of central authority acted as mediators between central government and the locality." See Braddick, "State Formation," 2; and Braddick, *State Formation*. On how a fluid boundary between the state and supporting institutions allows class interests to influence governance, see Jessop, *State Power*. My view of state formation as a broad process encompassing politics and culture comes from Brooke, Strauss, and Anderson, *State Formations*.

24. On cooperative federalism between levels of government, see Ablavsky, "Empire States." Also, see Balogh, *Government Out of Sight*; and Shankman, "Toward a Social History." A series of synthetic essays have sketched out how voluntary associations and state-chartered organizations acted as the building blocks of the American nation-state in the decades before the Civil War. See Brooke, "Cultures of Nationalism"; Neem, "Civil Society"; and Neem, "Taking Modernity's Wager." Most of this work focuses exclusively on the postrevolutionary period, while I draw connections back in time. For other works that cross the revolutionary divide, see Roney, *Governed by a Spirit*; and Moniz, *From Empire to Humanity*.

25. "On Learning"; and "On Literary Men and Colleges," both in Manning, *Key of Liberty*, 182, 174.

26. For a review of the literature on common schools, see Neem, "State of the Field."

27. Edling, *Hercules in the Cradle*; and Rao, *National Duties*.

28. On the paradox of Jeffersonians joining the most democratic and most proslavery Americans under one party head, see Riley, *Slavery and the Democratic*.

29. Main, *Political Parties*, 382–83; Appleby, *Capitalism and a New Social Order*, 47–48, 97; Murrin, "Great Inversion," 400; Young, *Democratic Republicans*, 51–54; Pasley, "*Tyranny of Printers*," 20–21; and for this transformation from the Federalist point of view, see

Koschnik, "Young Federalists." This view of the Jeffersonians even unites Gordon Wood and Alan Taylor, who are often described as representing opposite ends of the interpretive spectrum. Per Wood, Jeffersonians "challenge[d] the Federalist assumption that only well-to-do educated gentlemen were capable of exercising political authority." *Empire of Liberty*, 225–26. John Brooke suggests that "striving Republicans overwhelming rigidly hierarchical Federalists" is the central thread of Wood's interpretive project. "Trouble with Paradox," 556. For Taylor, see *American Revolutions*, 410–11; and Taylor, "From Fathers to Friends."

30. Discussion of the first party system is absent from most major work on early American education, even when the second party system figures into it. For example, see Kaestle, *Pillars of the Republic*, 37, 154–56; Beadie, *Education and the Creation*, 248–66. An exception is the long-embattled work of Cubberley, *Public Education*, esp. 108.

31. On the moderation of the Jeffersonian revolution, see Cotlar, *Tom Paine's America*, esp. 4–5, 11; Formisano, "Deferential-Participant Politics"; and Wiebe, *Opening of American Society*, xiii; and chapter 6 in this volume.

32. My understanding of pre–Civil War academies rests on a remarkable body of work by Kim Tolley and Nancy Beadie. Much of this casts academies as adaptable, middle-class institutions. See especially Tolley, "Rise of the Academies"; Beadie, "Academy Students." Also see Sizer, *Age of Academies*, 1–49; and Kett, *Rites of Passage*, 18–20, 126–30. I do not dispute their conclusions but rather show how the immediate postrevolutionary academies were distinct from what came later.

33. Huston, *American and British Debate*, ix–xiii; and Neem, *Democracy's Schools*, 5–30.

34. Some women founded academies—including incorporated academies—but "traces" of their stories are "rare," as Kim Tolley notes in *Heading South to Teach*, 5. Tolley's book is an exception, as is Brickley, "Sarah Pierce's Litchfield."

35. Thanks to Anelise Shrout for this observation.

36. This challenges Gordon Wood's argument that the revolutionary assault on aristocracy, such as it was in the United States, led directly to other forms of egalitarian change. See *Radicalism of the American Revolution*, 7–8.

37. Stewart, "Emergence of Racial Modernity"; and Polgar, "'To Raise Them to an Equal.'"

38. Demos, *Heathen School*; and Snyder, *Great Crossings*.

39. McMahon, *Mere Equals*, 18–41. Also see Rosemarie Zagarri's discussion of how the parties "thought with" women, especially Mary Wollstonecraft, in *Revolutionary Backlash*, 103–8.

40. Huston, *American and British Debate*, 91–96. See also the tables of school attendance and literacy in Vinovskis and Bernard, "Beyond Catharine Beecher."

41. Sklar, "Schooling of Girls"; Beadie, *Education and the Creation*, 154–67; and Archer, *Jim Crow North*, 10–12.

42. Moss, *Schooling Citizens*; Demos, *Heathen School*, 129–96; Guyatt, *Bind Us Apart*; and Snyder, *Great Crossings*, 12–14, 36–40, 272–96.

Chapter One

1. January 12, 1766; August 24, 1767; both in Trustee Minutes of the First Presbyterian Church, PHS, 7, 13–14.

2. Wood, *Radicalism of the American Revolution*, 21–22, 28, 38, 83–86; Beeman, *Varieties of Political Experience*, 8–30, and on New York manors, 95–126; and Brewer, "Entailing Aristocracy."

3. Wrightson, *English Society*, 191–93; and Stone, "Educational Revolution."

4. Cremin, *Colonial Experience*, 113–66; and Bailyn, *Education in the Forming*, 14–21.

5. "Extract from Minutes of Council of Virginia," *CSP*, item 1292, vol. 13 (1689–1692): 380.

6. Henry Hartwell and others to William Popple, *CSP*, item 1396, vol. 15 (1696–1697): 641–66.

7. Governor Seymour to the Council of Trade and Plantations, Maryland, *CSP*, item 410, vol. 24 (1709): 249–52.

8. Governor Johnston to the Council of Trade and Plantations, Edenton, NC, *CSP*, item 410, vol. 42 (1735–1736): 304–9.

9. Lieutenant Governor Spotswood to the Council of Trade and Plantations, Virginia, *CSP*, item 195, vol. 33 (1722–1723): 94.

10. Lieutenant Governor George Clarke to Council of Trade and Plantations, New York, *CSP*, item 268, vol. 44 (1738): 126–36.

11. Bailyn, *Education in the Forming*, 27; Lockridge, *Literacy in Colonial New England*, 49–50.

12. Zuckerman, *Peaceable Kingdoms*, 73–79.

13. Demos, *Little Commonwealth*, 142–44; and Lockridge, *Literacy in Colonial New England*, 51, 74.

14. Tully, "Literacy Levels"; and Lockridge, *Literacy in Colonial New England*, 74–75.

15. Lockridge, *Literacy in Colonial New England*, 79; and Levy, *Town Born*, 3, 263–88.

16. Zuckerman, *Peaceable Kingdoms*, 128–29.

17. Berkeley quoted in Schweiger, "Literate South," 332.

18. Morgan, *Virginians at Home*; Bailyn, "Politics and Social Structure"; and Taylor, *American Colonies*, 152–53.

19. Taylor, *American Colonies*, 246–47.

20. On Philadelphia, see Roney, *Governed by a Spirit*, 11–79. On the failure across Pennsylvania to establish social and political stability, see Smolenski, *Friends and Strangers*, 61–177; and Marietta and Rowe, *Troubled Experiment*.

21. Levy, *Quakers and the American Family*, 157–72; Smolenski, *Friends and Strangers*, 154–55, and on the schism's later echoes, 226–38.

22. Fogleman, "Migrations to the Thirteen."

23. Lodge, "Crisis of the Churches"; and Pearl, "'For the Good Order,'" 85–114.

24. On migration, see Fogleman, "Migrations to the Thirteen," 704–8; and Landsman, *Scotland and Its First American Colony*, 176–77. On Presbyterian ecclesiastical development, see Lodge, "Great Awakening," 28–30; Lodge, "Crisis of the Churches," 201; and Griffin, *People with No Name*, 114–16. On church rebuilding, see Butler, *Becoming America*, 185–224; and Butler, *Awash in a Sea*, 98–128.

25. Fogleman, *Hopeful Journeys*, 101–25; Engel, *Religion and Profit*, 71–79; and Lodge, "Great Awakening," 14–25.

26. On Reformed Protestantism's long influence on civil life, see Howe, "Evangelical Movement," 1233, 1237.

27. Lodge, "Crisis of the Churches"; and Kidd, *Great Awakening*, 1–12, 24–39.

28. Religious historians have questioned whether the old/new light/side dichotomy really captures the religious disputes at work, choosing instead to emphasize a spectrum of beliefs. See Winiarski, *Darkness Falls*, 14–15; and Kidd, *Great Awakening*, xiv, 37, 120. The divisions look starker when it comes to education.

29. Alexander, *Biographical Sketches of the Founder*.

30. May 30, 1737, in *Records of the Presbyterian Church*, 132–33.

31. Tennent quoted in Kidd, *Great Awakening*, 60. On the differing educational priorities of the Old and New Sides, see Heimert, *Religion and the American Mind*, 164–67.

32. On New Side schools, see Beam, "Dr. Robert Smith's Academy"; Wertenbaker, *Princeton*, 11; Funk, "Influence of the Presbyterian Church," 184–86; Turner, "Reverend Samuel Blair"; Sloan, *Scottish Enlightenment*, 55–61, and the list of schools, 281–84; Nybakken, "In the Irish Tradition"; Shereshewsky, "Academy Keeping"; Reid-Maroney, *Philadelphia's Enlightenment*; and Kidd, *Great Awakening*, 31–32.

33. Jonathan Dickinson to Theophilus Howell, January 30, 1746/7, Elizabeth Town, N.J., in Jonathan Dickinson Collection, PUL.

34. Samuel Finley to Joseph Bellamy, November 25, 1756, Nottingham, Samuel Finley Collection, PUL.

35. Mills, *History of West Nottingham Academy*, 23–25; and Reid-Maroney, *Philadelphia's Enlightenment*, 4, 95–114.

36. May 25, 1744, in Klett, *Minutes of the Presbyterian*, 197–99.

37. Pears Jr., "Francis Alison"; Munroe, *University of Delaware*, 11–14; Sloan, *Scottish Enlightenment*, 57–58; and Rowe, *Thomas McKean*, 7–8.

38. Franklin, *Idea of the English School*, 8. Also see, Heimert, *Religion and the American Mind*, 184.

39. Cremin, *Colonial Experience*, 402–5; and Landsman, *From Colonials to Provincials*, 80–82.

40. *Charter of a College*, 5.

41. Kling, "New Divinity Schools."

42. Lefavour, "Proposed College"; and Spring, *History of Williams College*, 42–44. Oliver Partridge to Dennis De Berdt, October 3, 1766, London, EM. 177, Emmet Collection, NYPL.

43. For other views of the 1758 reunion, see Landsman, *Scotland and Its First American Colony*, 250–55; Westerkamp, "Division, Dissension," 14–17; Fea, "In Search of Unity"; and Fea, *Way of Improvement*, 40–47.

44. Boonshoft, "Creating a 'Civilized Nation,'" 75–83.

45. Wallace to Witherspoon, Edinburgh, February 6, 1767, in Butterfield, *John Witherspoon Comes to America*, 26.

46. Ewing to Hannah Ewing, Edinburgh, July 5, 1774, folder 1, John Ewing Papers, UPenn.

47. Sloan, *Scottish Enlightenment*, 281–83. On academies in New Jersey, see Sloan, *Education in New Jersey*, 11–12. John Fea discusses one in *Way of Improvement*, 59–69.

48. Lodge, "Great Awakening," 280; Westerkamp, *Triumph of the Laity*, 204–5. While Lodge and Westerkamp differ vastly in their approaches to studying the Awakening, they both agree that the revivalists triumphed.

49. Bonomi, *Under the Cope of Heaven*, 73–75, 218–19; Winiarski, *Darkness Falls*, 436–40, 446–48; Kidd, *Great Awakening*, 72–75, 84–85; Winterer, *American Enlightenments*, 175–76; and Noll, *America's God*, 120–22.

50. Landsman, *From Colonials to Provincials*, 92–93; Hoeveler, *Creating the American Mind*; Landsman, "Legacy of British Union," 297–317; and May, *Enlightenment in America*, 49–65.

51. Hattem, "Past as Prologue," 43–45; and Winterer, *American Enlightenments*, 2–4, 227.

52. Sloan, *Scottish Enlightenment*, 61–63; Sloan, *Education in New Jersey*, 11; Nybakken, "In the Irish Tradition," 172–73; and Reid-Maroney, "Science and the Presbyterian Academies."

53. John Ewing's math notebook, papers of John Ewing, UPenn.

54. Watts, *Logick*. The first American edition was published in Philadelphia in 1789.

55. "Logick," in box 1, folder 7, Francis Alison Papers, PHS; and Notes on Robert Smith's "Lectures on Logic," in Robert Smith Papers, Notebooks vol. 1, PHS.

56. Robson, *Educating Republicans*, 73.

57. She discusses reading Watts on October 1, 1754, in Karlsen and Crumpacker, *Journal of Esther Edwards Burr*, 45.

58. Landsman, *From Colonials to Provincials*, 77–82; Ingersoll, "Francis Alison," 39–69; Sloan, *Scottish Enlightenment*, 73–102; and Noll, *America's God*, 95–102. For useful discussions of why Witherspoon came to terms with Hutcheson, see Landsman, "Witherspoon and the Problem"; and Diamond, "Witherspoon, William Smith." Compare with Mailer, *John Witherspoon's American Revolution*, 140–81. An edition of Witherspoon's moral philosophy lectures has been published as, *An Annotated Edition of Lectures*. On Edwards, see Norman Fiering, *Jonathan Edwards's Moral Thought*. Also see, Knott, *Sensibility and the American Revolution*, 7–8, 189–90; and Eustace, *Passion is the Gale*, 138–49.

59. Iverson, "Introduction," 218; see also Shovlin, "Emulation in Eighteenth-Century French"; Auricchio, "Laws of Bienséance"; Kaplan, "Virtuous Competition"; Caradonna, "Monarchy of Virtue"; and Caradonna, *Enlightenment in Practice*.

60. Priestley, *Miscellaneous Observations*, 54, 78.

61. The foundational work on emulation in American education is Opal, "Exciting Emulation," which focuses on the early republic and briefly notes European precedents, 455. For the late-colonial period, see Fea, *Way of Improvement*, 58–82.

62. *Poor Roger*, 1761.

63. Quote from "The Life of Dr. Smith," the introduction to *Sermons of Samuel Stanhope Smith*, 4.

64. *Seven Rational Sermons*, 72.

65. *Pennsylvania Gazette*, March 11, 1755.

66. August 24, 1767, Trustee Minutes of the First Presbyterian, PHS, 14.

67. Eustace, *Passion Is the Gale*, 197, 190.

68. *A Patern of Christian Education*, 2, 6–7 (emphasis mine). Interestingly, much of the published criticism of emulation in schools came from pamphlets and almanacs printed in Germantown. Other critical appraisals include Tobler, *Pennsylvania Town and Country-Man's Almanack*, 1754; and *Christian Education Exemplified*.

69. The line between emulation and ambition was porous. The *Oxford English Dictionary* defines the word emulation using the word ambition, but ambition often carried a negative connotation; "ambition, n;" and "emulation, n." OED Online, https://www.oed.com/view/Entry/61461, accessed December 2012. On fears of economic ambition, see Bushman, *Puritan to Yankee*, iv–v, 22–38, 135–43, 193, 267.

70. Hutcheson, *System of Moral*, 1:165.

71. Heimert, *Religion and the American Mind*, 53–54.

72. *Countryman's Lamentation*, 46.

73. For example, Samuel Davies to [David?] Cowel, September 14, 1758, Hanover, VA, in folder 2, Samuel Davies Papers, PHS. Earlier, while spearheading a fund-raising effort in Britain, Davies expressed anxieties about privileging college business over his church and family. See Pilcher, *Reverend Samuel Davies Abroad*, 3–4.

74. *Pennsylvania Town and Country-Man's Almanack, 1758*.

75. *Virginia Almanack, 1771*.

76. Barnard, *A Present for an Apprentice*, 81.

77. Corner, *Autobiography of Benjamin Rush*, 30–33. Benjamin Franklin also thought that schools should teach letter writing; see Franklin, *Idea of the English School*, 5.

78. *Constitutions of the Publick Academy*, 4.

79. "An Exercise to the Admonishing Club," Deerfield, N.J., March 16, 1773, in vol. 2, Philip Vickers Fithian Journals, PUL. See also Fea, *Way of Improvement*, 98–99.

80. See also Martin, *Men in Rebellion*, 128. I use the same estimate for the number of college graduates in the colonies as Martin (3,000) but calculate the rate relative to the estimated white male population rather than the total population. For estimates of the population of the North American colonies by race, see McCusker and Menard, *Economy of British America*, 54.

81. In a generous estimate, Jackson Turner Main surmised that 10 percent of white children could afford to go to academy; see *Social Structure of Revolutionary America*, 246.

82. Francis Alison to Ezra Stiles, Philadelphia, May 7, 1768, in Dexter, *Extracts from the Itineraries*, 433.

83. To come up with this figure, I combined data drawn from both McLachlan, *Princetonians, 1748–1768*, xxi; and Harrison, *Princetonians, 1769–1775*, xxix.

84. Harrison, *Princetonians, 1776–1783*, xxvi.

85. Elmer, *Elogy on Francis Barber*, 11–12.

86. Evidence that Reeve taught at the Elizabeth Town Academy is in August 24, 1767, Trustee Minutes of the First Presbyterian, PHS, 14. On the Elizabeth Town Academy teachers, see Murray, *Notes, Historical*, 87–88; and Hatfield, *History of Elizabeth*, 519–21.

87. See Landsman, "Witherspoon and the Problem"; and Noll, *America's God*, 102–3.

88. Mills, *West Nottingham Academy*, 23–25.

89. On the development of civil institutions and the opening of a provincial public sphere, see Greene, "Social and Cultural Capital"; and Roney, *Governed by a Spirit*. For the Awakening's role, see Breen and Hall, "Structuring Provincial Imagination"; and for an early take, see Brooke, *Heart of the Commonwealth*, 69–96.

90. On the colonial public sphere, see Brooke, "Ancient Lodges," 284–88; and Shields, *Civil Tongues*.

91. *New-York Gazette*, September 20, 1762; *Pennsylvania Gazette*, January 10, 1771. See also *New-York Journal*, May 7, 1767.

92. Lambert, "'Pedlar in Divinity'"; Hall, *Contested Boundaries*, 10, 75–84; and Parr, *Inventing George Whitefield*.

93. November 13, 1753; and October 22, 1753, both in Pilcher, *Reverend Samuel Davies Abroad*, 26, 22–23.

94. There were academies in several of the hinterland towns where Bradford's newspaper had subscribers, which are listed in Parkinson, *Common Cause*, 49, 704–7.

95. Pilcher, "Preacher of the New Light," 118–20, 123–24.
96. Moniz, *From Empire to Humanity*, 12–57.
97. Mader, "Politics and Pedagogy," 4; Boudreau, "Provost Smith and His Circle," 178; and Landsman, *From Colonials to Provincials*, 81.
98. Ingersoll, "Francis Alison," 85–87.
99. Fea, "Way of Improvement Leads Home."
100. January 24, 1766; May 12, 1767, both in vol. 1, Philip Vickers, Fithian Journals, PUL, 3, 173. Here my interpretation differs from John Fea's depiction of a distinct, locally constructed rural enlightenment; see *Way of Improvement*, 3, 7.
101. Gould, "Empire of Manners."
102. *Pennsylvania Gazette*, August 24, 1749.
103. May 26, 1757, Klett, *Minutes*, 256.

Chapter Two

1. Elmer, *Elogy on Francis Barber*, 12–13.
2. George Clinton Barber's Statement, Washington, D.C., June 20, 1802, in Pension and Bounty-Land-Warrant Application Files, DLAR.
3. Ebenezer Elmer, February 13, 1783, in "Military Notes," folder 16, Ebenezer Elmer Papers, N-JHS.
4. Elmer, *Elogy on Francis Barber*, 12.
5. Quote from a petition to Congress written by the trustees of the church in 1840 in Murray, *Notes, Historical*, 105.
6. The Revolution was not a religious event. Yet this generation of revolutionary elites represents one of the clearest links between the Great Awakening and the Revolution. This chapter can thus be read as a new entry in a stultifying debate on the existence and extent of the connections between the Awakening and the Revolution, the two great eighteenth-century ruptures. For a full discussion of the literature, see Boonshoft, "Great Awakening," 168–69, 364–65nn6–8. My interpretation is influenced by Mathews, "Second Great Awakening."
7. Greene, "An Uneasy Connection," esp. 35–36, 39–40.
8. Williams, *Philip Vickers Fithian*, 4.
9. Hutcheson, *System of Moral Philosophy*, 1:77.
10. Hutcheson, 1:164.
11. Sheridan, *British Education*, 533, 13.
12. Priestley, *An Essay on a Course*, 8–9, 4, 1.
13. The expansion of education for upper-middling and gentry ranks in late-sixteenth and seventeenth-century England helped consolidate a national ruling class; see Wrightson, *English Society*, 191–93; and Stone, "Educational Revolution in England."
14. Beneke, *Beyond Toleration*, 86, 93–94; and Robson, *Educating Republicans*, 30–33.
15. Jay, *A Letter to the Governors*, 39. This pamphlet was printed in 1771 in response to hostile questions from some of King's College's English patrons about whether their money had gone to good use.
16. See Cremin, *Colonial Experience*, 405–6; Landsman, *From Colonials to Provincials*, 159–62; and McCaughey, *Stand, Columbia*, 8–9. My arguments here most closely echo Hattem, "'Anglifying' an Empire."

17. Dickinson to [Theophilus Howell?], March 3, 1746/7, Elizabeth Town, Jonathan Dickinson Collection, PUL; and LeBeau, *Jonathan Dickinson and the Formative Years*, 172–80.

18. *Pennsylvania Packet*, June 15, 1772.

19. McAnear, "Raising of Funds," 594–99. On the emergence of lotteries in colonial America, see Millikan, "'Willing to Be in Fortune's Way,'" 54–87.

20. Beneke, *Beyond Toleration*, 79–112, and on education, 96–103.

21. *Pennsylvania Gazette*, November 21, 1754; and August 26, 1756.

22. *Pennsylvania Gazette*, September 12, 1754.

23. *Pennsylvania Gazette*, September 19, 1754.

24. The crisis of the Seven Years' War emboldened voluntary associations to challenge local government. See Roney, *Governed by a Spirit*, 131–57. On the ways in which the Seven Years' War fostered cooperation among Anglicans and New and Old Side Presbyterians against Quakers, see Eustace, *Passion Is the Gale*, 201–15.

25. Davies, *Religion and Public Spirit*; Davies, *Sermon Delivered at Nassau-Hall*; Pilcher, "Preacher of the New Light," 326–31; and Gould, *Persistence of Empire*, 6.

26. Davies, *Religion and Public Spirit*, 8, 6. The emphasis on leadership carried through to John Witherspoon's presidency; see Maloyed and Williams, "Reverend John Witherspoon's Pedagogy."

27. *Pennsylvania Gazette*, August 11, 1757; *Prayers, for the Use of the Philadelphia Academy*, 12; and Smith, *Charge*, 10. Also see Mailer, *John Witherspoon's American Revolution*, 159–60.

28. Watson, *Sermon, Preached*, 31, 34.

29. Colley, *Britons*, 167–70.

30. Brown, *Thoughts on Civil Liberty*, 23, 24.

31. Priestley, *Essay on a Course*, 143, 149, 151.

32. Brown, *Thoughts on Civil Liberty*, 172, 182.

33. Blackstone, *Commentaries*, 1:106–7.

34. Griffin, *America's Revolution*, 36–88; Gould, *Among the Powers*, 14–47, 79–110; and Gould, "Laws of War."

35. Sheridan, *British Education*, 184, 505.

36. Shields, *Civil Tongues*, 38–39; Braddick, *State Formation*, 337–425; Braddick, "Civility and Authority"; and Wilson, "Rethinking the Colonial State."

37. See Landsman, "British Union."

38. Breen, "Ideology and Nationalism," 26–27.

39. Zabin, *Dangerous Economies*, 87–99; Isaac, *Transformation of Virginia*, 81–87; Bushman, *Refinement of America*, 55–56; and Shields, *Civil Tongues*, 145–58.

40. Robbins, "'When It Is That Colonies May Turn Independent.'"

41. Kraus, "Development of a Curriculum," 67, 71.

42. Franklin, *Proposals Relating to the Education*, 11–12; and Efland, *History of Art Education*, 46–47.

43. *Pennsylvania Gazette*, December 12, 1754.

44. Fatherly, "'Sweet Recourse of Reason.'"

45. Kelley, *Learning to Stand & Speak*, 35–37; and Kerber, *Women of the Republic*, 190–99.

46. *Rivington's New-York Gazette*, May 5, 1774.

47. *Dunlap's Pennsylvania Packet*, October 9, 1775.

48. On the gendering of republicanism, see Bloch, "Gendered Meanings"; and Lewis, "Republican Wife." On luxury and republicanism, see Morgan, "Puritan Ethic"; Wood, *Creation of the American Republic*, 107–124, 418; and Isaac, *Transformation of Virginia*, 247–51.

49. *Four Dissertations*. John Morgan's essay critiqued imperial policy, 27–28.

50. Diamond, "Witherspoon, William Smith," 125–28; and Boudreau, "Provost Smith," 178–84.

51. On denominational and revolutionary affiliations, see Phillips, *Cousins' Wars*, 164–70; Clark, *Language of Liberty*, 335–62; and Bell, *War of Religion*.

52. Bonomi, *Under the Cope of Heaven*, 199–209; and Beneke, *Beyond Toleration*, 119–26.

53. McConville, *King's Three Faces*, 295–99.

54. Cohen and Gerlach, "Princeton in the Coming of the American Revolution." On the politicization of colleges; see Peckham, "Collegia Ante Bellum"; Miller, *Revolutionary College*, 79–94; Robson, *Educating Republicans*, 34–45, 58–93; Noll, *Princeton and the Republic*, 32–33, 48–54; and Hoeveler, *Creating the American Mind*, 241–346.

55. Fea, *Way of Improvement*, 42–49.

56. *Pennsylvania Chronicle*, October 31, 1772.

57. McDonnell, "Resistance to the Revolution"; and the essays by Aaron Sullivan, Michael McDonnell, and Travis Glasson in Zuckerman and Spero, *American Revolution Reborn*. The classic statement of this interpretation is Kim, "Limits of Politicization."

58. See Breen, *Marketplace of Revolution*, 235–93; Breen, *American Insurgents*, 160–84; and Gross, *Minutemen and Their World*, 50–52.

59. The state of Pennsylvania changed the College of Philadelphia's loyalty oath as part of an act "to conform the estates and interests of the College, Academy, and charitable School of Philadelphia . . . to the Revolution and to the Constitution and Government of this Commonwealth"; *Pennsylvania Packet*, November 20, 1779. The College of New Jersey amended its charter in 1780 to eliminate the oath to the king; see *Charter and By-Laws*, 25–26.

60. Braithwaite, "Development of Higher Education," 5–7.

61. O'Shaughnessy, *Empire Divided*, 21–27.

62. *Pennsylvania Packet*, June 15, 1772.

63. *Pennsylvania Packet*, June 29, 1772.

64. John Ewing to Hannah Ewing, London, March 3, 1772, folder 1, John Ewing Papers, UPenn.

65. *Norwich Packet*, July 27, 1779. This first appeared in the *Pennsylvania Packet*.

66. The following works demonstrate connections between denominational schools and revolutionary leadership: Beam, "Dr. Robert Smith's Academy," 152–53; Cohen and Gerlach, "Princeton in the Coming of the American Revolution," 69–92; Fea, "Rural Religion," 452–57; Landsman, "Presbyterians, Evangelicals," 170; Miller, *Revolutionary College*, 171–86; Mills, *History of West Nottingham Academy*, 23–25; Munroe, *University of Delaware*, 12; Noll, *Princeton and the Republic*, 20; Nybakken, "In the Irish Tradition," 173; Pears, "Francis Alison," 15; Robson, *Educating Republicans*, 22; Sloan, *Scottish Enlightenment*, 60–61n70; Tiedemann, "Presbyterianism and the American Revolution," 337–39; and Tiedemann, "Interconnected Communities," 15–16.

67. *Pennsylvania Packet*, November 19, 1784. This was in a "brief history" of the school, which was published in an advertisement.

68. *Pennsylvania Town*, 1758.

69. Benjamin Carp has told a similar but more urban story about a different civil institution, the fire company; see Carp, "Fire of Liberty."

70. On how ambition figured into officers' decisions to join the war effort, see Ruddiman, *Becoming Men*, 30–32.

71. Tiedemann, "Presbyterianism and the American Revolution," 339.

72. Lists of officers are in Heitman, *Historical Register*; and Stryker, *Official Register*.

73. For Deerfield, see Fea, "Rural Religion," 452–57; and for Elizabeth Town, see Boonshoft, "Great Awakening," 180.

74. On the Delaware line, see also Madron, *Presbyterian Patriots*; and Boonshoft, "Great Awakening," 180–81.

75. Francis Alison to the Committee of Safety, n.d., case 8, box 21, Simon Gratz Autograph Collection, HSP.

76. Lender, "Enlisted Line," 127–29, 190–93; and Ruddiman, *Becoming Men*, 30–31.

77. Royster, *Revolutionary People*, 87, 86–95. For a different take on the sense of honor that motivated officers, see Smith, *American Honor*, 98–166.

78. On sociability and sensibility among the officers, see Knott, "Sensibility and the American War."

79. January 14, 1777, Ticonderoga, "Journal," folder 8, Elmer Papers, N-JHS.

80. January 22, 1777, "Journal," folder 11, Elmer Papers, N-JHS.

81. May 5, 1777, "Journal," folder 11, Elmer Papers, N-JHS.

82. Lender, "Enlisted Line," 127.

83. Cox, *Proper Sense of Honor*, 41.

84. Martin, *Men in Rebellion*, 23–61. For New Jersey, see Purvis, "'High-Born, Long-Recorded"; and Adelberg, "Transformation of Local Governance." Brendan McConville has shown how land disputes rectified some of New Jersey's political immobility; see *Daring Disturbers*, 202–5, 249–55.

85. For New Jersey, I used a copy of the New Jersey Civil List, DLAR; and the list of assemblymen and councilors from 1760 to 1776 compiled in Gerlach, *Prologue to Independence*, apps. 1–2. For Delaware, I used the list of officeholders in Bushman, Hancock, and Homsey, *Proceedings of the Assembly*, 555–83.

86. Boonshoft, "Great Awakening," 181–82, 370–71nn71–79.

87. Harry M. Ward. "Brearly, David," *American National Biography* online.

88. February 27, 1777 in Baldwin, *Revolutionary Journal*, 94; and Washburn, *Brief History of Leicester Academy*, 39–40.

89. Greene, "The American Revolution," 100–101.

90. Some historians have argued that, along with a quantitative change in the socioeconomic makeup of officeholders, the American Revolution lessened the social distance between ruler and ruled. See Main, "Government by the People"; and Wood, *Radicalism of the American Revolution*, 294–95, 304. Michael Braddick argues that cultural and behavioral differences provided "the unarticulated legitimization for political power" throughout the early-modern British Atlantic; see Braddick, "Civility and Authority," 116–17.

91. "An Act for Settling the Militia of this Province," in *Laws of the Royal Colony of New Jersey*, 19.

92. Fischer, *Washington's Crossing*; and Leiby, *Revolutionary War in the Hackensack Valley*.

93. *Acts of . . . the State of New-Jersey*, 1778, chap. 12, pp. 29–31.

94. June [?], 1780, June 14, 1780, June 23, 1780, August 28, 1781, November 23, 1781, all in John Stockholm daybook, box 12, folder 16, Ashbel Green Materials, PUL.

95. *Royal Gazette*, January 29, 1780.

96. Quotations from Hatfield, *History of Elizabeth*, 473. Also see the petition of Elizabeth Town residents requesting funds to rebuild the academy; in Murray, *Notes, Historical*, 104–7; as well as Gigantino, *William Livingston's American Revolution*, 156–59.

97. *Royal Gazette*, January 29, 1780.

98. *New-Jersey Gazette*, February 2, 1780. See also Urquhart, *History of the City*, 331–34.

99. Newark Academy Claim, Essex County Claim #28, in Damages done by the British in Essex County, reel 1, Damages by the British and Americans, DLAR.

100. Wertenbaker, *Princeton*, 60–62.

101. Munroe, *University of Delaware*, 31.

102. N.d., box 10, folder 7, Fisher Family Papers, HSP.

103. *Pennsylvania Packet*, November 19, 1784.

104. Damages by the British in Middlesex County, in reel 2, Damages by the British and Americans, DLAR, 165, 176, 180, 328, 200.

105. Damages by the British in Somerset County, in reel 2, Damages by the British and Americans, DLAR, 188, 186.

106. Damages by the Americans in Hunterdon County, #46, reel 1, Damages by the British and Americans, DLAR.

107. British forces also caused significant damage to Presbyterian churches in New York City; see Linsley, "The American Reformation," 51–52.

108. Kulikoff, "'Such Things Ought Not,'" 147, 142, 147–55.

109. Elmer, *Elogy on Francis Barber*, 8, 15 (emphasis mine).

110. On the connections between the officer corps and postrevolutionary nationalism, see Burrows, "Military Experience"; Main, *Political Parties*, 385–87; Carp, "Origins of the Nationalist Movement"; and McDonnell, *Politics of War*, 346–47.

111. On connections between the periods, see Greene, "Colonial History and National History," and the forum that follows.

112. "Account of Money received towards the Bridge Town academy 1785," folder 16, Ebenezer Elmer Papers, N-JHS.

Chapter Three

1. Tocqueville, *Democracy in America*, vol. 2, book 2, chap. 5, p. 114 (emphasis mine).

2. In 1830, there was one academy for every 11,634 free people in New England, the region for which there is reliable data. In 1831, there were significantly more American Temperance Society auxiliaries per capita than academies: one for every 3,766 free people in free states. But academies outpaced American Bible Society auxiliaries, of which there was one for every 18,478 free people in free states in 1831. New England academy numbers come from Durnin, "New England's Eighteenth-Century Incorporated Academies"; and Opal, *Beyond the Farm*, 104. Data on American Bible Societies and American Temperance Society auxiliaries come from Brooke, "Cultures of Nationalism," 18. On religion and voluntarism, see Mathews, "Second Great Awakening"; Wiebe, *Opening of American Society*, 209–33; Young, *Bearing Witness against Sin*; Riordan, *Many Identities*, 173–208; Neem, "Civil Society and

American Nationalism"; Stamatov, "Activist Religion"; Stamatov, "Religious Field"; Conroy-Krutz, *Christian Imperialism*; and Moniz, *From Empire to Humanity*. Daniel Walker Howe has integrated education and academies, into this story; see "Church, State, and Education."

3. Linsley, "American Reformation," 187–93.

4. On the way in which ministers helped create a social order that lessened clerical authority, see Brown, "Spreading the Word."

5. Jacob Green, "Autobiography," typescript, folder 1, Jacob Green Papers, N-JHS, 19, 23–25, 29.

6. *New-Jersey Journal*, April 25, 1781.

7. Green, *Observations*. See also, Noll, "Observations on the Reconciliation"; and Rohrer, *Jacob Green's Revolution*, 107–94.

8. Noll, "Jacob Green's Proposal," 211–12.

9. Jacob Green, October 18, 1779, folder 7, Collection of Ashbel Green Materials, PUL.

10. Green, *View of a Christian Church*, 24.

11. Jacob Green, October 18, 1779, Collection of Ashbel Green Materials, PUL. See also Noll, "Jacob Green's Proposal," 216.

12. Green, "Autobiography," 39.

13. Green, *View of a Christian Church*, 52.

14. Green, 54.

15. Rohrer, *Jacob Green's Revolution*, 234.

16. Green, *View of a Christian Church*, 55–56. On voluntary associations as a model for church governance, see Linsley, "American Reformation," 174–223.

17. O'Brien, "Transatlantic Community."

18. Marshall, *Remaking the British Atlantic*, 293–310; and Engel, "SPCK and the American Revolution."

19. Moniz, *From Empire to Humanity*, 58–103.

20. Erskine to Witherspoon, February 5, 1784, London; [?] Hogg to Witherspoon, February 7, 1784, Edinburgh; Margaret [Watson?] to Witherspoon, February 12, 1784, all in folder 3, John Witherspoon Papers, N-JHS. On Nisbet, see Robson, "Enlightening the Wilderness."

21. Erskine to Witherspoon, February 5, 1784, London, folder 3, John Witherspoon Papers, N-JHS.

22. Franklin to Witherspoon, April 5, 1784, Passy, Benjamin Franklin Papers Online.

23. Jay to Witherspoon, April 6, 1784, John Witherspoon Collection, PUL.

24. Witherspoon to Franklin, March 27, 1784, London, Benjamin Franklin Papers Online.

25. "Memorial of the Trustees of the College of New Jersey to the Presbytery of New Brunswick," September 30, 1784, John Witherspoon Collection, PUL. See also Wertenbaker, *Princeton*, 67–69.

26. June 7, 1785, Minutes of the Trustees of Queen's College, typescript, box 2, folder 16, Boyd Historical Collection, RUL, 6.

27. Damages by the British in Middlesex County, reel 2, Damages by the British and Americans in New Jersey, DLAR, 176.

28. October 29, 1793, Minutes of the Trustees of Queen's College, 7. The idea was first floated in the 1760s; see Wertenbaker, *Princeton*, 74–75. On connections between Dutch

Reformed and Presbyterian congregations, see Ireland, "Ethnic-Religious Dimension," 427, 442–45.

29. Wertenbaker, *Princeton*, 143–50; and Miller, *Revolutionary College*, 246–50.

30. On the effective disestablishment of colleges, see Howe, "Church, State, and Education," 9–12.

31. July 11, 1782, in *Speeches of the Different Governors*, 19.

32. Bockelman and Ireland, "Internal Revolution," 155–56; and Ireland, "Ethnic-Religious Dimension," 430, 435–42.

33. The first board meeting was announced in *Pennsylvania Packet*, December 31, 1784. They met on January 3, 1785, Protestant Episcopal Academy Minutes, folder 7, box 36, Meredith family papers, HSP. For York, see *Maryland Journal*, July 15, 1785.

34. *Pennsylvania Packet*, January 20, 1785; and March 21, 1785; and for the catechism, *Freeman's Journal*, August 17, 1785.

35. *Pennsylvania Freeman's Journal*, January 19, 1785.

36. *Pennsylvania Freeman's Journal*, January 19, 1785.

37. Institutions that existed separate from the state regularly tried to claim they represented a unified body politic. On this "consensual public sphere," see Brooke, "Ancient Lodges," 296–309; Waldstreicher, *In the Midst*, 53–107; Koschnik, "Let a Common Interest," 15–23; and Neem, "Creating Social Capital."

38. *Pennsylvania Freeman's Journal*, January 26, 1785.

39. *Pennsylvania Evening Herald*, August 13, 1785.

40. *Freeman's Journal*, March 2, 1785. On the importance of charters, contracts, and constitutions to republican governance, see Wood, *Creation of the American Republic*, 283–84.

41. This is somewhat analogous to the rampant antiparty ideology of the period.

42. In the thirteen original states plus Vermont, only thirty-two counties claimed more than one academy before 1800, roughly 10 percent of the total counties and districts in those states. On my methods for identifying academies, see the appendix.

43. Early news of his efforts appeared in *Pennsylvania Evening Herald*, December 20, 1786.

44. Harrison, *Princetonians, 1769–1775*, 138–46.

45. For the list of trustees, see *Pennsylvania Evening Herald*, March 14, 1787. See also *Centennial Volume of the First Presbyterian Church*, 2–3.

46. *Pittsburgh Gazette*, September 2, 1786; reprinted in Marder, *Hugh Henry Brackenridge Reader*, 11.

47. *The Mail*, July 19, 1792.

48. *Republican Star*, February 1, 1803.

49. *New-York Daily Advertiser*, October 24, 1792.

50. Beadie, *Education and the Creation*, 116–22.

51. *New-Jersey Journal*, March 13, 1782.

52. *New-York Daily Advertiser*, February 28, 1792; and February 3, 1792, reel 1, Newark Academy Minutes, N-JHS.

53. *Federal Gazette*, July 2, 1792.

54. On demand's influence on postrevolutionary colleges, see Labaree, *A Perfect Mess*, 6–8, 27–34, 42.

55. *Maryland Journal*, March 7, 1786.

56. *Maryland Journal*, April 11, 1786.

57. Slonimsky, "'Engine of Free Expression'"; Brown, *Strength of a People*; and John, *Spreading the News*.

58. Benjamin Rush, "To the Citizens of Philadelphia," *Independent Gazetteer*, March 28, 1787.

59. "A Bill for the More General Diffusion of Knowledge," June 18, 1779, in Boyd, *Papers of Thomas Jefferson*, 2:526–35.

60. Onuf, "State Politics and Republican Virtue."

61. Neem, *Democracy's Schools*, 9–10, 78; Kaestle, *Pillars of the Republic*, 8–9; and Brown, *Strength of a People*, 75–77, 93–95, 101–3.

62. Nelson, "Perceived Dangers," 175–76; Yokota, *Unbecoming British*, 10–11; and Tamarkin, *Anglophilia*, 247–324.

63. Myers, *Liberty Without Anarchy*; and Irvin, *Clothed in Robes*, 229–38.

64. Bullock, *Revolutionary Brotherhood*, 121–33; Brooke, "Ancient Lodges," 296–303; and Ruddiman, *Becoming Men*, 78.

65. On Masonry and education, see Bullock, "'Sensible Signs'"; and Beadie, "'Encouraging Useful Knowledge.'"

66. Gigantino, *William Livingston's American Revolution*, 176–80.

67. Hough, *Origin of Masonry*, 11–12; and Sims, *Institution of the Society*. For biographical information on the Academy board, I relied on Hall, *History of the Presbyterian*, 162, 308, 327–39, 350, 448; and McLachlan, *Princetonians, 1748–1768*, 643–47.

68. *Virginia Journal*, September 15, 1785.

69. Chap. 52, December 1, 1791, Hening, *Virginia Statues at Large*, 13:293.

70. *The Mail*, Febraury 22, 1792.

71. June 24, 1798, sec. A, box 48, Phoenix Masonic Lodge No. 8 Records, Rubenstein Library, Duke University.

72. *Otsego Herald*, December 22, 1796; and January 4, 1798. See also, Taylor, *William Cooper's Town*, 209–10.

73. Lefavour, "Proposed College in Hampshire"; Spring, *History of Williams*, 42–44; and Durnin, "New England's Eighteenth-Century Incorporated Academies," 48–49. On the River Gods, see Murrin, "Review Essay," 267–68.

74. Levy, *Town Born*; and Hall, *Reforming People*.

75. Opal, "Labors of Liberality."

76. *Acts and Laws Passed by . . . the State of Massachusetts-Bay . . . 1779*, chap. 6.

77. "Report on the subject of Academies," February 27, 1797, in *MA Resolves, 1797*, 65–67, 66.

78. Vreeland, "Public Secondary Education," 394–405.

79. Brooke, *Heart of the Commonwealth*, 186–88.

80. Based on the 1790 census.

81. Hall, *Politics without Parties*, 190–226, esp. table 47, p. 195; Zagarri, *Politics of Size*, 15–16; and Brooke, "To the Quiet of the People."

82. April 7, 1784; July 4, 1785; June 26, 1786; May 23, 1787; and September 28, 1797; all in Trustee Records Octavo vol. 1, Leicester Academy Records, AAS.

83. More broadly, John Brooke argues that "elite voluntarism followed hard upon civil strife" in Worcester County. See *Heart of the Commonwealth*, 243, also 240–42, 186–87.

84. Rev. Sumner's Address, in Bancroft, *Importance of education*, 4. Bancroft also thought that the Federalists' restoration of public credit "brightened" the Academy's prospects, 14.

85. January 1, 1790, Minervaean Society records, AAS, 5. Though no Brookfield men were among the initial subscribers to Leicester Academy, the local Congregational minister began serving on the board of trustees during the 1790s; "A List of the Trustees of Leicester Academy," typescript, box 1, Leicester Academy Records.

86. Moynihan, *History of Worcester*, 109–11.

87. June 3, 1786; August 27, 1786; September 21, 1786; September 23, 1786; June 1, 1789; October 17, 1789; and December 4, 1789; all in vol. 3, Peabody Diaries, AAS.

88. Richards, *Shays's Rebellion*, 27–30; Condon, *Shays's Rebellion*, 88, 112, 119. On the lasting consequences for Shepard, see Boudreau and MacDonald, "New Commonwealth Votes," 88.

89. Shepard was listed first on the 1793 academy charter; see box 6, "1793 Bill" folder, Westfield Academy Records, Westfield Athenaeum.

90. Ely had initiated debt prosecutions against "inland farmers" who would become involved in the Regulation; see Szatmary, *Shays' Rebellion*, 101. Ely served on the first committee to build an academy building; April 20, 1797, box 3, "Records, Trustee Minutes," Westfield Academy Records.

91. For example, Seth Catlin was at Springfield alongside Shepard; see Starkey, *Little Rebellion*, 78. Catlin's opposition to civil unrest ran back to the 1770s and led neighbors to question his allegiances. In 1774, he and some friends chopped down a liberty pole in Deerfield. About a month later, as he tried to open the County Court in Springfield in his capacity as sheriff, he was "much abused" by a Whig mob. See July 28, 1774; and August 31, 1774, both in Ashley, *Romance, Remedies*, 98–99, 112. Joseph Stebbins was another known "friend of the government." See Sheldon, *Joseph Stebbins*, 15.

92. Brooke, "To the Quiet of the People," 435; and on prerevolutionary politics in Hampshire, see Nobles, *Divisions throughout the Whole*.

93. Sklar, "Schooling of Girls, 517–25.

94. Here, my point is analogous to neo-Progressive arguments about 1790s tax revolts; see Slaughter, *Whiskey Rebellion*; and Bouton, *Taming Democracy*. According to John Murrin, "the Revolution became revolutionary in Massachusetts precisely because it repudiated county rule"; see "Review Essay," 270.

95. Of 193 ballots cast for governor in Exeter in 1800, 3 went to the Republican candidate. See "New Hampshire Governor, 1800," *NNV*.

96. Here I rely on Van Beck Hall's "commercial-cosmopolitan continuum" for Massachusetts towns, including those in Maine. They ranged from "Group A towns," the most commercial and cosmopolitan, to "Group C towns," which displayed "little or no commercial activity and the least connection with the wider society"; Hall, *Politics without Parties*, 3. Group A and B towns were more likely to oppose debt relief and support the ratification of the U.S. Constitution; Hall, 270–71, 286–93. Only around 40 percent of Massachusetts towns fell into Groups A or B, but 90 percent of academies founded prior to 1800 were in Group A or B towns. Group C comprised nearly 60 percent of the total number of towns but was home only to 10 percent of academies founded before 1800. The list of town classifications is in the appendices to Hall's book, which are available on microfilm at Hillman Library, University of Pittsburgh (copy in author's possession).

97. Opal, "Exciting Emulation," 464–68.

98. "An Act for Appointing and Supporting Schools," *Revised Laws of Vermont*, 22–24.

99. "On Education," *Boston Magazine*, 176–78. Reprinted in *Massachusetts Centinel*, March 22, 1786.

100. [Untitled], *Boston Magazine*, 238–39.

101. "The Free Republican, no. X," *Independent Chronicle*, February 9, 1786.

102. Here I offer a different interpretation to Jason Opal, who finds intergenerational, intrafamily conflict at the root of academy debates. See Opal, *Beyond the Farm*, 119–24. Mary Babson Fuhrer carries Opal's interpretation forward; see *Crisis of Community*, 142–47.

103. *Maryland Gazette*, February 11, 1785; quoted in, Risjord, *Chesapeake Politics*, 215; and for the vote tabulation, 214.

104. *Maryland Journal*, May 20, 1785.

105. I agree with Daniel Walker Howe, that "if religious diversity was a problem for education, religious energy was an asset." However, Howe's argument that "religious impulses" drove academy expansion underestimates the importance of political upheaval. See Howe, "Church, State, and Education," 23, 16.

106. April 7, 1784; and July 4, 1785; both in Trustee Records Octavo vol. 1, Leicester Academy Records.

107. May 26, 1786; May 30, 1789; June 1, 1789; August 24, 1789; August 13, 1789; and September 21, 1789; all in vol. 3, Peabody Diaries. See also Opal, "Exciting Emulation," 464; and Larned, *History of Windham County*, 2:377.

108. *Pennsylvania Packet*, November 19, 1784.

109. "Act of Incorporation," November 1779, Minutes of Trustees of Washington Academy, MSA; and *Pennsylvania Packet*, November 19, 1784.

110. Reverend Jacob Kerr, who ran the school before the Revolution, led the founding trustees. November [?], 1779, Minutes of Trustees of Washington Academy.

111. May 17, 1784, Minutes of Trustees of Washington Academy, 4. They first asked Alexander McWhorter, of New Jersey, and then Thomas Read, a Presbyterian minister from Delaware. Both declined. September 4, 1783; October 21, 1783; and May 3, 1784; all in Minutes of Trustees of Washington Academy, 1–3.

112. May 17, 1784; July 5, 1784, both in Minutes of Trustees of Washington Academy, 4–5; and *Pennsylvania Packet*, November 19, 1784. On William Linn, who they hired, see Harrison, *Princetonians, 1769–1775*, 231–35.

113. Mary Claire Engstrom, "Hooper, William," in Powell, *Dictionary of North Carolina Biography*, 3:199–202.

114. November 1, 1783; and [n.d.]; both in Hillsborough Academy Papers, NCDAH, 6.

115. Trustee Minutes, Hillsborough Academy Papers, 7–8. Witherspoon to James Iredell, February 19, 1787, Princeton, John Witherspoon Collection, PUL. On Squire, see Princeton University, *General Catalogue*, 102.

116. Come, "Influence of Princeton."

117. *NJ Laws*, 1786, chap. 193.

118. *Brief Account of the Associated Presbyteries*, 12, 11–15. See also Rohrer, *Jacob Green's Revolution*, 236–39.

Chapter Four

1. *Pennsylvania Packet*, July 18, 1788.
2. *Pennsylvania Packet*, July 18, 1788. For academy students at another ratification celebration, see *Pennsylvania Packet*, July 10, 1788.
3. *Pennsylvania Packet*, July 18, 1788.
4. Wood, *Radicalism of the American Revolution*, 232–43, 341–42; Kett, *Merit*, 15–38; and Smith, *American Honor*, 167–211.
5. Yokota, *Unbecoming British*.
6. On "leadership," see Morgan, *Inventing the People*, 305–6.
7. Brewer, "Entailing Aristocracy."
8. Main, "Government by the People"; and Wood, *Radicalism of the American Revolution*, 287–305.
9. Wood, *Creation of the American Republic*, 393–429.
10. Bouton, "Road Closed."
11. Van Cleve, *We Have Not a Government*, 189–242.
12. "A Citizen of America," *New York Daily Advertiser*, February 19, 1788, in *DHRC*, 20:787.
13. John Forbes to John Quincy Adams, excerpts, Boston, January 19, 1788, in *DHRC*, 7:1532.
14. "The INTERESTS of this STATE," *New York Daily Advertiser*, October 15, 1787, in *DHRC*, 19:86.
15. "Helvedius Priscus," *Massachusetts Gazette*, February 5, 1788, in *DHRC*, 5:858.
16. Rufus King to James Madison, Boston, January 27, 1788, in *DHRC*, 7:1454.
17. Wilson quoted in Bouton, *Taming Democracy*, 179; and see Opal, *Avenging the People*, 64–66.
18. "Version of Wilson's Speech by Alexander J. Dallas," in *DHRC*, 2:349.
19. Wilson, *Works of the Honourable*, 1:436.
20. Carson, *Measure of Merit*.
21. Rozbicki, *Culture and Liberty*, 214–22.
22. Contrast Cutterham, "'What Ought to Belong to Merit'"; with Smith, *American Honor*, 98–166.
23. Chaussinand-Nogaret, *French Nobility*; Smith, *Culture of Merit*; and Blaufarb, *French Army*.
24. Knox, *Liberal Education*, 2:227.
25. Hemphill, *Bowing to Necessities*, pt. 2.
26. *Lord Chesterfield's Advice*, 22, 24.
27. *Pennsylvania Gazette*, August 15, 1787.
28. *Independent Gazetteer*, October 2, 1787.
29. Kett, *Merit*, 3–7, 27–38, 68–80. On merit and colleges, see Hessinger, "'Most Powerful Instrument.'"
30. Ramsay to Rush, Charleston, August 18, 1787, vol. 45, Rush Family Papers, LCP.
31. *Federal Gazette*, July 14, 1790.
32. "Proceedings of the Society of Associated Teachers," 274.
33. Waldstreicher, *In the Midst*, 8–9, 51–52; Koschnik, "Political Conflict and Public Contest"; and Newman, *Parades and the Politics*. Len Travers also notes the presence of students at patriotic events, in *Celebrating the Fourth*, 34–37.

34. "ORATION, Delivered by JAMES WILSON, Esq," *Pennsylvania Gazette* supplement, July 9, 1788.

35. Wood, *Creation of the American Republic*, 471–518, 553–62; and Brewer, *By Birth or Consent*, 126–27.

36. January 26, 1778, subscriptions folder, Washington-Henry Academy Trustee Records, VHS.

37. February 10, 1781, Trenton Academy Records, TFL, 1.

38. *New-Jersey Journal*, March 13, 1782.

39. *Pennsylvania Packet*, February 7, 1786.

40. *Maryland Journal*, March 7, 1786.

41. *Pennsylvania Packet*, February 10, 1787.

42. *Independent Gazetteer*, June 18, 1789.

43. *Pennsylvania Freeman's Journal*, March 9, 1785. Also see November 1, 1783, Hillsborough Academy Papers, NCDAH.

44. *Pennsylvania Freeman's Journal*, January 26, 1785.

45. *Independent Gazetteer*, June 29, 1782.

46. *Acts of . . . the State of New-Jersey . . . 1778*, chap. 12.

47. Opal, "Exciting Emulation"; and Reese, *Testing Wars*, 8–37.

48. Barrow, *Essay on Education*, I:90. For France, see Kaplan, "Virtuous Competition."

49. *Pennsylvania Mercury*, October 13, 1786.

50. *New-Jersey Gazette*, March 5, 1783; September 6, 1784; and December 27, 1784.

51. *Independent Gazetteer*, November 15, 1787.

52. *New-Jersey Gazette*, April 11, 1785.

53. *New-Jersey Gazette*, March 5, 1783.

54. For example, see Tolley "Chartered School in a Free Market," 71. For social and cultural capital, see Bourdieu, "Forms of Capital."

55. *United States Gazette*, August 7, 1805.

56. Kett, *Merit*, 74.

57. June 2, 1807, Diary of Daniel Mulford, NJHC, 130.

58. *Maryland Journal*, January 25, 1785.

59. *Mail*, July 19, 1792.

60. On venture schools' relationship to academies, see Miller, *Academy System*, 12–16; Sizer, *Age of Academies*, 4–6; Tolley, "Rise of the Academies"; Tolley, "Mapping the Landscape of Higher Schooling"; and Beadie, "Toward a History of Education Markets," 50–51.

61. Winterer, *Culture of Classicism*, 10–43.

62. "Tablet No. LXV," *Gazette of the United States*, November 25, 1789

63. *Baltimore Daily Intelligencer*, October 28, 1793.

64. *New-York Daily Advertiser*, October 2, 1790.

65. *Pennsylvania Packet*, October 27, 1784.

66. *Maryland Journal*, November 11, 1785.

67. *Freeman's Journal*, May 17, 1786.

68. April 6–10, 1786, "A Register of the Quarterly Examinations in the Academy of the Protestant Episcopal Church," box 36, folder 15, Meredith Family Papers, HSP.

69. As Carolyn Eastman argues, oratory "help[ed] demarcate class, racial, and gender boundaries when it was delivered by a privileged member of society." See *Nation of Speechifiers*, 9.

70. *New-York Daily Advertiser*, April 18, 1795.

71. *Claypoole's Daily Advertiser*, July 9, 1799.

72. *Maryland Journal*, January 3, 1786.

73. *Gazette of the United States*, July 15, 1789.

74. *Pennsylvania Packet*, October 13, 1784.

75. *Commercial Advertiser*, November 11, 1803 (emphasis mine).

76. *Maryland Journal*, March 7, 1786.

77. *Maryland Journal*, July 7, 1786.

78. *Independent Gazetteer*, April 11, 1787.

79. *New-York Daily Advertiser*, October 26, 1785.

80. *Gazette of the United States*, July 15, 1789.

81. Rush, "Observations Upon the Study of the Latin . . . ," in Rush, *Essays, Literary, Moral*, 14–15; and Webster, "On the Education of Youth in America," in Rudolph, *Essays on Education*, 47–49. Also see, Yokota, *Unbecoming British*, 39. On Federalists and classical education, see Kerber, *Federalists in Dissent*; and Foletta, *Coming to Terms*.

82. Opal, "Exciting Emulation," 451–52.

83. Based on the 1820 census, there were 261 free whites in this age range from Leicester, and twenty-six academy students. I use this age range because the teenage years were the most common time to attend academies. While there is a separate category of males sixteen to eighteen, there is not one for females. Therefore, I use sixteen as the cutoff. Data on Leicester Academy students are from the *Student, Teacher, and Trustee Database Project*.

84. There were actually twelve classical students from other Worcester towns. I could not identify with certainty the families of three students. The tax lists are in folio 14–15, Worcester County Records, AAS.

85. Here I push against scholarship that dismisses the idea that academies mostly served the elite as merely an echo of overblown critiques levied by antebellum reformers. See, for instance, Sizer, *Age of Academies*, 17–20; Kaestle, *Pillars of the Republic*, 118–20; and Beadie, "Internal Improvement," 100–102.

86. Judith Sargent Murray, quoted in Kelley, *Learning to Stand*, 66, numbers on 67.

87. Rush, "Thoughts upon Female Education . . . ," in Rush, *Essays, Literary, Moral*, 53. Also see, Nash, "Rethinking Republican Motherhood."

88. Murray, *Gleaner*, in Skemp, *Judith Sargent Murray*, 193–202, 234–43. On gendered discourses of equality, see McMahon, *Mere Equals*.

89. Rush, "Thoughts upon Female Education," 53.

90. *Independent Gazetteer*, September 15, 1788. At least two other female academies held exhibitions within the month; see *Independent Gazetteer*, September 9, 1788; and *Independent Gazetteer*, September 20, 1788.

91. *Aurora Gazette*, January 3, 1795.

92. For example, *Dunlap's American Daily Advertiser*, September 30, 1791.

93. See Vanderpoel, *Chronicles of a Pioneer School*, 84. On Litchfield, also see Brickley, "Sarah Pierce's Litchfield Female Academy."

94. Kerber, *Women of the Republic*, 185–232.

95. On this debate, see Eastman, *Nation of Speechifiers*, 53–82.

96. "Life of Harriet Beecher Stowe (by her son)," in Vanderpoel, *Chronicles of a Pioneer School*, 182.

97. Tolley, "Science for Ladies"; Nash, "'Cultivating the Powers"; and Winterer, *Culture of Classicism*, 22–25.

98. *New-Jersey Journal*, September 14, 1796.

99. January 26, 1802; January 27, 1802; and August 9, 1809; all in Newark Academy Minutes, reel 1, N-JHS, 35–37, 46.

100. Mary Bacon, "Woman of Merit Described," in Vanderpoel, *Chronicles of a Pioneer School*, 77.

101. Good, *Founding Friendships*; and McMahon, "'Of the Utmost Importance.'"

102. March 30, 1795, Newark Academy Minutes, reel 1, 17; and n.d., "Litigation Folder," Washington-Henry Academy Trustee Records, VHS. Generally, see Wilder, *Ebony and Ivy*.

103. November 15, 1787, Records of the New-York Manumission Society, N-YHS, 6:83–84.

104. *New-York Journal*, May 9, 1792.

105. Contrast with Polgar, "'To Raise Them,'" 230–32. Coming at these issues from the vantage of education reveals the limitations of early antislavery defenses of black citizenship.

106. *Greenleaf's New Daily Advertiser*, November 16, 1796.

107. Andrews, *History of the New-York African Free-Schools*, 84.

108. *Commercial Advertiser*, November 25, 1797.

109. Andrews, *History of the New-York African Free-Schools*, 37, 44, 47.

110. Hines, "Learning Freedom."

111. For example, see O'Neil, "Private Schools and Public Vision," 81–95, esp. table 5, on p. 94.

112. *Maryland Journal*, April 21, 1786; and March 7, 1786.

113. *Pennsylvania Mercury*, June 8, 1787.

114. April 6, 1786, "Register of the Quarterly Examinations in the Academy."

115. *Virginia Journal*, December 30, 1784.

116. See also, Brown, "Emergence of Urban Society"; Jaffee, "Village Enlightenment in New England"; and on academies, Kelly, *Republic of Taste*, 14–54.

117. Extract of a letter reprinted in *Albany Gazette*, July 8, 1790. On magazines, see Haberman, "Periodical Publics"; and Smith-Rosenberg, *This Violent Empire*. On the West and discourses of civility, see Griffin, *American Leviathan*.

118. *Maryland Journal*, November 11, 1785; and *Philadelphia Gazette*, April 14, 1791.

119. New-Jersey *Gazette*, July 4, 1785.

120. *Freeman's Journal*, August 10, 1785; and *Federal Gazette*, November 5, 1788.

121. *Maryland Journal*, February 4, 1785.

122. *Dunlap's American Daily Advertiser*, June 21, 1792.

123. Maryland *Herald*, February 6, 1800.

124. "Coroner, York County, 1805," NNV.

125. Wilson, *Works of the Honourable James Wilson*, 2:396.

126. *Mail*, July 19, 1792.

Chapter Five

1. On Quesnay, see Roberts, "An Exchange of Letters"; and Roberts, "American Career of Quesnay." Quesnay makes brief appearances in Silverman, *Cultural History of the American Revolution*, 446–47; Shields, *Civil Tongues*, 309–11; and Nelson, "Perceived Dangers of Study Abroad," 182–83, 190–91.

2. For previous work on French schools, see Farnham, *Education of the Southern Belle*; Fatherly, *Gentlewomen and Learned Ladies*; Kilbride, *American Aristocracy*, 53–77; Tolley, "Significance of the 'French School'"; and Kerrison, "French Education of Martha Jefferson Randolph."

3. Catherine Kelly offers the best account of the spread of polite education in academies. Kelly argues that "students pursued a distinctly republican, deeply politicized form of virtue." This "republican education" made them "pillars of the republic." Kelly, *Republic of Taste*, 21, 22, and 14–54. Academy boosters pitched polite education that way, but I emphasize both their unapologetic emulation of European schools and the opposition that engendered.

4. Golove and Hulsebosch, "Civilized Nation," 943, 972–75; and Gould, *Among the Powers*.

5. See Jones, *America and French Culture*. For a different take than mine on the French educational influence in the early United States, see Paulston, "French Influence in American Institutions." On French émigrés in early American elite culture, see Furstenberg, *When the United States Spoke French*.

6. See Allgor, *Perfect Union*; and a series of essays by Teute and Shields, "Confederation Court"; "Jefferson in Washington"; and "Court of Abigail Adams."

7. On dancing, see Haulman, "Rods and Reels"; and Zabin *Dangerous Economies*, 97–100. On dance as cultural diplomacy, see Prevots, *Dance for Export*.

8. Bushman, *Refinement of America*.

9. Sullivan, *Disaffected*; Smith, *Freedoms We Lost*, 179–80; Teute and Shields, "Meschianza"; and Arendt, "'Ladies Going About for Money,'" 163–65.

10. *Pennsylvania Packet*, December 28, 1779; and January 4, 1780.

11. *Pennsylvania Packet*, November 13, 1781.

12. *Pennsylvania Packet*, January 17, 1782.

13. *Political Intelligencer*, June 1, 1784.

14. *Independent Journal*, November 3, 1784.

15. *Pennsylvania Packet*, January 13, 1780.

16. *Pennsylvania Packet*, December 28, 1779.

17. *Pennsylvania Packet*, January 17, 1782.

18. *Independent Gazetteer*, September 24, 1782.

19. *Freeman's Journal*, January 23, 1782.

20. *Independent Gazetteer*, September 25, 1784.

21. *Pennsylvania Packet*, May 15, 1784.

22. *New-York Daily Advertiser*, July 8, 1789; and May 20, 1788; and *Federal Gazette*, September 11, 1789.

23. *Pennsylvania Packet*, September 11, 1789; and October 6, 1789.

24. *Independent Journal*, November 3, 1784. A New York teacher also offered architecture; see *New-York Packet*, November 28, 1785.

25. *Maryland Journal*, November 24, 1786; and December 1, 1786. On the gendering of art curriculum, see Fatherly, *Gentlewomen and Learned Ladies*, 71–72; and Kelly, *Republic of Taste*, 41–44.

26. *Pennsylvania Packet*, December 27, 1799.

27. Mr. and Mrs. Priest, in *Federal Intelligencer*, December 15, 1794; and Mr. and Mrs. DeSeze, in *American Minerva*, January 10, 1795.

28. Tolley, "Music Teachers."
29. New York *Packet*, September 9, 1784; *New-Jersey Gazette*, January 22, 1783; and *Maryland Journal*, April 11, 1786.
30. *Independent Gazetteer*, September 24, 1782.
31. *Pennsylvania Packet*, December 25, 1784. Knox, *Liberal Education*, I:142.
32. *Independent Gazetteer*, September 24, 1782.
33. Zabin, *Dangerous Economies*, 91–93; and Hemphill, *Bowing to Necessities*, 91–92.
34. Eastman, *Nation of Speechifiers*, 24–28; and Gustafson, *Eloquence Is Power*, 233–46.
35. *Independent Journal*, November 3, 1784.
36. *New-York Packet*, September 6, 1784.
37. *Pennsylvania Packet*, December 29, 1784. On fashion, see Haulman, "Fashion and the Culture Wars."
38. *Independent Gazetteer*, September 18, 1787. For New York, see *Independent Gazette*, December 27, 1783; *New-York Packet*, September 6, 1784; and *New-York Daily Advertiser*, September 28, 1789.
39. *Independent Gazetteer*, January 29, 1787.
40. *Independent Gazetteer*, September 18, 1787; and *Aurora General Advertiser*, May 29, 1798.
41. *Independent Journal*, January 8, 1785.
42. *Pennsylvania Packet*, January 4, 1780.
43. *Freeman's Journal*, January 23, 1782.
44. Silverman, *Cultural History of the American Revolution*, 377–82; Knott, "Sensibility and the American War," 24; Cray, "Major John André"; Kornblith and Murrin, "Dilemmas of Ruling Elites," 37–38; and Smith, *American Honor*, 159–62.
45. Editor's introduction to Tyler, *Contrast*, 1–34.
46. *Pennsylvania Packet*, January 17, 1782.
47. *Independent Journal*, December 8, 1784.
48. *Independent Journal*, January 1, 1785; and *New-York Packet*, May 9, 1789.
49. *Pennsylvania Packet*, December 29, 1784.
50. *Freeman's Journal*, November 21, 1787.
51. Webster, "On the Education of Youth in America," in Rudolph, *Essays on Education*, 44, 69, 70, 45, 66, 77. See also Kerber, *Federalists in Dissent*, 96–104.
52. Coram, "Political Inquiries," in Rudolph, *Essays on Education*, 82.
53. Murray, "On the Equality of the Sexes (contd.)," 223.
54. Bloch, "Gendered Meanings of Virtue"; and Lewis, "Republican Wife."
55. Wood, *Creation of the American Republic*, 107–13, 418; and Kelly, *Republic of Taste*, 32–33.
56. Steele, *Thomas Jefferson and American Nationhood*, 78–83.
57. *New-York Packet*, December 20, 1784.
58. *Pennsylvania Packet*, December 26, 1787.
59. *Dunlap's American Daily Advertiser*, January 20, 1791.
60. *New-York Packet*, September 14, 1790.
61. *Independent Journal*, January 1, 1785.
62. *Independent Journal*, November 3, 1784.
63. *New-York Packet*, July 13, 1786. See also, Silverman, *Cultural History*, 446–47.
64. Quesnay, "Memoir," 19.

65. Roberts, "American Career of Quesnay," 468–71.
66. It was originally published as Quesnay de Beaurepaire, *Mémoire, statuts et prospectus*. On its publication history, see Duveen and Klickstein, "Alexandre-Marie Quesnay De Beaurepaire's."
67. *Independent Journal*, November 3, 1784.
68. *Independent Journal*, November 3, 1784.
69. Quesnay, "Memoir," 23.
70. Quesnay, 16. On architecture, see Kennedy, *Orders from France*; and Bushman, *Refinement of America*, 100–138.
71. Yokota, *Unbecoming British*.
72. Quesnay, "Memoir," 24.
73. Quesnay, 16.
74. Quesnay, 23.
75. Furstenberg, *When the United States Spoke French*, 227–348.
76. Quesnay, "Memoir," 15.
77. Franklin, *Proposals Relating to the Education*, 24–25.
78. *Pennsylvania Packet*, August 30, 1783; and September 6, 1783.
79. *Pennsylvania Packet*, August 26, 1783.
80. June 26, 1786, in Taylor and Friedlaender, *Diary of John Quincy Adams*, 2:44–58.
81. October 2, 1786, in Taylor and Friedlaender, *Diary of John Quincy Adams*, 2:106–20.
82. *Independent Gazetteer*, June 29, 1782.
83. *Maryland Journal*, September 20, 1785.
84. *New-Jersey Gazette*, November 8, 1784; and Yokota, *Unbecoming British*, 17.
85. *New-York Daily Advertiser*, April 9, 1787.
86. *New-York Packet*, January 2, 1795; *New-York Packet*, May 5, 1789; New York *Mercantile Advertiser*, May 25, 1801; and *Philadelphia Gazette*, December 28, 1802.
87. Yokota, *Unbecoming British*, 39.
88. *Pennsylvania Gazette*, September 26, 1787.
89. Haulman, *Politics of Fashion*, 204–9; and Knott, *Sensibility and the American Revolution*, 250–52.
90. *Pennsylvania Gazette*, September 12, 1787.
91. *Pennsylvania Gazette*, August 15, 1787.
92. Tomlins, *Law, Labor, and Ideology*, 35–59; Novak, *People's Welfare*; and Gerstle, *Liberty and Coercion*, 55–88.
93. Madison, "Vices of the Political System of the United States, April 1787," in Hutchinson, *Papers of James Madison*, 9:353.
94. *Pennsylvania Gazette*, September 12, 1787.
95. *Independent Gazetteer*, September 17, 1787.
96. *Pennsylvania Gazette*, September 12, 1787.
97. Quoted in Tomlins, *Law, Labor, and Ideology*, 43.
98. Wilson, *Works of the Honourable James Wilson*, 1:33.
99. *Pennsylvania Gazette*, September 12, 1787.
100. *Independent Gazetteer*, September 7, 1787.
101. Golove and Hulsebosch, "Civilized Nation," 975, 985–86.
102. *Independent Gazetteer*, September 13, 1787.

103. *Independent Gazetteer*, September 15, 1787.
104. *Independent Gazetteer*, September 17, 1787.
105. *Independent Gazetteer*, September 15, 1787.
106. *Independent Gazetteer*, September 13, 1787.
107. Wilson, *Works of the Honorable James Wilson*, 1:353.
108. *Independent Gazetteer*, September 13, 1787.
109. *Independent Gazetteer*, September 15, 1787.
110. *Independent Gazetteer*, September 6, 1788.
111. Roberts, "American Career of Quesnay," 468–71; Duveen and Klickstein, "Alexandre-Marie Quesnay De Beaurepaire's," 281–82; and Roberts, "François Quesnay's Heir," 148–50.
112. Kelly, *Republic of Taste*, 14–54.
113. *Pennsylvania Gazette*, September 12, 1787.
114. *New-York Journal*, May 20, 1788.
115. *Pennsylvania Packet*, December 27, 1788.
116. *Mail*, December 19, 1791; and Philadelphia *General Advertiser*, January 4, 1792.
117. Philadelphia *General Advertiser*, January 10, 1794.
118. *Federal Gazette*, May 22, 1793; *Federal Gazette*, November 25, 1793; and *Philadelphia Gazette*, February 11, 1794.
119. Furstenberg, *When the United States Spoke French*, 89–136.
120. *New-York Daily Advertiser*, May 7, 1793.
121. *New-York Daily Gazette*, April 1, 1794; and *American Citizen*, August 16, 1800.
122. *New-York Daily Advertiser*, October 15, 1791. Also see, *New-York Daily Gazette*, October 10, 1792; *New-York Gazette*, April 19, 1802. Archibald Robertson eventually published *Elements of the Graphic Arts*. Also see Fort, "Archibald and Alexander Robertson."
123. *Albany Gazette*, January 22, 1796; and *American Spy*, September 20, 1796.
124. Kennedy, *Orders from France*, 59–78.
125. *Federal Intelligencer*, March 2, 1795; and *Gazette of the United States*, September 29, 1795.
126. *Federal Intelligencer*, December 29, 1795; *Baltimore Federal Gazette*, January 1, 1796; and March 17, 1796.
127. *Federal Gazette*, July 17, 1798; *Virginia Chronicle*, February 23, 1793; *Alexandria Daily Advertiser*, November 9, 1801; *Rights of Man*, September 5, 1798; and *Rights of Man*, October 4, 1798.
128. Trustees of the Winchester Academy Petition, October 27, 1786, Legislative Petitions of the General Assembly, Accession Number 36121, box 286, folder 8, LVA.
129. *Commercial Advertiser*, November 1, 1798.
130. The details are in Boonshoft, "Creating a 'Civilized Nation,'" 310n144.
131. Durnin, "New England's Eighteenth-Century Incorporated Academies," 92–96.
132. *Philadelphia Gazette*, October 17, 1801.
133. New York *Commercial Advertiser*, November 1, 1798.
134. Baltimore *Federal Gazette*, January 23, 1798.
135. For example, the Elizabeth Town Academy charged £20 for boarding and only £5 for tuition; see *New Jersey Journal*, March 3, 1790.
136. Quesnay, "Memoir," 20.
137. *Federal Gazette*, September 11, 1789; and *Porcupine's Gazette*, February 26, 1798.

138. R. Walsh to General Harper, Philadelphia, September 18, 1816, roll 3, Harper-Pennington Papers, MdHS. See also Kilbride, *An American Aristocracy*, 53–77.

139. September 30, 1785, Trenton Academy Records, TFL, 49–50. Elizabeth Town hired a teacher who was known for teaching a robust ornamental curriculum in nearby Hackensack; see *New-York Daily Advertiser*, May 18, 1789; *New-York Packet*, May 5, 1789; and *New-Jersey Journal*, July 21, 1790; June 8, 1791; and March 27, 1793. For Princeton, see *American Minerva*, May 20, 1795; and *Pennsylvania Packet*, September 4, 1790.

140. January 13, 1795; March 9, 1795; and March 30, 1795, all in reel 1, Newark Academy Minutes, N-JHS.

141. *Greenleaf's New York Journal*, April 22, 1797; and *Centinel of Freedom*, September 8, 1801.

142. New York information comes from the annual report of the state Board of Regents; see *American Minerva*, March 13, 1795. For Bordentown, see *Federal Gazette*, July 1, 1790; and *Porcupine's Gazette*, May 18, 1797.

143. *Aurora General Advertiser*, February 26, 1795.

144. François Furstenberg describes how American Republicans' support of the French Revolution exceeded the moderate sentiments of many French émigrés in Philadelphia. See Furstenberg, *When the United States Spoke French*, 115–16.

145. *Poulson's American Daily Advertiser*, April 1, 1802.

146. *Aurora General Advertiser*, November 7, 1803.

147. Baltimore *Federal Gazette*, October 10, 1798.

148. *Morning Chronicle*, January 22, 1805. Also see Yokota, "Postcolonialism and Material Culture."

149. *New-York Daily Advertiser*, October 20, 1792.

150. Du Courteil, *Proposal to Demonstrate*, 30, 28, 32.

151. Nelson, "Perceived Dangers of Study Abroad"; and Kilbride, *Being American in Europe*, 15–37.

152. See, for example, *Pennsylvania Packet*, November 19, 1784.

153. *Pennsylvania Packet*, August 28, 1787. See also, Haulman, *Politics of Fashion*, 205–9.

154. *Philadelphia Gazette*, May 17, 1794.

155. Well into the nineteenth century, American colleges continued to foster "pretensions to Englishness," according to Elisa Tamarkin. See Tamarkin, *Anglophilia*, 253, 247–324.

Chapter Six

1. Prince, *New Jersey's Jeffersonian Republicans*, 14, 21–23.

2. "New Jersey 1800 U.S. House of Representatives," *NNV*.

3. "Extracts from Papers Received from Mr. Israel Russell," 18–32; and Morris Academy of Morristown. "New Jersey 1800 U.S. House of Representatives"; "New Jersey 1800 Assembly, Morris County"; and "New Jersey 1803 Assembly, Morris County," all in *NNV*.

4. February 9, 1802; and March 9, 1802, in Daniel Mulford Diary, NJHC, 11, 12.

5. In Cheshire, Federalist candidates garnered four votes, combined, in the 1800 gubernatorial and U.S. House elections. "Massachusetts 1800 Governor"; and "Massachusetts 1800 U.S. House of Representatives, District Western 1"; both in *NNV*.

6. Pasley, "Cheese and the Words."

7. Ellis, *Jeffersonian Crisis*, 45–46.

8. July 4, 1801; October 8, 1801; January 8, 1802; and March 13, 1802; all in Daniel Mulford Diary, 4, 6–7, 10, 13.

9. Maier, "Revolutionary Origins"; and Bloch and Lamoreaux, "Voluntary Associations."

10. On Massachusetts and the rise of corporations, see Handlin and Handlin, *Commonwealth*; Hall, *Organization of American Culture*; Maier, "Revolutionary Origins"; and Neem, *Creating a Nation of Joiners*, 10–32.

11. All the New England states—besides Rhode Island, which incorporated its first academy in 1800—along with Maryland and Virginia, incorporated at least one academy before 1783. Georgia, North and South Carolina, and New Jersey incorporated their first between 1783 and 1786. Neither New York nor Pennsylvania incorporated a single academy before 1787, and Delaware waited until 1801.

12. Gordon, "First Disestablishment"; Grasso, "Religious and the Secular"; Bloch and Lamoreaux, "Voluntary Associations," 242–43.

13. *NYS Laws*, 7th session, 1784, chap. 51.

14. On L'Hommedieu's Federalist bona fides, see Young, *Democratic Republicans*, 145–46.

15. *NYS Laws*, 9th Session, 1786, chap. 54. The most complete account of the law's genesis is Sherwood, *University of the State of New York*, 58–81; but also see, Abbott, *Government Policy*, 12–14.

16. *NYS Laws*, 10th Session, 1787, chap. 82. On education and disestablishment, see Beadie, *Education and the Creation*, 118–20.

17. March 20, 1787, *NYSJ*, 10th Session, 1787, 61. For the Assembly debates, see March 31, 1787; and April 6, 1787, in *NYAJ*, 10th Session, 1787, 129–30, 142.

18. The list of Regents is in Hutchins, *Civil List*, 394. I determined partisanship through *NNV*, and for positions on ratification I used the biographical gazetteer in Schechter, *Reluctant Pillar*, 157–206.

19. For the assembly vote, see November 27, 1794, *NJ Assembly Journal*, 19th session, 1794, 92. *NJ Laws*, 19th session, 1794, chap. 499.

20. For one of these, see Taylor, *Liberty Men and Great Proprietors*, 35–36.

21. The state legislature noted "that the academy at Marblehead will probably only serve the purposes of a town school." See "Report on the Subject of Academies at Large," February 27, 1797, *MA Resolves*, 1797, chap. 44, p. 66; and January 5, 1792, Marblehead Academy Records, MHS.

22. Throughout, I use the lists of trustees in Durnin, "New England's Eighteenth-Century Incorporated Academies," 253–86.

23. Refer back, also, to chapter 3. On the lingering effects of Shays's Rebellion in Westfield and neighboring West Springfield, see Boudreau and MacDonald, "New Commonwealth Votes," 88–89.

24. They included Ebenezer Bridge and Joseph Varnum. For Bridge's partisanship, see "Massachusetts 1799 State Senate, Middlesex County," *NNV*. A few years earlier Varnum ran for office on the same slate as Bridge; see "Massachusetts 1793 State Senate, Middlesex County," *NNV*.

25. They were Oliver Prescott, Josiah Stearns, Joseph Moors, and Timothy Bigelow. For Bigelow: "Massachusetts 1798 State Senate, Middlesex County"; for Moors and Prescott: "Massachusetts 1809 House of Representatives, Groton"; and for Stearns: "Massachusetts 1796 State Senate, Worcester County," all in *NNV*.

26. They were Walter Spooner, William Baylies, and Elisha May. For the Massachusetts ratification vote, see *DHRC*, 6:1466. All three, along with David Cobb and Samuel Fales, stood for office as Federalists. Baylies: "Massachusetts 1806 House of Representatives, Bridgewater"; Spooner: "Massachusetts 1800 Electoral College, First Southern District"; May: "Massachusetts 1799 State Senate, Bristol County"; Cobb: "Massachusetts 1802 State Senate, Hancock, Kennebec, Lincoln and Washington Counties"; and Fales: "Massachusetts 1809 State Senate, Bristol County," all in *NNV*.

27. They were Simeon and Joseph Tisdale. See "Massachusetts 1811 House of Representatives, Taunton"; and "Massachusetts 1810 State Senate, Bristol County," both in *NNV*.

28. Brown, "Shays's Rebellion."

29. Cleves, *Reign of Terror*.

30. On 1793 as a turning point in Federalist organizing, see Brooke, "Ancient Lodges," 316–22.

31. *DHRC*, 6:1466.

32. "New Hampshire 1800 Governor," *NNV*.

33. Charter dates come from Durnin, "New England's Eighteenth-Century Incorporated Academies," 253–86.

34. Watson, "Man with the Dirty Black Beard"; Kaestle, *Pillars of the Republic*, 205–8; Neem, *Democracy's Schools*, 164–65; and Merritt, *Masterless Men*, 143–78. On taxation, see Einhorn, *American Taxation*.

35. On Federalists and education in North Carolina, see King-Owen, "North Carolina's Federalists," 34–37; Gilpatrick, *Jeffersonian Democracy in North Carolina*, 129–30, 142–44; and Risjord, *Chesapeake Politics*, 492–93.

36. Broussard, *Southern Federalists*, 248–51.

37. Cooper, *Statutes at Large of South Carolina*.

38. Millikan, "'Willing to Be in Fortune's Way.'"

39. Hening, *Virginia Statutes at Large*, 1777, chap. 23.

40. Smith, *Account of Washington College*, 49; *Virginia Journal*, September 16, 1784; and November 18, 1784; and *Maryland Journal*, May 31, 1785.

41. Coon, *North Carolina Schools*, 17–18.

42. "Act for granting a Lottery to Leicester Academy," June 14, 1785, in octavo vol. 1, Leicester Academy Records, AAS.

43. *New-Jersey Journal*, December 14, 1791.

44. November 3, 1791, *NJ Assembly Journal*, 16th session, 1791, 23–24; November 3, 1791, *NJ Council Proceedings*, 1791, 8–9; and *NJ Laws*, 16th session, 1791, chap. 347.

45. May 20, 1793, and May 23, 1793, in *NJ Assembly Journal*, 17th session, 1792, 113, and for the vote, 123. On the effort to get the lottery approved, see September 26, 1792; and April 13, 1793, both in Newark Academy Minutes, reel 1, N-JHS, 12–13.

46. *NJ Laws*, 18th session, 1793, chap. 461.

47. For the vote, see February 12, 1794 *NJ Assembly Journal*, 18th session, 1794, 111. In the final bill, the legislature added three more academy lotteries to the original bill, bringing the final total to seven. See, February 15, 1794, 118–19. For the Council, see February 7, 1794, *NJ Council Proceedings*, 18th session, 1793, 24–25.

48. *Laws of the State of New-York. Volume the Third*, chap. 38; and Marr, *Old New England Academies*, 19–32.

49. March 31, 1790; August 2, 1790; January 29, 1793, in NYSBR, 22, 26, 66.

50. *NYS Laws, 15th session, 1792*, chap. 69.

51. April 10, 1792, *NYS Senate Journal, 15th session, 1792*, 84. The assembly passed the bill without a roll call.

52. Banning, "Republican Ideology and the Triumph."

53. The trustees are listed in Boughton and Harter, *Chronicles of Erasmus Hall*, 33–34.

54. Foster, "Clinton Academy," trustees list, 182. Suffolk County's Federalist slate for the ratification convention is from *DHRC*, 21:1536. "Report of Committee on Application for Incorporation of East Hampton Academy by the Name of Clinton Academy," November 17, 1787, in box 1, folder 8, New York State Miscellaneous Collection, NYPL.

55. On Addison during ratification, see *DHRC*, 21:1542–44; and as a Federalist, "New York 1795 Assembly, Ulster County," *NNV*. He was a Republican again by decade's end; see "New York 1799 Council of Appointment," *NNV*.

56. For example, the initial 1792 application of the Schenectady Academy, which in 1795 became Union College, was denied; see March 27, 1792, NYSBR, 59.

57. February 7, 1793, NYSBR, 72–73.

58. Melancton Smith, New York Convention Debates, June 21, 1788, *DHRC*, 22:1751. Also see, Brooks, "Melancton Smith," 261. Manning quoted in Holton, *Unruly Americans*, 209.

59. Section 13 of the 1787 regents law provided that academies could not draw a yearly income greater than the value of 4,000 bushels of wheat. The best data I can find is that, in New York in 1790, a bushel of wheat cost $0.80; that would increase to $1.20 by 1795. See *History of Wages in the United States*, 21. A regents academy could thus have an income of somewhere between $3,200 and $4,800. At an exchange rate of $2.50 per English Pound, this works out to between £1,280 and £1,920. By contrast, churches could only take in £1,200 in New York, £500 in Pennsylvania, and £200 in North Carolina. See Gordon, "First Disestablishment," 322. For the exchange rate, see McCusker. "How Much Is That," 333.

60. Boonshoft, "Creating a 'Civilized Nation,'" 331–32.

61. Nancy Beadie argues that "corporate ownership represented an alternative to aristocratic proprietorship"; see *Education and the Creation of Capital*, 22. My analysis more closely follows Ruth Bloch and Naomi Lamoreaux, who argue that while the American Revolution expanded associational and corporate rights, lawmakers "tended to favor the same types of associations as those previously favored under colonial law," most of which were elite run; see "Voluntary Associations, Corporate Rights," 236.

62. "Scheme of the Newark Academy Lottery."

63. *New-Jersey Journal*, August 21, 1793; and September 18, 1793.

64. *New-Jersey Journal*, September 18, 1793.

65. [Untitled], *Boston Magazine*, 238.

66. "On Education," *Boston Magazine*, 177; and *Massachusetts Centinel*, March 22, 1786, and March 7, 1787.

67. April 2, 1791; and W. Mason to Bentley, April 26, 1792, both in Bentley, *Diary of William Bentley*, 1:242, 252. On Bentley, see Brown, *Knowledge is Power*, 197–217.

68. October 13, 1795, *VT Assembly Journal, 1795*, 39; and October 26, 1796, *VT Assembly Journal*, 1796, 95.

69. Adams speech, June 3, 1795, in *MA Resolves, 1795*, 7.

70. *Impartial Herald*, June 13, 1795. Also see Neem, *Creating a Nation of Joiners*, 28–30.

71. Beasley, "Emerging Republicanism and the Standing Order."

72. Cubberley, *Public Education in the United States*, 65–67.

73. Here, my interpretation differs from Rachel Hope Cleves' argument in *Reign of Terror in America*, 194–229. Cleves is right that Federalists' rhetorical commitment to education grew during the French Revolution. But their primary focus remained on academies, not common schools. Indeed, Cleves' chapter on education begins with an oration offered by Simeon Doggett at the opening of an academy. Considering the belief that academies hurt town schools, one might argue that public education had to be protected from Federalists. On New Hampshire, see Turner, *Ninth State*, 94–97.

74. September 14, 1801, in Bentley, *Diary of William Bentley*, 2:392.

75. February 27, 1797, *MA Resolves, 1797*, chap. 44, pp. 65–67.

76. *Philadelphia Gazette*, January 18, 1796.

77. For example, *New York Daily Advertiser*, January 4, 1790; and January 27, 1791; and *New York Journal*, July 30, 1791.

78. February 5, 1793, NYSBR, 70.

79. January 6, 1795; and February 28, 1795, both in *NYAJ, 18th session, 1795*, 5, 82. On the 1795 bill and Clintonian reform, see Young, *Democratic Republicans*, 526.

80. Here I am indebted to two unpublished papers; Shammas, "Extent and Duration"; and Koehler, "Measuring the Expansion of Schooling." Delaware took similar steps in 1796; see Opal, "Natural Rights," 303.

81. It is not entirely clear how the money was allocated, as only a partial report for one year exists. That year, the £20,000 appropriation was spread out over 1,300 schools, which worked out to about £0.34 per pupil and £14.8 per school. *NYS Assembly Journal, 21st session, 1798*, 282–85. The funding may have been spread even more thinly than this suggests, as no returns came back from seven counties. By comparison, in 1793—the year for which the records are most complete—the £1500 apportioned to the twelve Regents academies amounted to just shy of £2 per pupil, and just over £120 per school; see January 28, 1794, NYSBR, 88–89.

82. *NYS Laws, 18th session, 1795*, chap. 75; and Brooke, *Columbia Rising*, 239–41.

83. *NYS Laws, 19th session, 1796*, chap. 49.

84. Roberts, *Century in the Comptroller's Office*, 10–11.

85. January 31, 1797; February 1, 1797, in *NYSJ, 20th session*, 48–50.

86. February 7, 1797, *NYAJ, 20th session, 1797*, 90.

87. *NYS Laws, 20th session, 1797*, chap. 21. Also see, Hammond, *History of Political Parties*, 1:104–5; and Gunn, *Decline of Public Authority*, 88.

88. Murphy, "'Very Convenient Instrument.'"

89. Comptroller Memorandum Book, NYPL.

90. Brooke, *Columbia Rising*, 211–12, 313–15; and Klein and Majewski, "Economy, Community, and Law," 487–90. Edward Herring O'Neill shows that academy development in New York tracked with transportation development from 1800 to the Civil War, in "Private Schools and Public Vision." In Ohio, while education regularly became an issue over which parties could agree, it often started as a divisive partisan issue connected with internal improvements; see Neem "Path Dependence."

91. Pasley, *"Tyranny of Printers,"* 259.

92. Editorial note, Samuel Knox to Thomas Jefferson, January 22, 1810, *Papers of Thomas Jefferson, Retirement Series*, 2:74.

93. For the essays, see Justice, *Founding Fathers*. For the critique of the essays as unrepresentative, see Moroney, "Birth of a Canon."

94. Smith, *Remarks on Education*, 79.

95. "Academicus," "Plan for the Education of Youth," in Justice, *Founding Fathers*, 249.

96. "Freedom," "Concerning Education in Pennsylvania," in Justice, *Founding Fathers*, 266.

97. Knox, *Essay on the Best System*, 68, 84, 8.

98. Dubois, *Avengers of the New World*, 209–11.

99. The best recent work on the national university is Oberle, "Institutionalizing the Information Revolution." Also see Thomas, *Founders and the Idea*.

100. Alexander White to James Madison, December 2, 1796, in Hutchinson, Rachal, Rutland, and Stagg, *Papers of James Madison*, 16:421–22.

101. George Washington to Thomas Jefferson, March 15, 1795, in Boyd, *Papers of Thomas Jefferson*, 28:306–9.

102. Most recently, see Shankman, *Original Intents*.

103. Larson, *Internal Improvement*, 49–50; and Ellis, "Persistence of Antifederalism."

104. *American State Papers: Miscellaneous*, 1:153–54.

105. December 27, 1796, *Annals of Congress*, House of Representatives, 4th Congress, 2nd Session, 6:1711, 1706.

106. December 26, 1796, *Annals of Congress*, 6:1700.

107. December 26, 1796, *Annals of Congress*, 6:1699.

108. December 26, 1796, *Annals of Congress*, 6:1700.

109. Oberle, "Institutionalizing the Information Revolution," 44.

110. December 26, 1796, *Annals of Congress*, 6:1699, 1701.

111. For details on the fire, see *Philadelphia Gazette*, December 8, 1796; *Gazette of the United States*, December 6, 1796; and *Claypoole's American Daily Advertiser*, December 7, 1796. For the debate over the proposed new academy, see Baltimore *Federal Gazette*, January 3, 1797; January 6, 1797; January 7, 1797; January 10, 1797; January 11, 1797; and January 14, 1797.

112. *Maryland Journal*, May 20, 1785. On the debate over higher education in Maryland, see also Risjord, *Chesapeake Politics*, 213–16.

113. *Laws of Maryland*, 1798, chap. 107.

114. "Massachusetts 1794 U.S. House of Representatives, District Western 2," NNV.

115. Sharp, *American Politics in the Early Republic*, 17–52.

116. For the Massachusetts ratification votes, see "Convention Journal," February 6, 1788, in *DHRC*, 6:1461–68. The Williamstown trustees come from, Durnin, "New England's Eighteenth-Century Incorporated Academies," 286. On shifting partisan dynamics in this region, see Brooke, "To the Quiet," and on Lyman, 459–60; as well as Condon, *Shays's Rebellion*, 81, 91.

117. Opal, "Natural Rights," 305.

118. On these elections see Vrevich, "Mr. Ely's Amendment," 160–62.

119. I identified twenty academies founded in Pennsylvania before 1800. Town-level election results were available only for twelve of these. On the 1805 election, see Shankman, *Crucible of American Democracy*, 126–72, esp. 159–60. McKean served on the Newark Academy board from at least 1783 to 1791; see June 5, 1783; and September 21, 1791, both in Academy of Newark Board of Trustee Minute Book, UD Archives, 1, 22.

120. "Massachusetts 1804 House of Representatives, Groton"; "Massachusetts 1807 State Senate, Middlesex County"; and "Massachusetts 1807 Senate President," all in *NNV*.

121. Brooke, *Heart of the Commonwealth*, 220, 250, 254, 260.

122. Ellis, *Jeffersonian Crisis*, 87.

123. Brooke, "Ancient Lodges," 316–59; and Bullock, *Revolutionary Brotherhood*, 173–75.

124. Newman, "Principles or Men?"

125. MacWhorter, *Funeral Sermon*, iii.

126. On Masonry, Brooke, "Ancient Lodges," 328.

127. Based on the session laws for all three states.

128. Hume, "Virginia Society of the Cincinnati's Gift ... (Continued)," 201–3.

129. For a contemporary source that credits Washington with influencing the Cincinnati's decision, see *New-Jersey Journal*, January 18, 1803. Newspaper coverage of Washington's gifts can be found in, *Centinel of Liberty*, January 7, 1800; and *Federal Gazette*, February 8, 1800. See also Hume, "Virginia Society of the Cincinnati's Gift," 111–14.

130. Letter from several members to the President of the Virginia Society of the Cincinnati, December 1, 1803, in Hume, *Papers of the Society*, 266–67.

131. Washington Academy trustees to the Virginia Cincinnati, March 9, 1803, in Society of the Cincinnati in the State of Virginia papers, VHS.

132. For the initial decision to send the money to Washington Academy, see December 15, 1802, in Hume, *Papers of the Society*, 56. Some of the petitions from other academies are reprinted in Hume, "Virginia Society of the Cincinnati's Gift ... (Continued)," 203–7. For someone questioning whether to send the money to a single academy, see Alexander Balmain to the Virginia Society of the Cincinnati, November [?], 1803, Winchester, in Hume, *Papers of the Society*, 263.

133. Washington Academy trustees to the Virginia Cincinnati, March 9, 1803, in Society of the Cincinnati in the State of Virginia Papers, VHS.

134. For instance, see Robert Quarles to the Virginia Society of the Cincinnati, March 29, 1803, in Hume, *Papers of the Society*, 177.

135. James Wood to William Jackson, Richmond, August 20, 1812, folder 4F, box 13, Society of the Cincinnati Archives, SOC.

136. Brewer, "Entailing Aristocracy."

137. Hume, "Virginia Society of the Cincinnati's Gift ... (Continued)," 304–16.

138. *Porcupine's Gazette*, March 26, 1799. For another example, see *Aurora General Advertiser*, December 20, 1794. See also Dotts, "Democratic-Republican Societies," 180.

139. Young, *Democratic Republicans*, 411–12; and Kaestle, *Evolution of an Urban School System*, 60–64.

140. The Constitutional Association officers come from Foner, *Democratic-Republican Societies*, 443; and for the Academy board, see *New Jersey Journal*, February 24, 1790.

141. For the founding agreement and list of founding members, see June 27, 1783, Institutio Legalis Record Book, N-JHS, 1. On the society, see Skemer, "Institutio Legalis."

142. May [?], 1795; July 25, 1795; and October [?], 1795, all in Institutio Legalis Record Book, 195, 196, 199.

143. Boonshoft, "Litchfield Network."

144. Ellis, *Jeffersonian Crisis*; and Edwards, *People and Their Peace*.

145. On the connections between legal training, education, and Federalist conceptions of leadership, see Koschnik, "Young Federalists," 166–68.

146. Lewis, *History of Higher Education in Kentucky*, 23–24.

147. At the national level, this shared vision can be seen in the similar makeup of the executive departments through the Jeffersonian Revolution. See White, *Federalists*; White, *Jeffersonians*; and Richard R. John's useful review essay of the White oeuvre, "In Retrospect."

Chapter Seven

1. Rufus King to Noah Webster, May 25, 1807, box 3, folder 4, Noah Webster Papers, NYPL.

2. Rush Welter called these "the later republicans" and "liberal Whigs," in *Popular Education*, 29–36, 74–87.

3. Schocket, *Founding Corporate Power*.

4. Ogden, *View of the New-England Illuminati*, 8, 11, 18. See also Waterman, *Republic of Intellect*, 83–84.

5. Kerber, *Federalists in Dissent*, 95–134.

6. Rush, "Observations Upon the Study of the Latin . . . ," in Rush, *Essays, Literary, Moral*, 24, 25.

7. Octavo vol. 3, "Records of the Social Fraternity," Leicester Academy Records, AAS, 3.

8. Ogden, *View of the New-England Illuminati*, 14.

9. Ogden, *Address Delivered at the Opening*.

10. Knox, *Essay on the Best System*, 6.

11. On the Republican origins of the Whigs, see Ellis, *Jeffersonian Crisis*, 233–84; Roth, *Democratic Dilemma*, 172–78, 248–49; and Brooke, "Patriarchal Magistrates," 193–95.

12. Cleves, *Reign of Terror*, 194–229; Cutterham, *Gentlemen Revolutionaries*, 37–65; and Shalhope, *Roots of Democracy*, 113–17.

13. Lathrop, *Sermon, on the Dangers*, 12.

14. Lathrop, *Sermon, Preached at Westfield*, 10.

15. See Smith, *Remarks on Education*, 69–71; and Knox, *Essay on the Best System*, 111–12.

16. "Bill for the More General Diffusion of Knowledge," June 18, 1779, in Boyd, *Papers of Thomas Jefferson*, 2:526–35; and Steele, *Thomas Jefferson and American Nationhood*, 135.

17. Knox, *Essay on the Best System*, 115, 159.

18. "Plan for a Federal University," *Federal Gazette*, October 22, 1789.

19. Beresford, *Aristocracy the Bane of Liberty*, 37.

20. Melancton Smith, "Convention Debates," June 21, 1788, in DHRC, 20:1750. See also Cornell, "Aristocracy Assailed," 1157–68.

21. Cotlar, *Tom Paine's America*, 115–60.

22. Coram, "Political Inquiries," in Rudolph, *Essays on Education*, 113, 138, 130.

23. Foner, *Democratic-Republican Societies*, 13–15.

24. "Memorial to the [Delaware] Legislature on Schools," December 23, 1794; "Resolutions Adopted on the Importance of Establishing Public Schools," March 19, 1795; and "Celebration of the Nineteenth Anniversary of American Independence by the Joint

Societies," July 4, 1795, all in Foner, *Democratic-Republican Societies*, 108, 323, 225. See also Walsh, *Intellectual Origins of Mass Parties*, 46–55.

25. Manning, *Key of Liberty*, 140, 182.

26. Polgar, "'To Raise Them,'" 242–50; Alexander, *African or American*, 13–14; Neem, *Democracy's Schools*, 9–10; Cotlar, *Tom Paine's America*, 55–67; and Riley, *Slavery and the Democratic Conscience*, 50–93. On Manning, see introduction to Manning, *Key of Liberty*, 68–69.

27. *Albany Register*, February 18, 1799.

28. Taylor, *William Cooper's Town*, 286.

29. *NYS Laws*, 24th session, 1801, chap. 53. Also see Hobson, "Educational Legislation," 139.

30. March 4, 1801, *NYAJ*, 24th session, 1801, 144; and April 1, 1801, *NYSJ*, 24th session, 1801, 123.

31. Nancy Isenberg criticizes Gordon Wood for portraying early-nineteenth century democracy through "a 1950s notion of a meritocracy"; see "Empire Has No Clothes," 263n4. The language of merit is not as anachronistic as Isenberg suggests. Yet unlike Wood, my analysis suggests that the institutions built to create a merit-based society failed by the standards of the Jeffersonians who adopted the ideal, at least in 1800. See also Taylor, *Liberty Men*, 215–17; and Cotlar, "Federalists' Transatlantic Cultural Offensive."

32. "For the Balance No. IV," *Balance*, September 3, 1801; reprinted in *Spectator*, November 4, 1801.

33. "For the Balance No. V. SCHOOLS," *Balance*, November 12, 1801; republished in *Commercial Advertiser*, November 20, 1801. Also see, "Viator," "For the Balance, No. VII," *Balance*, December 24, 1801; "Historicus," "For the Balance No. X," *Balance*, November 26, 1801; and "Historicus," "For the Balance No. XIII and the last," *Balance*, December 17, 1801. For essays in support of academies, see *Balance*, June 11, 1801; June, 18, 1801; August 6, 1801; and August 13, 1801.

34. *Albany Centinel*, January 29, 1802.

35. *Balance*, February 9, 1802; *Albany Centinel*, February 2, 1802; and *Albany Gazette*, March 8, 1802.

36. *Albany Centinel*, November 9, 1804.

37. *Balance*, November 20, 1804, taken from *Evening Post*.

38. "Education," *Bee*, January 15, 1805; *Albany Register*, January 18, 1805; and *Otsego Herald*, February 21, 1805.

39. *Balance*, February 19, 1805.

40. *NYS Laws*, 28th session, 1805, chap. 66.

41. Cornog, *Birth of Empire*, 69–72.

42. *Morning Chronicle*, April 25, 1807.

43. *Political Barometer*, April 7, 1807; and "GATES," *Republican Crisis*, April 23, 1807.

44. Cornog, *Birth of Empire*, 78–83; and Taylor, *William Cooper's Town*, 351–52.

45. "Common Schools," *Independent American*, August 29, 1809; *Balance*, March 9, 1810, which was republished in *Northern Whig*, March 15, 1810; *New York Spectator*, March 17, 1810; and *Northern Post*, March 22, 1810. Also see "School Fund," *The American*, March 13, 1810; *Albany Balance*, March 20, 1810; *Independent American*, March 27, 1810; and *Northern Whig*, April 12, 1810.

46. *American Eagle*, March 28, 1810; *Suffolk Gazette*, March 31, 1810; and *American Monitor*, April 7, 1810.

47. *Political Barometer*, April 11, 1810.

48. *NYAJ*, 35th session, 1812, 103.
49. Folts, *History of the University*.
50. Bush, *History of Education in New Hampshire*, 13–15. On state politics, see Turner, *Ninth State*, 215–33.
51. Galusha quoted in, Huden, *Development of State School Administration*, 39. Cubberley, *Public Education in the United States*, 98. On Vermont politics, see Doyle, *Vermont Political Tradition*, 84–86; and Roth, *Democratic Dilemma*, 73–79.
52. Brooke, *Columbia Rising*, 342–62, 569n20; and Isenberg, *Fallen Founder*, 71–83.
53. Norton, "Communications."
54. Beadie, *Education and the Creation*, 154–57.
55. Martin, *Evolution of the Massachusetts*, 83–89, 91–94; and Sklar, "Schooling of Girls."
56. Williams, "Jedediah Peck," 231–32.
57. Buel, *America on the Brink*; Gilje, "'Free Trade and Sailors' Rights'"; Taylor, *Civil War of 1812*, 4–10, 81–83, 115–23; and Perl-Rosenthal, *Citizen Sailors*, 261–69.
58. Matson, "Mathew Carey's Learning Experience"; Shankman, "Capitalism, Slavery, and the New Epoch"; Sellers, *Market Revolution*, 70–102; and Larson, *Internal Improvement*, 39–108.
59. Eustace, "Introduction," in Eustace and Teute, *Warring for America*, 1–25.
60. Keyssar, *Right to Vote*, 31, 308–13.
61. Sylla, "Experimental Federalism," 489–502; Brooke, "Patriarchal Magistrates," for bank charters by region, 194; and Murphy, *Other People's Money*, 54–56.
62. Sylla, Legler, and Wallis, "Banks and State Public Finance"; Cubberley, *Public Education*, 99–103; Powell, *History of Education in Delaware*, 139–41; and Steiner, *History of Education in Maryland*, 52–56.
63. Kilpatrick, "Beginnings of the Public School," 6–7.
64. "Report on Education Made to the General Assembly of North Carolina at its Session of 1816," in Hoyt, *Papers of Archibald D. Murphey*, 2:51, 54.
65. "Report on Education Submitted to the Legislature of North Carolina, 1817," in Hoyt, *Papers of Archibald D. Murphey*, 2:63.
66. Addis, *Jefferson's Vision for Education*, 33–53; Neem, *Democracy's Schools*, 78–79; and on democracy in Virginia, Keyssar, *Right to Vote*, 29–33; and Sellers, *Market Revolution*, 113–17.
67. Haulman, *Virginia and the Panic*; Sellers, *Market Revolution*, 131–36; Rothbard, *Panic of 1819*, 1–16; Wilentz, *The Rise of American Democracy*, 202–9; and Opal, *Avenging the People*, 172–74.
68. Rothbard, *Panic of 1819*, 37–80, and appendix B, 259–62; Opal, *Avenging the People*, 174–85; Browning, *Panic of 1819*, 51–80; and Opal, "Natural Rights," 305–10.
69. VanBurkleo, "'That Our Pure Republican Principles,'" 73–94.
70. Opal, *Avenging the People*, 62–66; and Kidd, "Search For Moral Order," on moral critiques of relief, 345–55, and on antirelief solutions, 397–447.
71. December 2, 1816, *KYSJ*, 25th Session.
72. December 1, 1817, *KYSJ*, 26th Session, 13.
73. *Argus of Western America*, October 19, 1820.
74. VanBurkleo, "'That Our Pure Republican Principles,'" 211–12n114, 122. VanBurkleo describes Adair's policies as "anti-relief relief"; see 154–59.

75. All quotations from, *Report, &c., House of Representatives of the Commonwealth*, 5, 6, 9, 10, 14, 19, 20. See also Rothbard, *Panic of 1819*, 102–5; Wilentz, *Rise of American Democracy*, 210–13; and Lehman, "Explaining Hard Times," 359–61.

76. "To the Assembly with Documents from the Maryland Legislature relating to the Application of Public Lands to Public Education," March 8, 1821; and Hiester's 1821 Annual Message, both in *Pennsylvania Archives*, 5:257–69, 287–89.

77. Van Atta, *Securing the West*, 96–101; and "Appropriations of Public Lands for Schools."

78. Schulze, Inaugural Message, December 26, 1823, in *Pennsylvania Archives*, 5:495.

79. Opal, *Avenging the People*, 186–99, 199–203.

80. Kendall, *Autobiography of Amos Kendall*, 228–29; and Cole, *A Jackson Man*, 19, 26, 74–77.

81. "SKETCHES ON EDUCATION . . . NO. I," *Argus of Western America*, October 8, 1819.

82. M'Afee, "Speech of Robert B. M'Afee."

83. Cousins, *Horace Holley*, 141–44, 160–61.

84. "SKETCHES ON EDUCATION . . . NO. II," *Argus of Western America*, October 15, 1819.

85. "SKETCHES ON EDUCATION . . . NO. III," *Argus of Western America*, October 22, 1819.

86. "SKETCHES ON EDUCATION . . . NO. IV," *Argus of Western America*, October 29, 1819.

87. "SKETCHES ON EDUCATION . . . NO. V," *Argus of Western America*, November 12, 1819.

88. "SKETCHES ON EDUCATION . . . NO. VI," *Argus of Western America*, November 19, 1819.

89. VanBurkleo, "'That Our Pure Republican Principles,'" 55, 82, 93–94, 136–37, 180, 186.

90. *Argus of Western America*, September 3, 1823; and December 12, 1823.

91. Willard, *Address to the Public*, 4, 5, 34–35; and Brooke, *Columbia Rising*, 358–60.

92. Beecher, *Essay on the Education*; Tolley, *Heading South to Teach*, 150–53; Perlman and Margo, *Women's Work?*, 27–33; and Nash, *Women's Education*, 59–61, 65–67.

93. Scott, "Ever Widening Circle"; Kelley, *Learning to Stand & Speak*, 28; and Tolley, *Heading South to Teach*, 48–53.

94. Kelley, *Learning to Stand & Speak*, 191–244; Brickley, "Sarah Pierce's Litchfield Female Academy," 250–61; and Baker, *Affairs of Party*, 78–87. On earlier, less nationalistic, textbooks, see Nash, "Contested Identities."

95. Yokota, *Unbecoming British*, 38–61.

96. Schulten, "Map Drawing, Graphic Literacy," 196–98, 203–9.

97. Abbott, *Government Policy*, 28.

98. Miller, *Academy System*, 107–20; and Abbott, *Government Policy*, 35–39.

99. Quoted in Abbott, *Government Policy*, 37. Also see Cubberley, *Public Education in the United States*, 276–78.

100. M'Afee, "Speech of Robert B. M'Afee"; and "Public Schools," *American Farmer*, March 3, 1820.

101. Mercer, *Discourse on Popular Education*, 70; and Maclean, *Lecture on a School System*, 21, 30–32.

102. Beadie, "Internal Improvement," 99.

103. Hobson, "Educational Legislation," 38.

104. Neem, *Democracy's Schools*, 66.

105. The 1850 numbers come from Miller, *Academy System*, 34.

106. Goldin and Katz, "'Virtues' of the Past," 41–45; and Beadie, "Academy Students," 253–55.

107. Goldin and Katz, "'Virtues' of the Past," 44n75.

108. Sizer, *Age of Academies*, 37n55; and Axtell, *Wisdom's Workshop*, 154–59. Historians often describe academy students as middle-class, relying on data from the 1830s–1850s. See Kett, *Rites of Passage*, 18–20; Beadie, "Academy Students," 255–62; and Beadie, "Internal Improvement," 96–102. On nineteenth-century academies and communal change, see Beadie, *Education and the Creation*; Opal, *Beyond the Farm*; Fuhrer, *Crisis of Community*, 126–51; Kelly, *In the New England Fashion*; and Kelley, *Learning to Stand & Speak*.

109. In other words, it took reform to make academies less exclusive. Here I argue against Carl Kaestle, who suggests that a modern view of independent schools "tempts us to exaggerate the exclusive character of the academies." See Kaestle, *Pillars of the Republic*, 118, 118–20. On the reformers' view, see Glenn, *Myth of the Common School*, 219–22.

110. Mastromarino, "Fair Visions," 157–218; Ron, "Developing the Country," 69–71; and Kelly, "'Consummation of Rural Prosperity.'"

111. De Witt, *Considerations on the Necessity*, 3, 14, 27, 30–31.

112. Ron, "Developing the Country," 124–40; Ron, "Summoning the State"; and Cremin, *National Experience*, 337–42.

113. Lord, "Alden Partridge's Proposal."

114. Partridge, *Military Academy at West Point Unmasked*, 4.

115. Dwiggins, "Military Establishment and Democratic Politics," 76–151; and Green, *Military Education*.

116. Beadie, *Education and the Creation*, 249–53; and Bell, "Confronting Colorism."

117. Here and throughout, I push against a tendency in recent scholarship to emphasize the decentralized and voluntary origins of public schools, and instead foreground the role of state politics and law. See Tolley, *Transformations in Schooling*, 251–65; Go and Lindert, "Uneven Rise"; Beadie, "Education, Social Capital"; and Neem, *Democracy's Schools*, 61–93. For a review of this scholarship, see Neem, "State Of The Field." 347–49. For a critique of this literature, see Shammas, "Did Democracy Give the United States."

118. Burr, *Education in New Jersey*, 244–59.

119. Mercer, *Discourse on Popular Education*, 14, 53, 58, 62.

120. Maclean, *Lecture on a School System*, 7, 11, 12, 19–20.

121. Kidd, "Search for Moral Order," 262–84.

122. On Gales's moderate turn, see Cotlar, "Joseph Gales and the Making," 331–59. On Gales and the Raleigh academy, see Tolley, "Joseph Gales and Education"; and Tolley, "Chartered School in a Free Market." On North Carolina politics, see Gilpatrick, *Jeffersonian Democracy*, 129–30, 142–44; and Jeffrey, *State Parties*, 195–98.

123. Neem, *Democracy's Schools*, 5–60, 81–83.

124. Abbott, *Government Policy*, 33–41; Miller, *Academy System*, 29, 44–47; Folts, *History of the University*, 16; and Beadie, "From Student Markets," 3–6.

125. See the map in, Cubberley, *Public Education in the United States*, 262.

126. The literature on high schools is vast. See, Cubberley, *Public Education in the United States*, 252–64; Katz, *Irony of Early School Reform*, 51–53, 60–80; Kaestle, *Pillars of the Republic*, 120–21; Reese, *America's Public Schools*, 62–63; Neem, *Democracy's Schools*, 26–30; Vinovskis, *Origins of Public High Schools*; Labaree, *Making of an American High School*; and Ueda, *Avenues to Adulthood*.

127. Beadie, "Academy Students," 253; and Beadie, "Internal Improvement," 98–99.

128. Kett, *Rites of Passage*, 126–30.

129. Welter, *Popular Education*, 45–102; Walsh, *Intellectual Origins*, 226–40; and Neem, *Democracy's Schools*, 26–30.

130. Huston, *American and British Debate*, 91–96.

131. Kett, *Merit*, 99–111.

132. Opal, "Natural Rights," 313.

133. Neem, "Path Dependence."

134. Welter, *Popular Education*, 128–35; Watson, "Man with the Dirty Black Beard"; Merritt, *Masterless Men*, 143–78; Majewski, "Why Did Northerners Oppose"; Quintana, *Making a Slave State*, 164–65; and Hall, "Slaves of the State."

135. Griffin, "Antislavery Utopias"; Sinha, *Slave's Cause*, 180–82; and Wilentz, *Chants Democratic*, 176–80.

136. Wood, "'One Woman so Dangerous'"; Teute, "Roman Matron on the Banks"; Lewis, "Politics and the Ambivalence"; Kelley, *Learning to Stand & Speak*, 37–55; Zagarri, *Revolutionary Backlash*; and Zagarri, "Politics and Civil Society." On petitioning, see Zaeske, *Signatures of Citizenship*; and Portnoy, *Their Right to Speak*. On Stowe, see Brooke, "There Is a North."

137. Daggar, "Mission Complex," 477–80; Nichols, *Engines of Diplomacy*, 8–9, 153–59; Bowes, *Land Too Good*, 56–57; and Snyder, *Great Crossings*, 10–11. I also thank Samantha Seeley for sharing her forthcoming work on the topic.

138. Snyder, *Great Crossings*, 272–96.

139. Justice, *War That Wasn't*.

140. Kaestle, *Pillars of the Republic*, 98, 163–71; Glenn, *Myth of the Common School*, 196–204; and Neem, *Democracy's Schools*, 142–61.

141. Polgar, "'To Raise Them'"; and Gronningsater, "Delivering Freedom," chap. 3.

142. Steele, *Thomas Jefferson*, 169–86, esp. 180–82.

143. Hines, "Learning Freedom"; Alexander, *African or American?*, 82–84; and Archer, *Jim Crow North*, 43–56.

144. Neem, *Democracy's Schools*, 162–63; Wright, "Racial Integration in the Public Schools"; Davison, "Limits of Law," 684–97; Moss, *Schooling Citizens*, 18–20; and for the long arc, see Williams, *Prudence Crandall's Legacy*.

145. Cook, *Pricing of Progress*, 116–18.

146. Gronningsater, "Delivering Freedom," chap. 3.

147. Baumgartner, "Love and Justice."

148. Gronningsater, "Practicing Formal Politics."

149. Green, *Educational Reconstruction*; and Black, "Constitutional Compromise."

Epilogue

1. Guo, "What Are the Most Popular Street Names."

2. Leslie, "Where Have All the Academies Gone?"

3. See https://www.andover.edu/admission/tuition-and-financial-aid; and https://www.exeter.edu/admissions-and-financial-aid/tuition-financial-aid (both accessed September 16, 2019).

4. Kruse, *White Flight*, 169–79; Lassiter, *Silent Majority*, 165–74; Crespino, *In Search of Another Country*, 237–66; and Crosby, *Little Taste of Freedom*, 236–37.

5. Ayscue et al., "Charters as a Driver of Resegregation."

6. Frankenberg et al., "Choice without Equity."

7. Ravitch, *Reign of Error*.

8. Orfield et al., "Harming Our Common Future."

9. Putnam, *Our Kids*.

10. Chetty et al., "Mobility Report Cards."

11. Hayes, *Twilight of the Elites*, 31–64. See also Andrews, "New Ruling Class"; McClay, "Distant Elite"; and Frank, "Just Deserts."

Bibliography

Manuscript Collections

Albany, N.Y.
  New York State Archives
    Journal of Meetings Minutes, Board of Regents of University of New York, microfilm
Annapolis, Md.
  Maryland State Archives
    Minutes of Trustees of Washington Academy
Baltimore, Md.
  Maryland Historical Society
    Harper-Pennington Papers, MS. 431
Boston, Mass.
  Massachusetts Historical Society
    Marblehead Academy (Marblehead, Mass.) records, 1789–1792
Durham, N.C.
  Rubenstein Library, Duke University
    Freemasons Fayetteville, NC, Phoenix Masonic Lodge No. 8, Records
    Liberty Hall Academy Minutes of Board of Trustees
Morristown, N.J.
  North Jersey History & Genealogy Center, Morristown & Morris Township Library
    Diary of Daniel Mulford, typescript
Newark, Del.
  University of Delaware Archives
    Academy of Newark Board of Trustees Minute Book
Newark, N.J.
  New-Jersey Historical Society
    Ebenezer Elmer Papers, MG 38
    Institutio Legalis Record Book, MG 214
    Jacob Green Papers, MG 579
    John Witherspoon Papers, MG 58
    Joseph Black Collection, MG 125
    Newark Academy Minutes, MG 1303
New Brunswick, N.J.
  Alexander Library, Rutgers University
    Elizabeth R. Boyd Historical Collection on Rutgers
New York, N.Y.
  New-York Historical Society
    Records of the New-York Manumission Society, BV Manumission Society, MS 1465

New York Public Library, Manuscripts and Archives Division
    New York State Comptroller memorandum book 1799–1826, MssCol 2203
    New York State Miscellaneous Collection, MssCol 2212
    Noah Webster Papers, MssCol 3258
    Thomas Addis Emmet Collection, MssCol 927
Philadelphia, Pa.
  Historical Society of Pennsylvania
    Fisher Family Papers, Collection 2094
    Meredith Family Papers, Collection 1509
    Simon Gratz Autograph Collection, Collection 0250B
  Library Company of Philadelphia
    Rush Family Papers
  Presbyterian Historical Society
    Francis Alison Papers
    Robert Smith Papers, Notebooks
    Samuel Davies Papers
    Samuel Purviance Jr. Letters
    Trustee Minutes of the First Presbyterian Church of Elizabeth Town, New Jersey
  Rare Book and Manuscript Library, University of Pennsylvania
    John Ewing Papers, Ms. Coll. 284
Princeton, N.J.
  Firestone Library, Manuscripts Division, Department of Rare Books and Special
      Collections, Princeton University Library
    Philip Vickers Fithian Journals and commonplace books, 1766–1776. General
        Manuscripts Bound (C0199, no. 349)
    John Witherspoon Collection (C0274)
    Jonathan Dickinson Collection (C1046)
    Princeton University Library Collection of Ashbel Green Materials (C0257)
    Samuel Finley Collection (C1055)
Raleigh, N.C.
  North Carolina Department of Archives and History
    Hillsborough Academy Papers, 1776, 1783–1790 (Pc.596)
Richmond, Va.
  Virginia Historical Society
    Society of the Cincinnati in the State of Virginia Papers
    Washington Henry Academy Trustee Records
Trenton, N.J.
  Trentoniana Department, Trenton Free Public Library
    Records of the Proprietors of the Trenton Academy
Washington, D.C.
  Society of the Cincinnati
    Society of the Cincinnati Archives
Washington's Crossing, Pa.
  David Library of the American Revolution
    Damages by the British and Americans in New Jersey, film #437

New Jersey Civil List, 1664–1800, film #298
Revolutionary War Pension and Bounty Land Warrant Applications, B.L.11-450, reel 136
Westfield, Mass.
　Westfield Athenaeum
　　Westfield Academy Records
Worcester, Mass.
　American Antiquarian Society
　　Leicester Academy Records [manuscript], 1784–1963
　　Minervaean Society (Brookfield, Mass.) Records [manuscript], 1789–1794
　　Stephen Peabody Diaries [manuscript], 1767–1814
　　Worcester County (Mass.) Records [manuscript], 1665–1954

Newspapers

Albany Centinel (Albany, N.Y.)
Albany Gazette (Albany, N.Y.)
Albany Register (Albany, N.Y.)
Alexandria Daily Advertiser (Alexandria, Va.)
American Citizen (New York, N.Y.)
American Eagle (Catskill, N.Y.)
American Farmer (Baltimore, Md.)
American Minerva (New York, N.Y.)
American Monitor (Plattsburgh, N.Y.)
American Spy (Troy, N.Y.)
Argus of Western America (Frankfort, Ky.)
Aurora General Advertiser (Philadelphia, Pa.)
The [Albany] Balance (Albany, N.Y.)
The Balance (Hudson, N.Y.)
Baltimore Daily Intelligencer (Baltimore, Md.)
Baltimore Federal Gazette (Baltimore, Md.)
The Bee (Hudson, N.Y.)
Burlington Advertiser (Burlington, N.J.)
Carlisle Gazette (Carlisle, Pa.)
Centinel of Freedom (Newark, N.J.)
Centinel of Liberty (Georgetown, Washington, D.C.)
Claypoole's American Daily Advertiser (Philadelphia, Pa.)
Commercial Advertiser (New York, N.Y.)
Diary (New York, N.Y.)
Dunlap's American Daily Advertiser (Philadelphia, Pa.)
Dunlap's Pennsylvania Packet (Philadelphia, Pa.)
Evening Post (New York, N.Y.)
Federal Gazette (Philadelphia, Pa.)
Federal Intelligencer (Baltimore, Md.)
Freeman's Journal (Philadelphia, Md.)
Gazette of the United States (Philadelphia, Pa.)
General Advertiser (Philadelphia, Pa.)
Greenleaf's New York Journal (New York, N.Y.)
Independent Chronicle (Boston, Mass.)
Impartial Herald (Newburyport, Mass.)
Independent American (Ballston Spa, N.Y.)
Independent Gazetteer (Philadelphia, Pa.)
Independent Journal (New York, N.Y.)
Independent Reflector (New York, N.Y.)
The Mail (Philadelphia, Pa.)
Maryland Gazette (Baltimore, Md.)
Maryland Herald (Elizabethtown, Md.)
Maryland Journal (Baltimore, Md.)
Massachusetts Centinel (Boston, Mass.)
Morning Chronicle (New York, N.Y.)
National Gazette (Philadelphia, Pa.)
New-Jersey Gazette (Burlington and Trenton, N.J.)
New-Jersey Journal (Elizabeth Town and Chatham, N.J.)

New York Daily Advertiser (New York, N.Y.)
New-York Daily Gazette (New York, N.Y.)
New-York Gazette (New York, N.Y.)
New-York Journal (New York, N.Y.)
New York Mercantile Advertiser (New York, N.Y.)
New-York Packet (New York, N.Y.)
Northern Post (Salem, N.Y.)
Northern Whig (Hudson, N.Y.)
Norwich Packet (Norwich, Conn.)
Otsego Herald (Cooperstown, N.Y.)
Pennsylvania Chronicle (Philadelphia, Pa.)
Pennsylvania Evening Herald (Philadelphia, Pa.)
Pennsylvania Gazette (Philadelphia, Pa.)
Pennsylvania Mercury (Philadelphia, Pa.)
Pennsylvania Packet (Philadelphia, Pa.)
Petersburg Intelligencer (Petersburg, Va.)
Philadelphia Gazette (Philadelphia, Pa.)
Philadelphia General Advertiser (Philadelphia, Pa.)
Political Barometer (Poughkeepsie, N.Y.)
Political Intelligencer (New Brunswick, NJ.)
Porcupine's Gazette (Philadelphia, Pa.)
Poulson's American Daily Advertiser (Philadelphia, Pa.)
Republican Crisis (Albany, N.Y.)
Republican Star (Easton, Md.)
Richmond Enquirer (Richmond, Va.)
Rights of Man (Fredericktown, Md.)
Rivington's New-York Gazette (New York, N.Y.)
Rockbridge Repository (Lexington, Va.)
Royal Gazette (New York, N.Y.)
The Spectator (New York, N.Y.)
Suffolk Gazette (Sag Harbor, N.Y.)
The Times (Alexandria, Va.)
United States' Gazette (Philadelphia, Pa.)
Virginia Argus (Richmond, Va.)
Virginia Chronicle (Norfolk, Va.)
Virginia Journal (Alexandria, Va.)

Internet Resources

American National Biography, http://www.anb.org.
Benjamin Franklin Papers, Yale University, http://franklinpapers.org.
Hening, William Waller. *The Statutes at Large; Being a Collection of All the Laws of Virginia, from the First Session of the Legislature, in the Year 1619; Published Pursuant to an Act of the General Assembly of Virginia*, 13 vols. Richmond, Va.: Printed by and for Samuel Pleasants, 1809–1823, http://vagenweb.org/hening.
Legislative Petitions of the General Assembly, 1776–1865, Library of Virginia, http://www.virginiamemory.com/collections/petitions.
A New Nation Votes: American Election Returns, 1787–1825 (NNV), https://elections.lib.tufts.edu.
The Student, Teacher, and Trustee Database Project, 1800–1900, founded by Rich Morgan, American Antiquarian Society, http://morgan.mwa.org/studentnames/index.php.

Printed Government Documents

Acts and Laws Passed by the Great and General Court or Assembly, of the State of Massachusetts-Bay, in New-England: Begun and Held at Boston, in the County of Suffolk, on Wednesday the Twenty-Sixth Day of May, Anno Domini 1779; and from Thence Continued by Adjournments to Wednesday the Eighth of March Following, and Then Met. Boston: Printed by Benjamin Edes and Sons, printers to the Honorable Council of the state of Massachusetts-Bay, n.d.

American State Papers: Miscellaneous, 2 vols. Washington, D.C.: Gales and Seaton, 1832–1861.
Annals of Congress of the United States, 42 vols. Washington, D.C.: Gales and Seaton, 1834–1856.
Cooper, Thomas, ed. *The Statutes at Large of South Carolina*, vol. 5. Columbia, S.C.: A. S. Johnston, 1839.
Laws of Maryland, Made and Passed at a Session of Assembly, Begun and Held at the City of Annapolis, on Monday the Fifth of November, in the Year of Our Lord One Thousand Seven Hundred and Ninety-Eight. Annapolis, Md.: Printed by Frederick Green, printer to the state, [1799].
Laws of the State of New-York. Volume the Third. New York, N.Y.: Printed by Francis Childs and John Swaine, printers to the state, 1790.
The Laws of the Royal Colony of New Jersey, 1703–1745. Vol. 2. 3rd ser. Trenton, N.J.: New Jersey State Library, Archives and History Bureau, 1977.
Pennsylvania Archives: Papers of the Pennsylvania Governors, 12 vols. Harrisburg, Pa.: State of Pennsylvania, 1900.
Report, &c., House of Representatives of the Commonwealth of Pennsylvania. December 10, 1819. Harrisburg, Pa.: Peacock, [1819?].
Revised Laws of the State of Vermont. Passed by the General Assembly of the Representatives of the Freemen of the State, at Their Sessions in June and October, in the Year of Our Lord, One Thousand Seven Hundred and Eighty Two, and the Fifth Year of Their Sovereignty and Independence. Bennington, Vt.: Printed by Haswell & Russell, 1783.
The Speeches of the Different Governors, to the Legislature of the State of New-York, Commencing with Those of George Clinton, and Continued Down to the Present Time. Albany, N.Y.: J. B. Van Steenbergh, 1825.

Printed Primary Sources

Andrews, Charles C. *The History of the New-York African Free-Schools: From Their Establishment in 1787, to the Present Time; Embracing a Period of More Than Forty Years*. New York, N.Y.: M. Day, 1830.
"Appropriations of Public Lands for Schools." *North American Review* 13 (October 1821): 310–42.
Ashley, Elihu. *Romance, Remedies, and Revolution: The Journal of Dr. Elihu Ashley of Deerfield, Massachusetts, 1773–1775*. Edited by Amelia F. Miller and A. R. Riggs. Amherst, Mass.: University of Massachusetts Press, 2007.
Baldwin, Jeduthan. *The Revolutionary Journal of Col. Jeduthan Baldwin, 1775–1778*. Bangor [Maine?]: De Burians, 1906.
Bancroft, Aaron. *Importance of Education, Illustrated in an Oration, Delivered Before the Trustees, Preceptors & Students of Leicester Academy, on the Fourth of July, 1806; At Opening of a New Building for the Use of That Seminary*. Worcester [Mass.]: Printed by Thomas & Sturtevant, 1806.
Barnard, John. *A Present for an Apprentice: Or, A Sure Guide to Gain Both Esteem and Estate. With Rules for His Conduct to His Master, and in the World. More Especially, While an Apprentice, His Behaviour after He Is Free, Care in Setting Up, Company with the Ladies,*

Choice of a Wife, Behaviour in Courtship, and Wedding-Day, Complaisance after Marriage, Education of Children, &c. Philadelphia, Pa.: Re-printed by J. Crukshank, 1774.

Barrow, William. *An Essay on Education; In Which Are Particularly Considered the Merits and the Defects of the Discipline and Instruction in Our Academies*, 2 vols. London: Printed for F. and C. Rivington, 1802.

Beecher, Catharine. *An Essay on the Education of Female Teachers.* New York: Van Nostrand and Dwight, 1835.

Bentley, William. *The Diary of William Bentley, D.D. Pastor of the East Church, Salem, Massachusetts*, 4 vols. Salem, Mass.: The Essex Institute, 1905–1914.

Beresford, Richard. *Aristocracy the Bane of Liberty; Learning the Antidote. Designed to Recommend the General Establishment of Free Schools and Colleges in Republicks.* Charleston, S.C.: Printed by W. P. Young, 1797.

Blackstone, William. *Commentaries on the Laws of England.* 4 Vols. 3rd ed. Oxford: Clarendon Press, 1768.

[No Title], *Boston Magazine Containing, a Collection of Instructive and Entertaining Essays...* (April 1784): 238–39.

Boyd, Julian P. et al., eds. *Papers of Thomas Jefferson,* 41 vols. Princeton, N.J.: Princeton University Press, 1950–.

A Brief Account of the Associated Presbyteries; and a General View of Their Sentiments Concerning Religion and Ecclesiastical Order. By a Convention of Said Prespyteries [sic]. Catskill, N.Y.: Printed by M. Croswell, 1796.

Brown, John. *Thoughts on Civil Liberty: On Licentiousness, and Faction. By the Author of Essays on the Characteristics, &c.* Dublin: Printed for A. Leathley, 1765.

Bushman, Claudia L., Harold Bell Hancock, and Elizabeth Moyne Homsey, eds. *Proceedings of the Assembly of the Lower Counties on Delaware, 1770–1776, of the Constitutional Convention of 1776, and of the House of Assembly of the Delaware State, 1776–1781.* Newark, Del.: University of Delaware Press, 1986.

Butterfield, Lyman Henry, ed. *John Witherspoon Comes to America: A Documentary Account Based Largely on New Materials.* Princeton, N.J.: Princeton University Library, 1953.

The Charter and By-Laws of the Trustees of the College of New Jersey: Together with a Statement Concerning the Original Charter, and the Rules of Order of the Board. Princeton, N.J.: Printed by order of the Board of Trustees, 1892.

Charter of a College to Be Erected in New-Jersey, by the Name of Queen's-College. New York, N.Y.: Printed by John Holt, 1770.

Christian Education Exemplified Under the Character of Paternus Instructing His Only Son. Germantown, Pa.: Printed by Christopher Sower Junior, 1754.

Constitutions of the Publick Academy, in the City of Philadelphia. Philadelphia, Pa.: Printed by Benjamin Franklin, 1749.

Coon, Charles Lee, ed. *North Carolina Schools and Academies, 1790–1840: A Documentary History.* Raleigh, N.C.: Edwards & Broughton printing Company, state printers, 1915.

Corner, George Washington, ed. *The Autobiography of Benjamin Rush; His "Travels Through Life" Together with His Commonplace Book for 1789–1813.* Princeton, N.J.: Published for the American Philosophical Society by Princeton University Press, 1948.

The Countryman's Lamentation, on the Neglect of a Proper Education of Children; with an Address to the Inhabitants of New-Jersey. Philadelphia, Pa.: Printed and Sold by W. Dunlap, 1762.

Davies, Samuel. *Religion and Public Spirit. A Valedictory Address to the Senior Class, Delivered in Nassau-Hall, September 21, 1760. The Sunday before Commencement: By Samuel Davies, A.M. Late President of the College, Deceased*. Portsmouth, N.J.: Printed and sold by Daniel Fowle, 1762.

———. *A Sermon Delivered at Nassau-Hall, January 14. 1761. On the Death of His Late Majesty King George II. By Samuel Davies, A.M. Late President of the College of New-Jersey. Published by Request. To Which Is Prefixed, a Brief Account of the Life, Character, and Death, of the Author. By David Bostwick, A.M. Minister of the Presbyterian Congregation in New-York*. Boston, Mass.: Printed and sold by R. Draper, 1761.

De Witt, Simeon. *Considerations on the Necessity of Establishing an Agricultural College, and Having More of the Children of Wealthy Citizens Educated for the Profession of Farming*. Albany, N.Y.: Websters & Skinners, 1819.

Dexter, Franklin Bowditch, ed. *Extracts from the Itineraries and Other Miscellanies of Ezra Stiles, 1755–1794: With A Selection from His Correspondence*. New Haven, Conn.: Yale University Press, 1916.

Du Courteil, Amable-Louis-Rose De Lafitte. *Proposal to Demonstrate the Necessity of a National Institution in the United States of America, for the Education of Children of Both Sexes. To Which Is Joined, A Project of Organization*. Philadelphia, Pa.: Printed for G. Decombaz, 1797.

Elmer, Ebenezer. *An Elogy on Francis Barber, Esq., Lieutenant-Colonel Commandant of the Second New Jersey Regiment*. New York, N.Y.: Reprinted for C.F. Heartman, 1917.

"Extracts from Papers Received from Mr. Israel Russell, Relative to the Establishment of the First Academy, Library, and Printing Press in Morristown." *Proceedings of the New Jersey Historical Society* 8 (1856): 18–32.

Foner, Phillip S. *The Democratic-Republican Societies, 1790–1800: A Documentary Sourcebook of Constitutions, Declarations, Addresses, Resolutions, and Toasts*. Westport, Conn.: Greenwood Press, 1976.

Four Dissertations, on the Reciprocal Advantages of a Perpetual Union between Great-Britain and Her American Colonies. Written for Mr. Sargent's Prize-Medal. To Which (by Desire) Is Prefixed, an Eulogium, Spoken on the Delivery of the Medal at the Public Commencement in the College of Philadelphia, May 20th, 1766. Philadelphia, Pa.: Printed by William and Thomas Bradford, 1766.

Franklin, Benjamin. *Idea of the English School, Sketch'd Out for the Consideration of the Trustees of the Philadelphia Academy*. Philadelphia, Pa.: Printed by B. Franklin, 1751.

———. *Proposals Relating to the Education of Youth in Pennsylvania*. Philadelphia, Pa.: Printed by Franklin and Hall, 1749.

Green, Jacob. *Observations: On the Reconciliation of Great-Britain, and the Colonies: In Which Are Exhibited, Arguments For, and Against, That Measure. By a Friend of American Liberty*. Philadelphia, Pa.: Printed by Robert Bell, 1776.

———. *A View of a Christian Church and Church Government; Containing Many Interesting Matters; With an Address to Our Congregations, and an Appendix, Representing the Case and Circumstances of the Associate Presbytery of Morris County. To Which Is Subjoined,*

A Letter Relative to the Same Subject." By the Associated Presbytery of Morris County. Chatham, N.J.: Printed by Shepard Kollock, 1781.

Hoyt, William Henry. *The Papers of Archibald D. Murphey*, vol. 2. Raleigh, N.C.: E. M. Uzzell & Co., state printers, 1914.

Hutcheson, Francis. *A System of Moral Philosophy, In Three Books*, 2 vols. Glasgow: R. and A. Foulis, Printers to the University, 1755.

Hutchinson, William T., William M. E. Rachal, Robert A. Rutland, J. C. A. Stagg et al. *The Papers of James Madison: Congressional Series*, 17 vols. Chicago, Ill.: University of Chicago Press, 1962–1991.

Jay, Sir James. *A Letter to the Governors of the College of New York: Respecting the Collection That Was Made in This Kingdom in 1762 and 1763, for the Colleges of Philadelphia and New York. To Which Are Added, Explanatory Notes; and an Appendix, Containing the Letters . . . Between Mr. Alderman Trecothick and the Author*. London: Printed for G. Kearsly, 1771.

Kendall, Amos. *Autobiography of Amos Kendall*. Edited by William Stickney. Boston, Mass.: Lee and Shepard, 1872.

Klett, Guy. *Minutes of the Presbyterian Church in America 1706–1788*. Philadelphia, Pa.: Presbyterian Historical Society, 1976.

Knox, Samuel. *An Essay on the Best System of Liberal Education, Adapted to the Genius of the Government of the United States*. Baltimore, Md.: Printed by Warner & Hanna, 1799.

Knox, Vicesimus. *Liberal Education: Or, a Practical Treatise on the Methods of Acquiring Useful and Polite Learning*. 11th ed. London: Printed for Charles Dilly, 1795.

Lathrop, Joseph. *A Sermon, on the Dangers of the Times, from Infidelity and Immorality; and Especially from a Lately Discovered Conspiracy against Religion and Government, Delivered at West-Springfield, and Afterward at Springfield*. Springfield, Mass.: Printed by Francis Stebbins, 1798.

——— . *A Sermon, Preached at Westfield, January 1, 1800. At the Dedication of the Academy in That Town*. Suffield, Conn.: Printed by Edward Gray, 1800.

Looney, J. Jefferson et al., eds. *Papers of Thomas Jefferson: Retirement Series*, 15 vols. Princeton, N.J.: Princeton University Press, 2004–.

Lord Chesterfield's Advice to His Son, on Men and Manners: Or, A New System of Education; in Which the Principles of Politeness, and the Art of Acquiring a Knowledge of the World, Are Laid Down in a Plain, Easy, and Familiar Manner. To Which Are Annexed, The Polite Philosopher: Or, An Essay on the Art Which Makes a Man Happy in Himself, and Agreeable to Others. Also, Lord Burghley's Ten Precepts to His Second Son, Robert Cecil, Afterwards the Earl of Salisbury. Philadelphia, Pa.: Printed for T. Dobson, 1789.

Maclean, John. *A Lecture on a School System for New Jersey: Delivered, January 23, 1828, in the Chapel of Nassau-Hall, Before the Literary and Philosophical Society of New Jersey*. Princeton, N.J.: Princeton Press, Connolly & Madden, Printers, 1829.

MacWhorter, Alexander. *A Funeral Sermon, Preached in Newark, December 27, 1799. A Day of Public Mourning, Observed by the Town, for the Universally Lamented, General Washington, Late President of the United States. Who Died the Fourteenth of the Same Month. To Which Is Subjoined, His Last Address, to His Beloved Countrymen*. Newark, N.J.: Printed and sold by Jacob Halsey, 1800.

M'Afee, Robert B. "Speech of Robert B. M'Afee on Education." Broadside. Frankfort, Ky.: n.p., 1820.

Manning, William. *The Key of Liberty: The Life and Democratic Writings of William Manning, "a Laborer," 1747–1814*. Edited by Sean Wilentz and Michael Merrill. Cambridge, Mass.: Harvard University Press, 1993.

Marder, Daniel, ed. *A Hugh Henry Brackenridge Reader, 1770–1815*. Pittsburgh, Pa.: University of Pittsburgh Press, 1970.

Mercer, Charles Fenton. *A Discourse on Popular Education: Delivered in The Church at Princeton, the Evening Before the Annual Commencement of the College of New Jersey September 26, 1826*. Princeton, N.J.: Princeton Press, printed for the societies, by D. A. Borrenstein, 1826.

Murray, Judith Sargent. "On the Equality of the Sexes." *Massachusetts Magazine* 2 (March 1790): 132–35.

———. "On the Equality of the Sexes (contd.)." *Massachusetts Magazine* 2 (April 1790): 223–26.

Ogden, John Cosens. *An Address Delivered at the Opening of the Portsmouth Academy*. Portsmouth, N.H.: Printed by George Jerry Osborne, 1791.

———. *A View of the New-England Illuminati: Who Are Indefatigably Engaged in Destroying the Religion and Government of the United States; under a Feigned Regard for Their Safety—and under an Impious Abuse of True Religion*. Philadelphia, Pa.: Printed by James Carey, 1799.

"On Education." *The Boston Magazine, Containing, a Collection of Instructive and Entertaining Essays . . .* (March 1784): 176–78.

Partridge, Alden. *The Military Academy at West Point Unmasked, or, Corruption and Military Despotism Exposed*. Washington, D.C.: Sold at the Bookstore of J. Elliot, 1830.

A Patern [sic] of Christian Education, Agreable [sic] to the Precepts and Practice of Our Blessed Lord and Saviour Jesus Christ. Germantown, Pa.: Printed by Christopher Sower Junior, 1756.

Pilcher, George William, ed. *The Reverend Samuel Davies Abroad: The Diary of a Journey to England and Scotland, 1753–55*. Urbana, Ill.: University of Illinois Press, 1967.

Priestley, Joseph. *An Essay on a Course of Liberal Education for Civil and Active Life. . . .* London: Printed for C. Henderson under the Royal Exchange, 1765.

———. *Miscellaneous Observations Relating to Education. More Especially, as It Respects the Conduct of the Mind. To Which Is Added, An Essay on a Course of Liberal Education for Civil and Active Life*. Bath: Printed by R. Cruttwell, 1778.

The Pennsylvania Town and Country-Man's Almanack, for the Year of Our Lord 1758. Germantown, Pa.: Printed and sold by C. Sower, 1757.

Poor Roger, 1761. The American Country Almanack for the Year of Christian Account 1761. New York, N.Y.: Printed and Sold by James Parker, 1760.

Prayers, for the Use of the Philadelphia Academy. Philadelphia, Pa.: Printed by B. Franklin, and D. Hall, 1753.

"Proceedings of the Society of Associated Teachers." In New York [State] Department of Public Instruction, *Annual Report of the State Superintendent for the School Year Ending July 25, 1890*, vol. 37. Albany, N.Y.: State Printer, 1891.

Princeton University. *General Catalogue of Princeton University 1746–1906*. Princeton, N.J.: Published by the University, 1908.

Quesnay, Alexandre-Marie. "Memoir Concerning the Academy of the Arts and Science of the United States of America at Richmond, Virginia." In *Eighteenth Annual Report of the Library Board of the Virginia State Library, 1920–1921*. Translated by Roswell Page. Richmond, Va.: Davis Bottom, 1922.

Quesnay de Beaurepaire, Le Chevalier Alexandre Marie. *Mémoire, statuts et prospectus, concernant l'Académie des sciences et beaux-arts des Etats-Unis de l' Amérique, établie à Richemond ... Présentés à L. L. M. et à la famille royale, par le chevalier Quesnay de Beaurepaire*. Paris: Cailleau, 1788.

Records of the Presbyterian Church in the United States of America Embracing the Minutes of the General Presbytery and General Synod 1706–1788, Together with an Index and the Minutes of the General Convention for Religious Liberty, 1766–1775. Philadelphia, Pa.: Presbyterian Board of Publication and Sabbath-School Work, 1904.

Robertson, Archibald. *Elements of the Graphic Arts*. New York, N.Y.: David Longworth, 1802.

Rudolph, Frederick, ed. *Essays on Education in the Early Republic*. Cambridge, Mass.: Belknap Press of Harvard University Press, 1965.

Rush, Benjamin. *Essays, Literary, Moral and Philosophical*. Edited by Michael Meranze. Schenectady, N.Y.: Union College Press, 1988.

"Scheme of the Newark Academy Lottery, (of Only One Class) to Finish and Compleat an Academy in the Town of Newark, Agreeably to an Act of the Legislature of the State of New-Jersey." 1793.

Sermons of Samuel Stanhope Smith. Philadelphia, Pa.: S. Potter and Co., 1821.

Seven Rational Sermons, on the Following Subjects, Viz. I. Against Covetousness. II. On the Vanity of This Life. III. Against Revenge. IV. Of Mirth and Grief. V. The Cruelty of Slandering Innocent, and Defenceless Women. VI. The Duty of Children. VII. Advantages of Education. Written in England, by a Lady, the Translatress of Four Select Tales from Marmonte. Philadelphia, Pa.: Printed by Robert Bell, 1777.

Sheridan, Thomas. *British Education: Or, The Source of the Disorders of Great Britain*. London: Printed for R and J. Dodsley in Pall Mall, 1756.

Smith, Samuel Harrison. *Remarks on Education: Illustrating the Close Connection Between Virtue and Wisdom. To Which Is Annexed, A System of Liberal Education*. Philadelphia, Pa.: Printed by John Ormrod, 1798.

Smith, William. *An Account of Washington College, in the State of Maryland. Published by Order of the Visitors and Governors of the Said College, for the Information of Its Friends and Benefactors*. Philadelphia, Pa.: Printed by Joseph Crukshank, 1784.

———. *A Charge, Delivered May 17, 1757, at the First Anniversary Commencement in the College and Academy of Philadelphia, to the Young Gentlemen Who Took Their Degrees on That Occasion*. Philadelphia, Pa.: Printed by B. Franklin, and D. Hall, 1757.

Steiner, Bernard C. *History of Education in Maryland*. Washington, D.C.: U.S. Government Printing Office, 1894.

Taylor, Robert J., and Marc Friedlaender, eds. *The Adams Papers, Diary of John Quincy Adams*, 2 vols. Cambridge, Mass.: Harvard University Press, 1981.

Tobler, John. *The Pennsylvania Town and Country-Man's Almanack for the Year 1754*. Germantown, Pa.: Printed and sold by C. Sower, June, 1753.

Tocqueville, Alexis de. *Democracy in America*, 2 vols. New York, N.Y.: J. & H. G. Langley, 1835–1840.
Tyler, Royall. *The Contrast: Manners, Morals, and Authority in the Early American Republic*. Edited by Cynthia Kierner. New York, N.Y.: New York University Press, 2007.
Vanderpoel, Emily Noyes, ed. *Chronicles of a Pioneer School from 1792 to 1833, Being the History of Miss Sarah Pierce and Her Litchfield School*. Cambridge, Mass.: The University Press, 1903.
The Virginia Almanack for the Year of Our Lord, 1771 . . . Williamsburg, Va.: Printed and Sold by William Rind, 1770.
Watson, Daniel. *A Sermon, Preached on Occasion of the Brief for the American Colleges*. Newcastle: J. White, 1763.
Watts, Isaac. *Logick: Or, The Right Use of Reason in the Enquiry after Truth. With a Variety of Rules to Guard against Error, in the Affairs of Religion and Human Life, as Well as in the Sciences*. 16th ed. Philadelphia, Pa.: Printed for Thomas Dobson, at the stone house, in Second Street, between Market and Chesnut Street, 1789.
Willard, Emma. *An Address to the Public; Particularly to the Members of the Legislature of New-York, Proposing a Plan for Improving Female Education*. Albany, N.Y.: Printed by I. W. Clark, 1819.
Williams, John Rogers, ed. *Philip Vickers Fithian: Journal and Letters, 1767–1774*. Princeton, N.J.: Published by The University Library, 1900.
Wilson, James. *The Works of the Honourable James Wilson, L. L. D.: Late One of the Associate Justices of the Supreme Court of the United States, and Professor of Law in the College of Philadelphia*, 3 vols. Edited by Bird Wilson. Philadelphia, Pa.: At the Lorenzo Press, printed for Bronson and Chauncey, 1804.
Witherspoon, John. *An Annotated Edition of Lectures on Moral Philosophy*. Edited by Jack Scott. Newark, Del.: University of Delaware Press, 1982.
Yates, William. *Rights of Colored Men to Suffrage, Citizenship, and Trial by Jury: Being a Book of Facts, Arguments and Authorities, Historical Notices and Sketches of Debates—with Notes*. Philadelphia, Pa.: Merrihew & Gunn, 1838.

Secondary Sources

Abbott, Frank C. *Government Policy and Higher Education: A Study of the Regents of the University of the State of New York, 1784–1949*. Ithaca, N.Y.: Cornell University Press, 1958.
Ablavsky, Gregory. "Empire States: The Coming of Dual Federalism." *Yale Law Journal* 128 (May 2019): 1792–868.
Adelberg, Michael S. "The Transformation of Local Governance in Monmouth County, New Jersey, during the War of the American Revolution." *Journal of the Early Republic* 31 (Autumn 2011): 467–98.
Addis, Cameron. *Jefferson's Vision for Education, 1760–1845*. New York, N.Y.: Peter Lang, 2003.
Alexander, Archibald. *Biographical Sketches of the Founder and Principal Alumni of the Log College: Together with an Account of the Revivals of Religion under Their Ministry*. Philadelphia, Pa.: Presbyterian Board of Publication, 1851.

Alexander, Leslie. *African Or American?: Black Identity and Political Activism in New York City, 1784–1861*. Urbana, Ill.: University of Illinois Press, 2008.

Allgor, Catherine. *Parlor Politics: In Which the Ladies of Washington Help Build a City and a Government*. Charlottesville, Va.: University Press of Virginia, 2000.

———. *A Perfect Union: Dolley Madison and the Creation of the American Nation*. New York, N.Y.: Henry Holt and Company, 2006.

Andrews, Helen. "The New Ruling Class." *Hedgehog Review* 18 (Summer 2016): 20–35.

Appleby, Joyce O. *Capitalism and a New Social Order: The Republican Vision of the 1790s*. New York: New York University Press, 1984.

Archer, Richard. *Jim Crow North: The Struggle for Equal Rights in Antebellum New England*. New York: Oxford University Press, 2017.

Arendt, Emily J. "'Ladies Going About for Money': Female Voluntary Associations and Civic Consciousness in the American Revolution." *Journal of the Early Republic* 34 (Summer 2014): 157–86.

Auricchio, Laura. "The Laws of Bienséance and the Gendering of Emulation in Eighteenth-Century French Art Education." *Eighteenth-Century Studies* 36 (December 2003): 231–40.

Axtell, James. *Wisdom's Workshop: The Rise of the Modern University*. Princeton, N.J.: Princeton University Press, 2016.

Ayscue, Jenn, Amy Hawn Nelson, Roslyn Arlin Mickelson, Jason Giersch, and Martha Bottia. "Charters as a Driver of Resegregation." UCLA Civil Rights Project / Proyecto Derechos Civiles, January 2018.

Bailyn, Bernard. *Education in the Forming of American Society: Needs and Opportunities for Study*. Chapel Hill, N.C.: Published for the Institute of Early American History and Culture by the University of North Carolina Press, 1960.

———. "Politics and Social Structure in Colonial Virginia." In *Seventeenth-Century America: Essays in Colonial History*, edited by James Morton Smith, 90–115. Chapel Hill, N.C.: University of North Carolina Press, 1959.

Baker, Jean H. *Affairs of Party: The Political Culture of Northern Democrats in the Mid-Nineteenth Century*. Ithaca, N.Y.: Cornell University Press, 1983.

Balogh, Brian. *A Government Out of Sight: The Mystery of National Authority in Nineteenth-Century America*. New York, N.Y.: Cambridge University Press, 2009.

Banning, Lance. "Republican Ideology and the Triumph of the Constitution, 1789 to 1793." *William and Mary Quarterly* 31 (April 1974): 168–88.

Baumgartner, Kabria. "Love and Justice: African American Women, Education, and Protest in Antebellum New England." *Journal of Social History* 52 (Spring 2019): 652–76.

Beadie, Nancy. "Academy Students in the Mid-Nineteenth Century: Social Geography, Demography, and the Culture of Academy Attendance." *History of Education Quarterly* 41 (July 2001): 251–62.

———. *Education and the Creation of Capital in the Early American Republic*. New York, N.Y.: Cambridge University Press, 2010.

———. "Education, Social Capital, and State Formation in Comparative Historical Perspective: Preliminary Investigations." *Paedagogica Historica* 46 (2010): 15–32.

———. "'Encouraging Useful Knowledge' in the Early Republic: The Roles of State Governments and Voluntary Associations." In *The Founding Fathers, Education, and*

"The Great Contest": The American Philosophical Society Prize of 1797, edited by Benjamin Justice, 85–102. New York, N.Y.: Palgrave Macmillan, 2013.

———. "From Student Markets to Credential Markets: The Creation of the Regents Examination System in New York State, 1864–1890." *History of Education Quarterly* 39 (Spring 1999): 1–30.

———. "Internal Improvement: The Structure and Culture of Academy Expansion in New York State in the Antebellum Era, 1820–1860." In *Chartered Schools: Two Hundred Years of Independent Academies in the United States*, edited by Nancy Beadie and Kimberly Tolley 1727–1925, 89–115. New York, N.Y.: Routledge Press, 2002.

———. "Toward a History of Education Markets in the United States: An Introduction." *Social Science History* 32 (Spring 2008): 47–73.

Beadie, Nancy, and Kimberly Tolley. "A School for Every Purpose: An Introduction to the History of Academies in the United States." In *Chartered Schools: Two Hundred Years of Independent Academies in the United States, 1727–1925*, edited by Nancy Beadie and Kimberly Tolley, 3–16. New York, N.Y.: Routledge Press, 2002.

Beam, Jacob Newton. "Dr. Robert Smith's Academy at Pequea, Pennsylvania." *Journal of the Presbyterian Historical Society* 8 (December 1915): 145–61.

Beasley, James R. "Emerging Republicanism and the Standing Order: The Appropriation Act Controversy in Connecticut, 1793 to 1795." *William and Mary Quarterly* 29 (October 1972): 587–610.

Beeman, Richard R. *The Varieties of Political Experience in Eighteenth-Century America*. Philadelphia, Pa.: University of Pennsylvania Press, 2004.

Bell, James B. *A War of Religion: Dissenters, Anglicans, and the American Revolution*. New York, N.Y.: Palgrave Macmillan, 2008.

Bell, John Frederick. "Confronting Colorism: Interracial Abolition and the Consequences of Complexion." *Journal of the Early Republic* 39 (Summer 2019): 239–65.

Beneke, Chris. *Beyond Toleration: The Religious Origins of American Pluralism*. New York, N.Y.: Oxford University Press, 2006.

Black, Derek W. "The Constitutional Compromise to Guarantee Education." *Stanford Law Review* 70 (March 2018): 735–837.

Blaufarb, Rafe. *The French Army, 1750–1820: Careers, Talent, Merit*. Manchester: Manchester University Press, 2002.

Bloch, Ruth. "The Gendered Meanings of Virtue in Revolutionary America." *Signs* 13 (Autumn 1987): 37–58.

Bloch, Ruth, and Naomi R. Lamoreaux. "Voluntary Associations, Corporate Rights, and the State: Legal Constraints on the Development of American Civil Society, 1750–1900." In *Organizations, Civil Society, and the Roots of Development*, edited by Naomi R. Lamoreaux and John J. Wallis, 231–90. Chicago, Ill.: University of Chicago Press, 2017.

Bockelman, Wayne L., and Owen S. Ireland. "The Internal Revolution in Pennsylvania: An Ethnic-Religious Interpretation." *Pennsylvania History* 41 (April 1974): 124–59.

Bonomi, Patricia U. *Under the Cope of Heaven: Religion, Society, and Politics in Colonial America*. New York: Oxford University Press, 1986.

Boonshoft, Mark. "Creating a 'Civilized Nation': Religion, Social Capital, and the Cultural Foundations of Early American State Formation." Ph.D. Diss., Ohio State University, 2015.

———. "The Great Awakening, Presbyterian Education, and the Mobilization of Power in the Revolutionary Mid-Atlantic." In *The American Revolution Reborn*, edited by Michael Zuckerman and Patrick Spero, 168–83. Philadelphia, Pa.: University of Pennsylvania Press, 2016.

———. "The Litchfield Network: Education, Social Capital, and the Rise and Fall of a Political Dynasty, 1784–1833." *Journal of the Early Republic* 34 (Winter 2014): 561–95.

Boudreau, Daniel, and Bryan MacDonald, "A New Commonwealth Votes: Using GIS to Analyze the Politics of Turn-of-the-19th-Century Massachusetts." Worcester Polytechnic Institute, 2013.

Boudreau, George W. "Provost Smith and His Circle: The College of Philadelphia and the Transformation of Pennsylvania." In *"The Good Education of Youth": Worlds of Learning in the Age of Franklin*, edited by John Pollack, 168–87. New Castle, Del.: Oak Knoll Press, 2009.

Boughton, Willis, and Eugene Wendell Harter. *Chronicles of Erasmus Hall*. General Organization, Erasmus Hall High School, 1906.

Bourdieu, Pierre. "The Forms of Capital." In *Handbook of Theory and Research for the Sociology of Education*, edited by John G. Richardson, 241–58. New York: Greenwood Press, 1986.

Bouton, Terry. "A Road Closed: Rural Insurgency in Post-Independence Pennsylvania." *Journal of American History* 87 (December 2000): 855–87.

———. *Taming Democracy: "The People," the Founders, and the Troubled Ending of the American Revolution*. New York, N.Y.: Oxford University Press, 2007.

Bowes, John P. *Land Too Good for Indians: Northern Indian Removal*. Norman, Okla.: University of Oklahoma Press, 2016.

Bradburn, Douglas. *The Citizenship Revolution: Politics and the Creation of the American Union, 1774–1804*. Charlottesville, Va.: University of Virginia Press, 2009.

Braddick, Michael J. "Civility and Authority." In *The British Atlantic World, 1500–1800*, edited by David Armitage and Michael Braddick, 113–32. 2nd ed. New York: Palgrave Macmillan, 2009.

———. "State Formation and Social Change in Early Modern England: A Problem Stated and Approaches Suggested." *Social History* 16 (January 1991): 1–17.

———. *State Formation in Early Modern England, C. 1550–1700*. New York, N.Y.: Cambridge University Press, 2000.

Braithwaite, Lloyd. "The Development of Higher Education in The British West Indies." *Social and Economic Studies* 7 (March 1958): 1–64.

Breen, T. H. *American Insurgents, American Patriots: The Revolution of the People*. New York, N.Y.: Hill and Wang, 2010.

———. *George Washington's Journey: The President Forges a New Nation*. New York, N.Y.: Simon and Schuster, 2016.

———. "Ideology and Nationalism on the Eve of the American Revolution: Revisions Once More in Need of Revising." *Journal of American History* 84 (June 1997): 13–40.

———. *The Marketplace of Revolution: How Consumer Politics Shaped American Independence*. New York, N.Y.: Oxford University Press, 2004.

Breen, T. H., and Timothy Hall. "Structuring Provincial Imagination: The Rhetoric and Experience of Social Change in Eighteenth-Century New England." *American Historical Review* 103 (December 1998): 1411–39.

Brewer, Holly. *By Birth or Consent: Children, Law, and the Anglo-American Revolution in Authority*. Chapel Hill, N.C.: Published for the Omohundro Institute of Early American History and Culture by the University of North Carolina Press, 2005.

———. "Entailing Aristocracy in Colonial Virginia: 'Ancient Feudal Restraints' and Revolutionary Reform." *William and Mary Quarterly* 54 (April 1997): 307–46.

Brickley, Lynne Templeton. "Sarah Pierce's Litchfield Female Academy, 1792–1833." Ed. D. Diss., Harvard University, 1985.

Brooke, John L. "Ancient Lodges and Self–Created Societies: Voluntary Association and the Public Sphere in the Early Republic." In *Launching the "Extended Republic": The Federalist Era*, edited by Ronald Hoffman and Peter J. Albert, 273–377. Charlottesville, Va.: University Press of Virginia, 1996.

———. *Columbia Rising: Civil Life on the Upper Hudson from the Revolution to the Age of Jackson*. Chapel Hill, N.C.: Published for the Omohundro Institute of Early American History and Culture by the University of North Carolina Press, 2010.

———. "Cultures of Nationalism, Movements of Reform, and the Composite-Federal Polity: From Revolutionary Settlement to Antebellum Crisis." *Journal of the Early Republic* 29 (Spring 2009): 1–33.

———. "A Deacon's Orthodoxy: Religion, Class, and the Moral Economy of Shays's Rebellion." In *In Debt to Shays: The Bicentennial of an Agrarian Rebellion*, edited by Robert A. Gross, 205–38. Charlottesville, Va.: University of Virginia Press, 1993.

———. *The Heart of the Commonwealth: Society and Political Culture in Worcester County, Massachusetts, 1713–1861*. New York, N.Y.: Cambridge University Press, 1989.

———. "Patriarchal Magistrates, Associated Improvers, and Monitoring Militias: Visions of Self-Government in the Early American Republic, 1760–1840." In *State and Citizen: British America and the Early United States*, edited by Peter Thompson and Peter S. Onuf, 178–217. Charlottesville, Va.: University of Virginia Press, 2013.

———. *"There Is a North" Fugitive Slaves, Political Crisis, and Cultural Transformation in the Coming of the Civil War*. Amherst, Mass.: University of Massachusetts Press, 2019.

———. "To the Quiet of the People: Revolutionary Settlements and Civil Unrest in Western Massachusetts, 1774–1789." *William and Mary Quarterly* 46 (July 1989): 426–62.

———. "Trouble with Paradox: A Review of Gordon Wood, *Empire of Liberty*." *William and Mary Quarterly* 67 (July 2010): 549–57.

Brooke, John L., Julia C. Strauss, and Greg Anderson, eds. *State Formations: Global Histories and Cultures of Statehood*. New York, N.Y.: Cambridge University Press, 2018.

Brooks, Robin. "Melancton Smith: New York Anti-Federalist, 1744–1798." Ph.D. Diss., University of Rochester, 1964.

Broussard, James L. *The Southern Federalists, 1800–1816*. Baton Rouge, La.: Louisiana State University Press, 1978.

Brown, Richard D. "The Emergence of Urban Society in Rural Massachusetts, 1760–1820." *Journal of American History* 61 (June 1974): 29–51.

———. *Knowledge Is Power: The Diffusion of Information in Early America, 1700–1865*. New York, N.Y.: Oxford University Press, 1989.

———. "Shays's Rebellion and the Ratification of the Federal Constitution in Massachusetts." In *Beyond Confederation: Origins of the Constitution and American National Identity*, edited by Richard R. Beeman, Stephen Botein, and Edward Carlos Carter, 113–27. Chapel Hill, N.C.: Published for the Institute of Early American History and Culture by the University of North Carolina Press, 1987.

———. "Spreading the Word: Rural Clergymen and the Communication Network of 18th-Century New England." *Proceedings of the Massachusetts Historical Society* 94 (1982): 1–14.

———. *The Strength of a People: The Idea of an Informed Citizenry in America, 1650–1870*. Chapel Hill, N.C.: University of North Carolina Press, 1996.

Browning, Andrew H. *The Panic of 1819: The First Great Depression*. Columbia, Mo.: University of Missouri Press, 2019.

Buel, Richard. *America on the Brink: How the Political Struggle Over the War of 1812 Almost Destroyed the Young Republic*. New York, N.Y.: Palgrave Macmillan, 2005.

Bullock, Steven C. *Revolutionary Brotherhood: Freemasonry and the Transformation of the American Social Order, 1730–1840*. Chapel Hill, N.C.: Published for the Omohundro Institute of Early American History and Culture by the University of North Carolina Press, 1996.

———. "The Revolutionary Transformation of American Freemasonry, 1752–1792." *William and Mary Quarterly* 47 (July 1990): 347–69.

———. "'Sensible Signs': The Emblematic Education of Post-Revolutionary Freemasonry." In *A Republic for the Ages: The United States Capitol and the Political Culture of the Early Republic*, edited by Donald R. Kennon, 177–213. Charlottesville, Va.: Published for the United States Capitol Historical Society by the University Press of Virginia, 1999.

Burr, Nelson R. *Education in New Jersey, 1630–1871*. Princeton, N.J.: Princeton University Press, 1942.

Burrows, Edwin G. "Military Experience and the Origins of Federalism and Antifederalism." In *Aspects of Early New York Society and Politics*, edited by Jacob Judd and Irwin H. Polishook, 83–92. Tarrytown, N.Y.: Sleepy Hollow Restorations, 1974.

Bush, George Gary. *History of Education in New Hampshire*. Washington, D.C.: U.S. Government Printing Office, 1898.

Bushman, Richard L. *From Puritan to Yankee: Character and the Social Order in Connecticut, 1690–1765*. Cambridge, Mass.: Harvard University Press, 1967.

———. *The Refinement of America: Persons, Houses, Cities*. New York, N.Y.: A. A. Knopf, 1992.

Butler, Jon. *Awash in a Sea of Faith: Christianizing the American People*. Cambridge, Mass.: Harvard University Press, 1990.

———. *Becoming America: The Revolution before 1776*. Cambridge, Mass.: Harvard University Press, 2000.

Butterfield, Kevin. *The Making of Tocqueville's America: Law and Association in the Early United States*. Chicago, Ill.: University of Chicago Press, 2015.

Caradonna, Jeremy L. *The Enlightenment in Practice: Academic Prize Contests and Intellectual Culture in France, 1670–1794*. Ithaca, N.Y.: Cornell University Press, 2012.

———. "The Monarchy of Virtue: The 'Prix de Vertu' and the Economy of Emulation in France, 1777–91." *Eighteenth-Century Studies* 41 (July 2008): 443–58.

Carp, Benjamin L. "Fire of Liberty: Firefighters, Urban Voluntary Culture, and the Revolutionary Movement." *William and Mary Quarterly* 58 (October 2001): 781–818.

Carp, E. Wayne. "The Origins of the Nationalist Movement of 1780–1783: Congressional Administration and the Continental Army." *Pennsylvania Magazine of History and Biography* 107 (July 1983): 363–92.

Carson, John. *The Measure of Merit: Talents, Intelligence, and Inequality in the French and American Republics, 1750–1940*. Princeton, N.J.: Princeton University Press, 2007.

Centennial Volume of the First Presbyterian Church of Pittsburgh, PA., 1784–1884. Pittsburgh, Pa.: Wm. G. Johnston & Company, Printers, 1884.

Chaussinand-Nogaret, Guy. *The French Nobility in the Eighteenth Century: From Feudalism to Enlightenment*. Translated by William Doyle. New York, N.Y.: Cambridge University Press, 1985.

Chetty, Raj et al. "Mobility Report Cards: The Role of Colleges in Intergenerational Mobility." Working Paper, National Bureau of Economic Research, July 2017.

Clark, J. C. D. *The Language of Liberty, 1660–1832: Political Discourse and Social Dynamics in the Anglo-American World*. New York, N.Y.: Cambridge University Press, 1994.

Cleves, Rachel Hope. *The Reign of Terror in America: Visions of Violence from Anti-Jacobinism to Antislavery*. New York, N.Y.: Cambridge University Press, 2009.

Cohen, Sheldon S., and Larry R. Gerlach. "Princeton in the Coming of the American Revolution." *New Jersey History* 92 (Summer 1974): 69–92.

Cole, Donald B. *A Jackson Man: Amos Kendall and the Rise of American Democracy*. Baton Rouge, La.: Louisiana State University Press, 2004.

Colley, Linda. *Britons: Forging the Nation, 1707–1837*. New Haven, Conn.: Yale University Press, 1992.

Come, Donald Robert. "The Influence of Princeton on Higher Education in the South before 1825." *William and Mary Quarterly* 2 (October 1945): 359–96.

Condon, Sean. *Shays's Rebellion: Authority and Distress in Post-Revolutionary America*. Baltimore, Md.: Johns Hopkins University Press, 2015.

Connor, R. D. W. *North Carolina: Rebuilding an Ancient Commonwealth, 1584–1925*, vol. 1. Chicago, Ill.: The American Historical Society, 1929.

Conroy-Krutz, Emily. *Christian Imperialism: Converting the World in the Early American Republic*. Ithaca, N.Y.: Cornell University Press, 2015.

Cook, Eli. *The Pricing of Progress: Economic Indicators and the Capitalization of American Life*. Cambridge, Mass.: Harvard University Press, 2017.

Cornell, Saul. "Aristocracy Assailed: The Ideology of Backcountry Anti-Federalism." *Journal of American History* 76 (March 1990): 1148–72.

Cornog, Evan. *The Birth of Empire: DeWitt Clinton and the American Experience, 1769–1828*. New York, N.Y.: Oxford University Press, 1998.

Cotlar, Seth. "The Federalists' Transatlantic Cultural Offensive of 1798 and the Moderation of American Democratic Discourse." In *Beyond the Founders: New Approaches to the Political History of the Early American Republic*, edited by Jeffrey L. Pasley, Andrew W. Robertson, and David Waldstreicher, 274–99. Chapel Hill, N.C.: University of North Carolina Press, 2004.

———. "Joseph Gales and the Making of the Jeffersonian Middle Class." In *The Revolution of 1800: Democracy, Race, and the New Republic*, edited by James Horn, Jan Ellen Lewis, and Peter S. Onuf, 331–59. Charlottesville, Va.: University of Virginia Press, 2002.

———. *Tom Paine's America: The Rise and Fall of Transatlantic Radicalism in the Early Republic*. Charlottesville, Va.: University of Virginia Press, 2011.

Cousins, James P. *Horace Holley: Transylvania University and the Making of Liberal Education in the Early American Republic*. Lexington, Ky.: University Press of Kentucky, 2016.

Cox, Caroline. *A Proper Sense of Honor: Service and Sacrifice in George Washington's Army*. Chapel Hill, N.C.: University of North Carolina Press, 2004.

Cray, Robert E. "Major John André and the Three Captors: Class Dynamics and Revolutionary Memory Wars in the Early Republic, 1780–1831." *Journal of the Early Republic* 17 (October 1997): 371–97.

Cremin, Lawrence A. *American Education: The Colonial Experience, 1607–1783*. New York, N.Y.: Harper & Row, 1970.

———. *American Education: The National Experience, 1783–1876*. New York, N.Y.: Harper & Row, 1980.

Crespino, Joseph. *In Search of Another Country: Mississippi and the Conservative Counterrevolution*. Princeton, N.J.: Princeton University Press, 2007.

Crosby, Emilye. *A Little Taste of Freedom: The Black Freedom Struggle in Claiborne County*. Chapel Hill, N.C.: University of North Carolina Press, 2005.

Cubberley, Ellwood Patterson. *Public Education in the United States: A Study and Interpretation of American Educational History*. Rev. ed. Boston, Mass.: Houghton Mifflin, 1962.

Curtis, Robert I. "The Bingham School and Classical Education in North Carolina, 1793–1873." *North Carolina Historical Review* (July 1996): 328–77.

Cutterham, Tom. *Gentlemen Revolutionaries: Power and Justice in the New American Republic*. Princeton, N.J.: Princeton University Press, 2017.

———. "The International Dimension of the Federal Constitution." *Journal of American Studies* 48 (May 2014): 501–15.

———. "'What Ought to Belong to Merit Only': Debating Status and Heredity in the New American Republic." *Journal for Eighteenth-Century Studies* 40 (June 2017): 181–98.

Daggar, Lori J. "The Mission Complex: Economic Development, 'Civilization,' and Empire in the Early Republic." *Journal of the Early Republic* 36 (Fall 2016): 467–91.

Demos, John. *The Heathen School: A Story of Hope and Betrayal in the Age of the Early Republic*. New York, N.Y.: A. A. Knopf, 2014.

———. *A Little Commonwealth: Family Life in Plymouth Colony*. New York, N.Y.: Oxford University Press, 1970.

Diamond, Peter J. "Witherspoon, William Smith and the Scottish Philosophy in Revolutionary America." In *Scotland and America in the Age of the Enlightenment*, edited by Richard B. Sher and Jeffrey R. Smitten, 115–32. Edinburgh: Edinburgh University Press, 1990.

Dotts, Brian W. "The Democratic-Republican Societies: An Educational Dream Deferred." *Educational Horizons* 88 (2010): 179–92.

Douglas, Davison M. "The Limits of Law in Accomplishing Racial Change: School Segregation in the Pre-Brown North." *UCLA Law Review* 44 (1997): 677–744.

Doyle, William H. *The Vermont Political Tradition: And Those Who Helped Make It.* Rev. ed. Montpelier, Vt.: Leahy Press Inc., 2011.

Dubois, Laurent. *Avengers of the New World: The Story of the Haitian Revolution.* Cambridge, Mass.: Harvard University Press, 2004.

Durnin, Richard Gerry. "New England's Eighteenth-Century Incorporated Academies: Their Origin and Development to 1850." Ph.D. Diss., University of Pennsylvania, 1968.

Duveen, Denis I., and Herbert S. Klickstein. "Alexandre–Marie Quesnay De Beaurepaire's: Mémoire et Prospectus, Concernant l'Académie Des Sciences et Beaux Arts Des Etats–Unis de l'Amérique, Établie À Richemond, 1788." *Virginia Magazine of History and Biography* 63 (July 1955): 280–85.

Dwiggins, John. "The Military Establishment and Democratic Politics in the United States, 1783–1848." Ph.D. Diss., University of Pennsylvania, 2012.

Eastman, Carolyn. *A Nation of Speechifiers: Making an American Public after the Revolution.* Chicago, Ill.: University of Chicago Press, 2009.

Edling, Max M. *A Hercules in the Cradle: War, Money, and the American State, 1783–1867.* Chicago, Ill.: University of Chicago Press, 2014.

———. *A Revolution in Favor of Government: Origins of the U.S. Constitution and the Making of the American State.* New York, N.Y.: Oxford University Press, 2003.

Edwards, Laura F. *The People and Their Peace: Legal Culture and the Transformation of Inequality in the Post-Revolutionary South.* Chapel Hill, N.C.: University of North Carolina Press, 2009.

Efland, Arthur. *A History of Art Education: Intellectual and Social Currents in Teaching the Visual Arts.* New York, N.Y.: Teachers College Press, 1990.

Einhorn, Robin L. *American Taxation, American Slavery.* Chicago, Ill.: University of Chicago Press, 2006.

Ellis, Richard E. *The Jeffersonian Crisis: Courts and Politics in the Young Republic.* New York, N.Y.: Oxford University Press, 1971.

———. "The Persistence of Antifederalism after 1789." In *Beyond Confederation: Origins of the Constitution and American National Identity*, edited by Richard R. Beeman, Stephen Botein, and Edward Carlos Carter, 295–314. Chapel Hill, N.C.: Published for the Institute of Early American History and Culture by the University of North Carolina Press, 1987.

Engel, Katherine Carté. *Religion and Profit: Moravians in Early America.* Philadelphia, Pa.: University of Pennsylvania Press, 2011.

———. "The SPCK and the American Revolution: The Limits of International Protestantism." *Church History* 81 (March 2012): 77–103.

Eustace, Nicole. *Passion Is the Gale: Emotion, Power, and the Coming of the American Revolution.* Chapel Hill, N.C.: Published for the Ommohundro Institute of Early American History and Culture by the University of North Carolina Press, 2008.

Eustace, Nicole, and Fredrika J. Teute, eds. *Warring for America: Cultural Contests in the Era of 1812.* Chapel Hill, N.C.: Published for the Omohundro Institute of Early American History and Culture by the University of North Carolina Press, 2017.

Farnham, Christie Anne. *The Education of the Southern Belle: Higher Education and Student Socialization in the Antebellum South.* New York, N.Y.: New York University Press, 1994.

Fatherly, Sarah. *Gentlewomen and Learned Ladies: Women and Elite Formation in Eighteenth Century Philadelphia*. Bethlehem, Pa.: Lehigh University Press, 2008.

———. "'The Sweet Recourse of Reason': Elite Women's Education in Colonial Philadelphia." *Pennsylvania Magazine of History and Biography* 128 (July 2004): 229–56.

Fea, John. "In Search of Unity: Presbyterians in the Wake of the First Great Awakening." *Journal of Presbyterian History* 86 (Fall/Winter 2008): 53–60.

———. "Rural Religion: Protestant Community and the Moral Improvement of the South Jersey Countryside, 1676–1800." Ph.D. Diss., State University of New York at Stony Brook, 1999.

———. *The Way of Improvement Leads Home: Philip Vickers Fithian and the Rural Enlightenment in Early America*. Philadelphia, Pa.: University of Pennsylvania Press, 2008.

———. "The Way of Improvement Leads Home: Philip Vickers Fithian's Rural Enlightenment." *Journal of American History* 90 (September 2003): 462–90.

Fiering, Norman. *Jonathan Edwards's Moral Thought and Its British Context*. Chapel Hill, N.C.: Published for the Institute of Early American History and Culture by the University of North Carolina Press, 1981.

Fischer, David Hackett. *Washington's Crossing*. New York, N.Y.: Oxford University Press, 2004.

Folts, James D. *History of the University of the State of New York and the State Education Department 1784–1996*. Albany, N.Y.: New York State Education Department, 1996. https://eric.ed.gov/?id=ED413839.

Fogleman, Aaron. *Hopeful Journeys: German Immigration, Settlement, and Political Culture in Colonial America, 1717–1775*. Philadelphia, Pa.: University of Pennsylvania Press, 1996.

———. "Migrations to the Thirteen British North American Colonies, 1700–1775: New Estimates." *Journal of Interdisciplinary History* 22 (April 1992): 691–709.

Foletta, Marshall. *Coming to Terms with Democracy: Federalist Intellectuals and the Shaping of an American Culture, 1800–1828*. Charlottesville, Va.: University of Virginia Press, 2001.

Formisano, Ronald P. "Deferential-Participant Politics: The Early Republic's Political Culture." *American Political Science Review* 68 (1974): 473–87.

Fort, Megan Holloway. "Archibald and Alexander Robertson and Their Schools, The Columbian Academy of Painting, and The Academy of Painting and Drawing, New York, 1791–1835." Ph.D. Diss., City University of New York, 2006.

Foster, Sherrill. "Clinton Academy: Its History and Architecture." *Long Island Historical Journal* 12 (Spring 2000): 181–93.

Frank, Robert H. "Just Deserts." *Hedgehog Review* 18 (Summer 2016): 50–63.

Frankenberg, Erica, Genevieve Siegel-Hawley, and Jia Wang. "Choice without Equity: Charter School Segregation and the Need for Civil Rights Standards." UCLA Civil Rights Project / Proyecto Derechos, January 2010.

Fuhrer, Mary Babson. *A Crisis of Community: The Trials and Transformation of a New England Town, 1815–1848*. Chapel Hill, N.C.: University of North Carolina Press, 2014.

Funk, Henry D. "The Influence of the Presbyterian Church in Early American History." *Journal of the Presbyterian Historical Society* 12 (April 1924): 152–89.

Furstenberg, François. *When the United States Spoke French: Five Refugees Who Shaped a Nation*. New York: Penguin, 2014.

Gerlach, Larry R. *Prologue to Independence: New Jersey in the Coming of the American Revolution*. New Brunswick, N.J.: Rutgers University Press, 1976.
Gerstle, Gary. *Liberty and Coercion: The Paradox of American Government from the Founding to the Present*. Princeton, N.J.: Princeton University Press, 2015.
Gigantino, James J. *William Livingston's American Revolution*. Philadelphia, Pa.: University of Pennsylvania Press, 2018.
Gilje, Paul A. "'Free Trade and Sailors' Rights': The Rhetoric of the War of 1812." *Journal of the Early Republic* 30 (Spring 2010): 1–23.
Gilpatrick, Delbert. *Jeffersonian Democracy in North Carolina, 1789–1816*. New York, N.Y.: Columbia University Press, 1931.
Glenn, Charles Leslie. *The Myth of the Common School*. Amherst, Mass.: University of Massachusetts Press, 1988.
Go, Sun, and Peter Lindert. "The Uneven Rise of American Public Schools to 1850." *Journal of Economic History* 70 (March 2010): 1–26.
Goldin, Claudia, and Lawrence F. Katz. "The 'Virtues' of the Past: Education in the First Hundred Years of the New Republic." *NBER Working Paper No. 9958*, 2003.
Golove, David M., and Daniel J. Hulsebosch. "A Civilized Nation: The Early American Constitution, the Law of Nations, and the Pursuit of International Recognition." *New York University Law Review* 85 (2010): 932–1066.
Good, Cassandra A. *Founding Friendships: Friendships between Men and Women in the Early American Republic*. New York, N.Y.: Oxford University Press, 2015.
Gordon, Sarah Barringer. "The First Disestablishment: Limits on Church Power and Property before the Civil War." *University of Pennsylvania Law Review* 162 (2014): 307–72.
Gould, Eliga H. *Among the Powers of the Earth: The American Revolution and the Making of a New World Empire*. Cambridge, Mass.: Harvard University Press, 2012.
———. "An Empire of Manners: The Refinement of British America in Atlantic Perspective." *Journal of British Studies* 39 (January 2000): 114–22.
———. "The Laws of War and Peace: Legitimating Slavery in the Age of the American Revolution." In *State and Citizen: British America and the Early United States*, edited by Peter Thompson and Peter S. Onuf, 52–76. Charlottesville, Va.: University of Virginia Press, 2013.
———. *The Persistence of Empire: British Political Culture in the Age of the American Revolution*. Chapel Hill, N.C.: Published for the Omohundro Institute of Early American History and Culture by the University of North Carolina Press, 2000.
Grasso, Christopher. "The Religious and the Secular in the Early American Republic." *Journal of the Early Republic* 36 (Summer 2016): 359–88.
Green, Hilary. *Educational Reconstruction: African American Schools in the Urban South, 1865–1890*. New York, N.Y.: Fordham University Press, 2016.
Green, Jennifer R. *Military Education and the Emerging Middle Class in the Old South*. New York, N.Y.: Cambridge University Press, 2008.
Greene, Jack P. "The American Revolution." *American Historical Review* 105 (February 2000): 93–102.
———. "Colonial History and National History: Reflections on a Continuing Problem." *William and Mary Quarterly* 64 (April 2007): 235–50.

———. "Social and Cultural Capital in Colonial British America: A Case Study." *Journal of Interdisciplinary History* 29 (January 1999): 491–509.
———. "An Uneasy Connection: An Analysis of the Preconditions of the American Revolution." In *Essays on the American Revolution*, edited by Stephen G. Kurtz and James H. Huston, 32–80. Chapel Hill, N.C.: University of North Carolina Press, 1973.
Griffin, Patrick. *American Leviathan: Empire, Nation, and Revolutionary Frontier*. New York, N.Y.: Hill and Wang, 2007.
———. *America's Revolution*. New York, N.Y.: Oxford University Press, 2012.
———. *The People with No Name: Ireland's Ulster Scots, America's Scots Irish, and the Creation of a British Atlantic World, 1689–1764*. Princeton, N.J.: Princeton University Press, 2001.
Griffin, Sean. "Antislavery Utopias: Communitarian Labor Reform and the Abolitionist Movement." *Journal of the Civil War Era* 8 (June 2018): 243–68.
Gronningsater, Sarah L. H. "Delivering Freedom: Gradual Emancipation, Black Legal Culture, and the Origins of Sectional Crisis in New York, 1759–1870." Ph.D. Diss., University of Chicago, 2014.
———. "Practicing Formal Politics without the Vote: Black New Yorkers in the Aftermath of 1821." In *Emancipations, Reconstructions, and Revolutions: African American Politics and U.S. History from the First to the Second Civil War*, edited by David Waldstreicher and Van Gosse. Philadelphia, Pa.: University of Pennsylvania Press, Forthcoming.
Gross, Robert A. *The Minutemen and Their World*. New York, N.Y.: Hill and Wang, 1976.
Gunn, L. Ray. *The Decline of Authority: Public Economic Policy and Political Development in New York, 1800–1860*. Ithaca, N.Y.: Cornell University Press, 1988.
Guo, Jeff. "What Are the Most Popular Street Names in Every State?" *Washington Post* (Govbeat Blog), March 6, 2015. https://www.washingtonpost.com/blogs/govbeat/wp/2015/03/06/these-are-the-most-popular-street-names-in-every-state.
Gustafson, Sandra M. *Eloquence Is Power: Oratory & Performance in Early America*. Chapel Hill, N.C.: Published for the Omohundro Institute of Early American History and Culture by the University of North Carolina Press, 2000.
Guyatt, Nicholas. *Bind Us Apart: How Enlightened Americans Invented Racial Segregation*. New York, N.Y.: Basic Books, 2016.
Haberman, Robb K. "Periodical Publics: Magazines and Literary Networks in Post-Revolutionary America." Ph.D. Diss., University of Connecticut, 2009.
Hall, Aaron. "Slaves of the State: Infrastructure and Governance through Slavery in the Antebellum South." *Journal of American History* 106 (June 2019): 19–46.
Hall, David D. *A Reforming People: Puritanism and the Transformation of Public Life in New England*. New York, N.Y.: A. A. Knopf, 2011.
Hall, John. *History of the Presbyterian Church in Trenton, N. J.: From the First Settlement of the Town*. Trenton, N.J.: Anson D. F. Randolph, 1859.
Hall, Peter Dobkin. *The Organization of American Culture, 1700–1900: Private Institutions, Elites, and the Origins of American Nationality*. New York, N.Y.: New York University Press, 1982.
Hall, Timothy D. *Contested Boundaries: Itinerancy and the Reshaping of the Colonial American Religious World*. Durham, N.C.: Duke University Press, 1994.
Hall, Van Beck. *Politics Without Parties: Massachusetts, 1780–1791*. Pittsburgh, Pa.: University of Pittsburgh Press, 1972.

Hammond, Jabez Delano. *The History of Political Parties in the State of New-York: From the Ratification of the Federal Constitution to December, 1840*, vol. 1. Albany, N.Y.: C. Van Benthuysen, 1842.

Handlin, Oscar, and Mary Flug Handlin. *Commonwealth: A Study of the Role of Government in the American Economy: Massachusetts, 1774–1861*. Cambridge, Mass.: Harvard University Press, 1947.

Harrison, Richard A. *Princetonians, 1769–1775: A Biographical Dictionary*. Princeton, N.J: Princeton University Press, 1980.

———. *Princetonians, 1776–1783: A Biographical Dictionary*. Princeton, N.J: Princeton University Press, 1981.

Hatfield, Edwin Francis. *History of Elizabeth, New Jersey: Including the Early History of Union County*. New York, N.Y.: Carlton & Lanahan, 1868.

Hattem, Michael D. "'Anglifying' an Empire: Cultural Politics and Imperial Anglicanism in the Middle Colonies, 1749–1757." Unpublished manuscript, July 20, 2013.

———. "Past and Prologue: History Culture and the American Revolution." Ph.D. Diss., Yale University, 2017.

Haulman, Clyde. *Virginia and the Panic of 1819: The First Great Depression and the Commonwealth*. New York, N.Y.: Routledge, 2015.

Haulman, Kate. "Fashion and the Culture Wars of Revolutionary Philadelphia." *William and Mary Quarterly* 62 (October 2005): 625–62.

———. *Politics of Fashion in Eighteenth-Century America*. Chapel Hill, N.C.: University of North Carolina Press, 2011.

———. "Rods and Reels: Social Clubs and Political Culture in Early Pennsylvania." *Early American Studies* 12 (Winter 2014): 143–73.

Hayes, Christopher. *Twilight of the Elites: America after Meritocracy*. New York, N.Y.: Crown Publishers, 2012.

Heatwole, Cornelius Jacob. *A History of Education in Virginia*. New York, N.Y.: Macmillan, 1916.

Heimert, Alan. *Religion and the American Mind: From the Great Awakening to the Revolution*. Cambridge, Mass.: Harvard University Press, 1966.

Heitman, Francis Bernard. *Historical Register of Officers of the Continental Army During the War of the Revolution, April 1775, to December, 1783*. Washington, D.C.: Rare Book Shop Publishing Company, 1914.

Hemphill, C. Dallet. *Bowing to Necessities: A History of Manners in America, 1620–1860*. New York, N.Y.: Oxford University Press, 2002.

Hessinger, Rodney. "'The Most Powerful Instrument of College Discipline': Student Disorder and the Growth of Meritocracy in the Colleges of the Early Republic." *History of Education Quarterly* 39 (October 1999): 237–62.

Hines, Michael. "Learning Freedom: Education, Elevation, and New York's African-American Community, 1827–1829." *History of Education Quarterly* 56 (November 2016): 618–45.

History of Wages in the United States from Colonial Times to 1928. Washington, D.C.: United States Department of Labor, Bureau of Labor Statistics, 1934.

Hobson, Elsie Garland. "Educational Legislation and Administration in the State of New York from 1777 to 1850." Ph.D. Diss., University of Chicago, 1918.

Hoeveler, J. David. *Creating the American Mind: Intellect and Politics in the Colonial Colleges.* Lanham, Md.: Rowman & Littlefield, 2004.
Holton, Woody. *Unruly Americans and the Origins of the Constitution.* New York, N.Y.: Hill and Wang, 2007.
Hough, Joseph Howell. *Origin of Masonry in the State of New Jersey: And the Entire Proceedings of the Grand Lodge, from Its Organization. A. L. 5786.* Trenton, N.J.: J. H. Hough, 1870.
Howe, Daniel Walker. "Church, State, and Education in the Young American Republic." *Journal of the Early Republic* 22 (Spring 2002): 1–24.
———. "The Evangelical Movement and Political Culture in the North During the Second Party System." *Journal of American History* 77 (March 1991): 1216–39.
Huden, John C. *Development of State School Administration in Vermont.* Burlington, Vt.: Vermont Historical Society, 1944.
Hume, Edgar Erskine. *Papers of the Society of the Cincinnati in the State of Virginia, 1783–1824.* Fredericksburg, Va.: Published by the Society of the Cincinnati, 1938.
———. "The Virginia Society of the Cincinnati's Gift to Washington College." *Virginia Magazine of History and Biography* 42 (April 1934): 103–15.
———. "The Virginia Society of the Cincinnati's Gift to Washington College (Continued)." *Virginia Magazine of History and Biography* 42 (July 1934): 198–210.
———. "The Virginia Society of the Cincinnati's Gift to Washington College (Continued)." *Virginia Magazine of History and Biography* 42 (October 1934): 304–16.
Huston, James L. *The American and British Debate over Equality, 1776–1920.* Baton Rouge, La.: Louisiana State University Press, 2017.
Hutchins, Steven C. *Civil List and Constitutional History of the Colony and State of New York.* Albany, N.Y.: Weed & Parsons, 1879.
Hyde, Carrie. *Civic Longing: The Speculative Origins of U.S. Citizenship.* Cambridge, Mass.: Harvard University Press, 2018.
Ingersoll, Elizabeth A. "Francis Alison: American Philosophe, 1705–1799." Ph.D. Diss., University of Delaware, 1974.
Ireland, Owen S. "The Ethnic-Religious Dimension of Pennsylvania Politics, 1778–1779." *William and Mary Quarterly* 30 (July 1973): 423–48.
Irvin, Benjamin H. *Clothed in Robes of Sovereignty: The Continental Congress and the People Out of Doors.* New York, N.Y.: Oxford University Press, 2011.
Isaac, Rhys. *The Transformation of Virginia, 1740–1790.* Chapel Hill, N.C.: Published for the Institute of Early American History and Culture by the University of North Carolina Press, 1982.
Isenberg, Nancy. "The Empire Has No Clothes." *Journal of the Early Republic* 32 (Summer 2012): 261–77.
———. *Fallen Founder: The Life of Aaron Burr.* New York, N.Y.: Penguin, 2007.
Iverson, John. "Introduction: Forum on Emulation in France, 1750–1800." *Eighteenth-Century Studies* 36 (December 2003): 217–23.
Jaffee, David. "The Village Enlightenment in New England, 1760–1820." *William and Mary Quarterly* 47 (July 1990): 327–46.
Jeffrey, Thomas E. *State Parties and National Politics: North Carolina, 1815–1861.* Athens, Ga.: University of Georgia Press, 1989.
Jessop, Bob. *State Power: A Strategic-Relational Approach.* Cambridge: Polity, 2007.

John, Richard R. "In Retrospect: Leonard D. White and the Invention of American Administrative History." *Reviews in American History* 24 (1996): 344–60.
———. *Spreading the News: The American Postal System from Franklin to Morse.* Cambridge, Mass.: Harvard University Press, 1998.
Jones, Howard Mumford. *America and French Culture 1750–1848.* Chapel Hill, N.C.: University of North Carolina Press, 1927.
Jones, Martha. *Birthright Citizens: A History of Race and Rights in Antebellum America.* New York, N.Y.: Cambridge University Press, 2018.
Justice, Benjamin. *The War That Wasn't: Religious Conflict and Compromise in the Common Schools of New York State, 1865–1900.* Albany, N.Y.: SUNY Press, 2005.
———, ed. *The Founding Fathers, Education, and "The Great Contest": The American Philosophical Society Prize of 1797.* New York, N.Y.: Palgrave Macmillan, 2013.
Kaestle, Carl F. *The Evolution of an Urban School System: New York City, 1750–1850.* Cambridge, Mass.: Harvard University Press, 1973.
———. *Pillars of the Republic: Common Schools and American Society, 1780–1860.* New York, N.Y.: Hill and Wang, 1983.
Kaplan, Catherine O'Donnell. *Men of Letters in the Early Republic: Cultivating Forums of Citizenship.* Chapel Hill, N.C.: Published for the Omohundro Institute of Early American History and Culture by the University of North Carolina Press, 2008.
Kaplan, Nira. "Virtuous Competition among Citizens: Emulation in Politics and Pedagogy during the French Revolution." *Eighteenth-Century Studies* 36 (December 2003): 241–48.
Karlsen, Carol F., and Laurie Crumpacker, eds. *The Journal of Esther Edwards Burr, 1754–1757.* New Haven, Conn.: Yale University Press, 1986.
Katz, Michael, B. *The Irony of Early School Reform: Educational Innovation in Mid-Nineteenth Century Massachusetts.* New York, N.Y.: Teachers College Press, 1968.
Kaufman, Jason. "Corporate Law and the Sovereignty of States." *American Sociological Review* 73 (June 2008): 402–25.
Kelley, Mary. *Learning to Stand & Speak: Women, Education, and Public Life in America's Republic.* Chapel Hill, N.C.: Published for the Omohundro Institute of Early American History and Culture by the University of North Carolina Press, 2006.
Kelly, Catherine. "'The Consummation of Rural Prosperity and Happiness': New England Agricultural Fairs and the Construction of Class and Gender, 1810–1860." *American Quarterly* 49 (1997): 574–602.
———. *In the New England Fashion: Reshaping Women's Lives in the Nineteenth Century.* Ithaca, N.Y.: Cornell University Press, 1999.
———. *Republic of Taste: Art, Politics, and Everyday Life in Early America.* Philadelphia, Pa.: University of Pennsylvania Press, 2016.
Kennedy, Roger G. *Orders from France: The Americans and the French in a Revolutionary World, 1780–1820.* New York, N.Y.: A. A. Knopf, 1989.
Kerber, Linda K. *Federalists in Dissent: Imagery and Ideology in Jeffersonian America.* Ithaca, N.Y.: Cornell University Press, 1970.
———. *Women of the Republic: Intellect and Ideology in Revolutionary America.* Chapel Hill, N.C.: Published for the Institute of Early American History and Culture by the University of North Carolina Press, 1980.

Kerrison, Catherine. "The French Education of Martha Jefferson Randolph." *Early American Studies* 11 (Spring 2013): 349–94.

Kett, Joseph F. *Merit: The History of a Founding Ideal from the American Revolution to the Twenty-First Century.* Ithaca, N.Y.: Cornell University Press, 2012.

———. *Rites of Passage: Adolescence in America, 1790 to the Present.* New York, N.Y.: Basic Books, 1977.

Keyssar, Alexander. *The Right to Vote: The Contested History of Democracy in the United States.* Rev. ed. New York, N.Y.: Basic Books, 2008.

Kidd, Sarah A. "The Search for Moral Order: The Panic of 1819 and the Culture of the Early American Republic." Ph.D. Diss., University of Missouri, 2002.

Kidd, Thomas S. *The Great Awakening: The Roots of Evangelical Christianity in Colonial America.* New Haven, Conn.: Yale University Press, 2007.

Kilbride, Daniel. *An American Aristocracy: Southern Planters in Antebellum Philadelphia.* Columbia, S.C.: University of South Carolina Press, 2006.

———. *Being American in Europe, 1750–1860.* Baltimore, Md.: Johns Hopkins University Press, 2013.

Kilpatrick, William H. "The Beginnings of the Public School System in Georgia." *Georgia Historical Quarterly* 5 (September 1921): 3–19.

Kim, Sung Bok. "The Limits of Politicization in the American Revolution: The Experience of Westchester County, New York." *Journal of American History* 80 (December 1993): 868–89.

King-Owen, Scott. "North Carolina's Federalists in an Evolving Public Sphere, 1790–1810." M.A. Thesis, University of North Carolina at Wilmington, 2006.

Klarman, Michael. *The Framers' Coup: The Making of the United States Constitution.* New York: Oxford University Press, 2016.

Klein, Daniel B., and John Majewski. "Economy, Community, and Law: The Turnpike Movement in New York, 1797–1845." *Law & Society Review* 26 (1992): 469–512.

Kling, David W. "New Divinity Schools of the Prophets, 1750–1825: A Case Study in Ministerial Education." *History of Education Quarterly* 37 (July 1997): 185–206.

Knott, Sarah. *Sensibility and the American Revolution.* Chapel Hill, N.C.: Published for the Omohundro Institute of Early American History and Culture by the University of North Carolina Press, 2009.

———. "Sensibility and the American War for Independence." *American Historical Review* 109 (February 2004): 19–40.

Koehler, Rob. "Measuring the Expansion of Schooling in Early Republican New York." Paper presented at the New York State Historical Association conference, Albany, N.Y., November 2016.

Kornblith, Gary J., and John M. Murrin. "The Dilemmas of Ruling Elites in Revolutionary America." In *Ruling America: A History of Wealth and Power in a Democracy*, edited by Gary Gerstle and Steve Fraser, 27–63. Cambridge, Mass.: Harvard University Press, 2009.

Koschnik, Albrecht. *"Let a Common Interest Bind Us Together": Associations, Partisanship, and Culture in Philadelphia, 1775–1840.* Charlottesville, Va.: University of Virginia Press, 2007.

———. "Political Conflict and Public Contest: Rituals of National Celebration in Philadelphia, 1788–1815." *Pennsylvania Magazine of History and Biography* 118 (July 1994): 209–48.

———."Young Federalists, Masculinity, and Partisanship during the War of 1812." In *Beyond the Founders: New Approaches to the Political History of the Early American Republic*, edited by Jeffrey L. Pasley, Andrew W. Robertson, and David Waldstreicher, 159–79. Chapel Hill, N.C.: University of North Carolina Press, 2004.

Kraus, Joe W. "The Development of a Curriculum in the Early American Colleges." *History of Education Quarterly* 1 (June 1961): 64–76.

Kruse, Kevin M. *White Flight: Atlanta and the Making of Modern Conservatism*. Princeton, N.J.: Princeton University Press, 2005.

Kulikoff, Alan. "'Such Things Ought Not To Be': The American Revolution and the First National Great Depression." In *The World of the Revolutionary American Republic: Land, Labor, and the Conflict for a Continent*, edited by Andrew Shankman, 134–64. New York, N.Y.: Routledge, 2014.

Labaree, David F. *The Making of an American High School: The Credentials Market and the Central High School in Philadelphia, 1838–1939*. New Haven, Conn.: Yale University Press, 1988.

———. *A Perfect Mess: The Unlikely Ascendancy of American Higher Education*. Chicago, Ill.: University of Chicago Press, 2017.

Lambert, Frank. "'Pedlar in Divinity': George Whitefield and the Great Awakening." *Journal of American History* 77 (December 1990): 812–37.

Landsman, Ned C. "British Union and the American Revolution: Unions, Sovereignty, and the Multinational State." In *The American Revolution Reborn*, edited by Michael Zuckerman and Patrick K. Spero, 107–31. Philadelphia, Pa.: University of Pennsylvania Press, 2016.

———. *From Colonials to Provincials: American Thought and Culture, 1680–1760*. New York, N.Y.: Twayne Publishers, 1997.

———. "The Legacy of British Union for the North American Colonies: Provincial Elites and the Problem of Imperial Union." In *A Union for Empire: Political Thought and the British Union of 1707*, edited by John Robertson, 297–317. Cambridge: Cambridge University Press, 2006.

———. "Presbyterians, Evangelicals, and the Educational Culture of the Middle Colonies." *Pennsylvania History* 64 (July 1997): 168–82.

———. *Scotland and Its First American Colony, 1683–1765*. Princeton, N.J.: Princeton University Press, 1985.

———. "Witherspoon and the Problem of Provincial Identity in Scottish Evangelical Culture." In *Scotland and America in the Age of the Enlightenment*, edited by Richard B. Sher and Jeffrey R. Smitten, 29–45. Edinburgh: Edinburgh University Press, 1990.

Larned, Ellen Douglas. *History of Windham County, Connecticut: 1760–1880*, 2 vols. Worcester, Mass.: Printed by Charles Hamilton, 1880.

Larson, John Lauritz. *Internal Improvement: National Public Works and the Promise of Popular Government in the Early United States*. Chapel Hill, N.C.: University of North Carolina Press, 2001.

Lassiter, Matthew D. *The Silent Majority: Suburban Politics in the Sunbelt South*. Princeton, N.J.: Princeton University Press, 2006.

LeBeau, Bryan F. *Jonathan Dickinson and the Formative Years of American Presbyterianism*. Lexington, Ky.: University Press of Kentucky, 1997.

Lefavour, Henry. "The Proposed College in Hampshire County in 1762." *Proceedings of the Massachusetts Historical Society* 66 (1936): 53–79.
Lehman, J. David. "Explaining Hard Times: Political Economy and the Panic of 1819 in Philadelphia." Ph.D. Diss., University of California, Los Angeles, 1992.
Leiby, Adrian C. *The Revolutionary War in the Hackensack Valley: The Jersey Dutch and the Neutral Ground, 1775–1783*. New Brunswick, N.J.: Rutgers University Press, 1980.
Lender, Mark E. "The Enlisted Line: The Continental Soldiers of New Jersey." Ph.D. Diss., Rutgers University, 1975.
Leonard, Gerald. "Party as a Political Safeguard of Federalism: Martin Van Buren and the Constitutional Theory of Party Politics." *Rutgers Law Review* 54 (2001): 221–81.
Leslie, Bruce. "Where Have All the Academies Gone?" *History of Education Quarterly* 41 (July 2001): 262–70.
Levy, Barry. *Quakers and the American Family: British Settlement in the Delaware Valley*. New York, N.Y.: Oxford University Press, 1988.
———. *Town Born: The Political Economy of New England from Its Founding to the Revolution*. Philadelphia, Pa.: University of Pennsylvania Press, 2009.
Lewis, Alfred Fayette. *History of Higher Education in Kentucky*. Washington, D.C.: U.S. Government Printing Office, 1899.
Lewis, Jan. "Politics and the Ambivalence of the Private Sphere." In *A Republic for the Ages: The United States Capitol and the Political Culture of the Early Republic*, edited by Donald R. Kennon, 122–54. Charlottesville, Va.: Published for the United States Capitol Historical Society by the University Press of Virginia, 1999.
———. "The Republican Wife: Virtue and Seduction in the Early Republic." *William and Mary Quarterly* 44 (October 1987): 689–721.
Linsley, Susanna. "The American Reformation: The Politics of Religious Liberty, Charleston and New York 1770–1830." Ph.D. Diss., University of Michigan, 2012.
Lockridge, Kenneth A. *Literacy in Colonial New England: An Enquiry Into the Social Context of Literacy in the Early Modern West*. New York, N.Y.: W. W. Norton, 1974.
Lodge, Martin E. "The Crisis of the Churches in the Middle Colonies, 1720–1750." *Pennsylvania Magazine of History and Biography* 95 (April 1971): 195–220.
———. "The Great Awakening in the Middle Colonies." Ph.D. Diss., University of California, Berkeley, 1964.
Lord, Gary T. "Alden Partridge's Proposal for a National System of Education: A Model for the Morrill Land Grant Act." *History of Higher Education Annual* 18 (1998): 11–24.
Mader, Rodney. "Politics and Pedagogy in the American Magazine, 1757–58." *American Periodicals: A Journal of History, Criticism, and Bibliography* 16 (2006): 3–22.
Madron, Michael K. *Presbyterian Patriots: The Historical Context of the Shared History and Prevalent Ideologies of Delaware's Ulster-Scots Who Took up Arms in the American Revolution*. School of Advanced Military Studies, 2009. http://www.dtic.mil/cgi-bin/GetTRDoc?AD=ADA505604.
Maier, Pauline. "The Revolutionary Origins of the American Corporation." *William and Mary Quarterly* 50 (January 1993): 51–84.
Mailer, Gideon. *John Witherspoon's American Revolution*. Chapel Hill, N.C.: Published for the Omohundro Institute of Early American History and Culture by the University of North Carolina Press, 2017.

Main, Jackson Turner. "Government by the People: The American Revolution and the Democratization of the Legislatures." *William and Mary Quarterly* 23 (July 1966): 391–407.

———. *Political Parties before the Constitution*. Chapel Hill, N.C.: Published for the Institute of Early American History and Culture by the University of North Carolina Press, 1973.

———. *The Social Structure of Revolutionary America*. Princeton, N.J.: Princeton University Press, 1965.

Majewski, John. "Why Did Northerners Oppose the Expansion of Slavery?: Economic Development and Education in the Limestone South." In *Slavery's Capitalism: A New History of American Economic Development*, edited by Sven Beckert and Seth Rockman, 277–98. Philadelphia, Pa.: University of Pennsylvania Press, 2016.

Maloyed, Christie L., and J. Kelton Williams. "Reverend John Witherspoon's Pedagogy of Leadership." *American Educational History Journal* 39 (March 2012): 349–64.

Marietta, Jack D., and G.S. Rowe. *Troubled Experiment: Crime and Justice in Pennsylvania, 1682–1800*. Philadelphia, Pa.: University of Pennsylvania Press, 2006.

Marr, Harriet Webster. *The Old New England Academies: Founded Before 1826*. New York, N.Y.: Comet Press Books, 1959.

Marshall, P.J. *Remaking the British Atlantic: The United States and the British Empire after American Independence*. New York, N.Y.: Oxford University Press, 2012.

Martin, George Henry. *The Evolution of the Massachusetts Public School System: A Historical Sketch*. New York, N.Y.: D. Appleton & Company, 1894.

Martin, James Kirby. *Men in Rebellion: Higher Governmental Leaders and the Coming of the American Revolution*. New Brunswick, N.J.: Rutgers University Press, 1973.

Mastromarino, Mark Anthony. "Fair Visions: Elkanah Watson (1758–1842) and the Modern American Agricultural Fair." Ph.D. Diss., College of William and Mary, 2002.

Mathews, Donald G. "The Second Great Awakening as an Organizing Process, 1780–1830: An Hypothesis." *American Quarterly* 21 (April 1969): 23–43.

Matson, Cathy. "Mathew Carey's Learning Experience: Commerce, Manufacturing, and the Panic of 1819." *Early American Studies* 11 (Fall 2013): 455–85.

May, Henry F. *The Enlightenment in America*. New York, N.Y.: Oxford University Press, 1976.

McAnear, Beverly. "The Raising of Funds by the Colonial Colleges." *Mississippi Valley Historical Review* 38 (March 1952): 591–612.

McCaughey, Robert A. *Stand, Columbia: A History of Columbia University in the City of New York, 1754–2004*. New York, N.Y.: Columbia University Press, 2003.

McClay, Wilfred M. "A Distant Elite: How Meritocracy Went Wrong." *Hedgehog Review* 18 (Summer 2016): 36–49.

McConville, Brendan. *The King's Three Faces: The Rise & Fall of Royal America, 1688–1776*. Chapel Hill, N.C.: Published for the Omohundro Institute of Early American History and Culture by the University of North Carolina Press, 2006.

———. *These Daring Disturbers of the Public Peace: The Struggle for Property and Power in Early New Jersey*. Ithaca, N.Y.: Cornell University Press, 1999.

McCusker, John J. "How Much Is That in Real Money? A Historical Price Index for Use as a Deflator of Money Values in the Economy of the United States." *Proceedings of the American Antiquarian Society* 101 (October 1999): 297–373.

McCusker, John J., and Russell R. Menard. *The Economy of British America, 1607–1789.* Chapel Hill, N.C.: Published for the Institute of Early American History and Culture by the University of North Carolina Press, 1985.

McDonnell, Michael A. *The Politics of War: Race, Class, and Conflict in Revolutionary Virginia.* Chapel Hill, N.C.: Published for the Omohundro Institute of Early American History and Culture, by the University of North Carolina Press, 2007.

———. "Resistance to the Revolution." In *Companion to the American Revolution,* edited by Jack P. Greene and J. R. Pole, 342–51. London: Blackwell, 2000.

McLachlan, James. *Princetonians, 1748–1768: A Biographical Dictionary.* Princeton, N.J.: Princeton University Press, 1976.

McMahon, Lucia. *Mere Equals: The Paradox of Educated Women in the Early American Republic.* Ithaca, N.Y.: Cornell University Press, 2012.

———. "'Of the Utmost Importance to Our Country': Women, Education, and Society, 1780–1820." *Journal of the Early Republic* 29 (Fall 2009): 475–506.

Merritt, Keri Leigh. *Masterless Men: Poor Whites and Slavery in the Antebellum South.* New York, N.Y.: Cambridge University Press, 2017.

Miller, George Frederick. *The Academy System of the State of New York.* Albany, N.Y.: J. B. Lyon Company, 1922.

Miller, Howard. *The Revolutionary College: American Presbyterian Higher Education, 1707–1837.* New York, N.Y.: New York University Press, 1976.

Millikan, Neal Elizabeth. "'Willing to Be in Fortune's Way:' Lotteries in the Eighteenth-Century British North American Empire." Ph.D. Diss., University of South Carolina, 2008.

Mills, Scott A. *History of West Nottingham Academy, 1744–1981.* Lanham, Md.: Maryland Historical Press, 1985.

Moniz, Amanda Bowie. *From Empire to Humanity: The American Revolution and the Origins of Humanitarianism.* New York, N.Y.: Oxford University Press, 2016.

Morgan, Edmund S. *Inventing the People: The Rise of Popular Sovereignty in England and America.* New York: W. W. Norton, 1988.

———. "The Puritan Ethic and the American Revolution." *William and Mary Quarterly* 24 (Jan. 1967): 3–43.

———. *Virginians at Home: Family Life in the Eighteenth Century.* Williamsburg, Va.: Colonial Williamsburg Foundation, 1952.

Moroney, Siobhan. "Birth of a Canon: The Historiography of Early Republican Educational Thought." *History of Education Quarterly* 39 (Dec. 1999): 476–91.

The Morris Academy of Morristown, N.J.: A Brief Record of Its History until Merged in the Library and Lyceum. Morristown, N.J.: "The Jerseyman" office, 1905.

Moss, Hilary J. *Schooling Citizens: The Struggle for African American Education in Antebellum America.* Chicago: University of Chicago Press, 2009.

Moynihan, Kenneth J. *A History of Worcester, 1674–1848.* Charleston: History Press, 2007.

Munroe, John A. *The University of Delaware: A History.* Newark, Del.: University of Delaware Press, 1986.

Murphy, Brian Phillips. "'A Very Convenient Instrument': The Manhattan Company, Aaron Burr, and the Election of 1800." *William and Mary Quarterly* 65 (April 2008): 233–66.

Murphy, Sharon Ann. *Other People's Money: How Banking Worked in the Early American Republic*. Baltimore: Johns Hopkins University Press, 2017.

Murray, Nicholas. *Notes, Historical and Biographical, Concerning Elizabeth-Town, Its Eminent Men, Churches and Ministers*. Elizabeth-Town, N.J.: E. Sanderson, 1844.

Murrin, John. "The Great Inversion, or Court versus Country: A Comparison of the Revolutionary Settlements in England (1688–1721) and America (1776–1816)." In *Three British Revolutions: 1641, 1688, 1776*, edited by J. G. A. Pocock, 368–454. Princeton, N.J.: Princeton University Press, 1980.

———."Review Essay." *History and Theory* 11 (January 1972): 226–75.

Myers, Minor. *Liberty Without Anarchy: A History of the Society of the Cincinnati*. Charlottesville, Va.: University Press of Virginia, 1983.

Nash, Margaret A. "Contested Identities: Nationalism, Regionalism, and Patriotism in Early American Textbooks." *History of Education Quarterly* 49 (November 2009): 417–41.

———. "'Cultivating the Powers of Human Beings': Gendered Perspectives on Curricula and Pedagogy in Academies of the New Republic." *History of Education Quarterly* 41 (July 2001): 239–50.

———. "Rethinking Republican Motherhood: Benjamin Rush and the Young Ladies' Academy of Philadelphia." *Journal of the Early Republic* 17 (Summer 1997): 171–91.

———. *Women's Education in the United States, 1780–1840*. New York, N.Y.: Palgrave Macmillan, 2005.

Neem, Johann N. "Civil Society and American Nationalism, 1776–1865." In *Politics and Partnerships: The Role of Voluntary Associations in America's Political Past and Present*, edited by Elisabeth S. Clemens and Doug Guthrie, 29–53. Chicago, Ill.: University of Chicago Press, 2010.

———. *Creating a Nation of Joiners: Democracy and Civil Society in Early National Massachusetts*. Cambridge, Mass.: Harvard University Press, 2008.

———. "Creating Social Capital in the Early American Republic: The View from Connecticut." *Journal of Interdisciplinary History* 39 (Spring 2009): 471–95.

———. *Democracy's Schools: The Rise of Public Education in America*. Baltimore, Md.: Johns Hopkins University Press, 2017.

———. "Path Dependence and the Emergence of Common Schools: Ohio to 1853." *Journal of Policy History* 28 (2016): 48–80.

———. "State Of The Field: What Is the Legacy of the Common Schools Movement? Revisiting Carl Kaestle's 1983 Pillars of the Republic." *Reviews in American History* 44 (June 2016): 342–55.

———. "Taking Modernity's Wager: Tocqueville, Social Capital, and the American Civil War." *Journal of Interdisciplinary History* 41 (Spring 2011): 591–618.

Nelson, Adam R. "The Perceived Dangers of Study Abroad, 1780–1800: Nationalism, Internationalism, and the Origins of the American University." In *The Founding Fathers, Education, and "The Great Contest": The American Philosophical Society Prize of 1797*, edited by Benjamin Justice, 175–97. New York, N.Y.: Palgrave Macmillan, 2013.

Nelson, Eric. *The Royalist Revolution: Monarchy and the American Founding*. Cambridge, Mass.: Harvard University Press, 2014.

Newman, Simon P. *Parades and the Politics of the Street: Festive Culture in the Early American Republic*. Philadelphia, Pa.: University of Pennsylvania Press, 1997.

———. "Principles or Men? George Washington and the Political Culture of National Leadership, 1776–1801." *Journal of the Early Republic* 12 (Winter 1992): 477–507.

Nichols, David Andrew. *Engines of Diplomacy: Indian Trading Factories and the Negotiation of American Empire*. Chapel Hill, N.C.: University of North Carolina Press, 2016.

Nobles, Gregory H. *Divisions Throughout the Whole: Politics and Society in Hampshire County, Massachusetts, 1740–1775*. New York, N.Y.: Cambridge University Press, 1983.

Noll, Mark A. *America's God: From Jonathan Edwards to Abraham Lincoln*. New York, N.Y.: Oxford University Press, 2002.

———. "Jacob Green's Proposal for Seminaries." *Journal of Presbyterian History* 58 (Fall 1980): 210–22.

———. "Observations on the Reconciliation of Politics and Religion in Revolutionary New Jersey: The Case of Jacob Green." *Journal of Presbyterian History* 54 (Summer 1976): 217–37.

———. *Princeton and the Republic, 1768–1822: The Search for a Christian Enlightenment in the Era of Samuel Stanhope Smith*. Princeton, N.J.: Princeton University Press, 1989.

Norton, Mary Beth. "Communications." *William and Mary Quarterly* 48 (October 1991): 639–45.

Novak, William J. "The Legal Transformation of Citizenship in Nineteenth-Century America." In *The Democratic Experiment: New Directions in American Political History*, edited by Meg Jacobs, Julian Zelizer, and William Novak, 64–84. Princeton, N.J.: Princeton University Press, 2003.

———. "The Myth of the 'Weak' American State." *American Historical Review* 113 (June 2008): 752–72.

———. *The People's Welfare: Law and Regulation in Nineteenth-Century America*. Chapel Hill, N.C.: University of North Carolina Press, 1996.

Nybakken, Elizabeth. "In the Irish Tradition: Pre-Revolutionary Academies in America." *History of Education Quarterly* 37 (July 1997): 163–83.

Oberle, George. "Institutionalizing the Information Revolution: Debates over Knowledge Institutions in the Early American Republic." Ph.D. Diss., George Mason University, 2016.

O'Brien, Susan. "A Transatlantic Community of Saints: The Great Awakening and the First Evangelical Network, 1735–1755." *American Historical Review* 91 (October 1986): 811–32.

O'Neil, Edward Herring. "Private Schools and Public Vision: A History of Academies in Upstate New York, 1800–1860." Ph.D. Diss., Syracuse University, 1984.

Onuf, Peter S. "State Politics and Republican Virtue: Religion, Education, and Morality in Early American Federalism." In *Toward a Usable Past: An Inquiry into the Origins and Duplications of State Protections of Liberty*, edited by Paul Finkelman and Stephen E. Gottlieb, 91–116. Athens, Ga.: University of Georgia Press, 1991.

Opal, J. M. *Avenging the People: Andrew Jackson, the Rule of Law, and the American Nation*. New York, N.Y.: Oxford University Press, 2017.

———. *Beyond the Farm: National Ambitions in Rural New England*. Philadelphia, Pa.: University of Pennsylvania Press, 2008.

———. "Exciting Emulation: Academies and the Transformation of the Rural North, 1780s–1820s." *Journal of American History* 91 (September 2004): 445–70.

———. "The Labors of Liberality: Christian Benevolence and National Prejudice in the American Founding," *Journal of American History* 94 (March 2008): 1082–1107.

———. "Natural Rights and National Greatness: Economic Ideology and Social Policy in the American States, 1780–1820." In *The World of the Revolutionary American Republic: Land, Labor, and the Conflict for a Continent*, edited by Andrew Shankman, 295–323. New York, N.Y.: Routledge, 2014.

Orfield, Gary, Erica Frankenberg, Jongyeon Ee, and Jennifer B. Ayscue. "Harming Our Common Future: America's Segregated Schools 65 Years after Brown." UCLA Civil Rights Project / Proyecto Derechos Civiles, May 2019.

O'Shaughnessy, Andrew Jackson. *An Empire Divided: The American Revolution and the British Caribbean*. Philadelphia, Pa.: University of Pennsylvania Press, 2000.

Pangle, Lorraine Smith, and Thomas L. Pangle. *The Learning of Liberty: The Educational Ideas of the American Founders*. Lawrence, Kan.: University Press of Kansas, 1993.

Parkinson, Robert G. *The Common Cause: Creating Race and Nation in the American Revolution*. Published for the Omohundro Institute of Early American History and Culture by the University of North Carolina Press, 2016.

Parr, Jessica M. *Inventing George Whitefield: Race, Revivalism, and the Making of a Religious Icon*. Oxford, Miss.: University Press of Mississippi, 2015.

Pasley, Jeffrey L. "The Cheese and the Words: Popular Political Culture and Participatory Democracy in the Early American Republic." In *Beyond the Founders: New Approaches to the Political History of the Early American Republic*, edited by Jeffrey L. Pasley, Andrew W. Robertson, and David Waldstreicher, 31–56. Chapel Hill, N.C.: University of North Carolina Press, 2004.

———. *"The Tyranny of Printers": Newspaper Politics in the Early American Republic*. Charlottesville, Va.: University Press of Virginia, 2001.

Paulston, Roland G. "French Influence in American Institutions of Higher Learning, 1784–1825." *History of Education Quarterly* 8 (July 1968): 229–45.

Pearl, Christopher R. "'For the Good Order of Government': The American Revolution and the Creation of the Commonwealth of Pennsylvania, 1740–1790." Ph.D. Diss., Binghamton University, 2013.

Pears, Thomas Clinton, Jr. "Francis Alison, Colonial Educator." *Delaware Notes* 17 (1944): 9–22.

Peckham, Howard H. "Collegia Ante Bellum: Attitudes of College Professors and Students toward the American Revolution." *Pennsylvania Magazine of History and Biography* 95 (January 1971): 50–72.

Perl-Rosenthal, Nathan. *Citizen Sailors: Becoming American in the Age of Revolution*. Cambridge, Mass.: Harvard University Press, 2015.

Perlman, Joel, and Robert A. Margo. *Women's Work? American Schoolteachers, 1650–1920*. Chicago, Ill.: University of Chicago Press, 2001.

Phillips, Kevin. *The Cousins' Wars: Religion, Politics, and the Triumph of Anglo-America*. New York, N.Y.: Basic Books, 1999.

Pilcher, George William. "Preacher of the New Light, Samuel Davies, 1724–1761." Ph.D. Diss., University of Illinois, Urbana-Champaign, 1963.

Polgar, Paul J. "'To Raise Them to an Equal Participation': Early National Abolitionism, Gradual Emancipation, and the Promise of African American Citizenship." *Journal of the Early Republic* 31 (Summer 2011): 229–58.

Portnoy, Alisse. *Their Right to Speak: Women's Activism in the Indian and Slave Debates.* Cambridge, Mass.: Harvard University Press, 2005.

Powell, Lyman Pierson. *The History of Education in Delaware.* Washington, D.C.: U.S. Government Printing Office, 1893.

Powell, William Stevens, and Jay Mazzocchi, eds. *Encyclopedia of North Carolina,* 6 vols. Chapel Hill, N.C.: University of North Carolina Press, 1979–1996. https://www.ncpedia.org.

Prevots, Naima. *Dance for Export: Cultural Diplomacy and the Cold War.* Hanover, N.H.: University Press of New England, 1998.

Prince, Carl E. *New Jersey's Jeffersonian Republicans: The Genesis of an Early Party Machine, 1789–1817.* Chapel Hill, N.C.: University of North Carolina Press, 1964.

Purvis, Thomas L. "'High-Born, Long-Recorded Families': Social Origins of New Jersey Assemblymen, 1703 to 1776." *William and Mary Quarterly* 37 (October 1980): 592–615.

Putnam, Robert D. *Our Kids: The American Dream in Crisis.* New York, N.Y.: Simon and Schuster, 2015.

Quintana, Ryan A. *Making a Slave State: Political Development in Early South Carolina.* Chapel Hill, N.C.: University of North Carolina Press, 2018.

Rao, Gautham. *National Duties: Custom Houses and the Making of the American State.* Chicago, Ill.: University of Chicago Press, 2016.

———. "William J. Novak's The People's Welfare and the New Historiography of the Early Federal State." *American Journal of Legal History* 57 (June 2017): 226–31.

Ravitch, Diane. *Reign of Error: The Hoax of the Privatization Movement and the Danger to America's Public Schools.* New York, N.Y.: A. A. Knopf, 2013.

Reese, William J. *America's Public Schools: From the Common School to "No Child Left Behind,"* updated edition. Baltimore, Md.: Johns Hopkins University Press, 2011.

———. *Testing Wars in the Public Schools.* Cambridge, Mass.: Harvard University Press, 2013.

Reid-Maroney, Nina. *Philadelphia's Enlightenment, 1740–1800: Kingdom of Christ, Empire of Reason.* Westport, Conn.: Greenwood Press, 2001.

———. "Science and the Presbyterian Academies." In *Theological Education in the Evangelical Tradition,* edited by R. Albert Mohler and Darryl G. Hart, 203–16. Grand Rapids, Mich.: Baker Books, 1996.

Richards, Leonard L. *Shays's Rebellion: The American Revolution's Final Battle.* Philadelphia, Pa.: University of Pennsylvania Press, 2002.

Riley, Padraig. *Slavery and the Democratic Conscience: Political Life in Jeffersonian America.* Philadelphia, Pa.: University of Pennsylvania Press, 2015.

Riordan, Liam. *Many Identities, One Nation: The Revolution and Its Legacy in the Mid-Atlantic.* Philadelphia, Pa.: University of Pennsylvania Press, 2007.

Risjord, Norman K. *Chesapeake Politics, 1781–1800.* New York, N.Y.: Columbia University Press, 1978.

Robbins, Caroline. "'When It Is That Colonies May Turn Independent': An Analysis of the Environment and Politics of Francis Hutcheson (1694–1746)." *William and Mary Quarterly* 11 (April 1954): 214–51.

Roberts, Arthur. *1797 to 1897. A Century in the Comptroller's Office, State of New York.* Albany, N.Y.: J. B. Lyon, printer, 1897.

Roberts, John G. "The American Career of Quesnay de Beaurepaire." *The French Review* 20 (May 1947): 463–70.
———. "An Exchange of Letters between Jefferson and Quesnay De Beaurepaire." *Virginia Magazine of History and Biography* 50 (April 1942): 134–42.
———. "François Quesnay's Heir." *Virginia Magazine of History and Biography* 50 (April 1942): 143–50.
Robertson, Andrew W. "'Look on This Picture ... And on This!': Nationalism, Localism, and Partisan Images of Otherness in the United States, 1787–1820." *American Historical Review* 106 (October 2001): 1263–80.
Robinson, Dale Glenwood. *The Academies of Virginia, 1776–1861*. Richmond, Va.: Dietz Press, 1977.
Robson, David W. *Educating Republicans: The College in the Era of the American Revolution, 1750–1800*. Westport, Conn. Greenwood Press, 1985.
Robson, David W. "Enlightening the Wilderness: Charles Nisbet's Failure at Higher Education in Post-Revolutionary Pennsylvania." *History of Education Quarterly* 37 (October 1997): 271–89.
Rohrer, S. Scott. *Jacob Green's Revolution: Radical Religion and Reform in a Revolutionary Age*. University Park, Pa.: Pennsylvania State University Press, 2014.
Ron, Ariel. "Developing the Country: 'Scientific Agriculture' and the Roots of the Republican Party." Ph.D. Diss., University of California, Berkeley, 2012.
———. "Summoning the State: Northern Farmers and the Transformation of American Politics in the Mid-Nineteenth Century." *Journal of American History* 103 (September 2016): 347–74.
Roney, Jessica Choppin. *Governed by a Spirit of Opposition: Origins of American Political Practices in Colonial Philadelphia*. Baltimore, Md.: Johns Hopkins University Press, 2014.
Roth, Randolph A. *The Democratic Dilemma: Religion, Reform, and the Social Order in the Connecticut River Valley of Vermont, 1791–1850*. New York, N.Y.: Cambridge University Press, 1987.
Rothbard, Murray N. *The Panic of 1819: Reactions and Policies*. New York, N.Y.: Columbia University Press, 1962.
Rowe, G. S. *Thomas McKean: The Shaping of an American Republicanism*. Boulder, Co.: Colorado Associated University Press, 1978.
Royster, Charles. *A Revolutionary People at War: The Continental Army and American Character, 1775–1783*. Chapel Hill, N.C.: Published for the Institute of Early American History and Culture by the University of North Carolina Press, 1979.
Rozbicki, Michal Jan. *Culture and Liberty in the Age of the American Revolution*. Charlottesville, Va.: University of Virginia Press, 2011.
Ruddiman, John A. *Becoming Men of Some Consequence: Youth and Military Service in the Revolutionary War*. Charlottesville, Va.: University of Virginia Press, 2014.
Schechter, Stephen L., ed. *The Reluctant Pillar: New York and the Adoption of the Federal Constitution*. Troy, N.Y.: Russell Sage College, 1985.
Schocket, Andrew M. *Founding Corporate Power in Early National Philadelphia*. DeKalb, Ill.: Northern Illinois University Press, 2007.
Schulten, Susan. "Map Drawing, Graphic Literacy, and Pedagogy in the Early Republic." *History of Education Quarterly* 57 (May 2017): 185–220.

Schweiger, Beth Barton. "The Literate South: Reading before Emancipation." *Journal of the Civil War Era* 3 (September 2013): 331–59.
Scott, Anne Firor. "The Ever Widening Circle: The Diffusion of Feminist Values from the Troy Female Seminary 1822–1872." *History of Education Quarterly* 19 (Spring 1979): 3–25.
Sellers, Charles. *The Market Revolution: Jacksonian America, 1815–1846.* New York, N.Y.: Oxford University Press, 1994.
Shalhope, Robert E. *The Roots of Democracy: American Thought and Culture, 1760–1800.* Lanham, Md.: Rowman & Littlefield, 1990.
Shammas, Carole. "Did Democracy Give the United States an Edge in Primary Schooling?" *Social Science History* 39 (Fall 2015): 315–38.
———. "The Extent and Duration of Formal Schooling in Eighteenth-Century America." Paper presented at the McNeil Center for Early American Studies, Philadelphia, Pa., December 7, 2012.
Shankman, Andrew. "Capitalism, Slavery, and the New Eopch: Matthew Carey's 1819." In *Slavery's Capitalism: A New History of American Economic Development*, edited by Sven Beckert and Seth Rockman, 243–62. Philadelphia, Pa.: University of Pennsylvania Press, 2016.
———. *Crucible of American Democracy: The Struggle to Fuse Egalitarianism & Capitalism in Jeffersonian Pennsylvania.* Lawrence, Kans.: University Press of Kansas, 2004.
———. *Original Intents: Hamilton, Jefferson, Madison, and the American Founding.* New York, N.Y.: Oxford University Press, 2017.
———. "Toward a Social History of Federalism: The State and Capitalism To and From the American Revolution." *Journal of the Early Republic* 37 (Winter 2017): 615–53.
Sharp, James Roger. *American Politics in the Early Republic: The New Nation in Crisis.* New Haven, Conn.: Yale University Press, 1993.
Sheldon, George. *Joseph Stebbins, a Pioneer at the Outbreak of the Revolution.* Salem, Mass.: Salem Press Company, 1916.
Shereshewsky, Murray S. "Academy Keeping and the Great Awakening: The Presbyterian Academies, College of New Jersey, and the Creation of a New Jersey Way, 1727–1768." Ph.D. Diss., New York University, 1980.
Sherwood, Sidney. *The University of the State of New York: History of Higher Education in the State of New York.* Washington, D.C.: U.S. Government Printing Office, 1900.
Shields, David S. *Civil Tongues & Polite Letters in British America.* Chapel Hill, N.C.: Published for the Institute of Early American History and Culture by the University of North Carolina Press, 1997.
Shields, David S., and Frederika J. Teute. "The Court of Abigail Adams." *Journal of the Early Republic* 35 (Summer 2015): 227–35.
———. "The Meschianza: Sum of All Fêtes." *Journal of the Early Republic* 35 (Summer 2015): 185–214.
———. "The Republican Court and the Historiography of a Women's Domain in the Public Sphere." *Journal of the Early Republic* 35 (Summer 2015): 169–83.
Shovlin, John. "Emulation in Eighteenth-Century French Economic Thought." *Eighteenth-Century Studies* 36 (December 2003): 224–30.
Silverman, Kenneth. *A Cultural History of the American Revolution: Painting, Music, Literature, and the Theatre in the Colonies and the United States from the Treaty of Paris to*

the Inauguration of George Washington, 1763–1789. New York, N.Y.: Thomas Y. Crowell Company, 1976.

Sims, Clifford Stanley, *The Institution of the Society of the Cincinnati: Together with the Roll of the Original, Hereditary, and Honorary Members of the Order, in the State of New Jersey, from 1783 to 1866.* Albany, N.Y.: Printed for the Society by J. Munsell, 1866.

Sinha, Manisha. *The Slave's Cause: A History of Abolition.* New Haven, Conn.: Yale University Press, 2016.

Sizer, Theodore R. *The Age of Academies.* New York, N.Y.: Bureau of Publications, Teachers College, 1964.

Skemer, Don C. "The Institutio Legalis and Legal Education in New Jersey: 1783–1817." *New Jersey History* 96 (Autumn/Winter 1978): 123–34.

Skemp, Sheila L. *Judith Sargent Murray: A Brief Biography with Documents.* New York, N.Y.: Bedford St. Martins, 1998.

Sklar, Kathryn Kish. "The Schooling of Girls and Changing Community Values in Massachusetts Towns, 1750–1820." *History of Education Quarterly* 33 (Winter 1993): 511–42.

Slaughter, Thomas P. *The Whiskey Rebellion: Frontier Epilogue to the American Revolution.* New York, N.Y.: Oxford University Press, 1986.

Sloan, Douglas. *Education in New Jersey in the Revolutionary Era.* Trenton, N.J.: The New Jersey Historical Commission, 1975.

———. *The Scottish Enlightenment and the American College Ideal.* New York, N.Y.: Teachers College Press, 1971.

Slonimsky, Nora. "'The Engine of Free Expression': The Political Economy of Copyright in the Colonial British Atlantic and Early National United States." Ph.D. Diss., City University of New York, 2017.

Smith, Barbara Clark. *The Freedoms We Lost: Consent and Resistance in Revolutionary America.* New York, N.Y.: New Press, 2010.

Smith, Craig Bruce. *American Honor: Creating the Nation's Ideals in the Revolutionary Era.* Chapel Hill, N.C.: University of North Carolina Press, 2018.

Smith, Jay M. *The Culture of Merit: Nobility, Royal Service, and the Making of Absolute Monarchy in France, 1600–1789.* Ann Arbor, Mich.: University of Michigan Press, 1996.

Smith-Rosenberg, Carroll. *This Violent Empire: The Birth of an American National Identity.* Chapel Hill, N.C.: Published by the Ommohundro Institute of Early American History and Culture by the University of North Carolina Press, 2010.

Smolenski, John. *Friends and Strangers: The Making of a Creole Culture in Colonial Pennsylvania.* Philadelphia, Pa.: University of Pennsylvania Press, 2010.

Snyder, Christina. *Great Crossings: Indians, Settlers, and Slaves in the Age of Jackson.* New York, N.Y.: Oxford University Press, 2017.

Spring, Leverett Wilson. *A History of Williams College.* Boston, Mass.: Houghton Mifflin, 1917.

Stamatov, Peter. "Activist Religion, Empire, and the Emergence of Modern Long-Distance Advocacy Networks." *American Sociological Review* 75 (2010): 607–28.

———. "The Religious Field and the Path-Dependent Transformation of Popular Politics in the Anglo-American World, 1770–1840." *Theory and Society* 40 (2011): 437–73.

Starkey, Marion. *A Little Rebellion.* New York, N.Y.: A. A. Knopf, 1955.

Steele, Brian Douglass. *Thomas Jefferson and American Nationhood*. New York, N.Y.: Cambridge University Press, 2012.

Steiner, Bernard Christian. *History of Education in Maryland*. Washington, D.C.: Government Print Office, 1894.

Stewart, James Brewer. "The Emergence of Racial Modernity and the Rise of the White North, 1790–1840." *Journal of the Early Republic* 18 (Summer 1998): 181–217.

Stone, Lawrence. "The Educational Revolution in England, 1560–1640." *Past & Present* 28 (July 1964): 41–80.

Stryker, William S. *Official Register of the Officers and Men of New Jersey in the Revolutionary War*. Trenton, N.J.: Wm. T. Nicholson & Co., Printers, 1872.

Sullivan, Aaron. *The Disaffected: Britain's Occupation of Philadelphia During the American Revolution*. Philadelphia, Pa.: University of Pennsylvania Press, 2019.

Sumner, Margaret. *Collegiate Republic: Cultivating an Ideal Society in Early America*. Charlottesville, Va.: University of Virginia Press, 2014.

Swift, Fletcher Harper. *A History of Public Permanent Common School Funds in the United States, 1795–1905*. New York, N.Y.: Henry Holt and Co., 1911.

Sylla, Richard. "Experimental Federalism: The Economics of American Government, 1789–1914." In *The Cambridge Economic History of the United States*. Vol. 2, *The Long Nineteenth Century (1789–1920)*, edited by Stanley L. Engerman and Robert Gallman, 483–542. New York, N.Y.: Cambridge University Press, 2000.

Sylla, Richard, John B. Legler, and John J. Wallis. "Banks and State Public Finance in the New Republic: The United States, 1790–1860." *Journal of Economic History* 47 (June 1987): 391–403.

Szatmary, David P. *Shays' Rebellion: The Making of an Agrarian Insurrection*. Amherst, Mass.: University of Massachusetts Press, 1980.

Tamarkin, Elisa. *Anglophilia: Deference, Devotion, and Antebellum America*. Chicago, Ill.: University of Chicago Press, 2007.

Taylor, Alan. *American Colonies: The Settling of North America*. New York, N.Y.: Penguin, 2001.

———. *American Revolutions: A Continental History, 1750–1804*. New York, N.Y.: W. W. Norton & Company, 2016.

———. *The Civil War of 1812: American Citizens, British Subjects, Irish Rebels, & Indian Allies*. New York, N.Y.: A. A. Knopf, 2010.

———. "From Fathers to Friends of the People: Political Personas in the Early Republic." *Journal of the Early Republic* 11 (Winter 1991): 465–91.

———. *Liberty Men and Great Proprietors: The Revolutionary Settlement on the Maine Frontier, 1760–1820*. Chapel Hill, N.C.: Published for the Ommohundro Institute of Early American History and Culture by the University of North Carolina Press, 1990.

———. *William Cooper's Town: Power and Persuasion on the Frontier of the Early American Republic*. New York, N.Y.: A. A. Knopf, 1995.

Teute, Fredrika. "Roman Matron on the Banks of Tiber Creek." In *A Republic for the Ages: The United States Capitol and the Political Culture of the Early Republic*, edited by Donald R. Kennon, 98–121. Charlottesville, Va.: Published for the United States Capitol Historical Society by the University Press of Virginia, 1999.

Teute, Fredrika, and David Shields. "The Confederation Court." *Journal of the Early Republic* 35 (Summer 2015): 215–26.

———. "Jefferson in Washington: Domesticating Manners in the Republican Court." *Journal of the Early Republic* 35 (Summer 2015): 237–59.

Thomas, George. *The Founders and the Idea of a National University*. New York, N.Y.: Cambridge University Press, 2014.

Tiedemann, Joseph S. "Interconnected Communities: The Middle Colonies on the Eve of the American Revolution." *Pennsylvania History* 76 (Winter 2009): 1–41.

———. "Presbyterianism and the American Revolution in the Middle Colonies." *Church History* 74 (June 2005): 306–44.

Tolley, Kim. "A Chartered School in a Free Market: The Case of Raleigh Academy, 1801–1823." *Teachers College Record* 107 (January 2005): 59–88.

———. *Heading South to Teach: The World of Susan Nye Hutchison, 1815–1845*. Chapel Hill, N.C.: University of North Carolina Press, 2015.

———. "Joseph Gales and Education Reform in North Carolina, 1799–1841." *North Carolina Historical Review* 86 (January 2009): 1–31.

———. "Mapping the Landscape of Higher Schooling, 1727–1850." In *Chartered Schools: Two Hundred Years of Independent Academies in the United States, 1727–1925*, edited by Nancy Beadie and Kim Tolley, 19–43. New York, N.Y.: Routledge Press, 2002.

———. "Music Teachers in the North Carolina Education Market, 1800–1840." *Social Science History* 32 (Spring 2008): 75–106.

———. "The Rise of the Academies: Continuity or Change?" *History of Education Quarterly* 41 (July 2001): 225–39.

———. "Science for Ladies, Classics for Gentlemen: A Comparative Analysis of Scientific Subjects in the Curricula of Boys' and Girls' Secondary Schools in the United States, 1794–1850." *History of Education Quarterly* 36 (July 1996): 129–53.

———. "The Significance of the 'French School' in Early National Female Education." In *The Founding Fathers, Education, and "The Great Contest": The American Philosophical Society Prize of 1797*, edited by Benjamin Justice, 133–54. New York, N.Y.: Palgrave Macmillan, 2013.

———, ed. *Transformations in Schooling: Historical and Comparative Perspectives*. New York, N.Y.: Palgrave Macmillan, 2007.

Tomlins, Christopher L. *Law, Labor, and Ideology in the Early American Republic*. New York, N.Y.: Cambridge University Press, 1993.

Travers, Len. *Celebrating the Fourth: Independence Day and the Rites of Nationalism in the Early Republic*. Amherst, Mass.: University of Massachusetts Press, 1997.

Tully, Alan. "Literacy Levels and Educational Development in Rural Pennsylvania, 1729–1775." *Pennsylvania History* 39 (July 1972): 301–12.

Turner, J. D. Edmiston. "Reverend Samuel Blair, 1712–1751." *Journal of the Presbyterian Historical Society* 29 (December 1951): 227–36.

Turner, Lynn W. *The Ninth State: New Hampshire's Formative Years*. Chapel Hill, N.C.: University of North Carolina Press, 1983.

Tyack, David. "Forming the National Character: Paradox in the Educational Thought of the Revolutionary Generation." *Harvard Educational Review* 36 (April 1966): 29–41.

Ueda, Reed. *Avenues to Adulthood: The Origins of the High School and Social Mobility in an American Suburb*. New York, N.Y.: Cambridge University Press, 1987.

Urquhart, Frank John. *A History of the City of Newark, New Jersey: Embracing Practically Two and a Half Centuries, 1666–1913*, 3 vols. New York, N.Y.: The Lewis Historical Publishing Co., 1913.

Van Atta, John R. *Securing the West: Politics, Public Lands, and the Fate of the Old Republic, 1785–1850*. Baltimore, Md.: Johns Hopkins University Press, 2014.

VanBurkleo, Sandra F. "'That Our Pure Republican Principles Might Not Wither': Kentucky's Relief Crisis and the Pursuit of 'Moral Justice.'" Ph.D. Diss., University of Minnesota, 1988.

Van Cleve, George William. *We Have Not a Government: The Articles of Confederation and the Road to the Constitution*. Chicago, Ill.: University of Chicago Press, 2017.

Vinovskis, Maris. *The Origins of Public High Schools: A Reexamination of the Beverly High School Controversy*. Madison, Wis.: University of Wisconsin Press, 1985.

———, and Richard M. Bernard. "Beyond Catharine Beecher: Female Education in the Antebellum Period." *Signs* 3 (Summer 1978): 856–69.

Volk, Kyle G. "Apply Liberalism Liberally: Incest and the Troubled American State." *Reviews in American History* 45 (March 2017): 50–56.

Vreeland, Herbert Harold, Jr. "Public Secondary Education in Connecticut in the Seventeenth and Eighteenth Centuries: With Special Reference to Its Support by Private Bequests and Gifts." Ph.D. Diss., Yale University, 1941.

Vrevich, Kevin. "Mr. Ely's Amendment: Massachusetts Federalists and the Politicization of Slave Representation." *American Nineteenth Century History* 19 (2018): 159–76.

Waldstreicher, David. *In the Midst of Perpetual Fetes: The Making of American Nationalism, 1776–1820*. Chapel Hill, N.C.: Published for the Omohundro Institute of Early American History and Culture by the University of North Carolina Press, 1997.

Walsh, Julie M. *The Intellectual Origins of Mass Parties and Mass Schools in the Jacksonian Period: Creating a Conformed Citizenry*. New York, N.Y.: Garland Publishing, 1998.

Ward, W. R. *The Protestant Evangelical Awakening*. Cambridge: Cambridge University Press, 1992.

Washburn, Emory. *A Brief History of Leicester Academy*. Boston, Mass.: Phillips, Sampson, and Company, 1855.

Waterman, Bryan. *Republic of Intellect: The Friendly Club of New York City and the Making of American Literature*. Baltimore, Md.: Johns Hopkins University Press, 2007.

Watson, Harry L. "The Man with the Dirty Black Beard: Race, Class, and Schools in the Antebellum South." *Journal of the Early Republic* 32 (Spring 2012): 1–26.

Welter, Rush. *Popular Education and Democratic Thought in America*. New York, N.Y.: Columbia University Press, 1962.

Wertenbaker, Thomas Jefferson. *Princeton, 1746–1896*. Princeton, N.J.: Princeton University Press, 1946.

Westerkamp, Marilyn J. "Division, Dissension, and Compromise: The Presbyterian Church During the Great Awakening." *Journal of Presbyterian history* 78 (Spring 2000): 3–18.

———. *Triumph of the Laity: Scots-Irish Piety and the Great Awakening, 1625–1760*. New York, N.Y.: Oxford University Press, 1988.

White, Leonard D. *The Federalists: A Study in Administrative History*. New York, N.Y.: Macmillan, 1947.

———. *The Jeffersonians: A Study in Administrative History.* New York, N.Y.: Macmillan, 1951.
Wiebe, Robert H. *The Opening of American Society: From the Adoption of the Constitution to the Eve of Disunion.* New York, N.Y.: A. A. Knopf, 1984.
Wilder, Craig Steven. *Ebony and Ivy: Race, Slavery, and the Troubled History of America's Universities.* New York, N.Y.: Bloomsbury Press, 2013.
Wilentz, Sean. *Chants Democratic: New York City and the Rise of the American Working Class, 1788–1850.* New York, N.Y.: Oxford University Press, 1984.
———. *The Rise of American Democracy: Jefferson to Lincoln.* New York, N.Y.: W. W. Norton, 2005.
Williams, Donald E., Jr. *Prudence Crandall's Legacy: The Fight for Equality in the 1830s, Dred Scott, and Brown v. Board of Education.* Middletown, Conn.: Wesleyan University Press, 2014.
Williams, Sherman. "Jedediah Peck: The Father of the Public School System of the State of New York." *Journal of the New York State Historical Association* 5 (October 1920): 219–40.
Wilson, Kathleen. "Rethinking the Colonial State: Family, Gender, and Governmentality in Eighteenth-Century British Frontiers." *American Historical Review* 116 (December 2011): 1294–1322.
Winiarski, Douglas L. *Darkness Falls on the Land of Light: Experiencing Religious Awakenings in Eighteenth-Century New England.* Chapel Hill, N.C.: Published for the Omohundro Institute of Early American History and Culture by the University of North Carolina Press, 2017.
Winterer, Caroline. *American Enlightenments: Pursuing Happiness in the Age of Reason.* New Haven, Conn.: Yale University Press, 2016.
———. *The Culture of Classicism: Ancient Greece and Rome in American Intellectual Life, 1780–1910.* Baltimore, Md.: Johns Hopkins University Press, 2004.
Wood, Gordon S. *The Creation of the American Republic, 1776–1787.* Chapel Hill, N.C.: Published for the Institute of Early American History and Culture by the University of North Carolina Press, 1969.
———. *Empire of Liberty: A History of the Early Republic, 1789–1815.* New York, N.Y.: Oxford University Press, 2009.
———. *The Radicalism of the American Revolution.* New York, N.Y.: A. A. Knopf, 1992.
Wood, Kirsten E. "'One Woman so Dangerous to Public Morals': Gender and Power in the Eaton Affair." *Journal of the Early Republic* 17 (July 1997): 237–75.
Wright, Marion Thompson. "Racial Integration in the Public Schools in New Jersey." *Journal of Negro Education* 23 (Summer 1954): 282–89.
Wrightson, Keith. *English Society 1580–1680.* New Brunswick, N.J.: Rutgers University Press, 1982.
Yokota, Kariann. "Postcolonialism and Material Culture in the Early United States." *William and Mary Quarterly* 64 (January 2007): 263–70.
———. *Unbecoming British: How Revolutionary America Became a Postcolonial Nation.* New York, N.Y.: Oxford University Press, 2011.
Young, Alfred F. *The Democratic Republicans of New York: The Origins, 1763–1797.* Chapel Hill, N.C.: Published for the Institute of Early American History and Culture by the University of North Carolina Press, 1967.

Young, Michael P. *Bearing Witness against Sin: The Evangelical Birth of the American Social Movement*. Chicago, Ill.: University of Chicago Press, 2006.
Zabin, Serena. *Dangerous Economies: Status and Commerce in Imperial New York*. Philadelphia, Pa.: University of Pennsylvania Press, 2011.
Zaeske, Susan. *Signatures of Citizenship: Petitioning, Antislavery, and Women's Political Identity*. Chapel Hill, N.C.: University of North Carolina Press, 2003.
Zagarri, Rosemarie. "Politics and Civil Society: A Discussion of Mary Kelley's Learning to Stand and Speak." *Journal of the Early Republic* 38 (Spring 2008): 75–82.
———. *The Politics of Size: Representation in the United States, 1776–1850*. Ithaca, N.Y.: Cornell University Press, 1987.
———. *Revolutionary Backlash: Women and Politics in the Early American Republic*. Philadelphia, Pa.: University of Pennsylvania Press, 2007.
Zuckerman, Michael. *Peaceable Kingdoms: New England Towns in the Eighteenth Century*. New York, N.Y.: A. A. Knopf, 1970.
Zuckerman, Michael, and Patrick K. Spero, eds. *The American Revolution Reborn*. Philadelphia, Pa.: University of Pennsylvania Press, 2016.

Index

academies: and American Revolution, 39–40, 41–43, 45–46; British Empire's support of, 33–37; careers of colonial alumni, 27, 43; clergy educated at, 19, 21–22; colonial curriculum, 14, 22–24, 26, 27–28, 37–38; and colonial public sphere, 28–30; curriculum, 2, 3, 72, 76, 85–87, 93, 103–4, 111, 113, 114, 132, 149, 150, 169–70; costs of attendance, 65, 76, 88, 113; demographics of attendance, 26–27, 87–88, 175; elite demand for, 50, 60–61, 76, 87, 92–93, 96–100, 105, 114, 117, 145; and elite formation, 2–5 50, 60, 72, 79, 83–85, 86–87, 94–95, 97, 99–100, 103, 108–110, 117, 143–46, 148–49, 153–54 171; exhibitions at, 5, 45, 82–85, 86, 90, 91; Federalists' support of, 3–4, 67, 72, 75–76, 78–79, 95, 114, 121–22, 125–29, 130–32, 136–37, 144, 151, 154, 156–57, 164, 170; funding of, 55, 92–93, 129–31, 132–33, 155; Great Awakening and, 19–21; and inequality, 68, 86–87, 93–94, 110, 131–33, 137–38, 178; Jeffersonian Republican positions on, 3, 7–8, 114–15, 121–22, 127–29, 131, 136–37, 139–41, 142–43, 144, 148, 152–55, 156–57; legacy of, 181; and local communities, 5, 28–30, 55, 63–65, 92–94; as middle-class institutions, 169–71, 191n32, 225n108; opposition to, 2, 7–8, 63–69, 87, 90, 101–4, 132–37, 148, 153–54, 155, 165–66, 182; ornamental education at, 37–38, 111–14; and patriotism, 82–83; regional variations in, 122–25, 130–31, 140–41, 147; religion in early republic and, 49–50, 55–59, 69–72, 123–24, 140; replaced by high schools, 174–75; as rural institutions, 5, 28–29; secularization of in colonial period, 25–28, 34–36; satires of, 38, 101, 103; and Shays's Rebellion, 65–68, 126, 140, 141–42, 143; social networks forged at, 26–28, 84; state support, 2, 5, 54, 67–68 122–31, 132–33, 134–35, 137, 144, 147, 155–56; and teacher training, 159, 168–70, 173, 175; voluntary associations within, 91, 122

Academy of Polite Arts (Richmond, Va.), 104–7, 111

Adair, John, 164, 167

Adams, John Quincy, 78, 106–7

Adams, Samuel, 134, 135

African American education, 9–10, 91–92, 136, 154–55; and political culture, 179; white ideas about, 75, 88, 128, 138, 155, 178

agricultural colleges, 171–72, 175

Alexandria (Va.) Academy, 84, 86

Alison, Francis, 20, 23, 27, 29, 30, 42

Allison, Burgiss, 86

American Literary, Scientific, and Military Academy (Norwich University), 172

American Philosophical Society 1795 essay contest, 137–38, 139, 151–52

American Revolution: allegiances during, 39–40; education and coming of, 39–41; destruction during, 44–47, 55, 130; impact on religion, 52–53

André, John, 100, 115

Andrews, Charles, 91–92

Anglican Church, 17, 22, 39, 46, 124; and education in colonial era, 33–35; and education in the Confederation era, 57–9; transformation into Episcopal Church, 55–57

Anti-Catholicism, 33–34, 36, 178

Anti-Federalists, 64, 78, 102, 126–27, 129, 132, 139, 141, 146, 153

antirelief: during Panic of 1819, 163, 164; and education, 163, 165, 166–67
antislavery and education, 91, 154, 172–73, 176, 178–79
aristocracy: education and, 2, 7, 10, 78–79, 81–82 87, 133, 137–38, 139, 145–46; 166–67, 171, 172, 175; hereditary, 10, 61, 76, 77, 79, 82, 95, 138, 144, 173; ideas about, 3–4, 14, 16, 76, 78, 100 138; merit-based, 76, 79, 81–82, 86, 95, 145–46, 149, 168, 170, 172, 175; modern meritocracy, 182; opposition to merit-based, 150, 152, 153, 171, 182
art education, 37–38, 96, 98, 99, 102, 104, 111–13, 115
Atkinson (N.H.) Academy, 66, 67 70

Baldwin, Jeduthan, 43–44
Baltimore (Md.) Academy, 83, 87, 92, 94 140
banking, 46, 163, 166; and education, 136–37, 157, 161, 164, 167, 173
Bank of the United States, 139
Barber, Francis, 27, 31, 41, 42, 44, 47–48, 130
Barnard, Henry, 174
Barr, Samuel, 59
Barrow, William, 84
Bartlett, Josiah, 128
Beccaria, Cesare, 109
Beecher, Catharine, 168
Bentley, William, 134
Beresford, Richard, 152
Blackstone, William, 36
Blair, Samuel, 20
Bloomfield, Joseph, 62
Blyth, Benjamin, 99
Bordentown (N.J.) Academy, 86, 114, 115
Brackenridge, Hugh Henry, 58, 59, 78
Brearley, David, 43, 62
Breckenridge, John, 121–22
Bridgewater (Mass.) Academy, 150–51
British support of American schools: during the colonial period, 33–37; decline in 1780s, 53–4
Brown, Andrew, 98–99, 106
Brown, John, 35–36

Brown v. Board of Education, 182
Burr, Aaron, 137, 156–57
Burr, Aaron, Sr., 50, 146
Burr, Esther Edwards, 23

Campfield, William, 121
Carey, Mathew, 160–61
Carrier, Joseph, 106
Carroll, William, 166
Catholic education, 57, 58, 178
celebrations, 75–76, 81, 84–85
Channing, William Ellery, 174
charters of incorporation: for academies, 2, 5, 64, 67–68, 71, 126–37, 140–42, 144, 147, 150; in colonial period 21, 33–34, 40, 58, 64; regional variations in, 122–25, 126, 131
charter schools, 182–3
Chesterfield, Lord, 80
Choctaw Academy, 178
civility: education and ideas about, 9, 36, 93–94, 97, 105–7, 109, 177
civil society: in colonial era, 28–31; in early republic, 49–50, 72, 150, 200n2
Clarkson, Matthew, 131
classics, 2–4 ,14, 76, 85, 88–89, 90, 132, 137; as basis for merit, 86, 106; opposition to, 87, 126 150, 169
Clinton Academy, 131
Clinton, DeWitt, 157, 158
Clinton, George, 55, 125, 130, 136, 156
Clintonian Republicans, 130, 136–37
Codrington, Christopher, 40
Cohansie (region of N.J.), 29, 39
colleges: and the American Revolution, 37–41; in Confederation era, 53–55; modern, 184; religious support of, 13, 16, 21, 33–36, 70–71
College and Academy of Philadelphia (University of Pennsylvania): in colonial era, 21, 26, 27, 34, 35, 38, 39; reorganization of, 55–56
College of New Jersey (Princeton University): in colonial period, 20, 23, 27, 29, 33–34, 35, 50, 146; during American Revolution, 37, 39, 40, 41–42, 46; in

Confederation era, 53–55, 71; in early republic, 149, 150, 173
College of William & Mary, 17, 60
Collin, Nicholas, 80–81, 111, 115; "Foreign Spectator" essays, 107–10, 116
Collins, Isaac, 62
common schools. *See* public schools
Congregational Church, 64, 68, 70, 123, 149–50
Connecticut: education in, 64, 70, 90, 123, 134–35, 158, 169, 174, 179
Constitution, U.S.: rationale behind, 1–4; education and debate over, 77–79, 126
Continental Army: academy students and teachers in, 31, 42–43, 47; and merit, 79–81; officers' political beliefs, 61, 62, 77; officers' political careers, 43–44; officers' support for academies, 49, 62, 100–101; and ornamental education, 96, 100–101
Coram, Robert, 102, 153, 154
Courteil, Amable-Louis-Rose De Lafitte Du, 115
Cox, James, 99, 114
Crandall, Prudence, 179
Cruzeau, Charles, 112

dancing instruction: in colonial period, 37–38; in early republic, 97, 98, 99–101, 104 106, 109, 111, 113, 115
Dartmouth College, 21, 63, 149, 172
Davies, Samuel, 29, 34–35
Deerfield (Mass.) Academy, 67, 127, 150, 151
Deerfield (N.J.) Academy, 42, 47
Delaware: and American Revolution, 42, 43 45–46; in colonial period, 17–18, 20; education in, 24, 32, 34, 38; public schools, 161, 179
Democratic Party, 175, 176
Democratic-Republican Societies, 145, 154
denominational education: in colonial period 19–22, 23, 25, 33–37; decline of, 26–29, 55–59
De Witt, Simeon, 170, 171–72
Dickinson College, 53, 57, 58, 84
Dickinson, Jonathan, 33, 50

disestablishment, 50, 52, 124–25
D'Orsiere, Louis, 98, 99
Doughty, John, 121
Duane, William, Jr., 164–65
Dummer, William, 21, 63
Dutch Reformed Church, 18, 46, 54–55, 59, 125

Edwards, Jonathan, 21, 24
elite: and academies in revolutionary era, 41–44, 48; and academies in early republic, 50, 60, 68–69, 72, 79, 83–85, 86–87, 94–95, 97, 99–100, 103, 108–110, 117, 143–46, 148–49, 153–54 171; American ideas about, 5, 60–65, 67, 77–79 152–55, 163, 171–72; basis for in colonial period, 14–17, 19; colonial academies and, 21–22, 25–28, 30, 33, 36–38; demand for academies, 2–3, 50, 60–61, 76, 87, 92–93, 96–100, 105, 114, 117, 145; influence on modern education, 183
Elizabeth Town, N. J., 13, 45; Academy during American Revolution, 31, 42; Academy in early republic, 98, 114, 130, 146; Constitutional Association, 146; Presbyterian academy, 13, 24, 27, 30, 146
Elmer, Ebenezer, 42, 47–48, 49
Embargo Act, 8
emulation: at colonial academies, 24; in early national academies, 83–84, 85, 86, 99; at female academies, 89–90, 99; opposition to, 25
Episcopal Academies, 56–58, 86, 93
Erasmus Hall Academy (N.Y.), 131, 181
Erskine, John, 53, 54
Essex County, N.J., 46
European education: American fears of, 115–16; American writers on, 84, 101–102, 106–7, 137–38; English writers on, 32–33, 35–36
Ewing, John, 22, 27, 41
exhibitions: academies, 5, 45, 83–85, 86, 114; African American students at, 91–92; female academies, 90, 177; visitors at, 84–85

Fagg's Manor (Pa.) Academy, 20, 58
Fayetteville (N.C.) Academy, 63
Federalists, 67, 72, 94, 109, 146: and academies, 3–4, 8–9, 77–79, 114–15, 121–22, 125, 128–29, 131–32, 136–37, 141, 147, 151, 154, 155, 157, 164, 170, 178; and African American education, 178; and Constitution, 3–4, 75–76, 77–79, 95; criticisms of, 149–50, 152, 156–58, 164, 166; decline of, 148, 157–58; and education reform in 1820s, 170–73; and Illuminati conspiracy, 143, 152; and merit, 79–82; national policies of, 121–22, 139–40; opposition to public schools, 149, 152, 166; support for public schools, 162; and women's education, 10, 159, 168
female academies. *See* Women's education
fencing instruction, 96, 100 106, 112, 113, 115
Finley, Samuel, 20, 26, 27
Fithian, Philip Vickers, 26, 29, 32, 42
"Foreign Spectator." *See* Collin, Nicholas
France: American admiration of culture, 97, 112; ideas about education in, 24, 80, 103; influence on American education, 104–5, 115
Franklin, Benjamin, 21, 30, 37–38, 53, 86, 106
Free Masons, 43, 61–62; and academies, 62–63, 104; and partisan politics, 143–44
French language instruction, 37–38, 97–98
French Revolution, 111, 138; in United States, 97, 114, 122, 126, 143, 148, 150, 218n73

Gales, Joseph, 173–74
Galusha, Jonas, 159
gender: and American Revolution, 38–39, 88; and education, 9–10, 16, 38–39, 75, 88–91; and ornamental education, 96, 101–3
geography curriculum, 85, 111, 169
George-Town Academy, 86, 113
Georgia: academies, 61, 128, 161; public schooling, 161, 176
Genesee Wesleyan Seminary (Syracuse University), 173

Gerry, Elbridge, 127, 142
Gilman, John T., 127, 135
grammar schools, 16, 21, 63, 67
Great Awakening, 2, 13; clergy shortages and, 18–19; and education, 19–22, 50–51, 71–72
Green, Ashbel, 50, 55
Green, Enoch, 42
Green, Jacob, 50–52, 55, 71–72

Hagerstown (Md.) Academy, 94
Haitian Revolution, 112, 138
Hall, David, 42
Hall, Primus, 154
Hamilton, Alexander, 4, 109, 125, 157
Hampden-Sydney Academy (Va.), 129
Hancock, John, 127, 134
Harvard College, 15, 16, 21, 22, 50, 106
Hatfield Academy. *See* Queen's College (Mass.)
Hiester, Joseph, 165, 166
high schools, 174–75
Hillsborough (N.C.) Academy, 70–71
history teaching, 169
Holley, Horace, 167
Hooper, William, 70–71
Hopkinson, Francis, 34
Houston, William Churchill, 62
Hutcheson, Francis, 23, 25, 32
Hutchison, Susan Nye, 169

Illuminati, Bavarian, 143, 152
immigration, 18–19, 112, 114–15
imperial crisis. *See* American Revolution
Indians: white views of, 36, 93; education and dispossession of, 9, 63, 108–110, 160, 177–78; public schools created by, 178
inequality: 1, 8, 9, 23; education and, 10, 42–44, 76, 80, 85–92, 94, 95, 110, 117, 131–33, 138, 148, 153, 158, 166–67, 176–77, 182
informed citizenship: African Americans and, 9, 91, 128, 138, 179–80; education and, 10, 16, 75, 94–95, 152–55, 160, 174, 184; republican commitment to, 1, 5, 60, 71, 89, 106, 111, 150, 152, 163, 174

interdenominational cooperation: and colleges, 55; and academies, 58–59
internal improvements: education and, 108, 116, 132, 136–37, 161, 164, 166, 176

Jackson, Andrew, 111, 166
Jay, John, 54, 137, 155, 156
Jefferson, Thomas: on African American education, 178–79; on European education, 103; and public schools, 60–61, 152; and University of Virginia, 162
Johnson, Richard Mentor, 178

Kendall, Amos, 166–67
Kentucky: academies, 147, 166, 170; and Panic of 1819, 163–64; public schools, 166–67, 178
King's College (Columbia University), 33, 34 125
King, Rufus, 77, 148
Knox, Samuel, 137–38, 151, 152
Knox, Vicesimus, 80, 99

Lafayette, Marquis de, 100, 101
land grants for schools, 130, 135, 147, 172
Lathrop, Joseph, 151–52
Latin. *See* classics
latitudinarianism, 22–23, 33–34, 37
Lawrence (Mass.) Academy, 143
legal education, 146
Leicester Academy, 66, 68, 70, 143, 150; founding of, 43–44, 64–65; student body of, 88–89, 150
Leland, John, 121
Lewis, Morgan, 157
L'Hommedieu, Ezra, 125, 131
Liberty Hall Academy (Va.), 71
Litchfield (Conn.) Female Academy, 90, 169
Litchfield (Conn.) Law School, 146, 149, 150
literacy: rates, 10, 16, 179; and slavery, 92, 128; women's, 159
Little, Woodbridge, 141
Livingston, Edward, 140
Livingston, John, 131

Livingston, William, 45
Log College, 19–20
lotteries, 34, 129–30, 137, 155; opposition to, 132–33, 156
Louverture, Toussaint, 138
luxury, 38, 102–3, 108, 116
Lyman, William, 140, 141

Maclean, John, 170, 173
Madison, James, 78, 108, 139
M'Afee, Robert, 167, 170
magazines, 29, 68, 89, 93–94, 134–34
Mann, Horace, 7, 169, 174
manners, 99–104, 109–110, 115
Manning, William, 7, 154
manual-labor schools, 172–73
Marblehead (Mass.) Academy, 126
Maryland: academies, 41, 46, 58 69, 70, 82, 83, 99, 113 129, 140, 144; public schools, 161, 165
Massachusetts: academies, 21, 43, 63–65, 67–68, 123–24, 126–27, 129, 134–35, 140–42, 150, 171; politics of education in, 65–69, 82, 126–27, 134–35, 140–43, 150, 151, 154; public schools, 16, 158, 159–60, 171, 174, 175
Maxcy, Virgil, 165, 170, 178
McKean, Thomas, 142
McWhorter, Alexander, 83, 144
Mercer, John Fenton, 162, 170, 173
merit: academies define, 82, 85–86, 95, 147; American understandings of, 81–82, 92, 150, 152, 163, 182, 184; and aristocracy, 76, 79, 145, 149, 170, 176; criticisms of academies' role in defining, 150, 152, 175; European understanding of, 80; gendered understanding of, 89–91; in modern U.S., 182, 184; school reform and, 168, 170–72, 174, 176
mid-Atlantic: academies in, 124–25; colonial education in, 2, 13–14, 17–18, 19–21; immigration to, 18
middle class: access to academies, 88, 140, 170–71, 225n108–9; curriculum directed at, 85, 132, 169–70

military education, 172
Milton (Mass.) Academy, 150, 151
Minervaean Society (Brookfield, Mass.), 66
Moderate Enlightenment, 5, 23, 27, 61–62
Moderate Jeffersonians: and academies, 8, 122, 141–43, 144, 147, 148–49, 151, 155, 174; and African American education, 154; and Free Masonry, 143–44; and legal education, 146; and public schools, 149, 152, 156–57, 174; and women's education, 159, 168
moral philosophy, 23–24, 32, 39
Morgan, John, 27, 40–41
Morrill Land Grant Act, 172
Morris Academy (Morristown, N.J.), 121–22
Mulford, Daniel, 121–22
Murphey, Archibald, 161–62, 173–74
Murray, Judith Sargent, 89–90, 102

Nationalists (Confederation era), 61; and academies, 5, 49–50, 55, 59, 60–62, 63, 66
National University, 96, 104, 109–110, 111, 152; congressional debates about, 139–40
nation-building. *See* state formation
New Brunswick, N.J., 46, 55
New England: academies in, 63–69, 126–27, 123, 134–35; colonial education in, 16, 21; early republic education in, 10, 63–69, 113, 159–60, 161; town life, 64–65, 123, 160
New Hampshire education, 66, 123, 127–28, 135, 159
New Jersey: academies, 113, 114–15, 130, 132–33; education during colonial period 13, 17; education during American Revolution, 43–45; education during confederation era, 47–48, 62, 98, 113; politics of education, 62, 113, 121–22, 125, 132–33; public schools, 161, 170, 173, 179; Revolutionary War in, 41–42, 44–45
New Salem (Mass.) Academy, 126, 142
New York: education, 55, 59, 112; politics of education, 136–37, 155–59, 172, 169; state support for academies, 125, 130, 131–32, 170; state support for public schools, 136, 158–59, 174; women's education, 168
New York African Free School, 91, 136, 154, 179
New York City Society of Associated Teachers, 82, 146
New York State Board of Regents, 4, 125, 130, 131–32, 135–36, 150–51, 158, 169–70, 171, 174, 217n59
Newark (Del.) Academy: in colonial era, 20, 22, 24, 27, 33–34; during American Revolution, 38–40, 45–46; in early republic, 142
Newark (N.J) Academy, 45, 62–63, 83, 91, 98, 114, 130, 132–33
Nicholas, John, 140
Nisbet, Charles, 53
North Carolina: academies, 61, 63, 70–71, 129, 144, 169; in the colonial era, 15; public schooling, 161–62, 173–74, 183
Northwest Ordinance, 2, 165

Oberlin College, 173
Ogden, Aaron, 27
Ogden, John Cosens, 149–51
Old Republicans, 141, 146
oratory, 76, 86–87, 93, 99; women's, 90
ornamental education: in colonial period, 37–38; and commerce, 105–6; criticism of, 101–3; at early national academies, 111–14, 114–15; elite demand for, 96, 106; at female academies, 89, 97–98, 111; political justification of, 96–97, 104–6, 108–110, 114–15

Panic of 1819, 8, 148, 162–64, 173, 177; and public schooling, 165–68, 171, 173
Partridge, Alden, 172
Peabody, Stephen, 66, 70
Peck, Jedediah, 155, 157–58, 160
Pennsylvania: academies, 78–79, 135, 142; colonial-era education, 17, 19–20; Confederation-era education, 55–59, 60; debate over Constitution in; 78–79;

politics during Panic of 1819, 164–65, 167; public schools in, 167
Pennsylvania Abolition Society, 154
Pequea (Pa.) Academy, 20, 24
Philadelphia: in colonial era, 17, 29; during American Revolution, 97; education in, 21, 57, 84, 86, 96–98, 102, 106, 112, 114; French community in, 98, 112
Phillips Andover (Mass.) Academy, 64, 182, 183
Phillips Exeter (N.H.) Academy, 67, 135, 182
Pierce, Sarah, 169
Pittsburgh Academy, 58–59, 78
Plainfield (Conn.) Academy, 64
Platt, Jonas, 157
polite education. *See* ornamental education
Poor, John, 90, 145
postcolonial: American elite, 3, 61; American education, 3, 96–97, 107–8, 117, 138, 168
Potts, Stacy, 62
Presbyterian Church: and academies, 13, 19–20, 22, 51–52; and American Revolution, 39–40, 45, 46; ecclesiastical development of, 18–19; and education in Confederation era, 53–56, 58–59, 70–71; and education in early republic, 146, 149–50; schism, 19, 21; and Seven Years' War, 34–36
Presbytery of New Brunswick, 54
Priestley, Joseph, 24, 33, 36
Princeton Theological Seminary, 55
public schools: and African Americans, 178–80; competition with academies, 132–34, 155–56, 158, 168; constitutional support of, 2; in modern era, 183–84; opposition to, 152; political support for, 7–9, 60–61, 67–68, 148–49, 155–59, 166–67, 170, 173; reformers' visions for, 152–55, 156, 166–67, 173–74; regional differences in, 7–9, 10, 135, 152, 158–59, 161–62, 168, 176; religion and, 178; and women, 159–60, 177
Putnam, Rufus, 43

Quakers, 17, 34, 56, 57, 157, 177
Queen's College (Mass.), 21, 63, 67
Queen's College (Rutgers University), 21, 54, 55
Quesnay de Beaurepaire, Alexandre-Marie: career of, 96, 97–98, 99, 100, 104–5, 111; justifies polite education, 103–6

racial inequality, 75, 138, 154–55, 176–80, 182–83
Radical Jeffersonians, 7, 8, 82, 145–46, 149; and African American education, 154–55; and public schools, 82, 153–54, 155–59, 165; and women, 159
Raleigh (N.C.) Academy, 174
Ramsay, David, 81
Reeve, Tapping, 27, 146
relief measures: in 1780s, 3, 146, 164; during Panic of 1819, 163, 164; and public schools, 163, 165–67, 170
religious pluralism, 55–59
Republican Party (1850s–1860s), 172
Republicans, Jeffersonian (*see also* Moderate Jeffersonians, and Radical Jeffersonians): acceptance of academies, 114–15, 121–22, 127, 139–41, 157; opposition to academies, 132, 136–38; democracy and, 122, 143–44; and public schools, 136–37, 155–59, 174
Richmond Academy. *See* Academy of Polite Arts
River Gods (Hampshire County, Mass.), 21, 63, 67
Robertson, Andrew and Alexander, 112
Rousseau, Jean-Jacques, 24
Rush, Benjamin, 26, 27, 53, 81; on Classics, 87, 150; on national university, 139, 152; and public schools, 60; on religion and education, 57–58; on women's education, 89–90

Schulze, John, 166
Scottish Enlightenment, 37
Sedgwick, Theodore, 141

segregation, 10, 179–80, 182–82; opposition to, 173, 183–84
segregation academies, 182
Seven Years' War: education and, 33–37
Shays's Rebellion, 65–68, 126, 140, 141–42, 143
Shepard, William, 66–67, 141
Sheridan, Thomas, 32–33, 36
Shippen, Edward, 27
Skinner, Thompson, 141
Slaughter, Gabriel, 164, 166
slavery, 8, 9, 50, 160–61; in academies, 91; education and, 10, 16–17, 36, 40, 92, 128, 138, 149, 176, 178
Smith, Melancton, 132, 153, 171
Smith, Robert, 20, 23, 24
Smith, Samuel Harrison, 137–38, 152
Smith, William, 29, 35, 39, 55–56
Society of the Cincinnati, 43, 61, 77, 80, 81, 82; support for academies, 62, 144–45
Society in London for Promoting Religious Knowledge (SPRK), 29
Society for the Propagation of the Gospel (SPG), 40
Somerset (Md.) Academy. *See* Washington Academy (Md.)
South: debates over academies in, 30, 50, 61, 128–29, 140; 147, 168; education in, 7, 10, 70–71, 112–13, 124, 176; public schools in, 152, 161–62, 176
South Carolina: education in, 128, 152
Spangler, John, 75–76, 86, 94–95
Squire, Zadoc, 71
state formation: British, 36–37; education and in U.S., 3–4, 53–54, 83, 96–97, 104–5, 107, 108–110, 116
Stockholm, John, 44–45
Stono Rebellion, 128
Stowe, Harriet Beecher, 90, 177
subscribers of academies, 5, 40, 47–48, 62, 65, 92
Sullivan, James, 142
Synod of New York, 18–19, 54–55
Synod of Philadelphia, 18–19, 20, 30, 54–55

Taney, Roger, 84
Taunton (Maas.) Academy, 126
Teachers: entrepreneurial, 98–99, 111–12, 113–14; European credentials of, 107, 112, 115; as immigrants to U.S., 106, 112; training in academies 168–69; women, 99, 168–69
Tennent, Gilbert, 20, 50
Tennent, William, 19
Tennessee, 166
Tocqueville, Alexis de, 49, 61
Tompkins, Daniel, 157–58
Transylvania University, 166, 167
Trenton (N.J.) Academy, 62, 71, 84, 94, 114, 125
trustees of academies: cosmopolitanism of, 67–69; during American Revolution, 37, 40; patriotic claims of, 82–83, 93–94; power over curriculum, 84, 86, 93–94
turnpikes. *See* internal improvements
Tyler, Royall, 100

Union Hall Academy (N.Y.), 59, 114
United Irishmen, 146
University of the State of Pennsylvania, 56–57
University of Virginia, 137, 162

Van Rensselaer, Stephen, 170, 172
Varnum, Joseph, 143
venture schools, 85, 93
Vermont education, 68, 134, 135, 159, 168
Virginia: academies, 62, 71, 82, 91, 96, 104, 113, 128–29, 144–45; education in, 15–17, 60–61, 93, 152, 162; religion in, 18, 20, 34–35;
Voluntary Associate Presbyteries, 51–52, 71–72

War of 1812, 8, 148, 158, 160–62, 165, 171
Washington Academy (Md.), 46, 58, 70
Washington, George, 44, 45, 84, 100, 101, 144; support for academies, 144–45; support for national university, 139–40
Washington-Henry Academy (Va.), 71, 82, 91, 145

Watson, Daniel, 35
Watson, Elkanah, 171, 172
Watts, Isaac (*Logic*), 23
Webster, Noah: 1–2, 3, 4, 102, 148, 151; views on classics, 87, 150
The West, 108–9, 163, 177–78
Westfield (Mass.) Academy, 66–67, 126, 141, 152
Westford (Mass.) Academy, 126, 143
West Indies, 40–41
West Nottingham Academy, 26, 27
Whig Party, 149, 151, 174, 175, 176
Whitefield, George, 28, 34, 50
Willard, Emma, 168–69
Williams, Israel, 63
Williamson, Hugh, 40
Williamstown (Mass.) Academy (Williams College), 64, 141
Wilmington (Del.) Academy, 45–46, 81
Wilson, James, 78–79, 82, 86, 87 95, 109, 110; and Fort Wilson Riot, 97
Witherspoon, John, 21, 24, 53–54, 71
Wollstonecraft, Mary, 89
women's education: curriculum of, 88–90, 169; debates over, 89–91; expansion after American Revolution, 88–89; in female academies, 9–10; and nation-building, 83, 116, 169, 177; and ornamental curriculum, 97–98, 111, 116; school reform and, 159–60, 177; and women's status, 88–91
Woodruff, Aaron Dickinson, 62
Woodstock (Conn.) Academy, 70

Yale College, 16, 149, 150
York (Pa.) Academy, 75–76
Young Ladies' Academy of Philadelphia, 89, 90, 145

www.ingramcontent.com/pod-product-compliance
Lightning Source LLC
Chambersburg PA
CBHW030527230426
43665CB00010B/800